Modern Europe
1870 -1966

History Essays for Leaving Cert.

(Higher Level)

Eileen O'Brien

MENTOR PUBLICATIONS

Mentor Publications, 43 Furze Road, Sandyford Ind. Est., Dublin 18
Tel: (01) 2952112/3   Fax (01) 2952114

© **Mentor Publications 1995**
All Rights Reserved

Author:	Eileen O'Brien
Typeset by:	Aisling Glennon
Cover Design:	Christine Warner
Published in Ireland by:	Mentor Publications 43 Furze Road, Sandyford Industrial Estate, Dublin 18 Tel: (01) 2952112/3; Fax: (01) 2952114
Printed in Ireland by:	Colour Books Ltd. Baldoyle, Dublin 13.
ISBN:	0 947548 14 9

1 3 5 7 9 10 8 6 4 2

Contents

GERMANY, 1871-1918

1. Bismarck's Domestic Policy, 1871-1890 … … … … … … … … … … …   7
2. Bismarck's Foreign Policy, 1871-1890 … … … … … … … … … … …   11
3. *"Bismarck's Diplomatic and Political Juggling was
   Triumphantly Successful"* Discuss … … … … … … …   15
4. Treat of Wilhelm II's Involvement in German Affairs
   from 1888 to 1918 … … … … … … … … … … … … … … … …   19
   Past Exam Questions … … … … … … … … … … … … … … …   22

FRANCE, 1870-1914

5. Treat of Politics, Instability and Scandals in France
   during the period 1870-1914 … … … … … … … … … … … …   24
6. French Foreign Policy, 1870-1914 … … … … … … … … … … …   28
7. Church-State Relations in France, 1870-1914 … … … … … … …   32
8. La Belle Époque … … … … … … … … … … … … … … … …   36
   Past Exam Questions … … … … … … … … … … … … … … …   39

RUSSIA, 1870-1924

9. Alexander III, 1854-1894 … … … … … … … … … … … … … …   41
10. Nicholas II, 1868-1918 … … … … … … … … … … … … … …   45
11. Describe the Circumstances that led to the
    Revolution in Russia, 1917 … … … … … … … … … … … …   49
12. Treat of Russia in Revolution, 1917 … … … … … … … … … …   53
13. Lenin, 1870-1924 … … … … … … … … … … … … … … … …   57
    Past Exam Questions … … … … … … … … … … … … … … …   61

BRITAIN, 1870-1914

14. Treat of the Reforms brought about in Great Britain
    during the period 1870-1914 … … … … … … … … … … … … …   62
15. Britain's Foreign Policy, 1870-1914 … … … … … … … … … … …   66
    Past Exam Questions … … … … … … … … … … … … … … …   70

THE AGE OF IMPERIALISM

16. European Expansion Overseas, 1870-1914 … … … … … … … …   72
17. Treat of European Involvement in Africa, 1870-1914 … … … … … …   77
    Past Exam Questions … … … … … … … … … … … … … … …   81

WAR AND PEACE

18. The Causes of World War I 82
19. Account for the Early Successes but Final Defeat for
    Germany during World War I 86
20. Treat of Main Developments in Warfare during
    World War I, 1914-1918 90
21. The Treaty of Versailles 94
22. The League of Nations 98
    Past Exam Questions 102

WEIMAR GERMANY

23. The Weimar Republic, 1919-1933 103
24. Gustav Stresemann, 1878-1929 108
25. Weimar Culture 113
    Past Exam Questions 117

MUSSOLINI'S ITALY

26. Benito Mussolini, 1883-1945 118
27. Account for the Rise of Fascism in Italy under Mussolini 123
28. Mussolini's Domestic Policy 128
29. Mussolini's Foreign Policy 133
    Past Exam Questions 137

HITLER'S GERMANY

30. Adolf Hitler, 1889-1945 140
31. Account for Hitler's Rise to Power in Germany 145
32. Hitler's Domestic Policy, 1933-1939 150
33. Hitler's Foreign Policy, 1933-1939 155
    Past Exam Questions 159

FASCISM

34. Discuss the Principal Characteristics of European
    Fascism in the Inter-War Period 160
35. Treat of Relations between Fascist Italy and Nazi
    Germany during the Period 1933-1945 165
    Past Exam Questions 169

RUSSIA UNDER STALIN

36. Stalin, 1879-1953 170
37. Stalin's Domestic Policy 175
38. Stalin's Foreign Policy 179
    Past Exam Questions 183

CIVIL WAR IN SPAIN

39. The Spanish Civil War … … … … … … … … … … … … … …   184
Past Exam Questions … … … … … … … … … … … … … … …   188

WORLD WAR II

40. Assess the Part Played by Great Britain in W.W.II. … … … … … … …   190
41. Treat of the Part Played by the USSR in World War II … … … … … …   195
Past Exam Questions … … … … … … … … … … … … … … …   199

POST-WAR FRANCE

42. Charles De Gaulle, 1890-1970 … … … … … … … … … … …   200
43. The Fourth Republic, 1946-1958 … … … … … … … … … … … … …   205
44. The Fifth Republic, 1958-1969 … … … … … … … … … … … …   209
Past Exam Questions … … … … … … … … … … … … … … …   213

POST-WAR GERMANY

45. *"Both as a national leader and as an international
statesman Konrad Adenauer had outstanding achievements
to his credit".* Discuss … … … … … … … … … … … … … …   214
Past Exam Questions … … … … … … … … … … … … … … …   218

POST-WAR BRITAIN

46. British Foreign Policy, 1945-1966 … … … … … … … … … … …   219
47. Treat of the Domestic Policies pursued by successive British
Governments during the period 1945-1966 … … … … … … … …   224
Past Exam Questions … … … … … … … … … … … … … … …   228

POST-WAR RUSSIA

48. Nikita Khrushchev, 1894-1971 … … … … … … … … … … … …   229
Past Exam Questions … … … … … … … … … … … … … … …   233

POST-WAR GENERAL TOPICS

49. The United Nations … … … … … … … … … … … … … … …   234
50. Treat of the Movement towards European Unity
from 1945 to 1966 … … … … … … … … … … … … … … …   239
51. Treat of Decolonisation from 1945 onwards … … … … … … … …   244
52. The Cold War … … … … … … … … … … … … … … … …   248
Past Exam Questions … … … … … … … … … … … … … … …   252

RESEARCH TOPICS … … … … … … … … … … … … … … …   255
"Bleeding the French White" — Gen. Erich von Falkenhayn
and the Battle of Verdun (Feb-Dec 1916) … … … … … … … …   257
The Mission of Count Claus von Stauffenberg … … … … … … …   260

GERMANY, 1871-1918

1. Bismarck's Domestic Policy, 1871-1890

Creation of the German Empire

The German victory in the Franco-Prussian war led to a wave of nationalist feeling in Germany and consequently to the declaration of a German *Reich*, or Empire, on 18th January 1871. Over the following years, Bismarck - the man chiefly responsible for unification - set about shaping the policies of the new Germany. Above all, he sought to protect Prussia's powerful position in Germany and to ensure that the real power was held by the crown, nobility and Junker class. Disliking the idea of collective government, Bismarck wished to exercise tight control over affairs. The constitution of 1871, for example, was largely the product of his own thought and will. It guaranteed the position of the Kaiser as head of state. Only the King of Prussia could become Kaiser, whose power was considerable. He controlled foreign policy, was Commander-in-Chief of the army and could declare war. The Kaiser alone could appoint or dismiss the Chancellor and other federal officials. In turn, the Chancellor was responsible for his actions only to the Kaiser. From 1870 until his death in 1888, Wilhelm I assumed the position of Kaiser while Bismarck, until his resignation in 1890, was Chief Minister or Chancellor. A strong chancellor could, by manipulating the Kaiser, rule the empire almost single-handedly. In effect, Bismarck, for as long as Wilhelm lived, exercised virtually unshakeable influence.

Constitution - Prussian Dominance

The German empire was made up of 25 states with a federal constitution, i.e. there were 25 local state governments and above these was a federal government, which was made up of representatives of all the states but which was controlled by the Kaiser and the Chancellor. It was mainly concerned with foreign affairs but also had control of trade, banking, coinage and railways. The state governments retained their own rulers, along with their own administrative, religious, parliamentary and taxation systems. The federal parliament, for its part, consisted of two houses, the *Bundesrat* and the *Reichstag*. The *Bundesrat* was the upper house and was composed of representatives from each of the states. The number of members was determined by the size and power of each state. Prussia, covering two-thirds of the country, held 17 seats and the next largest was Bavaria with 6; the majority of states had only one seat. As a motion to alter the constitution could be defeated by 14 votes, Prussia could always prevent constitutional change. The lower house, the *Reichstag*, was made up of representatives sent there by various states. These were elected by all men over the age 25 years. Prussia had 236 out of the 397 seats. Although the *Reichstag* could introduce legislation, its powers were severely limited and it had little real role to play. And while opposition parties were allowed to develop, they were unable to achieve much. Thus it was that while a veneer of democracy was created, in practice Germany bordered on a dictatorship with Bismarck exercising what amounted to a free hand.

1. Bismarck's Domestic Policy, 1871-1890

The Kulturkampf [I]

While the new empire was dominated by Lutheran Prussia, it did contain a population which was about one-third Catholic. To protect their interests, German Catholics organised themselves into a new political party, the Centre Party. They demanded a firm guarantee of the freedom of the Catholic church in Germany. Bismarck was irritated by their demands. He disliked the Catholics for a number of reasons:

1. Catholics had a divided loyalty: to the Pope in Rome and the Kaiser in Berlin.
2. The Catholic Centre Party was growing in strength. Bismarck disliked opposition.
3. Bismarck himself was a Lutheran so, on a personal level, he was suspicious of the Catholics.

Bismarck's opportunity to weaken the Catholics came in 1870 when Pope Pius IX issued a decree on Papal Infallibility. This stated that when the Pope spoke on matters of faith or morals, he was divinely inspired and could not err. Some Catholics objected to the dogma and became known as *'old Catholics'*. Bismarck used the quarrel within the Catholic church as the opportunity to launch his attack on Catholicism. The *Kulturkampf*, defined as a *'struggle for civilisation'*, was a church-state conflict which was largely fought out over control of education. In July 1871, the Catholic bureau in the Prussian Ministry of Education and Public Worship was abolished. This was followed by the Pulpit Law which forbade the Catholic clergy to raise political issues in their sermons. The Falk Laws of 1872 made all schools subject to state inspection. At the same time, the Jesuit order was banned and other religious groups were forbidden to teach in Germany.

The Kulturkampf [II]

The full attack on Catholicism came with the May Laws of 1873, 1874 and 1875. Under these laws,

1. appointments of priests would be recognised only if they had graduated from a German university,
2. there was to be a government veto on clerical appointments by bishops,
3. civil marriage was made compulsory,
4. education was placed completely under state control,
5. state funds for Catholic activities were removed,
6. church property was confiscated.

In consequence, by 1876 all Prussian bishops were either in prison or in exile. By 1877 over one-third of the 4,500 Catholic parishes were without a priest. Not surprisingly, reaction to these laws was swift. Pius IX cut off diplomatic relations with Berlin, declared the laws null and void and called for a general policy of civil disobedience. The Church, meanwhile, gained strength from persecution and the Centre Party actually grew in numbers. Protestants also reacted to the laws, fearful of any sort of religious persecution. Even the Kaiser was wary of the laws. Instead of uniting Germany, Bismarck had succeeded in dividing Germans. Realising his mistake, Bismarck made a political U-turn. His opportunity for a change of course came when in 1878 Leo XIII succeeded Pius IX. Relations with the Papacy were now improved. Falk was dismissed in 1879 as Bismarck sought to shift the blame away from himself and the May Laws were themselves greatly modified. In any event, Bismarck now needed the support of the Catholic Centre Party against a more serious threat - the Socialists.

Bismarck and the Socialists

In 1869 various socialist groups in Germany joined together to form the Social Democratic Party. They did so under the leadership of Ferdinand Lassalle and over the following years, they became Bismarck's most bitter opponents in the *Reichstag*. He disliked and feared them because:

1. of their international character,
2. Socialists wanted to overthrow the state and Bismarck feared revolution,
3. Bismarck was a member of the Junker class and did not understand the problems and needs of the working people.

Up to 1875, the Socialists presented little or no problem for Bismarck because they only had a few seats in the *Reichstag*. Thereafter, they became more organised and determined. In 1875, for example, the Social Democratic Party held an important conference at Gotha where it drew up a programme. Private business was condemned and a state takeover of industry was advocated. The Socialists proclaimed their loyalty to the workers rather than to the state. Around the same period of time, Germany's rapid industrialisation ensured the continuing growth of an urban workforce. Dissatisfied with conditions, they turned to socialism. In 1877 the Social Democrats had 12 seats in the *Reichstag* (9% of the votes) and their numbers were on the increase. The opportunity to suppress the Socialists came to Bismarck in 1878. In that year there were two assassination attempts on the life of the Kaiser. Bismarck blamed the Socialists and proceeded to deal with them through a mixture of coercion and conciliation.

The Socialists - Coercion and Conciliation

Bismarck dissolved the *Reichstag*, and the general election which followed was fought on a campaign of anti-socialism. The electorate returned a right-wing majority and Bismarck now had the necessary support to introduce anti-socialist legislation. The Exceptional Law, October 1878, banned socialism in Germany. Local police were given the power to ban any organisation supporting left-wing activities; public meetings or collections for the cause were banned, while socialist newspapers were suppressed. During the years of enforcement, 1878-1890, 1,350 publications were banned, 900 people were expelled and some 1,500 Socialists were sent to prison. But Bismarck knew that force alone would not destroy socialism. Thus, he introduced a policy of *'State Socialism'*. Laws were passed to protect workers against the three major threats to their social livelihood - sickness, accident and old age or incapacity. Germany was the first country in the world to introduce such reforms, yet they failed to allay the hostility of the Socialists since their practical value did not become apparent for some years. Bismarck's 'carrot and stick' approach, therefore, failed to break the socialists. They were driven underground but they continued to meet in secret or abroad. The working class of Germany wanted not just reform but a real say in the running of the government. Succeeding *Reichstag* elections saw the Socialists increase their vote. By 1890 their vote had trebled and by 1912 the SDP was the largest party in the *Reichstag*.

1. Bismarck's Domestic Policy, 1871-1890

Industrialisation

An enormous expansion took place in German economic development in the years after 1870. Unification gave a tremendous boost to industrialisation, in that Germany now possessed enormous resources of raw material in the Ruhr, the Saar, Silesia and Alsace-Lorraine. Manufacturers also had one large market at their disposal. For his part, Bismarck's economic programme centred around his desire to impose a system of tariffs, thereby protecting home industry, and to encourage heavy industry. To this end, he was influenced by Friedrich List and his book *'The National System of Political Economy'*. Germany's greatest progress took place in the coal, metallurgical and engineering industries. Steel production, for example, increased from 130,000 tonnes in 1870 to 2,100,000 in 1890. At the same time, great strides were made in the chemical industry and in electrical engineering. One of the most famous industrial firms was Alfred Krupp's. His steel factory at Essen became famous for the producton of arms and railway equipment. The factories of Werner von Siemens became world famous for their electrical and telegraphic equipment. Modern factories and equipment accelerated economic growth. Simultaneously, railway construction underwent a boom. In 1870, Germany had 27,000 kilometres of railway line, by the 1880s this had grown to 65,000 kilometres and it continued to grow thereafter. That Germany was, next to America, the world's greatest economic power by 1914, was undoubtedly helped by Bismarck's attempts to link up schools, universities and industry, thereby attracting the brains of the country to industry.

Agriculture - Evaluation

The Industrial Revolution was accompanied by progress and prosperity in agriculture. In spite of the temporary setback in 1873, caused by a depression, agriculture became more mechanised. It was further aided by government assistance and subsidies, as well as the policy of protection by high tariffs. This favoured the production of cereals. The new sugar beet industry grew rapidly and the establishment of co-operatives proved very successful in encouraging savings and providing credit. The fact that through the Bismarck era, only 12% of Germany's annual financial investment was in non-German ventures, ensured a ready availability of capital. In this, as in other areas, Bismarck exploited opportunities as they arose. He did so with varying degrees of success. One important repercussion of unification, for example, was the creation of national minorities within the new Germany. These included the Danish population in North Schleswig, the Poles to the east of the empire and the French in Alsace-Lorraine. These groups remained continually hostile to the *Reich* and although there can be no doubting Bismarck's tremendous skill in holding the new federal structure together and in ensuring that Germany forged confidently ahead into the twentieth century, much of his successes depended on his own personality and his ability to see them through. The faults became more apparent following his resignation in 1890. In the meantime, Bismarck showed that he had a genius for granting concessions *"in form but not in substance"*. The man who once maintained *"I want to play only the music I myself like or no music at all"* seldom deviated from that belief.

2. Bismarck's Foreign Policy, 1871-1890

Consequences of Unification - Aims

The emergence of the German empire, following the Franco-Prussian war (1870-1871) changed the balance of power in Europe. As a nation of 70 million people and lying at the very centre of Europe, Germany was now the strongest Continental power. The military and diplomatic balance had shifted from Paris to Berlin and it was unclear whether Bismarck would be able to keep the momentum of German nationalism within the frontiers of 1871. Germany's geographic position constituted a threat to her neighbours, both east and west. It also made Germany vulnerable to a two-front attack from France and Russia combined, or a sea blockade by Britain. Unification was thus not simply a German question but a European one. Bismarck, however, sought to do *"everything to stave off the consequences of his own work"* by declaring Germany to be a *"satiated"* power. He made Germany great by war and after 1871 he intended to keep her great by peace. Fearful of a war of revenge, Bismarck further aimed to keep France in isolation and to prevent her from forming an alliance with any other European power. In order to do this, Bismarck would have to prove his skill on the international plane as he prepared to enter into alliances with former enemies. And although the quality of German diplomats was of the highest calibre, Bismarck's diplomatic system was largely 'a one-man band'. In many respects, Bismarck's position after 1871 was rather like that of the unscrupulous businessman, who, having made his millions, becomes a philanthropist and chairman of innumerable charitable boards.

Dreikaiserbund, 1873 - Conflict with France

Bismarck believed that Europe consisted of five major powers - Germany, Austria-Hungary, Russia, Great Britain and France. He knew that alliances of some sort were inevitable and he sought to ensure that Germany would always be one of at least three. As a first step, Bismarck sought to ensure the friendship of Austria-Hungary and Russia. In September 1872 tripartite talks took place in Berlin between Franz Joseph, Alexander II and Wilhelm I. These led to a series of summits which, in turn, produced the agreements of 6th June and 22nd October of the following year. The *Dreikaiserbund* or League of Three Emperors (1873) was not a formal military alliance. Rather it was a statement of common interests. The three powers stressed their desire for peace and thereby their agreement to maintain the status quo and to honour existing borders. They also decided on mutual consultation before taking unilateral action in the event of war. Above all, the *Dreikaiserbund* revealed the conservative and anti-revolutionary bias of its members. Bismarck valued the alliance as a means of isolating France, but there can be no doubting that he would have liked further agreement of a more concrete nature. His attempts to get this were seriously hindered by a number of crises in the period from 1875 onwards. The first threat was from France and its origin lies with Bismarck's alarm at the speed with which France had paid its war indemnity and rebuilt its army. Resorting to *'crude sabre-rattling'*, Bismarck caused a series of articles, including *'Is war in sight?'*, to be written. This suggested that Bismarck was going to launch a pre-emptive strike against France. France protested and in this she was backed up by Great Britain and Russia. The crisis thereafter abated as Germany was forced to repudiate the article. Yet it was important in that

1. it enabled France to escape isolation temporarily
2. it exposed the essential weakness of the *Dreikaiserbund*

The Balkan Crisis - Congress of Berlin

The diplomacy of Bismarck was subjected to a more testing challenge as a result of the Austro-Russian conflict in the Balkans. The conflict began in June 1875 with uprisings in Bosnia and Herzegovina and the possible collapse of Turkish power. If that were to happen, a vacuum would be created which Austria and Russia would compete to fill. The situation reached a further crisis point when, in April 1877, Russia invaded Turkey. Fighting was concluded in March 1878 with the Treaty of San Stefano. Russia managed to secure the creation of a new state of Bulgaria at Turkey's expense. Austria-Hungary, fearing the increase of Russian influence, threatened war. So too did Britain, concerned as she was about any Russian advance towards the Mediterranean. Bismarck had himself no ambition or interest in the Balkans but he knew that war would put an end to German security. He also wished to avoid choosing between Austria-Hungary and Russia. Consequently, Bismarck offered himself as *'honest broker'* and suggested that a conference be held in Berlin to settle the problem. The congress was attended by Great Britain, Russia, Austria-Hungary, Turkey, France, Italy and Germany. The terms of the negotiated settlement included a revision of the Treaty of San Stefano and the infliction of a diplomatic defeat on Russia. To this extent, the congress was more favourable to Austria-Hungary than to Russia and showed which country Bismarck was more likely to favour in the future. But while war on a European scale was avoided, in the long term, the problems which created the crisis remained. A further result of the congress was that Russia felt very bitter and distrustful towards Germany, complaining that what had happened in Berlin was *"a European coalition against Russia under the leadership of Prince Bismarck"*.

Dual Alliance (1879) - Triple Alliance (1882)

In the immediate aftermath of the Congress of Berlin, Bismarck tried to revise the *Dreikaiserbund* but it soon became apparent that this was not possible. For better or worse, Bismarck now began to commit himself to an Austrian alliance. His reasons for doing this were varied. In the first place, Bismarck in 1879 was embarking on a foreign policy in which considerations of maintaining a status quo played a large part. An alliance with Austria appealed to many sections of German society—Catholics, National Liberals, Conservatives and the army. Secondly, Bismarck may have been trying to pacify Austria-Hungary and to compel *'Prussia'* to adopt a more peaceful policy. Some historians suggest that the alliance was *"the logical completion of German unification begun in the 1860s"*. In any case, the Dual Alliance which was signed in 1879 pledged each country to support the other against a Russian attack. If either were attacked by another power, the other would remain benevolently neutral. Two years later, in 1881, the French (encouraged by Bismarck) formally declared their protectorate over Tunis. Italy, bitterly resentful of the French action, joined with Germany and Austria in May 1882 to convert the Dual Alliance into a Triple Alliance. This alliance gave a promise of aid in the event of an attack by France and was renewed every five years until 1915. Bismarck had reservations about the alliance in that he felt the Italian monarchy was not a strong one. It was, nonetheless, advantageous in that it further isolated France.

The Dreikaiserbund renewed - Reinsurance Treaty (1887)

Tsar Alexander II of Russia was assassinated early in 1881 and his successor, Alexander III, was anxious to achieve better relations with Germany. In June 1881, a new *Dreikaiserbund* was agreed on between Germany, Austria-Hungary and Russia. By the terms of this *Dreikaiserbund*, which were formal though secret, it was agreed that if any of the three powers became involved in a war with a fourth power, the others would remain neutral. Russia, fearing she might be at war with Britain over the Balkans, was pleased with the agreement while Germany, once again, ensured that should she find herself at war with France, Russia would not force her into fighting a two-front war. The *Dreikaiserbund* was renewed in 1884 but thereafter it foundered on the rocks of Austro-Russian rivalry. Thus in 1881, Alexander III refused to renew it, but he did agree to negotiate with Germany alone. The result was the Reinsurance Treaty (1887), which was to be renewed every three years. Both Germany and Russia promised to remain neutral if the other went to war unless Germany attacked France, or Russia attacked Austria-Hungary. At the same time, Bismarck secretly acknowledged Russia's right to exert a dominant influence in Bulgaria and agreed to the closure of the Dardenelles Straits to warships of all foreign powers. The Reinsurance Treaty was Bismarck's last desperate effort to maintain his system in Europe, but it did not stop tension between Germany and Russia, or between Russia and Austria-Hungary. Nor did it contain any clauses to protect Russia's economic needs, a situation that forced Russia to turn to France for assistance.

Colonisation [I]

Bismarck had long resisted suggestions from various quarters that Germany should acquire colonies. He did so on the grounds that
1. the acquisition of colonies could easily upset the delicate equilibrium he had established,
2. colonies were an expensive luxury which could dissipate Germany's economic resources - Bismarck likened the idea of Germany needing colonies to *"a poverty stricken Polish gentleman providing himself with silks and sables when he needed shirts"*,
3. colonies meant having a navy to protect them - Bismarck fully realised that any effort to enlarge Germany's navy would arouse Britain's hostility,
4. colonisation required adequate time and preparation.

However this was the era when the European powers were involved in the *'scramble for Africa'* and many Germans wanted their *'place in the sun'*. Consequently, in 1882, the German Colonial Society was founded to encourage overseas acquisitions. This received support from industrialists, merchants, missionaries and adventurers. Desire for government support of colonial expansion gained momentum in 1884 when Bismarck called a conference in Berlin of the major European powers, where it was decided to draw the line of so-called *'spheres of influence'* in Africa. In 1883, Namibia was declared a German protectorate. Then, in 1884, Togo and the Cameroons became

German colonies. 1885 saw Germany lay claim on Tanzania and thereafter, she expanded in New Guinea and the Marshal Islands. Bismarck's behaviour or aberration during these few years has prompted one source to compare him to a sober industrious farmer who suddenly makes off with a barmaid on market day!

Colonisation [II]

The speed with which Bismarck created a colonial empire five times the size of the German *Reich*, and the reason why, is rather obscure and proves to be one of the more controversial aspects of his chancellorship. Several explanations have been put forward. One possibility is that Bismarck's imperialism was motivated by short-term domestic objectives; that he sought, for example, to strengthen the appeal of the National Liberals in the 1884 elections or that he was attempting to divert attention away from divisive domestic problems. Bismarck may also have been trying to stir up a little trouble with England, conscious as he was of the imminent accession of the Anglophile crown prince. Simultaneously, Bismarck, by using England as a possible enemy, may have been trying to terrify the electorate into returning his supporters. Certainly he called England's bluff and tested her real strength. A further explanation is that Bismarck might have simply wished to cash in on the colonial bonanza. For Bismarck, this was more an experiment than a commitment and once they proved to be a financial and administrative burden, he became disillusioned and withdrew his support. Thus, while the colonies proved a valuable source of raw materials and provided a market for goods, there was little German emigration, and as already suggested, the cost of conquering and maintaining them was high.

Conclusion

After 1871 Europe enjoyed over twenty years of unbroken peace and much of the credit for this must go to Bismarck, the acknowledged master of international relations. Through his diplomatic manoeuvres and alliances, he kept France isolated and prevented the Russians and Austrians from fighting each other. Bismarck used Germany's influence to stabilise international affairs and as long as Germany continued to play that role, European peace was reasonably secure. Yet Bismarck was forced to resign in 1890 and Germany started on a bumpier and thornier road thereafter, which profoundly affected not just Germany's internal affairs but the very nature of international relations themselves. As one historian so aptly suggested of Bismarck, *"with the egotism that accompanies greatness"*, he failed to prepare any successor. Thus, in the years after 1890 no chancellor emerged who was either capable or permitted to fill the gap. It may also be possible that by 1890, Bismarck had exhausted his genius for improvisation; that he was running out of long-term solutions for the problems and dilemmas facing the *Reich*. That things were beginning to fail by 1890 is suggested by the fact that Russia, in spite of the Reinsurance Treaty, was becoming increasingly alienated from Germany and that France was moving out of isolation towards Russia. At the same time, Bismarck had failed to secure the friendship of Britain, while Austria-Hungary was an ally that could present as many problems for Germany in the future, as it appeared to solve. Whatever the truth, there can be no taking away from the fact that Bismarck was an almost superhuman figure, who, in retirement, became *"an archetypal figure and a national genius"*.

3. *"Bismarck's Diplomatic and Political Juggling was Triumphantly Successful."* Discuss.

Introduction - Process of Unification

Having entered parliament in 1847, Bismarck's rise up the political ladder to the position of Prussian Chancellor (1862) was helped by his ability to resolve a crisis in the *Landtag* (Prussia's parliament) over army reforms. He now set about fulfiling his own ambitions and plans and, in so doing, he showed himself to be a diplomat of some considerable skill. A conservative member of the Junker class, Bismarck wished to expand Prussia's influence. To this end, he manipulated the question of German nationalism as he put into operation a plan for German unification. In the war with Denmark (1864) Bismarck cunningly persuaded Austria to join with Prussia in acquiring the province of Schleswig-Holstein. Austria, lulled into a false sense of security by a promise of a share in the spoils, had been deceived about Bismarck's real intentions. Bismarck then turned against Austria, his former ally. Before launching the Austro-Prussian war in 1866, Bismarck shrewdly succeeded in acquiring the promise of French neutrality. Thereafter, Bismarck ended Austria as a factor in German affairs. Bismarck's diplomatic juggling was taken a step further in 1870 when he successfully created a situation - through the Ems telegram - where France declared war on his country. Not only had Bismarck succeeded in making the French responsible for the war, but he had triumphantly managed to compel the four southern German states (previously unwilling to join a united Germany) to unite against the common enemy.

The New Germany - Constitution

From early on, Bismarck sought to steer the course of German affairs. Reluctant states were given inducements to join a united Germany. In the case of Bavaria, for example, King Ludwig of Bavaria was bribed with money. Behind the scenes, the threat of economic and political isolation furthered Bismarck's cause. Essentially, Bismarck exploited the differences between individual states and negotiated separately with them. Such was his success that on 18th January 1871 the German empire was proclaimed. Bismarck then set about drafting a new constitution, a cleverly engineered piece of work, which became law in April 1871. For nearly 20 years Bismarck worked the constitution in a way that might indeed be considered *'triumphantly successful'*. Only the King of Prussia could become Kaiser and his powers were considerable. He had sole charge of foreign affairs, was Commander-in-Chief of the armed forces and was responsible for appointing and dismissing the Chancellor. In return, the Chancellor, who was responsible for all other ministers, was answerable to the Kaiser alone. While Wilhelm I was Kaiser (1871-1888), he was happy to take a back seat to Bismarck and allow him to rule the empire almost single-handedly. Bismarck's position was further aided by the workings of parliament. Despite a veneer of democracy, both houses, the *Bundesrat* and *Reichstag*, were Prussian dominated. Prussia held 17 of the 58 seats in the *Bundesrat* but since only 14 negative votes were needed to prevent constitutional change, in practice Prussia had control. The *Reichstag* had 397 seats and Prussia held 236 of them. In this and other ways, therefore, Bismarck assumed what amounted to dictatorial powers.

3. Bismarck's Diplomatic and Political Juggling

The Kulturkampf

The *Kulturkampf*, or church-state conflict which developed in Germany in the 1870s, is further evidence of Bismarck's political juggling. Motivated by his dislike of opposition and of Catholicism in general, Bismarck's political opportunism was such that he seized the chance to weaken the Catholics when they themselves were divided over the issue of Papal Infallibility in 1870. He proceeded to introduce a series of laws (Pulpit, Falk and May) which severely eroded the power of the Catholic church in Germany. In this, Bismarck was not triumphant, for reaction to the laws was swift and came from many quarters. But Bismarck's political talent was such that he was capable of extricating himself from the predicament. Realising his mistake, he made a political U-turn. Relations with the Vatican were renewed when Leo XIII succeeded to the papacy, and in 1879 Adalbert Falk was dismissed from his position as Minister for Education and Public Worship. The burden of blame for the laws was shifted upon Falk. It might therefore be argued that Bismarck was victorious, to the extent that he emerged unscathed from the *Kulturkampf*. Further evidence of his success can be seen in the way Bismarck managed to play political partners off against one another and he frequently juggled rival groups and manoeuvred them around to his way of thinking. In the fields of federal administration and the economy, Bismarck allied with the National Liberals. Their insistence on the development of parliamentary rights irked him and in the mid 1870s, Bismarck decided that his interests were best served by closer co-operation with the Conservative and Centre Parties in the *Reichstag*. The introduction of tariffs was the means by which their support was won. Then in the late 1870s Bismarck decided that he now needed (and he got!) the support of the Catholics against the Socialists.

Socialists - Economy

Bismarck had no time for socialism and resented the re-organisation and growth of the Social Democratic Party in the period after 1875. He awaited his chance to attack. This came with the assassination attempts on the life of the Kaiser in 1878. Bismarck conveniently blamed the Socialists and introduced the Exceptional Law. The Socialists were banned from Germany, their leaders arrested, meetings banned and newspapers suppressed. Yet Bismarck was too clever a politician to stop there and chance creating socialist martyrs. He decided to wean workers away from socialism. This was to be done through a programme of *'State Socialism'* which offered protection to workers against sickness, accidents and in old age. In his efforts to reduce the political influence and power of the Socialists, however, Bismarck was not very successful and by 1890 the Socialists' vote had trebled. Workers in Germany wanted not just reforms but a real say in the running of the country. Bismarck was more successful in exploiting Germany's natural resources and in ensuring that substantial economic progress was made in the period 1871-1890. Communications, heavy industry, chemical industry and engineering all made a substantial leap forward and were helped by Bismarck's system of protection through the imposition of tariffs. Agriculture, too, was aided by such a policy and, although it led to a clash with the National Liberals who favoured free trade, the support of the Conservative and Centre parties ensured that the Chancellor won the argument. Protectionism also ensured that Bismarck became less dependent on individual states.

3. Bismarck's Diplomatic and Political Juggling

Foreign Policy - Dreikaiserbund

With regard to his foreign policy after 1871, Bismarck can again be seen as a shrewd and wily politician. Having used war to unite Germany and to make her great, Bismarck now believed that his ambitions could best be served by peace. His aims of keeping hostile France in diplomatic isolation and of preserving peace, required considerable diplomacy and involved the playing off of other powers against each other, to Germany's advantage. The *Dreikaiserbund* of 1873 between Germany, Austria-Hungary and Russia was a first step towards doing just that. The alliance ensured that Germany would not have to fight a two-front war and decreased France's chance of finding an ally. But although the *Dreikaiserbund* owed much to Bismarck's diplomatic juggling, it could not be deemed to be in all respects triumphant. In the first place, the *Dreikaiserbund* was a gentleman's agreement rather than a formal military alliance and secondly, and more significantly, it foundered upon the rocks of Austro-Russian conflict in the Balkans. Russia's defeat of Turkey and the subsequent Treaty of San Stefano, 1878, brought matters to a head. Many European powers were upset and war was threatened. To manoeuvre European affairs at that time, and to avoid open conflict, proved to be a significant test of Bismarck's skill as a negotiator.

Congress of Berlin - Dual and Triple Alliances

Bismarck's answer to the Balkan crisis was to offer himself as *'honest broker'* and call for a congress to be held in Berlin. He wished, together with Britain and the other major powers, to work for a solution acceptable to all. The terms of the negotiated settlement, which involved a revision of the San Stefano agreement, ensured that European war was avoided and, in so far as that was the case, the Congress of Berlin is often considered to be a spectacular success for Bismarck, demonstrating his diplomacy at its very best. But long-term problems remained, created especially by Russia's belief that the Berlin outcome was more favourable to Austria-Hungary, *"a coalition of Europe against Russia under the chairmanship of Prince Bismarck"*. The resulting threat to the *Dreikaiserbund* was realised soon after, as Russia withdrew from the agreement. This led to the Dual Alliance of 1879 with Austria. This promised mutual support in the event of a war with Russia and benevolent neutrality with regard to any other power. Bismarck cleverly saw the treaty as a means of fobbing off the demands of those Germans who wanted a greater Germany and also of keeping Austria-Hungary from an alliance with Britain and France. Bismarck was not entirely happy with the alliance, however, and in 1882 he used a disagreement between France and Italy as the opportunity to incorporate Italy into a Triple Alliance. Though not perfect, the alliance gave Bismarck some of the security he desired.

Renewal of the Dreikaiserbund - Reinsurance Treaty

Bismarck knew that while Russia was on her own, there would always be a danger of her drifting into an alliance with France. Thus, when Alexander III came to power in 1881, Bismarck used the occasion to revive the *Dreikaiserbund*. He managed to get both Austria-Hungary and Russia to agree to the clause that if any one of the three became involved in a war with a fourth power, the others would remain neutral. The Chancellor had once more successfully manipulated the course of political events by the use of his diplomatic skills. But his negotiations were not 'triumphantly' successful, for although the Dreikaiserbund was renewed in 1884, Russia refused to sign it in 1887 as a result of a fresh outburst of tension between Russia and Austria-Hungary. Bismarck, anxious about what Russia might do, invited the Tsar to Berlin. Again Bismarck was forced to use his juggling ability to save the country from a difficult situation. The result was the Reinsurance Treaty of 18th June 1887. Both countries agreed to remain neutral unless Germany attacked France, or Russia attacked Austria-Hungary.

Colonies - Conclusion

The diplomatic juggling and great manipulative skills of Bismarck are also obvious in his dealings with the issue of colonies. Although he was *"no man for colonies"*, he entered the *'scramble for Africa'* between the years 1884 and 1885. His involvement led to the establishment of a conference in Berlin of the major European powers in 1884 and the subsequent diplomatic drawing of the so-called *'spheres of influence'*. While Bismarck's reasons for becoming involved were many and varied, they did involve the juggling of public and other opinion to fulfil the Chancellor's own needs. Beyond doubt, Bismarck was a fine politician whose character contained a blend of cunning and perception. A confirmed juggler, words such as subterfuge, hoodwinking, bluffing and outwitting sit easily with him. Nothing pleased Bismarck more than to achieve a simple result by complex manoeuvres. This is why he preferred diplomacy to government. But in spite of apparent success, the legacy of Bismarck's work in Germany and in Europe proved disastrous. By ensuring that the Kaiser had ultimate power, Bismarck allowed for his own dismissal with the enthronement of Wilhelm II. Likewise, in terms of his foreign policy, the complex system which Bismarck created, depended largely on the Chancellor's own genius for survival, but had the potential for disaster in less capable hands. This was just what happened after 1890. In the final analysis, therefore, Bismarck's diplomatic and political juggling could not be said to be *'triumphantly successful'*.

4. Treat of Wilhelm II's Involvement in German Affairs from 1888 to 1918

Introduction - Clash with Bismarck

Wilhelm II was born in Berlin on 27th January 1859. He suffered many physical disabilities including a withered left arm and deafness in his left ear. These handicaps ensured that Wilhelm had little time for formal education. Although a man of some intelligence, Wilhelm lacked discipline, was impetuous, arrogant and capable of bad temper. He also showed considerable preoccupation with self and frequently proved a poor judge of character. In June 1888, at only 29 years of age, and following the premature death from throat cancer of his father, Frederick III, after only 99 days as emperor, Wilhelm succeeded to a position of great power. The role of Kaiser was one which called for tact, diplomacy and strength of character, but Wilhelm lacked political and personal maturity. Over the following years, he proved to be a decided liability to the *Reich*, all too often making spur-of-the-moment decisions and wild speeches, sometimes undoing months of work by politicians and civil servants alike. From the beginning, Wilhelm II was eager to exert his own authority and made clear his unwillingness to take a back seat to Bismarck, *"I will give the old man six months' breathing space, then I will rule myself"*. The expected clash between the two men occurred over their treatment of the Socialists and over the direction of German foreign policy. The result was Bismarck's forced resignation in March 1890.

Autocratic Rule - Wilhelm's Chancellors

A firm autocrat, Wilhelm believed absolutely in the divine right of kings. As early as 1891, he maintained: *"I regard my whole position as having been imposed on me from heaven"*. Consequently, Wilhelm refused to listen to prolonged discussions and came increasingly to direct government as he sought to show Germany and the world that he was the real ruler. Following Bismarck's resignation, Wilhelmine Germany saw a decline in the Chancellor's authority. Although generally well meaning, the men who now assumed this position did not possess Bismarck's political skills and all too often found themselves caught between the Kaiser and the parliament. Von Caprivi, who held the post of Chancellor from 1890-1894, had no real political experience so that, while he was a man of considerable integrity and oversaw the introduction of a number of bills in the *Reichstag* aimed at improving working conditions, he ultimately fell victim to the continued growth of the Social Democrats. This in turn led to a clash with Wilhelm, and von Caprivi's resignation following the defeat of an anti-socialist bill. Hohenlohe, 1894-1900, was elderly when he became Chancellor. He was a man without strong ideas and most of his appointments, bills and gestures were made on the Kaiser's orders. Hohenlohe was succeeded by von Bülow, 1900-1909. Since his primary aim seemed to have been to stay in power, he had no hesitation in appealing to Wilhelm's vanity. Von Bülow's downfall, when it came, was over a defeat of his tax proposals. Bethmann-Hollweg, who remained in office from 1909-1917, was an efficient administrator but the tide of events proved unfavourable.

Change in Foreign Policy - Alliance Systems

Under Wilhelm II, Germany adopted a 'new course' in foreign affairs. For the most part, his handling of events was a byword for clumsiness. On the alliance front, Wilhelm favoured closer alliance with Austria-Hungary and with Britain, and outright hostility towards Russia. Not surprisingly, therefore, he allowed himself to be convinced by von Caprivi, who, himself, was influenced by a senior Foreign Office official, Friedrich von Holstein, to allow the Reinsurance Treaty, which was due for renewal in 1890, to lapse. Holstein had argued that the Reinsurance Treaty gave more advantages to Russia than to Germany. Wilhelm also forbade German banks to lend money to Russia, hoping, through blackmail, to influence the course of events. What actually happened was that French bankers took the place of German ones and the Franco-Russian friendship was born. The economic link was cemented with the Franco-Russian alliance of 1894. This agreement promised aid, each to the other, in the event of war with Germany. After just a few years in power, Wilhelm had ensured that Bismarck's hard work at avoiding a two-front war, was undone. Meanwhile, not only did Britain fail to join an alliance with Germany, but in 1904 she actually joined France in a non-military alliance, the *Entente Cordiale*. Germany, through her change in direction and policy, was paving the way for a difficult and uncertain future.

Weltpolitik

Weltpolitik, the desire to make Germany a great world power by finding her *'rightful place in the sun'*, originated from a domestic crisis, namely the growth of socialism and the determination to organise a general rallying of all groups behind the regime. An expansionist foreign policy would enable Germany to acquire raw materials, markets, profits and prestige. It was aided by the Colonial Society, founded, though uninfluential, during the chancellorship of Bismarck and the Pan German League in 1890. As Germany sought to expand her influence to many parts of the globe, problems were created. Friction with Britain occurred in 1895-1896 over the Jameson Raid. This was when 500 Britishers, led by Dr. Jameson, invaded the Transvaal. The raid was repulsed but in its aftermath, Wilhelm sent a telegram to the Boer President, Paul Kruger, congratulating him on *"restoring peace in face of armed bands"*. The British were angered by such blatant interference. Germany's acquisition of naval bases in Kiao Chow, China (1898) furthered the tension, not just with Britain but also with Russia. Relations with Britain deteriorated still further in 1899 when Wilhelm supported German construction of the Berlin-Baghdad railway. Traditionally, Turkey had been an ally of Britain but the massacre of Armenian Christians by Turks around this time horrified British public opinion and led to a cooling of relations. Again, during the Boer War (1899-1902), German support for the Boers and opposition to the British damaged relations between Germany and Great Britain still further. In any event, by the early 1900s, Germany, as well as her friendship with the Turks, had established a substantial overseas empire, consisting of vast territories in Africa and naval bases in the Pacific.

Naval Conflict

The policy of Weltpolitik required naval *(Flottenpolitik)* as well as colonial expansion. Admiral von Tirpitz was a major advocate of German naval enlargement. He hoped that the German fleet would be capable of standing up to any fleet in the world and won support through his *'risk theory'*, i.e. as long as Britain had the upper hand on the naval front, there was a risk of war. Seeing himself as *'Admiral of the Atlantic'*, the idea of naval expansion was one which was dear to Wilhelm's heart. The *Reichstag* was persuaded to approve the monies required and in 1898, the first Naval Law was passed. This provided for a vast programme of shipbuilding which included 19 battleships and over 40 cruisers and torpedo boats. The British, who had traditionally adopted a two-power standard* were alarmed and indeed, antagonistic. Churchill expressed popular sentiment when he pointed out that *"the Royal Navy is a dire necessity - the German fleet a luxury"*. Germany and Britain now became involved in a *'naval race'* which continued until 1914 and which changed dramatically in 1906 with the building of the first British dreadnoughts. These had more speed, fire power and better design than any other warship and made all previous battleships obsolete. Meanwhile, as the naval race persisted, Germany and Britain were pushed further apart, with no possibility of an alliance between the two.

Morocco

The year 1904 had seen a growing understanding between Britain and France which included British acceptance of French influence in Morocco. In 1905 the French put pressure on the Sultan of Morocco to grant them more concessions. Germany protested and at a meeting with the Sultan at Tangier, Wilhelm promised to support the Sultan against France. He demanded that an international conference be held at Algeciras (Spain) to discuss the issue. Wilhelm hoped that the conference, which met between January and April 1906, would drive a wedge between Britain and France and felt confident that a ruling would be made against France. But the international powers were suspicious of Germany, fearing she would use Morocco as an excuse for war with France. Only Austria-Hungary supported Germany, all other powers recognised French predominance in Morocco. Germany had suffered her first rebuff. In 1911 the problem flared up again. In May of that year, the French claimed that their position in Algeria was being endangered by unrest in Morocco and consequently sent in troops to Fez, the capital. Germany again protested, pointing out that the action violated the Algeciras Conference. In July, a German gunboat, the *Panther*, arrived off the port of Agadir. The Germans sought compensation, financial and otherwise. Feelings ran high, argument was followed by counter-argument. In November 1911, however, Wilhelm effectively admitted defeat for a second time.

Moving towards War

The Moroccan Convention of November 1911 saw Wilhelm recognise French claims to Morocco. Germany's only compensation was a large tract of wasteland in the French Congo. Meanwhile, the German newspaper *'Der Post'* questioned Wilhelm's acceptance of defeat: *"Have we become a nation of women?"*. Wilhelm now became even more determined that in the future he would stand firm and that if Germany was portrayed as a warmonger, she would live up to her name. Thus, over the following years, preparations for war went ahead in earnest. The Kaiser's plans for war were helped by the Schlieffen Plan, 1905. Count von Schlieffen devised a scheme which allowed Germany to cope with an enemy on both sides - France and Russia. An initial

---

* Britain's naval strength should be equal to the combined forces of any two European powers.

all-out effort against France would crush her in four to six weeks. In the assumption that Russian mobilisation would be slow, owing to her backwardness, the Germans would then turn to the east and pulverise Russia. This plan dominated all German military thinking in the lead up to war. By then, Wilhelm had already ensured that Germany had become a militaristic state where the army enjoyed a privileged position. The German Army law of 1913 sought an increase of army peace-time strength by 117,000 men and 19,000 officers. Improvements in weaponry, logistics and organisation also took place. The readiness to envisage the possibility of war was accompanied by an awareness of the need for striking the first blow and by assurances of support for Austria in the pursuit of her aggressive foreign policy.

War - Conclusion

The assassination of Franz Ferdinand (heir to the Austrian throne) and his wife in Sarajevo, June 1914, was followed by an Austrian ultimatum to the Serbs. When all demands were not met, events escalated and on 1st August, Germany declared war on Russia, Serbia's ally. Thereafter, Britain, France and others became involved. The German war machine clicked into action, the German military staff insisting on the need for speed. Wilhelm, for his part, continued to act with characteristic volatility and irresponsibility but after some early successes, Germany was put on the defensive. The Schlieffen plan failed and by 1918, after all the fanfares of victory, the war was in fact lost. Slogans such as *'The Kaiser is a scoundrel'* and *'Hang the Kaiser'* were reflective of the growing desire for Wilhelm's departure. Wilhelm, however, stubbornly held on, continuing to indulge in fantasies of Germany's greatness. The stubborn retention of office destroyed the last chance of survival of his dynasty. In November 1918, the state that Bismarck had founded collapsed, to be replaced by a republic which had 14 years of troubled life before expiring miserably. On the 9th November, Wilhelm was left with no alternative but to abdicate. He fled to the neutral Netherlands where he was given protection, and where he lived until his death in 1941. The man whose reign is chiefly remembered for its repercussions on international relations, presided over calamity after calamity, leading to the catastrophe of World War I. Although Wilhelm should not be expected to assume the totality of responsibility, he was undoubtedly a man lacking in discipline, with an overdeveloped sense of theatre and a fundamental misreading of history. His ministers thereby had to contend with an absolutist and with a warrior prince.

Germany, 1871-1918: Past Exam Questions

1995

C1. Bismarck

Evaluate Bismarck's domestic and foreign policies.

1994

C1. Bismarck

"During the period 1871-1890 Bismarck acted with considerable skill and success to keep the peace in Europe." Discuss.

C2. Germany, 1870-1914

Treat of circumstances that led to the growth of German military power in the years preceding World War I.

1993

C3. The German and British Economies, 1870-1914

"From 1870 the German economy grew so rapidly that it had overtaken Britain by 1914 to become the leading industrial power in Europe." Discuss.

1992

E4. Essay

(ii) The contrasting fortunes of British and German industry, 1870-1914.

1991

E4. Essay

(ii) Bismarck's domestic policies.

1990

C2. France and Germany, 1870-1914

Treat of relations between France and Germany during the period 1870-1914.

1989

C2. Anglo-German Relations

Treat of relations between Germany and Great Britain during the period 1870-1914.

1988

C1. Bismarck

Treat of Bismarck's management of the affairs of the German empire from 1871 onwards.

1987

C5. Kaiser William II

"Kaiser William II of Germany, 1888-1918, by his personality and actions, contributed to the outbreak of World War I." Discuss.

1986

C2. Bismarck

Analyse the part played by Bismarck in the history of the German Empire, 1871-1890.

1985

C2. Bismarck

Discuss the domestic policies pursued by Bismarck as Chancellor of the German Empire, 1871-1890.

FRANCE, 1870-1914

5. Treat of Politics, Instability and Scandals in France during the period 1870-1914

Introduction - The Making of the Third Republic

The Second Empire was not ended by the will of the people, nor was it destroyed by revolution. Rather, it had been overthrown by the Franco-Prussian war. The decisive battle of Sedan in 1870 effectively witnessed the capitulation by France to the German invader. But the abdication of Napoleon III without a predestined successor and the collapse of the Second Empire left only a void. Thus, while the Third Republic, proclaimed by the National Assembly and led by Leon Gambetta and Adolphe Thiers, sought to fill the vacuum, the reality was that France had been thrust accidentally and prematurely into a new age. Perhaps not surprisingly, a period of great difficulty, confusion and instability ensued as crisis followed upon crisis. One of the first tasks which the National Assembly at Bordeaux set itself was to get France out of the German war as quickly as possible. The Treaty of Frankfurt, May 1871, was especially harsh and increased the tension that existed at all levels of French society. France agreed to the surrender of Alsace-Lorraine to Germany. This involved the loss of a population of nearly 1.5 million, though there was considerable migration to France from the surrendered territories. France also lost valuable mines and industries. War indemnities, amounting to five billion francs, furthered the strain. The fact that these were paid more rapidly than had been expected ensured the ending of German occupation of France by September 1873. Feelings of bitterness, engendered as a result of defeat, proved much more difficult to erase.

The Paris Commune, 1871

"Paris is trembling with anger". This anger was to erupt on 18th March 1871 and subsequently took the form of civil war. The Paris Commune reflected clearly the discontent and instability in French society. Parisians, who had undergone a four-month siege by the Germans, after the rest of the country had given up the struggle, resented the fact that the seat of government was in Bordeaux (and then in Versailles) rather than in Paris itself. Parisians were also offended by the humiliating terms of the Treaty of Frankfurt. They were fearful, too, about the election of Thiers, a former Monarchist, as head of government and about the large Monarchist representation in parliament. Thiers sparked off the civil war when he ordered the National Guard, Paris' own militia, to hand over their arms, insisting that the country could not afford to pay local soldiers who were not needed. Consisting of left-wing Republicans, Socialists, Communists, the National Defence and others, the *Communards* (including Raoul Rigault, Emile Duval and Jules Vallés) sought to rival the authority of Thiers' National Assembly. Fighting began on the Butte of Montmartre in Paris and lasted 73 days. Of the spectacle of Frenchmen fighting Frenchmen, George Clemenceau wrote *"The mob was in the grip of some kind of frenzy. All were shrieking like wild beasts"*.

Yet the Commune was not properly organised and its members had to contend with in-fighting. The 21st-28th May, *La Semaine Sanglante*, was the week that witnessed the most terrible bloodshed. Between 20,000 and 25,000 people died, both sides took hostages and shot them (among those shot was the Archbishop of Paris) and some of the finest buildings of Paris were demolished. A newspaper recorded *"one could see on the Seine a long stream of blood flowing with the current"*. In the end Paris was subjugated, the Communards having been ruthlessly suppressed.

Monarchists versus Republicans

During the 1870s the main political struggle in France was between Republicans and Monarchists. The Republic, so dramatically proclaimed by the *'men of 4th September'* had, at the time, no legal backing. To complicate matters still further, the elections of February 1871 returned a majority of Monarchists, so that a restoration of the Monarchy seemed likely. But those who wished to see an end to the Republic could not agree among themselves on a suitable candidate for the throne. Loyalties were split in three ways:

1. Napoleon III or his son (Bonapartists)
2. Comte de Paris (Orleanists)
3. Comte de Chambord (Bourbons)

Meanwhile, Thiers remained as head of government until he was replaced as President, in 1873, by Marshal MacMahon (a royalist). 1875 witnessed yet more political manoeuvrings in the National Assembly and in that year, in the absence of a constitution, a number of laws were passed. The President was to hold office for seven years and parliament was to consist of two bodies, the Chamber of Deputies and the Senate. Subsequent elections showed the country's approval of the Republic and cemented the regime. The clash between the two groups came to the fore again in 1877, however, with the *Seize Mai* crisis. In that year the Republican Chamber of Deputies refused to co-operate with MacMahon. The result was a victory for the Republicans and MacMahon had to witness a curtailment of his powers. Thereafter, the Republicans became more confident, but the strategic conflict between Left and Right remained. Many of the Republic's political leaders lived in fear of the old forces and Republicans continued to hold important positions at all levels of French society.

The Boulanger Affair, 1886-1889

The Boulanger Affair was one of the many crises that rocked the Republic to its foundations. General George Boulanger was appointed Minister for War in 1885. He was given the task of remodelling the army, which he did with great aplomb. Armaments were improved, the lot of the ordinary soldier was bettered and legislation was prepared to reduce military service. All of Boulanger's actions were accompanied by tremendous publicity as were his fighting speeches against Bismarck's Germany. Boulanger captured the imagination of French people, who nicknamed him *'General Revanche'*(the Revenge General). They saw him as another Napoleon who would restore France to her former glory. The French government, however, was alarmed by Boulanger's recklessness, fearing that he was planning to lead France into an unprepared war with Germany. In March 1888 he was dismissed from his post. Boulanger now became the darling of the discontented (conservative Monarchists, the army, church, fickle Parisian masses) and the idol of the Paris crowds. Songs were written about him and the cult of hero worship developed. In January 1889, Boulanger was persuaded to stand for election in Paris. An overwhelming victory for Boulanger seemed to pave the way for his forceful takeover of power - *coup d'état* - but although urged by his supporters to do so, Boulanger's nerve failed him at the last moment and he fled to Belgium where he committed suicide two years later. Thus, although Boulangerism ended as a farce, its importance lies not in the man or his actions, but in the support the movement attracted and the desperate need among the French people for a strong political figure, and the danger that it posed to the Third Republic.

The Panama Scandal

No sooner had the Boulanger episode died down than a fresh problem appeared, the Panama scandal. A new example of political corruption, the origin lies with Ferdinand de Lesseps and his attempt to repeat his triumph of the Suez canal with a Panama canal. The Panama Canal Company was launched and in 1881 construction began. Difficulties were encountered immediately. Miles of rock and mosquito-ridden swamps, combined with insufficient funds, made progress slow and difficult. Meanwhile, politicians and journalists were bribed to keep problems a secret and maintain public confidence. Then, in 1888, the government authorised the issue of lottery bonds to finance the venture. Not enough money was raised, the project was abandoned and in 1889 the company went bankrupt with debts in the region of £60m. Some 800,000 Frenchmen lost their money. Bowing to public pressure, the chamber set up an inquiry and the whole story of bribes and pay-offs was revealed. Several prominent parliamentarians and the Jewish financiers, Jacques de Reinach and Cornelius Herz, were implicated. Between 1892 and 1893 three French governments fell. The Republican regime was accused of being incurably corrupt and, in the ensuing months and years, Jews were to become convenient whipping boys for those who had lost their savings.

The Dreyfus Affair, 1894-1906

In 1894 a document known as the *bordereau* was found and this caused a huge scandal which was highly dramatic and full of tension, suspicion and bitterness. The discovery of the *bordereau* made clear that there was a leakage of military information to the German embassy. The suspicion fell on a Jewish military officer, Captain Alfred Dreyfus, who was found guilty of treason and sentenced to life imprisonment on Devil's Island. His family, among others, protested his innocence, maintaining that Dreyfus was a convenient scapegoat. When in March 1896, another document was found, General Picquart took up the case. Picquart believed that a man named Esterhazy was guilty of this crime. In January 1898, Esterhazy was tried by court martial and found not guilty. Thereafter Esterhazy fled to England where he lived under an assumed name until his death in 1923. Meanwhile, Picquart was dismissed from his position in the army and sent to Tunisia. The novelist Emile Zola then took up the case and, in an open letter to the President of the French Republic entitled *'J'accuse'*, the war office was accused of aiding and abetting a serious miscarriage of justice. Zola's letter roused passions to fever pitch and forced all French citizens to take sides. The Right believed Dreyfus to be guilty while the Left protested his innocence. Civil war was threatening. In 1899 a new trial was ordered. Dreyfus was found guilty *"with extenuating circumstances"*. A pardon was granted and a general amnesty for all involved followed. It was not until 1906, however, that Dreyfus was exonerated, reinstated into the army and awarded the Legion of Honour.

Conflict between Church and State

The Left-Right divide was again apparent in France with regard to the Catholic Church. The Church was closely identified with the interests of the Right (upper and middle classes) and the Left argued that it was the key danger to the Republic and responsible for most of France's ills. To this end, the Republic wished to reduce the Church's power. Education became the battlefield. In 1882 Jules Ferry, a determined opponent of clerical influence, sought to make education free, compulsory and secular. Jesuits were expelled from the country and the other orders debarred from teaching unless authorised by the government. Despite all the opposition to these laws, Pope Leo XIII regarded a faithful France as crucial to the future of Catholicism and urged Catholics there to both accept the Republican regime and meet their social obligations. The *Ralliement* was a failure, however, as feelings of hostility between Church and State were too deeply ingrained. The Dreyfus affair and the attitude adopted by the Church made the Republican government more determined to reduce the power of the Church. In 1901 the Premier, Waldeck-Rousseau, passed a Law of Associations which required members of all religious groups to obtain permission for their activities from the National Assembly. A new Premier, Emile Combes, saw to it that few permissions were granted. Finally, in 1905, under Aristide Briand, the law of Separation of Church and State was passed. The law was greeted by riots and, in the short term, the political cost was considerable, because, instead of healing old wounds, the Left and Right became more antagonistic. By 1914 the Church was, nonetheless, beginning to see that freedom from state interference and patronage could be beneficial and salutary.

Conclusion

The Third Republic, whose beginnings were so difficult, lasted until 1940. By 1914 it had in fact long outlasted all previous regimes since 1789. Although seeming to stagger from crisis to crisis, it was the form of government that divided Frenchmen least. The consolidation of the Republican position had started to take root as early as 1879 when parliament moved back to Paris. Around the same time, the Republicans had ensured that the *Marseillaise* was adopted as the national anthem, that the 14th July, Bastille Day, became a national holiday and that the slogan *'liberty, equality and fraternity'* became the motto of the Republic. Yet real and meaningful progress was severely hampered by the nature of French politics and the underlying divisions and tensions. Many of the political groupings were themselves fragmented and for the period in question, no single group could gain sufficient support to provide long and lasting government. The shifting panorama of temporary coalitions which dominated French political life, can be shown by adding up the number of cabinet governments - between 1870 and 1940 there were 108. An average length of a ministry was between eight and ten months. Such statistics should not, however, cloud the fact that the Third Republic did hold conflicting political interests together in one situation and that progress was made on several fronts. Included among the strengths of the Republic are the payment to Germany of war indemnities, the reorganisation of the army, educational reforms, industrial and foreign progress and the very considerable colonial expansion that took place.

6. French Foreign Policy, 1870-1914

The Franco-Prussian War and its Aftermath

The cause of the Franco-Prussian war in 1870 is undoubtedly related to the progress of German unification and to Bismarck's *"never-ending pursuit of Prussian interests"*. Also closely related to the outbreak of the war is Napoleon III's lack of insight and understanding on the foreign front, a situation which caused France to stand idly by, while Prussia defeated Austria in 1866. Thereafter, the war grew out of Bismarck's desire to unite the northern German states with the southern ones. His opportunity to do just this came with the Spanish succession issue and his successful 'doctoring' of the Ems telegram. Believing themselves to have been insulted, the French declared war on Prussia on 19th July 1870. Although it was widely believed that the French army was ready *"down to the last gaiter button"*, equipped as it was with capable leaders like MacMahon and Bazaine and new weapons, the Chaissepot rifle and the Mitrailleuse machine gun, the reality was very different. Supplies were inadequate and unevenly distributed, uniforms were in short supply and confusion and delay were widespread. Meanwhile, battles at Saarbrücken, Worth, Wissenbourg and Metz, as well as Sedan in September 1870, ensured German victory. Napoleon was captured, the monarchy collapsed and France was declared a Republic. By January 1871, Paris, too, was forced into submission. The Treaty of Frankfurt which was now concluded between Germany and France forced France to cede the two provinces of Alsace and Lorraine to Germany as well as pay 5 billion francs in indemnities. There would be German occupation of France until the money was paid.

Aims - Imperialism

The harsh terms of the Treaty of Frankfurt, published in May 1871, greatly angered Frenchmen and led to a deep psychological hatred of Germans. Thus, although the war indemnities were cleared by 1873, the loss of Alsace-Lorraine remained a burning issue. As a constant reminder of the loss, the Strasbourg (capital of Alsace) monument in Paris was solemnly draped in black. The desire for revenge against Germany was well demonstrated by the support and popularity of General Boulanger in the 1880s. Yet, France could never hope to defeat Germany on her own, and potential allies were all monarchies and suspicious of the Republican regime. At the same time, Bismarck's complicated web of alliances after 1871 ensured that France was kept in diplomatic isolation. Seeking compensation, and encouraged to do so by Bismarck, French foreign policy thereby concentrated on the acquisition of colonies. The *'expansive urge'* of the 1880s was particularly promoted by Jules Ferry. France had already taken possession of Algeria, one of the most fertile areas of the world. They knew that the next logical step was to take Tunisia, Algeria's neighbour, but the cost and bloodthirsty wars in Algeria made her hesitate. Only when Italy showed interest in Tunisia did the French make a move. 40,000 troops were sent to Tunisia and after a brief military campaign, France took control. The cost of the campaign, however, made Premier Jules Ferry very unpopular with the Assembly and before long his government was brought down.

Imperialism

Over the following years, France lost her historic links with Egypt. Egyptian bankruptcy had compelled France and Britain to take financial control of the government in Cairo. But when an Egyptian nationalist revolt broke out in 1882 under Colonel Arabi Pasha and the British 'responded' by sending in troops, the French, remembering what had happened to Ferry, refused to take any part in the operation. In so doing, they effectively abandoned Egypt to the British. Ferry, a convinced imperialist, became Premier again in 1883. Disgusted by the timidity of the previous French government over Egypt, Ferry now sought colonies elsewhere. French control over Madagascar was established. The explorer, Savorgnav de Brazza, then claimed part of the Congo basin for France. Indo-China was the next step for the French as they sought to expand their trading interest there. Fierce outbreaks of fighting before French occupation was accepted, ensured that these efforts proved very expensive. Perhaps not surprisingly, the Assembly in Paris was annoyed by Ferry's insistence on more and more money to pay for the conquests. In March 1885, Ferry was voted out of office. Meanwhile, relations with Germany, which had eased somewhat between 1879 and 1885, again worsened during the Boulanger crisis and the Schnaebele incident in 1887, when a French espionage agent was arrested on German soil, once again prompted a war scare. The coming to power in Germany of Wilhelm II in 1888 was to see relations deteriorate still further.

Franco-Russian Alliance, 1894

After Bismarck ceased to be German Chancellor in 1890, his successors abandoned the careful delicacy of his diplomacy. They allowed the Reinsurance Treaty with Russia to lapse. Faced with the obvious hardening of the German-Austrian alliance, feeling isolated and in need of an ally, Russia became more responsive to French overtures of friendship. Russia also urgently required financial aid to finance programmes of railway building, to develop armaments and industry and to service its huge national debt. France, for her part, isolated and vulnerable since 1870, was anxious to do all she could to improve her position. Consequently by 1891, France had lent Russia two billion francs and Russian stock was in great demand on the French market. After two years of negotiation, a military convention was signed between the two powers, leading to the Franco-Russian alliance of 1894. France would come to the aid of Russia in the event of an attack by Germany, or by Italy supported by Germany. Thus, it was at the expense of throwing in her lot with Russia that France had defeated the central purpose of Bismarck's diplomacy since 1871 - the necessity to avoid a two-front war. Provided that Russian promises could be trusted, France would not again find herself fighting Germany alone.

Conflict at Fashoda, 1898

Throughout the 1890s, the French continued to create a vast colonial empire. This was the period of the so-called *'scramble for Africa'* and France was determined that she, too, should take her cut. From Senegal in West Africa, France established a vast Saharan empire. But with Britain, Germany, France, Portugal, Belgium and Italy all seeking a share of the spoils, a clash between the European powers was almost inevitable. The French were involved in such a clash at Fashoda in 1898 when they met the British head on. Captain Marchand had led a small French force across Africa from the French Congo. He hoped to claim the source of the Nile for France. On reaching Fashoda in July 1898, Marchand hoisted the French flag. Shortly afterwards, General Kitchener, accompanied by a larger British force, consisting of five gunboats and 2,000 men, claimed Fashoda for the British. A serious crisis loomed. Neither Kitchener nor Marchand wished to take responsibility for opening hostilities, however, and they decided to refer the matter to their respective governments. Delcassé, the French Foreign Minister, recognised the weakness of Marchand's military position. Prudence and realism dictated that Delcassé ask Marchand to withdraw, which he duly did in March 1899. While the crisis might have led to war, a peaceful settlement was reached. The Nile Valley was recognised as a British sphere of influence and Western Africa as a French sphere.

The Entente Cordiale, 1904

Relations with Britain remained strained over the next few years and were aggravated by the pro-Boer sentiments of the French during the Boer War, 1899-1902. However, thereafter, mutual fears of Germany brought about a reconciliation. An accord between both countries was helped by a successful state visit to Paris by Edward VII in May 1903. Two months later, President Loubet, accompanied by Delcassé, visited London. Prolonged discussions between both countries culminated in the signing of the *Entente Cordiale*, or 'Friendly Understanding', on 8th April 1904. This was not a military alliance, nor was it an agreement directed against any specific enemy. Rather it cleared away outstanding differences and remaining obstacles to Anglo-French co-operation. In the most important section of the agreement, France agreed not to obstruct British action in Egypt, while Britain recognised France's interests in Morocco. Secret clauses allowed for a future British protectorate in Egypt and a French protectorate in Morocco. The agreement opened the way for the possibility of a military alliance between two old enemies, at some time in the future.

The Moroccan Crisis, 1905-1911

Following the *Entente Cordiale*, French involvement in Morocco increased. Delcassé hoped to establish a French protectorate in Morocco by gaining control of the Moroccan debt. His plans to achieve this were so successful that Germany became alarmed. In March 1905, Kaiser Wilhelm II paid a call on the Sultan of Morocco in Tangiers. Claiming to defend Morocco's independence, Wilhelm demanded an international conference to discuss the position of Morocco. The Algeciras Conference of 1906 was a complete rebuff to Germany. The independence of Morocco was recognised but French influence remained dominant in policy and finance. In the aftermath of the Conference, the situation in Morocco continued to be unstable. Late in 1910, France decided on a military takeover. Using various pretexts, French troops occupied the Moroccan town of Fez and moved into the interior. The Germans claimed that their action was in breach of the Algeciras agreement and responded by sending a gunboat, the *Panther,* to Agadir. The Germans also demanded compensation in the French Congo. The second Moroccan crisis threatened a major international conflict but at the Moroccan Convention of November 1911, Germany, realising that France had greater support, backed down and accepted that Morocco would become a French protectorate.

Triple Entente - Conclusion

One outcome of the Moroccan crisis was that Britain and Russia, France's ally, drew closer together. In August 1907 the main areas of friction were settled and this, in turn, cleared the way for the Triple Entente between Britain, France and Russia. Yet while the collective arrangements of the Triple Entente completed the division of Europe into armed camps (the Triple Alliance and Triple Entente), it is important to realise that French foreign policy on the eve of World War I was not intended to provoke conflict in Europe and that her relations, for the most part, were more cautious than aggressive. Further, it should be noted that right up until the outbreak of war, France was uncertain of British military support. Meanwhile, in the years immediately before war, French foreign policy was dominated by the French President Raymond Poincaré. Overseas expansion continued and, by 1914, General Lyautey, one of the greatest of all colonial administrators, had rounded off French control of north-west Africa. France had, by then, some 11 million square kilometres of Africa, and her entire empire was second only to Britain's, thus giving credence to Jules Ferry's vision that France *"should carry everywhere its flag, its arms, its genius"*. Lack of continuity in government however, meant that while the empire gave a great psychological boost to France's status as a great world power, there was often no thought-out policy from Paris and resources were frequently wasted, neglected or abused. The empire was very much the creation of men on the spot.

7. Church-State Relations in France, 1870-1914

Background - 1870 Position

The conflict between the Catholic Church and the French government during the period 1870-1914 did not spring up overnight but dated back to the French Revolution (1789) and its aftermath, when the French government confiscated and sold church property. At the same time, all citizens of France were allowed to elect bishops and priests. The Church, for its part, strenuously opposed the revolution and the Republican doctrines which inspired it. Peace was brought to the religious conflict in 1801 when Napoleon I and Pius VII signed a *Concordat* (agreement). Henceforth, the clergy were to receive state salaries and, while the French government could nominate bishops, the Pope retained the right to confirm the nominations. This *Concordat* remained in force after the collapse of the Second Empire (1870). Meanwhile, the Church was seen as an integral part of French life, controlling as it did, almost all elementary and secondary education. Over half the boys and almost all girls attended Catholic parochial schools. The Church was also involved in charitable work such as looking after the poor, the sick and the old. Around 30,000 men and 120,000 women belonged to religious orders or congregations in France in 1870. The Sacré Coeur church, on the Butte of Montmartre in Paris, became an impressive symbol of the Church's power. The huge, white-domed church which dominates the skyline was built from donations given by supporters of the Right.

Areas of Tension in the Third Republic

To some commentators, the Third Republic, which was created after the defeat of France in the Franco-Prussian war, existed simply because it was *"the form of government that divided Frenchmen least"*. Certainly, it had low prestige and this was reflected by its poor showing at the polls. Politicians viewed the Church as the key danger to the Republic, accusing the clergy of indoctrinating people with anti-Republican ideas in their sermons and in the schools which they controlled. As Gambetta so aptly put it in 1877 - *"le cléricalisme, voilà l'ennemi"*(the Church is the enemy). The political conservatism of the clergy was matched by a philosophical and scientific conservatism. Thus, it was that many French intellectuals saw the destruction of clerical influence as a necessary first step to social progress and scientific and technological advancement. A further problem lay in the association of the French Church with the monarchists and imperialists. The aristocracy was solidly Catholic and many of the hierarchy came from the nobility. At the same time, the wealthier middle classes and higher officials supported the Church. Yet, the Republican politicians who now controlled France were, in the main, middle and lower middle class men, so that social and class tensions were added to the political and philosophical ones.

Jules Ferry and Education

Education had long been a battlefield between the Right, who wanted the Catholic Church to keep its control over the schools and the Left, who wanted to extend state control. Jules Ferry, who was appointed Minister for Education in 1879, was a determined opponent of clerical influence. Ferry expelled clerics from the Higher Council of Education and he declared that the granting of degrees and diplomas should be confined to the state. In 1882 Ferry put a bill through the Assembly which made primary education free, secular and compulsory. Women's training colleges were founded throughout France as a first step to breaking religious control of female education. Ferry also sought to stop anybody from teaching who was not authorised by the state to do so, and their premises were closed down by troops and police. Meanwhile, the schools set up by the state were theoretically neutral in religious matters. Their teachers were expected to love the Republic, to hate its enemies and to abhor ignorance and superstition.

Other Attacks

Since the Church opposed such reforms, it was inevitable that there would be confrontation between Ferry and the major religious orders. This led to the expulsion of powerful religious groups like the Jesuits from France. Other orders, whose schools were closed down, quit the country. An outcry from supporters of the Church followed and this, combined with the fact that there were relatively few state schools, meant that these early measures had little effect. Yet even though some of the orders were allowed back, the Catholic Church in France inevitably became the enemy of the Republic. Feelings of animosity were deepened by other laws which were enacted over the years. Salaries paid to the clergy, for example, were reduced, seminarists had to perform military service, civil marriage was made compulsory and divorce was instituted. Simultaneously, public displays of religion were forbidden. Nuns were expelled from the hospitals, and chaplains were removed from the army. In 1891 the Assumptionists, the most anti-Republican of all religious orders, were dissolved.

The Ralliement (Rapprochement)

While Pius IX remained on the Papal throne there was no possibility of any relations between the Church and the Republic other than a state of open, or barely concealed, war. In 1878, with the ascension of Leo XIII, the opportunity of a détente was brought about. Leo XIII, though an elderly man when elected Pope, was remarkably open-minded and diplomatic and prepared to make concessions to improve the position of the Church in France. Thus, while he publicly deplored the many anti-religious acts carried out by the French parliament, he admitted that the government's anti-clericalism was caused by the anti-republicanism of the clergy. Consequently, in 1884, a papal encyclical enjoined the French bishops not to exhibit hostility to the established authorities of the state. A further step was taken towards a *rapprochement* with the Republic in 1890 when Cardinal Lavigerie, primate of Africa and a noted royalist, advised French Catholics to rally to the Republic and defend the interests of the Church by taking part in political life. This was reinforced in 1892 when Leo XIII issued the encyclical *'Au Milieu des Sollicitudes'*. While some Catholics and royalists did now enter public life and place their considerable talents at the disposal of the state, the Pope's instructions, for the most part, fell on deaf ears. Dislike of the Republic was too deeply ingrained and the clergy were too hostile to the Republicans to change the habits of a lifetime.

Dreyfus Affair - Waldeck-Rousseau/Emile Combes

The *ralliement* was dealt a further death blow by the attitude adopted by the Church during the Dreyfus affair (1894-1906). Though innocent, Catholic newspapers accepted evidence against Dreyfus as genuine and were particularly virulent in their anti-semitism and in their opposition to the Liberals and Republicans who championed Dreyfus' cause. Meanwhile in June 1899, a cabinet of Republican defence was formed under Waldeck-Rousseau, a former colleague of Gambetta and Ferry. Soon afterwards, Waldeck-Rousseau put forward a scheme compelling religious congregations to apply to the National Assembly for legal recognition - the Law of Associations. Having denounced the Church as a rival power within the state, this was the means by which Waldeck-Rousseau sought to control religious orders. Such a policy was further endorsed by the passionately anti-clerical Emile Combes. Combes brought the whole administrative machinery into play in support of his campaign. He saw to it that those who asked for recognition under the new law found, with few exceptions, their requests rejected. The orders were dissolved. Their members were forced to emigrate and their property was confiscated and sold cheaply by the government to its own supporters. About ten thousand schools were closed and clerics were forbidden to teach.

Pius X - Law of Separation, 1905

The law of July 1904 forbade the religious orders to teach in any school, whether it was controlled by them or not. At the same time, priests were excluded from the state examination for the *agrégation* (teaching diploma); responsibility for burials was attributed to the secular authorities and crucifixes were removed from law courts. In that same year - 1904 - Pius X succeeded Leo XIII. The conflict with Rome now worsened as Pius protested against the state visit of the French President, Émile Loubet, to the King of Italy. The Vatican did not recognise the new Italian kingdom and resented the fact that France did. Further differences between Rome and Paris arose over the appointment and dismissal of bishops. Within this context, the Law of Separation of church and state (first tabled by Combes in 1904) secured passage in 1905 under Aristide Briand. Freedom of worship was granted to all religions and state support was withdrawn from the Catholic Church. Traditionally, the state had contributed 40 million francs annually to maintain church buildings and to pay clergy. All property was confiscated and would later be handed over to elected *Associations Culturelles*, whose members might, or might not, be Catholic. These societies would then be charged with the task of arranging public worship.

Effects of Separation

The Law of Separation was considered by the Catholic Church to be neither just nor generous. It was greeted by riots as angry parents, priests and nuns tried to defy officials and police. Pius X condemned the law in an encyclical letter *'Vehementer'* but Combes and his successor, Briand, had won. In the aftermath of the separation law there was confusion, poverty, a curbing of the Church's power and influence, and a decline in vocations to the priesthood as only those prepared to lead a life of extreme hardship now entered. There was also a decline in church attendance and membership, a drop in the number of baptisms and a rise in civil marriages. Yet, while the Church in

7. Church-State Relations in France, 1870-1914

France was poorer and smaller, it enjoyed, for the first time in years, freedom from state interference. The papacy could appoint bishops without taking into account the preferences of the French government. The general quality of the clergy greatly improved and *curés* (priests) and *vicaires* (vicars) gained more respect now that they were no better off than their parishioners. At the same time, the state benefited. The National Assembly no longer spent a disproportionate amount of time quarrelling with the Church. Thus, it was that while separation temporarily exacerbated relations, in the end it tended to reduce the tension between church and state. Although the majority of Catholics were not yet reconciled to the Republic by 1914, with the decline of clerical influence in politics, the violence of anti-clerical sentiment abated.

8. La Belle Époque

Introduction - Fashion

La Belle Époque (The Beautiful Era) was the label given to the decades either side of the turn of the century. What made this one of the great ages of French history was, more than anything else, its achievement in art, letters and sciences. A renaissance occurred and subsequent generations, looking back, maintained that it was the *"time in which we'd most like to have lived"*. The worldwide reputation that Paris had in fashion, for example, helped to portray the years of the Third Republic as a time of 'wine and roses'. One name that stands out in the fashion industry is Charles Frederick Worth. Although an Englishman by birth, Worth set himself up in Paris and it was there that he created an immense luxury industry that stood up against international fashion competition for forty years. Exhibiting a genius for original design and a flair for elegance, the *Times* of London wrote in March 1894 that Worth *"set the taste and ordained the fashion of Paris"*. Worth also introduced many features into the fashion world which were to become standard in the 20th century. Mannequins were used to show his clothes. These delighted private customers and helped to boost sales. Not surprisingly, Paris couture was much in demand by the well-to-do.

Art - Impressionism [I]

Nowhere was the vigour and vitality of France's cultural genius shown to better effect than in the originality and experimentation of her painters and in the ascendancy she established over European painting in these decades. The Third Republic produced a galaxy of brilliant artists. A list of their names is a roll call of the famous. Monet and Renoir led the way. Other Impressionists included Pissarro, Dégas, Sisley and Morisot. And although Van Gogh was Dutch and Picasso Spanish, both found their cultural homes in France. These artists were concerned with pure aestheticism, the doctrine of *'art for art's sake'*, which now became a cult. Objective reality was entirely subordinated to the personal emotions and taste of the painter himself. Artists must paint regardless of any public, only to satisfy themselves or at most to please their fellow artists, who alone might be expected to share their sensitivity. It was an aristocratic, not a democratic, conception. Freed from all social and moral considerations, the artists belonging to this new school of Impressionism, were prepared to risk shocking their contemporaries. Therefore, when the Impressionists held their first exhibition in Paris in 1874, they were regarded as rebels by the orthodox critics. Gone was the classical emphasis on composition that had been in vogue under the Second Empire. Concerned above all with registering an immediate impression of transient beauty, the artists depicted refractions and reflections of light and shade, as well as the play of light which produced delicate tints of colour.

Art - Impressionism [II]

The Impressionists revolutionised painting with their shimmering, colourful pictures. Bright colours were applied boldly side-by-side and the effect was sometimes rather similar to a mosaic. They painted rapidly, preferring to work outdoors in the natural light. No longer seeing the photographer as a rival, many Impressionists were influenced by the new forms of photography. It was Monet's painting *'Impression'* that gave the movement its name. It is a painting of the sun rising over the sea and shows the effect of light and shade out-of-doors as it had struck Monet's eye. Monet was especially interested in subtle changes in atmospheric effects. Renoir loved to show the effect of sunlight on figures and flowers. *'Two Sisters (On the Terrace)'* does just that. *'Moulin de la Galette'* is another Renoir painting. Monet was a realistic painter. He departed from the symbolic and storytelling qualities of earlier art and dealt with pure, everyday, visual images. Pissarro and Sisley painted the French countryside and river scenes. Dégas did not use the divided colour technique, but his paintings are spontaneous and immediate. *'The Dancers'* is one such example and, as well as painting ballet dancers, Degas also enjoyed portrayals of horse-racing. Morisot painted women in scenes of everyday domestic life. The group of Impressionists held eight joint exhibitions of their paintings, the last in 1886. Thereafter, as artists continued to develop their own interests and techniques, the period of Post-Impressionism began.

Post-Impressionism

The Post-Impressionists added other dimensions to the visual effects of the Impressionists. Above all, they sought greater independence and simplicity. The most important post-Impressionists in France were Cézanne, Gaugin, Van Gogh, Seurat and Toulouse-Lautrec. Cézanne lived at the same time as the earlier Impressionists. Like them, he was interested in light, colour and atmospheric effects. But he refused to disregard deliberate composition and architectural form, emphasising instead their solidity. *'Mont Sainte Victoire'* was a landscape which the artist painted many times. Gaugin left France altogether to live in the South Sea islands, where he painted colourful, decorative pictures in a style influenced by primitive art. Van Gogh expressed his passionate emotions in colourful paintings of everyday objects and events. Seurat carried to extremes the Impressionist interest in technical theories of colour and light. His large pictures had an almost architectural order. *'Sunday Afternoon on the Island of La Grande Jatte'*, made up from tiny dots of colour demonstrates his use of the Pointillist technique. Toulouse-Lautrec painted dance hall and circus scenes with biting satirical overtones. *La Belle Époque* also saw the development of a style which was called Cubism and which was eventually to develop into abstract art. Picasso was a leading exponent of this art form.

Literature [I]

The Third Republic witnessed a period of realism in literature. Writers sought to express the immediate sensations of the world and events. In particular, the novelist became a kind of social scientist, registering and recording life. The Goncourt brothers, Edmond and Jules, wrote a series of novels describing, on the basis of a careful documentation, the more sordid aspects of French life. They were followed by Emile Zola and Anatole France, popular novelists of *La Belle Époque*, who introduced a note of naturalism into their writings and who also provided a large dose of social criticism. Zola's *'Les Rougan-Macquart'* is psychological in essence and traces through a series of novels - twenty novels were written between 1871 and 1893 - the case history of a degenerating French family. Each of the novels describes the adventures of one of the several members of the Rougan-Macquart family, and each treats a different profession, trade, or class of society. Thus, the characters range from scheming senators or financiers to the degraded and wretched victims of social injustice. *'The Belly of Paris'* (1873), for example, gives a vivid picture of the central markets of Paris, *'The Grog Shop'* (1877) is a terrifying portrait of the effect of alcoholism on industrial workers in Paris and *'Nana'* (1880) is a study of prostitution and other vices. Zola excelled in writing descriptions.

Literature [II]

Anatole France was another ardent critic of his age. His first successful novel was *'The Crime of Sylvester Bonnard'* (1881), but it was the famous Dreyfus affair that led him to write more specifically about political and social issues. His novels of the 1900s reflect his part in the struggle for social justice that took place in the country. *'Penguin Island'* (1908), *'The Gods are Athirst'* (1912) and *'The Revolt of the Angels' (1914)* ridicule society and its institutions. Such was his clear and elegant style and the subtlety of his observation that Anatole France won the Nobel Price for literature in 1921. Guy de Maupassant, another prominent writer of La Belle Époque, is considered to be one of the world's great short story writers. De Maupassant wrote clearly and simply and his tales deal with many subjects - the middle class, peasants, government officials, the Franco-Prussian war, outdoor life, animals and the supernatural. The best known include *'The Tellier House'* (1881), *'Yvette'* (1885), *'Toine'* (1886) and *'The Horla'* (1887). Such tales are realistic reflections of life and portray their author's brutally sarcastic and pessimistic attitude toward people. Sympathy was reserved for the poor and the outcasts. A number of Catholic writers also gained popularity and renown. J.K. Huysman's *'La Cathédrale'* portrayed the deep mysticism of the French Catholic mind at the end of the nineteenth century, while Charles Péguy achieved a marriage of Catholicism and patriotism in his poetry. His best known poem *'Le Mystère de la Charité de Jeanne d'Arc'*, reflected the nostalgia which was felt in 1912 on the 500th anniversary of Joan of Arc.

Sculpture - Music - Entertainment

Sculpture reached a level of mastery during this period with the powerful and popular work of Auguste Rodin. Rodin gave his sculpture figures a look of surface movement and used extraordinary momentary poses. One of his best known works is *'The Thinker'*. It is of a man deep in thought, leaning forward with his chin resting on his hand. The position of the man's body, as well as his face, give the feeling of concentration. *'The Citizens of Calais'* is another Rodin sculpture. It showed six men, walking in single file, to give themselves up to Edward III in the hope that he would spare Calais and all the rest of the citizens from destruction. Rodin also made portraits in sculpture. The sculptor Maillol won appreciation for his nudes. In music, too, France was prolific in genius. Massnet and Saint-Saëns, César Frank, Gabriel Fouré, Maurice Ravel and Claude Debussy, formed an unrivalled group of young composers in all the main musical forms. Debussy, for example, wrote music with sounds that call forth such images as moonlight, waterfalls and fireworks. 1902 saw the production of his *'Pelléas et Mélisande'*. The Frenchman, Jacques Offenbach acquired international fame for his light music and operettas. But as well as offering high culture, Paris also presented popular entertainment. The *Folies-Bergères* and the *Moulin Rouge* music halls were as much frequented by artists and the working classes as the *Opéra* and *Comédie Française* were by the bourgeoisie.

Science - An Evaluation

The important cultural achievements made during *La Belle Époque* include not just those made in art, letters and music, but also the advances made in science and technology. Pierre and Marie Curie discovered radium and, in so doing, helped to carry further the inquiry into the secret relationship between energy and matter. In biology Louis Pasteur studied micro-organisms and devised the modern germ theory. He developed many kinds of vaccination, as well as the pasteurisation of milk. The Pasteur Institute, opened in 1888, was dedicated to research in work he had started. New standards and techniques were widespread. Little wonder, then, that Paris became the *'Athens of the West'*, attracting artists, poets and philosophers from all over the world. Yet, in looking back over the period, we must be careful not to see it through rose-coloured spectacles. The period was by no means *'belle'* for many French people. Coinciding with France's spectacular achievements were the internal tensions of the day and the inability, at times, to solve domestic problems. Political quarrels, long hours, little security for many workers, and public concern that France was losing in the race for international prestige, all played a part and may have inspired, to some extent, *'La Belle Époque'*. Perhaps even the artist's senses were *"honed by his suffering"*.

France, 1870-1914: Past Exam Questions

1995

E4. Essay

(ii) Relations between the Catholic Church and the State in France and Italy, 1870-1914.

1994

C4. France, 1870-1914

Treat of political instability and cultural achievement in France during the period 1870-1914.

1993

C1. The Franco-Prussian War, 1870-1871

Account for the defeat of France in the Franco-Prussian War and assess the impact of that war on France.

C2. Church-State Relations, 1870-1914

Treat of relations between the Roman Catholic Church and the state in each of two of the following countries, Italy, France, Germany, during the period 1870-1914.

1992

C2. France, 1870-1914

"Although France was a deeply divided country between 1870 and 1914, the period saw considerable cultural achievement at home, and expansion overseas." Discuss.

1991

C2. France

Treat of the Third French Republic, 1870-1914, under two of the following headings:

(i) The establishment of the Third French Republic

(ii) Church-State relations

(iii) Cultural achievements

(iv) Economic developments

(v) Political scandals

1990

C2. France and Germany, 1870-1914

Treat of relations between France and Germany during the period 1870-1914.

1989

C3. Church-State Relations

Treat of relations between the Roman Catholic Church and the state in each of two of the following countries, Italy, France, Germany, during the period 1870-1914.

1988

E4. Essay

(ii) Church-State relations in France, 1870-1914

1987

C4. France, 1870-1919

Account for the defeat of France in the Franco-Prussian War, 1870-1871, and assess the impact of that war on France up to the Versailles Settlement, 1919.

1986

E4. Essay

(ii) Literature and the Arts in France, 1870-1914.

1985

C3. France, 1870-1914

Treat of three of the following aspects of French history in the period 1870-1914:

(i) Cultural developments

(ii) Church-State relations

(iii) Political scandals

(iv) Overseas expansion

RUSSIA, 1870-1924

9. Alexander III, 1854-1894

Introduction - The Reactionary Tsar

Since the seventeenth century, Russia had been ruled by the Romanov dynasty. Their rule was the perfect example of autocracy* and through the centuries the Tsars had blindly adhered to the status quo, managing to survive without providing much of a *raison d'être*. Their autocracy came under threat in the nineteenth century, and in 1881 Alexander II's assassination at the hands of a terrorist group, the People's Will, showed clearly what enemies of the state could do. Alexander's son, Alexander III succeeded him. A giant of a man, Alexander III believed that the murder of his father, which he witnessed, was evidence that the reformist policies of his father were a failure. Consequently, Alexander *"mounted the throne as a soldier mounts the breach"*, determined to crush all opposition. He refused to listen to appeals for a national assembly and a free social order, and on 25th April 1881, he issued a manifesto in which he made known his determination to uphold and consolidate his God-given autocracy. To this end, Alexander was influenced by Konstantin Pobedonostsev, the procurator of the Holy Synod. Pobedonostsev believed that the only salvation for Russia lay in obedience to the absolute authority of the monarchy. *"Parliamentarianism"*, he said *"is the great lie of our time"*. Therefore, come hell or high water, the autocracy had to be preserved. The pure theory of repression which was advocated ensured that the years after 1881 were reactionary ones, a time when the government and its supporters in the Church and among the landowners, did all they could to undo the advances made under Alexander II.

Repression

The reign of Alexander III is known for the severity of its repression. Liberal members of government, including Loris Melikov and his plans of a new course for Russian history, were ousted and a more conservative group took over. Among these was the new Minister of the Interior, Dmitri Tolstoi, who until his death in 1889, was in charge of implementing the reactionary measures now taken. The powers of the *Okrana,* or state police, were widened. The job of these men was to seek out persons suspected of opposition to the Tsar. There was no need to prove that a prisoner was plotting against the emperor, nor was it necessary to hold a trial before a suspect could be exiled. In 1887 a group of terrorists, among whom was Lenin's brother, Alexander, was captured and executed for attempting to assassinate the Tsar. Meanwhile, the *Okrana* worked through secret agents who joined suspected organisations, or enrolled as students in a university. The state police was unwilling to admit a mistake and its headquarters contained the *'black room'* where mail was opened and read before being sent on its way. It also had the power to censor. Newspapers and books were rigidly

---

* government by one person

controlled and writers forced to go into hiding or abroad. Freedom of speech was removed. These repressive measures were felt especially in the area of education. All student organisations were forbidden and whatever independence the universities had exercised in the past, was taken away.

Privileges of the Nobility

Since the tsarist regime depended on the support of the nobility, steps were taken to improve their political, economic and social position. Under Alexander III, the nobility was given more privileges than ever before. Credit banks were established for large estate owners. In 1885, for example, the Nobles' State Bank was founded, which gave loans to landowners at far more favourable terms than did the Peasants' Bank. The land-owning classes were also exempt from paying tax. Added to that, land captains - who had to be members of the nobility - replaced the former justices of the peace, previously the main link between the *Zemstvos** and the peasantry. The land captains wielded almost omnipotent power in the villages and sought to keep the peasants in bondage. A revision of the constitution of *Zemstvos* in 1889 guaranteed paramount power to the noble element, with a 57% majority. The peasant element was correspondingly diminished to 43%. In education, too, a system of privilege was introduced under a new education minister, Delyanov. In 1887 fees in secondary schools were raised so that *"children of coachmen, servants, laundresses, small shop-keepers and the like"* would not be able to attend. Access to university education was even more elitist. Not surprisingly, the peasants felt bitterly resentful of this system of privilege.

Russification

The Russian empire had grown over the years from the state of Muscovy to include many different races and religions. In effect, it had become a *"huge multi-national conglomerate"*. To the west and south of the empire were Finns, Poles, Lithuanians, Estonians, Latvians and Ukranians. In the nineteenth century, nationalist movements had grown up among some of these minority peoples, a situation that was deemed 'disloyal'. Pobedonstsev's answer was to impose on all subjects a policy of *Russification*, thereby extending the repressive policies to the non-Russian people of the empire. Russification was based on a sacred belief in the destiny of Russian people *(Narodnost)*. It concerned itself with the breakdown of any traces of a separate identity through a process of forced assimilation i.e. a united nation would be created by imposing on all subjects one religion, one language, one culture and one central authority. The Russian Orthodox church, for example, was promoted and property relating to other churches was secularised. In schools, minority languages were disallowed as the teaching of Russian was enforced. Schools that showed resistance were closed down. Simultaneously, business with court or government officials had to be conducted in Russian. Through an army of state officials, some centralisation was brought about on the administrative level. The policy of Russification was enforced with special harshness in the Polish parts of the empire but there, as elsewhere, it failed. National groups remained as independent as ever and looked forward to political independence.

* Established in 1864, the Zemstvos were democratically elected district/provisional councils.

Anti-Semitism

It was probably the Russian Jews who had to undergo the worst torments. The European part of the empire contained a high percentage of Jews. They were seen as a distinct and threatening minority but, although anti-semitism had been endemic in Russia for generations, it was only now that it was used as an instrument of government policy. According to Pobedonostsev *"one third of the Jews of Russia must die, one third emigrate and one third assimilate"*. A Jewish girl, Hessia Helfmann, had been one of Alexander II's assassins. This was the pretext for a wave of government inspired pogroms (215 in all) which brought terror, death and rape to more than a hundred Jewish localities in the spring and summer of 1881. The May laws of 1882 followed. They forbade Jews to settle in rural districts. They were henceforth forcibly 'resettled' in the ghettos of the interior. Jewish doctors were excluded from employment with public authorities and in 1887 a quota system was introduced which kept Jewish children attending schools and universities to a minimum. In 1889, Jews were forbidden from practising law and in 1890 they lost their franchise rights in the *Zemstvos*, even though they were required to pay *Zemstvo* taxes. This process reached its climax in 1891 and 1892. At the same time as these laws were making themselves felt, Jewish homes and businesses were attacked by mobs of Russians. The police made no effort to interfere.

Opposition Groups

Such harassment inevitably bred opposition and led to revolutionary ideas. Throughout the late nineteenth century political movements in Russia were forced to organise in secret. The vigilance of the tsarist police made this a necessity. One opposition group was the *Narodniks*. This was a movement *"to the people"*. It was comprised of students, usually the offspring of the middle and well-educated classes, who put on peasant dress and went out into the country. Living with the peasants, the *Narodniks* helped them by teaching and nursing them. When they failed, they became extreme. 'The People's Will', responsible for Alexander II's assassination, was an offshoot of the *Narodniks*, as were other 'populist' movements. A further group was the Anarchists or Nihilists. They were a very idealistic group who wanted no type of government at all. There also existed a small liberal organisation who wanted to westernise Russia and bring about a constitutional monarchy, through reform rather than revolution. While Marxism was not yet widespread, George Plekhanov succeeded in founding the Emancipation of Labour and thus laid the foundation for a future political party, the Social Democrats.

Industrialisation

Only in one area did Alexander III act with any enlightenment. This was in industrialisation. Up to 1885, Russia's rate of industrial growth had been extremely low. Thereafter a coherent and determined policy of industrial expansion was initiated, much of it under the guidance of Sergei Witte, Minister of Finance from 1892. Some re-organisation of state finances was attempted while a protective tariff system was also introduced. At the same time a stable currency linked to gold was established. Meanwhile, foreign investment was encouraged by the offer of high interest rates. Russian state railway bonds were sold abroad and by this means the necessary capital to undertake the vast railway enterprises was acquired. In 1891, the Trans-Siberian railway from Moscow to Vladivostok, a distance of four to five thousand miles, commenced. This was essential for any successful industrial revolution. In 1894, the manufacture of vodka was nationalised, thus bringing in a substantial revenue for state expenses. The production of coal, iron, steel, wool and cotton was encouraged. Yet many of the implications of industrialisation were disastrous. Heavy foreign borrowing led to heavy taxation at home. Added to this were the primitive slum conditions in which the newly emerging proletariat was forced to live. The agricultural sector, for its part, was neglected and remained backward.

Foreign Policy - Conclusion

As far as foreign policy was concerned, Alexander III reopened negotiations for a *Dreikaiserbund* in 1881, by which it was agreed that if Russia, Austria-Hungary or Germany were involved in a war with a fourth power, then the other two would remain neutral. Although renewed in 1884, Russia refused to sign the agreement three years later as a result of continuing tensions in the Balkans. She did, however, agree to sign a Reinsurance Treaty with Germany but in the final analysis, this treaty amounted to nothing. A change in German foreign policy with the advent of Wilhelm II to power and failure to assist Russia financially, pushed Alexander III into closer relations with France, culminating in the military links of the Russian alliance, 1894. In October of that year, Alexander III, formerly a man of great strength and physique, died from nephritis. Often hailed as *'the best forgotten Tsar'*, his physical strength was not necessarily matched by an intellectual one and his reign proved to be one of almost unmitigated reaction on the political front. By 1894, Russia was replete with unsolved problems, lacking in 'real government' and unfit to face the storms of the twentieth century. The inefficiency of the tsarist regime was aggravated by Alexander's blind inflexibility and ignorance. In many ways, Alexander harked back to the dark days of Nicholas I with their slogans of *'autocracy, orthodoxy and nationalism'*. But the late nineteenth century was incomparably more difficult. The taste for freedom, given under the reign of Alexander II, was not lightly lost and restraining and discriminatory laws which fell thick and fast, served only to encourage the development of a more self-conscious revolutionary movement. To achieve the same result as his predecessors, therefore, Alexander's regime had to be more repressive than earlier ones. The question that was now begging was, to whom did the twentieth century belong — the Tsar and his successors, or revolutionaries?

10. Nicholas II, 1868-1918

Introduction - Repression Continues

The 26-year-old Nicholas II ascended to the throne in 1894 upon the death of Alexander III. More sensitive than his father, Nicholas was a man of great personal charm, deeply religious and devoted to his family. But Nicholas was also weak willed, unimaginative and misguided. Like his father, Nicholas had been tutored by Pobedonostsev and he had a blind faith in the autocracy. Thus, although the hope had been strong among liberals that Nicholas might resume the reforms of his grandfather, Alexander II, Nicholas made it clear that he would *"uphold the principle of autocracy as firmly and unflinchingly as my late, unforgettable father"*. His wife, the German born Princess Alexandra, was likewise devoted to autocracy. Nicholas' sole ambition in power was, in fact, to pass on the empire intact to his son, Alexis. Of the representatives of the Zemstvos who sought political reform, Nicholas insisted that they were *"carried away by senseless dreams"*. Nicholas encouraged Pobedonostsev's reactionary activities and Plehve, the new Minister of the Interior was described as the *"symbol of autocracy gone mad"*. These men gave the police even stronger powers than before. Press censorship remained in existence as did university surveillance. Russification, the process of uniting the empire by imposing on all subjects one language, culture, religion and central authority continued to discriminate against minority groups. Perhaps even more severe was the anti-semitism evident in Russia and the approval of still more pogroms.

Industrialisation

Under the inspiration of Sergei Witte, Minister of Finance from 1892-1903, all branches of Russian industry and production showed a remarkable upsurge. Witte proved to be an outstanding negotiator and organiser and his superiority in the cabinet was manifest. He was convinced that Russia's future greatness lay in industrialisation. The emphasis was to be on heavy industry and railways. Coal, iron, steel, wool and cotton production was encouraged. In the last decade of the nineteenth century, the smelting of pig iron, for example, increased by 190%. The growth of factories was such that by 1902, 49.8% of the working population was engaged in factories employing a thousand or more workers. The number of such factories had increased between 1879 and 1902 by 123%. Railway construction, for its part, expanded from 30,000 km in 1890 to 53,000 km in 1900. By 1904, the Trans-Siberian railway, one of the greatest engineering achievements of all times, was completed. Such growth was helped by Witte's re-organisation of state funds and his protective tariff system. A stable currency linked with gold was established while foreign investment, Witte's special preserve, was encouraged. The nationalisation of vodka in 1894 had also brought in substantial revenue for state expenses. The human accompaniment to all this, however, was a sudden, gigantic growth in the size of the urban working class whose slums were squalid, unhygienic and overcrowded. Workers were frequently exploited.

Oppositon Groups

Although certain progress was being made on the industrial front, real and fundamental discontent remained. Around the turn of the century, three distinct opposition movements existed in Russia, each of them offering a solution to the country's problems.

1. The Liberals proposed a western-style solution. They wanted to end autocracy and to create a constitutional monarchy with a parliament elected by universal male suffrage. Reforms would be achieved by peaceful rather than revolutionary means. This group found support among the *Zemstvo* politicians, the more enlightened gentry and the professional middle classes. In 1904 they formed themselves into a political party known as the Constitutional Democrats (Kadets).

2. Next came the Social Revolutionaries (S.R.), an offshoot of the earlier populist movement, driven underground by the persecutions of Alexander III. The S.R. came into existence in 1901 and its members called for the setting up of a fully socialist society. The group concentrated on the peasants to whom they promised all the land they wanted.

3. The third and final group were the Social Democrats (S.D.), founded in 1898. Prominent figures included Lenin, Trotsky, Plekhanov and Martov. These, too, sought the implementation of a socialist state but they did not overlook the role of the newly formed proletariat. Following a dispute over how to organise a revolution, this group split in 1903 into Bolsheviks (meaning 'majority') and Mensheviks (meaning 'minority').

The Russo-Japanese War, 1904-1905

In the course of the nineteenth century Russia had expanded considerably. Pushed out of the Balkans after her defeat at the Congress of Berlin, 1878, Russia turned to the Far East. Her special area of penetration was Manchuria and Korea. This created tension with Japan who requested that Russian troops be removed from Korea. The Russians, however, were in no mood for compromise or negotiation. Governing circles, and the Tsar himself, welcomed war, Plehve insisting that *"a short victorious war would stem the tide of revolution"*. The war came in February 1904 when Japanese torpedo boats launched a surprise attack on the Russian fleet at Port Arthur. The Russians were no match for the Japanese and after a long siege, Port Arthur surrendered in January 1905. Russia lost her entire eastern fleet. In March 1905, Russia suffered a second defeat, this time on land. The battle of Mukden lasted 10 days and saw the loss of 90,000 men, as well as Russia's retreat from Manchuria. One last desperate gamble was invested in Russia's Baltic fleet which had set out for the Far East in October 1904. By May 1905 it had reached the Gulf of Korea. A battle in the Straits of Tsushima followed and lasted only a matter of hours. It was a disaster for the Russians who had 20 battleships destroyed. This, combined with mounting trouble at home, forced Nicholas to end the war. President Roosevelt was accepted as mediator by both sides and in August 1905 the Treaty of Portsmouth enabled Japan to take over Korea and the southern half of Manchuria.

The 1905 Revolution

The Russo-Japanese war had weakened and humiliated Russia. Discontent swept through the country. As early as July 1904, Plehve was killed by a terrorist bomb but the rebellious mood of the people was more clearly expressed throughout 1905. In January of that year a strike was organised in St. Petersburg's largest metallurgical factory, the Putilov works. Within a week it spread to other factories in the city. Then on 22nd January 1905, a priest, Fr. Gapon, led a large procession to the Tsar's Winter Palace. The group was orderly, peaceful and unarmed, and sought merely to petition the Tsar for reform. The Tsar was absent from the palace and the troops guarding it opened fire, killing approximately 500 people and wounding thousands. News of the massacre is often considered to be the *"spark that set alight the flame of revolution"*. Disorder now flared up throughout Russia. In February, the Social Revolutionaries assassinated Grand Duke Sergei, the Tsar's uncle. That summer, peasant revolts became widespread. Terrorism in the countryside included the murder of landlords and the destruction of property. In June the crew of the battleship *Potemkin* mutinied and sailed her away from the port of Odessa. A general strike followed whereby public services ceased, postal and telegraph systems stopped work, no trains ran, and shops, banks and law courts closed. The whole life of the country was paralysed. Meanwhile, the workers had organised themselves in *soviets,* or workers' councils. The most important soviet was in St. Petersburg. Through the year many of the minority nations made a bid for freedom from Russian rule. Under such pressure, Nicholas issued his October manifesto, promising sweeping changes which included an elected parliament, or *duma*, and a Council of Ministers led by a Prime Minister.

Dumas - Stolypin

The first duma met in 1906. Members, most of whom were liberals or S.R.s, demanded a full share in the government, the transfer of nobles' land to the peasants and the freeing of political prisoners. The Tsar replied that this was *"inadmissible"*. Shortly afterwards the duma was dissolved. A second duma was dismissed after only three months. The third and fourth dumas lasted longer (around 5 years) and were controlled by conservative groups tolerated by the Tsar. Little meaningful legislation was introduced. Pieter Stolypin, Prime Minister from 1906-1911, was regarded as very significant in nullifying the gains of 1905. Strongly conservative and a supporter of the regime, Stolypin was, nonetheless, intelligent enough to take practical steps to prevent revolution from breaking out. The development of industry was encouraged, laws which forbade the peasant to move from his village were ended, land captains were abolished and a Peasants' Land Bank which provided loans to enable peasants to buy land was set up. The *Zemstvos* were encouraged to carry out extensive health programmes and a vast drive to remove illiteracy was launched in 1908. Yet Stolypin's rule is perhaps best remembered for its cruelty and repression. *'Stolypin's necktie'* (the gallows) ensured that thousands lost their lives. Thousands more were sent into exile, and in some villages Stolypin ordered every tenth man to be flogged. A plot to murder Stolypin got under way and in September 1911 he was assassinated at the opera house in Kiev.

Outbreak of War - February Revolution

World War I broke out on 1st August 1914. For a short while the war united the Russian people. Divisions were forgotten and there were mass demonstrations of loyalty. The war was all things to all people and Russians were optimistic about the outcome. In the meantime, there was an outbreak of hatred for everything German. Despite some initial successes, however, the war went badly for Russia. Her officers were poorly trained and treated their men cruelly while arms were in short supply. In September 1915, Nicholas assumed control of the army. This proved a serious error of judgment for not only was Nicholas no soldier but the Tsarina *'the hated German woman'* was left in charge. Alexandra lacked tact and diplomacy and was very much under the influence of Gregory Rasputin, who increasingly became *'the real ruler of Russia'*. Under Rasputin's influence, a game of *'ministerial leapfrog'* took place and in less than two years, 21 ministers were dismissed and replaced by Rasputin's choices. Even the noblemen lost faith in the Tsarina. Rasputin's murder in 1916 was at the hand of a group of princes, led by Yusopov. By this stage, the war had imposed tremendous strains on Russia's backward economy. Rising prices, food shortages and strikes were common. Frustration came to a head with the February revolution of 1917.

Fall of the Romanov Dynasty - Conclusion

The revolution began spontaneously on 23rd February. Food was scarce and there were angry scenes outside bakers' shops. Demonstrators protesting about bread shortages merged with crowds holding a procession to celebrate International Woman's Day. Simultaneously, workers at the Putilov armaments factory went out on strike. They were joined by other strikers as the unrest spread. 40 people were killed on 24th February as the police opened fire but thereafter the authorities lost control as the soldiers joined the revolutionaries. Public buildings were taken over, prisoners released and police stations and barracks captured. The duma pressed the government to provide emergency services but the Tsar was unwilling to take advice. Persistingly refusing to acknowledge the seriousness of the situation, the Tsar now dissolved the duma. Only too late did Nicholas II decide to return to Petrograd* but the train on which he was travelling stopped at Pskov because the railway line was in the hands of the rebels. The grim reality of the situation hit home and Nicholas decided to abdicate in favour of his brother, Grand Duke Mikhail. Knowing that he did not command widespread support, the Grand Duke declined the honour. Thus did the 300-year-old Romanov dynasty come to an end. Clearly, Nicholas had proved unequal to the tasks that confronted him. He had failed consistently to understand the new forces at work in Russia so that increasingly the empire deteriorated into a ramshackle, dilapidated and inefficient condition. The man who is perhaps best described as *'the wrong man in the wrong place at the wrong time'* was murdered, along with his family, in July 1918 by Bolshevik order.

* Name given to St. Petersburg during the war. St. Petersburg was considered to sound too German.

11. Describe the Circumstances that led to Revolution in Russia, 1917

" Why did you engage in this revolt, young man? Don't you realise you're up against a wall? Yes, a wall, but a rotten one; one kick and it will crumble"

— Vladimir Ulyanov (Lenin)

Autocracy - Alexander II

Russia, in the years prior to 1917, provided a good example of autocracy. The Tsar had absolute power and was answerable only to God. Such a system had been necessary in the time of the early tsars, who were cruel and ruthless in order to prevent power slipping into the hands of powerful landowners. As time went on, however, the problems of government became less simple and it proved much more difficult to make autocracy work. By the reign of Alexander II (1855-1881), there was widespread demand for change. Alexander feared that his empire was on the brink of revolution and tried to weaken the oppositon through a programme of social reform. Many thousands of people were removed from police supervision, restrictions on university students were lifted, there was a revision of censorship regulations, and in 1861 an edict liberating the serfs was introduced. This was followed in 1864 by a system of local self government. Each district set up a *Zemstvo* with powers to provide roads, schools and medical services. Changes were also made in the legal system and in the army. Yet the result of the reforms was disappointing. The *'revolution from above'* that Alexander seemed to have proclaimed at the beginning of his reign never came. Alexander was not prepared to clip his autocratic wings and the failure to introduce a constitutional monarchy can only be described as an opportunity lost. Further, it must be noted that Alexander's reforming zeal was blunted in the 1870s, mainly due to the growth of socialism, reluctance to antagonise the nobility and to the several attempts on his life. But the people had had a taste of freedom and wished for more. Thus, the seeds of later rebellions were sown. Meanwhile, on 1st March 1881, an extreme group, The People's Will, succeeded in assassinating Alexander II.

Alexander III - The Reactionary Tsar

The backwardness of Russia, the cruelty of the government and the miserable living conditions of the peasants led to continued attacks on the autocracy. This fuelled the determination of the new tsar, Alexander III, to crush all opposition and to undo the advances made under Alexander II. The appeal by the People's Will for a national assembly and a free social order fell on deaf ears. Rather, Alexander made clear his determination to uphold and consolidate his God-given powers. To this end, Alexander III was influenced by Konstantin Pobedonostsev, a trusted advisor and confidant. Together these men introduced a veritable reign of terror in Russia. A new police force, the *Okrana*, was set up to crush all radical groups, censorship was widespread and schools and universities were closely monitored. Professors, for example, were to be chosen by the government while students were forbidden to join clubs. Police spies were enrolled as students to ensure that lectures contained no criticism of the government, and to seek out secret organisations among the students. An even more evil side to the reaction was the persecution of the non-Russian people in the empire. *Russification*, the policy of enforcing everything Russian on the minorities, worked to the detriment of Poles, Finns, Latvians and others. Many non-Russian groups were not allowed to hold official jobs and their own language and traditions were outlawed in the hope of creating in Russia one large united nation. Worst were the pogroms. Jews were singled out for persecution, their property was attacked, they were assaulted and some were killed. The police made no effort to interfere. Anti-semitic laws hindered the movement of Jews at all levels of society. Hardly surprising, therefore, was the growing level of discontent.

Growing Discontent

If these actions were not enough to spur the people to rebellion, Alexander seemed to cap the situation by granting concessions to those who needed them least, the nobility. They became exempt from paying taxes, acquired loans on favourable terms, had education limited to them alone and took effective control of the *Zemstvos*. The fact that Nicholas II, who succeeded Alexander III in 1894, proved to be no better a ruler than his father, continuing to pursue unpopular policies and failing dismally to meet the demands of his people, guaranteed that by the end of the nineteenth century Russia faced an almost nationwide state of unrest. Opposition made itself felt in the upsurgence of groups such as the liberals, who advocated reform and political liberty. Hoping to achieve this by peaceful means, the liberals in 1904 formed the Constitutional Democratic Party (Kadets). A second political grouping, the Social Revolutionaries grew from earlier populist movements. They called for radical reform - a socialist society - and concentrated on the peasants, to whom they promised land. More important were the Social Democrats, from which the Bolsheviks derived. The Bolsheviks were a disciplined party led by Lenin, who recognised the important role of the industrial proletariat. Although repressed, underground and sometimes even operating from outside of Russia, these groups grew in support and credibility. For the moment they operated on the fringes but sooner or later, someone was going to throw a match on what was already an explosive situation.

Negative Repercussions of Industrialisation - War with Japan

Even in the one area where Alexander III, and later Nicholas II, had many outward successes - industrialisation - it can be seen that their policies and the actions of finance minister, Sergei Witte, only contributed to the seething disquiet within the country. Many of the implications of industrial development were disastrous. A result of the heavy borrowings, for example, was high taxes at home. Another negative result of the industrial expansion was the serious under-investment in agriculture and the continued backwardness of that sector of the economy. Famine was widespread. Yet even when there were poor harvests, grain had to be exported to pay off debts. At the same time, the newly created urban proletariat lived in slum conditions where overcrowding and poor sanitation were the norm. Unrest became evident. Driven to desperation by the failure to stop opposition from growing, it was believed that *"a short victorious war"* with Japan was the one thing that could save the regime. Such a conflict developed in 1904 and had its origins in Russia's growing influence in the Far East. In February 1904 the Japanese attacked the Russian fleet at Port Arthur. The

Russians were no match for the Japanese and Port Arthur was finally forced to surrender. The ten-day battle at Mukden in Manchuria in March 1905 saw the Russians suffer a major defeat, as they did in May 1905 in the straits of Tsushima. Annihilating defeat weakened and humiliated Russia and aggravated problems at home.

Revolution, 1905

The situation in Russia became a crisis. A strike in the Putilov works, St. Peterburg's largest metallurgical factory, in January 1905, inspired other strikes throughout the city. Then on 22nd January 1905, a procession of workers, carrying a petition to the Tsar, was fired on by the police. Hundreds were killed and many more were wounded on this Bloody Sunday. Disorder now spread. The Tsar's uncle, Grand Duke Sergei, was assassinated in February. In June there were mutinies aboard several warships, notably the *Potemkin*. The country was ablaze with peasant violence but the culmination came in October 1905 when there was a gigantic strike in Russia. Public services ceased, no trains ran, postal and telegraph systems stopped, bakers quit baking bread, shops, banks and law courts closed. The strike had been directed by Soviet Committees. They organised essential supplies, arranged demonstrations and published pamphlets and posters. Feeling powerless in the face of such general disorder, Nicholas II promised sweeping changes in his October Manifesto. There was to be an elected parliament, or *duma,* and the autocratic government of the Tsar was to be replaced by a Council of Ministers and led by a Prime Minister. Yet while four dumas met between 1906 and 1917, Nicholas went back on many of his promises. He dissolved the dumas when they suggested reform and replaced liberal prime ministers. Clearly, Nicholas was as firmly rooted as ever in his autocratic and illiberal ways. He consistently ignored the fact that his people were not prepared to be repressed indefinitely.

Repression Continues - The Pre-War Years

Nicholas' precarious position was not helped by Pieter Stolypin, who became Prime Minister in 1906. Although much of his administration showed an enlightened quality and reforms in agriculture, industry, education and health were plentiful, Stolypin was notorious for his cruelty to peasants and revolutionaries, and was disliked by both extremes of Left and Right. His ruthless treatment of Poles and Jews furthered his reputation for sternness. In his first year in office, for example, over 1,000 people were executed. The hanging of 3,500 in 1907 ensured that the gallows became known as *'Stolypin's necktie'.* Simultaneously, thousands were exiled to the harsher areas of Siberia. In some villages, Stolypin ordered every tenth man to be flogged as a warning to others. Little wonder, therefore, that Stolypin was assassinated in 1911. Efforts at conciliation in the form of modest social security schemes in 1912 were counterbalanced by further repression. 170 strikers were shot down in the Lena goldfield in that same year. A rapidly rising population made it ever more difficult to satisfy restless industrial workers and land-hungry peasants. Yet for all that, the Tsar's autocratic rule might have continued for many years had it not been for the outbreak of World War I in 1914. This idea is reinforced by the protestations of loyalty at the tercentenary celebrations of the Romanov dynasty in 1913.

World War I

In August 1914 World War I broke out. For a short time the war united the Russian people. Songs of *"God save the Tsar"* were sung as never before. Troubles were forgotten as the people united against the common enemy. Members of the duma, for instance, made extravagant speeches of support. An outbreak of hatred for everything German ensured that the German embassy in St. Petersburg was attacked while the name of the capital was changed to Petrograd. But Russia's optimism was short-lived. The war served only to highlight the inefficiencies of the army. By 1916, more than a third of all men of working age had been recruited into the army of 15 million troops. A third of the troops had already been killed or wounded. Poor training and equipment, cruelty, defeat, hardship and desertion destroyed the support the Tsar had had in 1914. Nicholas' decision to assume control of the army exacerbated the problems. He was no soldier and in his absence, his wife, Tsarina Alexandra, took charge of government. She had little understanding of politics and showed no tact or diplomacy. Being half-German complicated the situation but she was disliked mainly because of the faith she placed in Gregory Rasputin. Rasputin became the real power in Russia and continually recommended old, sick and unfit men for top government positions. Even noblemen lost faith in the way government was being managed. Rasputin was murdered in 1916, but his murder only made the Tsar more obstinate. He ignored warnings of the empress' unpopularity and of trouble at home caused by food shortages, hunger and disillusionment.

Revolution 1917 - Conclusion

The war destroyed any confidence that the people still had in the government. A police department report noted *"a marked increase in hostile feelings among the peasants"* and stated that *"the proletariat of the capital is on the verge of despair"*. Thus it was that the grotesque mixture of tragedy and farce which gave many Russian novels their 'Russian' flavour boiled over in February 1917. The people were tired of cruelty, injustice, squalour, starvation and the Tsar's blind adherence to the status quo. Spontaneous strikes and protests flared as the people hit back. What made the February revolution different from earlier ones, however, was that the soldiers and police went over to the side of the people. This ensured that the authorities lost control. The Tsar remained unwilling to take advice and only too late he realised the seriousness of the situation. His attempt to return to the capital was blocked and his subsequent abdication ensured the ending, once and for all, of the three hundred-year-old Romanov rule.

> *"Like the chewed stump of a fag*
> *we spat their dynasty out".*
>
> —Vladimir Mayokovsky (Russian poet)

A new epoch in Russian history had opened up. From Republicanism to Communism, the absence of the tsar as the centre of power led to the emergence of new personalities and new concepts. But the irony of history is such that while Russia in 1917 had undertaken to proceed along a very different course, that very difference was not always perceptible in the years ahead - so very different and yet so much alike!

12.   Treat of Russia in Revolution, 1917

Instability and Discontent, 1917

The real effect of war could well and truly be felt in Russia by early 1917. The country had experienced enormous losses: human, material and territorial. Conscription, lists of the war dead and the return of an endless stream of wounded from the front had ensured that the initial enthusiasm for war soon dissipated. Nicholas' decision to take command of the army was an undisputed mistake while the war minister, Sukhomlinov was incompetent and failed to inspire confidence. Many officers were poorly trained and treated their men cruelly. Inadequate supplies and the general backwardness of Russia complicated the situation. Not surprisingly, inflation, recourse to paper money, rising prices and food shortages (or at best, problems of inefficient distribution) and a fall in real wages gave vent to slogans such as *"Down with the Tsar"*. Nicholas II's unpopularity was furthered by opposition to his wife, the empress Alexandra, who was half German and suspected of being in sympathy with the German army. Lacking in tact and diplomacy, Alexandra believed absolutely in the divine rights of kings and urged her husband *"Don't yield. Be the boss"*. That advice proved disastrous under the circumstances and had the effect of uniting the nation against the Tsar and the Tsarina. Indignation grew and, in the absence of any hope of real and meaningful reform, revolution became an ever more attractive option. The revolution had been talked over and fought for during many years of tsarist rule. Yet the fact remains that many of those who had done the fighting and the talking, the plotting and the propaganda, who had served their time in Siberia or abroad and run the gauntlet of the secret police, were now taken unawares.

The February Revolution [I]

The February revolution began spontaneously, even 'unpolitically', on 23rd February. It was set in motion by rank and file workers and was confined at first to Petrograd. The first signs of trouble were in January when workers at the Putilov factory - where the 1905 revolution began - demanded a 50% increase in wages. Their demands were flatly refused. A management declaration of a lock-out thereafter ensured that 40,000 workmen at the factory were refused work. These workers were joined by a crowd holding a procession to celebrate International Women's Day. Simultaneously, food shortages led to angry scenes outside bakers' shops. Many people resorted to theft. Years of repression coupled with the hardships of war were now making themselves felt as the unrest spread, yet it must be noted that the movement took the revolutionaries by surprise as much as anyone else. Nonetheless, within 48 hours 240,000 people were out on strike and life in Petrograd became paralysed. On 26th February, troops opened fire. 40 people were killed and many more were wounded. After this, tempers rose still higher. The rioters attacked police stations, public buildings were taken over and prisoners released. On 27th February, the troops and police refused to go into the streets to disperse the rioters, preferring to mutiny rather than fire on their fellow Russians with whom they openly sympathised. On that same day, the revolution spread across the country. A collapse of authority was clear.

The February Revolution [II]

On the day that the revolution had begun, Nicholas had left Petrograd to inspect troops at the front. He believed that the food riots and strikes were no more serious than others in the previous years of war. At his headquarters at Mogilev, Nicholas was warned by Rodzianko, the president of the duma, that *"The position is serious. There is anarchy in the capital... The general dissatisfaction grows. Disorderly firing takes place in the streets. A person trusted by the country must be charged immediately to form a ministry"*. Nicholas, however, remained astonishingly apathetic, maintaining *"That fat Rodzianko has sent me some nonsense"*. All Nicholas did was to call for the duma to be disbanded. Its members disobeyed the order, Alexander Kerensky* announcing that the duma had to set up a *"provisional government"*. While the duma had hoped to restore order and to persuade Nicholas to accept a constitutional monarchy, it became increasingly clear that it was taking over from the tsar and his ministers. Meanwhile, on 27th February, the Tauride Palace in Petrograd (where the duma sat) was invaded by workers who set up a Soviet of Workers' and Soldiers' Deputies, modelled on the 1905 soviet. Members were elected by their workmates in barracks, factories, workshops and public enterprises. Similar soviets were formed in Moscow, the provincial towns and the countryside. The soviet did not function as a government but it had great power. It controlled the factories and services such as railways and electricity. In some places, the soviet even controlled food distribution and Soviet Order No. 1 enjoined all soldiers to obey only the soviet and to safeguard their arms.

From Autocracy to Republic

Only too late did Nicholas realise the seriousness of the situation. On 1st March, he set out for the capital. The railway line was by then in the hands of rebels and Nicholas' train was stopped at Pskov. Ready now to make concessions, Nicholas offered to appoint a prime minister who was acceptable to the duma. This time he was told by Rodzianko that *"it is too late to make concessions, it is time to abdicate"*. Nicholas was offered the chance to abdicate in favour of his son, Alexi, but Nicholas was unwilling, insisting that Alexi was delicate and only 13 years of age. Nicholas thus gave up the throne in favour of his brother, Grand Duke Mikhail. Mikhail realised that he did not have the backing of the majority of the provisional government. He refused the throne and on 2nd March 1917, the Romanov dynasty ended as Russia became a republic. Power was then divided between the provisional government, or duma, and the soviets. The former was headed by Prince Lvov. Its most important ministers included Milyukov, Guchkov and Kerensky. In the seven months of its existence it freed political prisoners, allowed for freedom of speech and of the press, abolished secret courts and reformed criminal law and the death penalty. It also promised elections for a constituent assembly. But the provisional government, in its calls for patience, failed to satisfy the burning demands for peace and land, and to that extent, proved to be of no fundamental difference from the tsarist regime to ordinary men. The soviet, on the other hand, was Marxist in character and had the support of many Russian people. It had the potential to pose as a rival government and continued to assert its authority. Kerensky was one of the few personalities to provide a link between the two bodies.

* A leading Socialist. Also a member of the Petrograd soviet.

Lenin's Return - July Days - Kornilov Affair

Lenin, the Bolshevik leader, was in Zurich when the February revolution broke out. He saw it as the first step to the greater revolution of the proletariat and was anxious, in its aftermath, to return to Petrograd. In April 1917, he was given safe passage through Germany en route to Russia, the Germans believing that his anti-war attitudes would weaken the Russian army and people even further. On his arrival in Petrograd, Lenin began to denounce the provisional government. His *'April Theses'* were concerned with a plan for a Bolshevik takeover. The Bolsheviks campaigned for *'Peace, Bread and Land'*, the things most wanted by the masses. Lenin also realised the potential of the soviets and insisted that *'all power'* should be given to them. Meanwhile, the revolution was rolling on under its own momentum. News of the defeat of the Russians by the Germans in June 1917 came at a bad time for Russia as food supplies were short, prices were rising and jobs were being lost. Demonstrations against the government in July took the form of still more strikes and a revolt by soldiers from the naval base of Kronstadt. 400 people were killed in two days. Kerensky, who in late July became Prime Minister, took firm action and quickly ended the rising. In its wake the Bolsheviks were blamed. Arrests were made and Lenin himself went into hiding in Finland. But Kerensky's triumph did not last long. People in Russia were looking for strong leadership. General Kornilov, Commander-in-Chief of the army, was seen by many as the man capable of restoring law and order in Petrograd. In September he sought to stage a coup d'état. Kerensky only defeated him with the help of the Petrograd soviet and about 25,000 Red Guards, the armed followers of the Bolsheviks. And while the July Days had discredited the Bolsheviks, the Kornilov affair made them respectable. Time was running out for the provisional government.

Plans For a Bolshevik Coup

The Bolsheviks had fostered Bolshevism and, following the Kornilov affair, they gained in membership and popular support. The number of party members increased to over 200,000, while majorities in the Petrograd and Moscow soviets were readily obtained. This pattern was followed in many local and provincial soviets. Increasingly *'all power to the soviets'* meant *'all power to the Bolsheviks'*. The party's policies were realistic and closely echoed those of the soldiers and workers. A new wave of peasant violence and increasing lawlessness in the cities, combined with the hopeless economic situation, all played into the hands of the Bolsheviks and ensured the party's strengthening position. In October, Lenin returned to Petrograd in disguise. Revolution was clearly on the agenda, Lenin maintaining that *"History will never forgive us if we do not seize power now"*. On 10th October, at a meeting of the Central Committee of the Bolshevik party, the supreme decision was taken. By a majority of 10 to 2* it was resolved to initiate an armed insurrection. Lenin wanted immediate action on the decision. Trotsky, the leader of the Red Guard, favoured delay. Eventually it was decided that the revolution should take place on the night of 24th-25th October, the day before the Second All Russian Congress of Soviets was scheduled to meet. Meanwhile on 12th October, a Military Revolutionary Committee under the presidency of Trotsky was established. Room 10 in the Smolny Institute became the Bolsheviks' headquarters. From there plans were drawn up. These included the taking

---

* Only Zinoviev and Kamenev voted against the motion, believing that an insurrection would be crushed.

over of key points in the city and the distribution of arms. That Trotsky had succeeded in winning over the garrison of the Peter and Paul fortress to the Bolsheviks guaranteed an almost endless supply of guns.

The October/Bolshevik Revolution

The provisional government had heard rumours of a planned coup. Only on 24th October, however, did Kerensky begin to take action. He closed Bolshevik newspapers and ordered the cruiser *Aurora*, anchored near the Winter Palace, to be put to sea. Telephones at the Smolny Institute were disconnected and the Winter Palace was guarded by the Women's Battalion of Death. Trotsky, in turn, reopened the newspaper offices, fortified the Smolny Institute and countermanded Kerensky's orders to the cruiser *Aurora*. The signal for the start of operations came at 2 a.m. on the night of 24th October when the siren of the *Aurora* sounded. The Bolsheviks thereafter methodically occupied key points in Petrograd. Railway stations, the state bank, the post office, the telegraph exchange and power stations were all taken. So too were key bridges along the river Neva. Everything happened very quickly, so that by the next morning Kerensky found Petrograd already in the grip of the Bolsheviks. Little resistance was given other than Kerensky's failed attempt to find troops in the provinces who would lead an attack against the revolution. Kerensky succeeded only in raising a small force of 700 Cossacks who were easily repulsed. He subsequently fled Russia, finding refuge in the U.S. By nightfall of 25th October only the Winter Palace, the headquarters of the provisional government, was untaken. This was captured in the early hours of 26th, and was helped by the arrival of sailors from Kronstadt, who took command of the *Aurora* and fired a shell into the Palace. The nerve of the defenders was now broken and they, along with the members of the government, surrendered.

Bolsheviks in Power - Conclusion

The October revolution had seen the death of no more than six members of the Red Guard and has consequently gone down in history as an almost *'bloodless coup'*. On 26th October Lenin told the delegates of the National Congress of Soviets that *"we shall have a soviet government, without the participation of a bourgeoisie of any kind. The oppressed masses will themselves form a government"*. But while the Bolsheviks had come to power relatively easily, maintaining that power was going to prove much more difficult. The Bolsheviks, renamed *Communists* in 1918, were a minority party in Russia as a whole, and on almost every front they now faced opposition. But the Bolsheviks had no intention of relinquishing power. Alongside his decrees on land and peace, Lenin adopted stern and cruel measures to deal with counter-revolutionaries. The establishment of a new Russian secret police, the *Cheka*, was followed by the *'Red Terror'* whereby legalised acts of brutality, assassinations and execution were all carried out in the name of the state. Of the Russian civil war, 1918-1921, Lenin argued *"Do you really think we shall be victorious without using the most cruel terror... If we cannot shoot a man who sabotages a member of the Red Guard, then what kind of revolution is this?"* Consequently over 8 million Russians were wiped out as a result of war, famine and disease. Mass emigration also took place. Thus it is that in Russia it proved impossible to *"praise the day* (October revolution) *before evening comes* (aftermath)*"*. Of the loss of kindness and forbearance involved in shaping Russia's destiny, Trostky wrote that *"something snapped in the heart of the revolution"*.

13.   Lenin, 1870-1924

Background/Early Influences

Lenin was born Vladimir Ilych Ulyanov on 20th April 1870 in Simbirsk on the middle Volga. His father was a progressive minded school teacher who, in time, became inspector for the province of Simbirsk. Lenin was consequently not strictly 'of the people'. He had a brilliant record as a high school student and was described as *"highly gifted, industrious and punctual"*. Before long, however, he was in trouble. In 1887 his brother, Alexander, was executed for an attempt on the life of the reactionary Tsar, Alexander III. Lenin swore *"I'll make them pay for this"* and became a determined opponent of autocracy. But he began to doubt whether the People's Will group, of which his brother had been a member, was following the right path. Their terrorist activities did not alter the system under which Russia was governed. Likewise, the policies of the liberals did not go deep enough. Lenin thus became a Marxist and over the following years he displayed a remarkable mastery of Marxist thought. Energetic, serious and determined, he quickly made a strong impression on his comrades. While he was not always liked, Lenin was nonetheless recognised as having potential leadership qualities. In the meantime, however, he continued his studies. He entered the university of Kazan but was expelled because of his involvement in student demonstrations. This did not halt him and he was to become a fully qualified lawyer at 21 years of age, emerging with a first class diploma and top results in every subject. Thereafter, Lenin continued his Marxist activities. In 1895 he took the lead in setting up the League for the Liberation of Labour. This led to his arrest, imprisonment and subsequent exile to Siberia. While there, he married Nadezhda Krupskaya, a young school teacher and wrote his major historical work, *'The Development of Capitalism in Russia'*.

From Social Democratic Party to Bolsheviks

In 1898, several groups of Marxists came together to form the Social Democratic Labour Party (S.D.L.P.), headed by George Plekhanov. It was to be *"the class movement of the organised working masses"*. Freed from his enforced exile in 1900, Lenin headed back to western Russia, and immediately became involved with the SDLP. As editor to the party newspaper, *Iskra* (The Spark) which proved impossible to publish in Russia, Lenin moved abroad, living in Germany, England and Switzerland. The paper was smuggled into Russia and helped to keep alive the revolutionary tradition. Then in 1902, Lenin wrote his most famous pamphlet, *"What is to be done?"*. This showed a recognition of differences within the party. Lenin attacked those Social Democrats, such as Martov, who favoured building up a mass party from the factory workers. He argued that a disciplined corps of professional revolutionaries should take charge and upon this small group of dedicated disciples would lie responsibility for decision making. The issue was raised at the second Congress of the Social Democrats in 1903 and amidst anger, hostility and bitterness, the movement split. The Bolsheviks (meaning 'majority') sided with Lenin while the Mensheviks (meaning 'minority') opposed his ideas. In terms of support, the names are something of a misnomer, however, for while the Bolsheviks had achieved a majority at Congress, the Mensheviks had the largest support among Russian workers. Various efforts to unite the party amounted to nothing and after a conference in Prague in 1912, Lenin decided the Bolsheviks would try to achieve power on their own. Before this decision was reached, the 1905 revolution had occurred in Russia. Although Lenin had played no part in the events, he saw that revolution was possible in underdeveloped Russia. Lenin was determined that the *soviets* (workers' councils), formed first in 1905, should become the tool of the Bolsheviks.

World War I to 1917

Lenin believed that the war was against the interests of working men and he headed a small group of anti-war socialists. His views were outlined in a pamphlet, *'The Seven Theses on War'*. Lenin hoped that the war would lead to the exhaustion and collapse of tsarism and rejoiced in every disaster that befell Russia, maintaining that *"it was better that Russia, not Germany, should lose the war"*. Yet Lenin was taken unawares at the speed and suddenness of the overthrow of Tsar Nicholas II in February 1917. When news reached Lenin in Switzerland he telegraphed the Bolsheviks in Russia *"Our tactics: absolute distrust, no support of the new government, Kerensky particularly suspect"*. Lenin knew that it was necessary to return home to Russia and readily agreed to a German offer of a free passage home. Following his return home, Lenin sought to teach the workers that the February revolution was only the first step to the greater revolution of the proletariat. Based upon the popular slogans *'Peace, Bread, Land'* and *'All power to the Soviets'*, Lenin outlined his plan of action in his *'April Theses'*. The July rising, which took the form of demonstrations against the provisional government, strikes and a revolt from the naval base at Kronstadt, came too early for Lenin's plans and, although the Bolsheviks participated to some extent, they sought, above all, to prevent the rising going too far. The Bolsheviks were, nonetheless, blamed for the July Days and in their aftermath, Bolshevik leaders were hunted down and Lenin went into hiding in Finland. Yet the Kornilov affair, which occurred in September 1917 when Kornilov, Commander-in-Chief of the army, sought to establish a military dictatorship, played into the hands of the Bolsheviks. Kerensky and the provisional government were saved by the soviet and Bolshevik Red Guard, 25,000 strong.

The October Revolution

The popularity of the Bolsheviks soared. Soviets in towns, villages and army units passed into Bolshevik control. The Bolsheviks were further helped by peasant violence and industrial unrest. Lenin, who had observed the Kornilov affair from his hiding place in Finland, decided in October 1917 to return to Petrograd and prepare for an immediate seizure of power, *"History will never forgive us if we do not assume power now"*. On 10th October, the central committee of the Bolsheviks agreed by a 10 to 2 majority to start a revolution. Two days later, on 12th October, a Military Revolutionary Committee, under Trotsky, was formed. Preparations for a coup got into full swing. These involved the seizure of the Peter and Paul fortress, the takeover of railway stations, the telegraph exchange, the post office, the state bank and power stations. Key bridges on the river Neva were also held while the cruiser *Aurora* pointed its guns on the Winter Palace. Little resistance was forthcoming and the Bolsheviks methodically gained control of the city between the 24th-26th October. The Winter Palace, the headquarters of the provisional government, was taken, and

Kerensky's ministers were arrested. Kerensky himself had fled the country. As a result of this almost 'bloodless' revolution, the Bolsheviks, with Lenin as their chairman, assumed power, maintaining that power was going to prove much more difficult than its seizure.

Lenin in Power - Rule by Decree

It was now necessary to consolidate the revolution. The desire to do so was given a tremendous impetus by the forces of counter revolution. From early on, Lenin's government was one which ruled by decree. A land decree abolished private land ownership and transferred the land to peasant committees. The power of the Russian Orthodox Church was cut away, civil marriages were made compulsory, all ranks and titles removed and women were declared equal to men. Censorship of the press was introduced in March 1918. Large-scale industry and banks were nationalised, labour discipline and duties were enforced and strikes were declared treason to the state. As early as November 1917, the only 'free' elections since the February revolution were held. It was the Social Revolutionaries rather than the Bolsheviks (25% of the vote) who polled an absolute majority, so Lenin decided that the Russian people were not yet ready for democracy and after only one meeting, the Constituent Assembly was forcibly dissolved. Thereafter, Lenin and the Communists allowed nobody to argue with them. In December, the *Cheka*, a secret police force which surpassed its tsarist counterpart, the *Okrana*, in ruthlessness, was set up. Led by Felix Djerzhinsky, the *Cheka* became the 'eyes and ears' of the Bolsheviks. It had the authority to arrest and even pass sentence of death so that by the end of 1918, 50,000 opponents of the Communists had been executed by the *Cheka*. In March 1918, the Bolsheviks who were officially renamed the Communist Party, signed the treaty of Brest-Litovsk with Germany. This was the means by which Russia obtained peace but it involved the surrender of one third of Russia's agricultural land and its population, the loss of more than four fifths of Russia's coal mines and over half of her industry. Despite anger and indignation, both within and outside the party, Lenin demanded peace at all costs, insisting that the very survival of the regime depended on it.

Civil War

The forces of counter revolution became much more serious after the treaty of Brest-Litovsk. Opposition (called the White forces) consisted of a confusing mixture of Social Revolutionaries, Mensheviks, liberals, tsarist supporters and others. They were helped by peasants' discontent at the Communists' treatment of the Social Revolutionaries. As the Bolsheviks sought to retain power, Red armies fought against the Whites. Among the first victims of the civil war were the Tsar and the royal family. Their murders at Ekaterinburg on 16th July 1918 were carried out on the order of Lenin and sought to ensure that the Romanovs would not become the figureheads of opposition to the Communists. This was followed by the command *'shoot and deport'* which was to be applied equally to all who threatened the regime. An attempt on the life of Lenin in August 1918 by Fanya Kaplan only worsened the situation. Yet in the early stages of war, the Whites seemed to have all the advantages. Led by professional and experienced war generals, such as Kornilov, they contrasted sharply with the workers' detachment within the Red army. The Whites also had the support of the Allied Powers. By the end of 1918, approximately 20 different governments were functioning on Russian soil. Things continued to go badly for the Reds throughout 1919. Perhaps the main threat came from Admiral Kolchak's armies. In 1919 they moved steadily westwards across the Urals and at one point were within 200 miles of Moscow. But Lenin and Trotsky displayed savage energy as they worked to save communism. The Reds were also more united than the Whites, and Trotsky, who had his headquarters in a railway carriage, proved to be a superb military commander. Allied support lessened as time went on but, in any case, Allied intervention was resented by the peasants. One further advantage for the Reds was that they controlled a compact area, capable of being defended.

The Tide of War Changes - War Communism

Thus it was that the Red Army slowly gained the upper hand. By the end of 1919, Kolchak's army had disintegrated while he, himself, had fallen into the hands of the Reds (He was executed early in 1920). Hardly had this threat been repelled than the southern front under the White Army's General Denikin came alive. Denikin, too, was forced to retreat. With British aid he moved to the Crimea and subsequently turned over his command to General Wrangel, who had no hope of resuming the struggle. The next threat came from the Polish army but it was also beaten off in 1920. And even though the war continued through 1921/'22, there was little more than mopping up to do after 1920. By then, famine ravaged Russia and bands of starving men, women and children were commonplace. It is estimated that as many as 5 million died of starvation, typhoid and cholera during these years. The situation was emphatically not helped by Lenin's policy of *'war communism'*, 1918-1921. This was concerned with state control over every aspect of the economy and involved the forcible requisitioning and expropriation of food and essential supplies. The system was harsh and although it allowed the Reds to win the war, it gave the peasants no incentive to produce surplus food and consequently resulted in economic collapse. Sailors at the naval base of Kronstadt rose once again in March 1921 but this time it was against communist dictatorship. The mutiny was ruthlessly suppressed and in the process a thousand sailors were killed. As a realist, Lenin knew that some change in the policy of war communism was needed; *'new gangways to communism'* had to be built if the Communists were to stay in power.

New Economic Policy - Death of Lenin - An Evaluation

This change, or gangway, came in the form of the New Economic Policy (N.E.P.), March 1921. As a result of N.E.P. the government kept control of the 'commanding heights': heavy industry, banks, power supplies, transport and foreign trade. 80% of the industrial workforce remained employed in state industries. Small industries were, however, allowed to operate under private management and this allowed for the emergence of *Nepmen*, or small businessmen. Concessions were also made to the peasants. Part of their crops continued to be paid in tax but any surplus could be sold privately. The *Kulak*, or richer peasants, came into existence during this period. Some Communists argued that N.E.P. was pushing Russia down the road to capitalism but Lenin used his personal influence to have the policy accepted, maintaining that *"we must take a step backwards in order to go two steps forward at a later date"*. Having already suffered a number of strokes, Lenin died on 21st January 1924, aged 53 years. His death was greatly mourned and in his memory, Petrograd was renamed Leningrad.

That Lenin's body was also embalmed and placed in a mausoleum in Moscow's Red Square is further evidence of the veneration in which he was held. Any assessment of his life and work shows him to be completely dedicated, even single-minded, in his pursuit of the cause. While a supreme realist, a great orator and a political genius, Lenin was not above ruthless and undemocratic tactics, and fully endorsed the *'red terror'* of his party during the civil war years. He was, nonetheless, the undisputed *"engine driver of the revolution"* (Trotsky), the founder of Soviet Russia, the father of Communism.

Russia, 1870-1924: Past Exam Questions

1995
C3. Russia, 1917
Describe the circumstances that led to revolution in Russia, 1917.

1993, 1986
E4. Essay
(i) Czarist Russia

1992
C3. Czarist Russia, 1870-1914
Discuss developments in Russia under the Czars, 1870-1917.

1991
C5. Lenin
Treat of the part played by Lenin in the history of Russia.

1988
C4. Russia, 1917
Why were there revolutions in Russia in 1917?

1987
C1. Czarist Russia, 1855-1917
Treat of reform, reaction and revolution in Czarist Russia, 1855-1917.

1986
D1. Lenin
Analyse the part played by Lenin in the history of Russia.

1985
C4. Russia
Compare and contrast the 1905 and 1917 revolutions in Russia under such headings as the following:- background; revolutionary groups; role of the Czar; international involvement; outcomes; etc.

BRITAIN, 1870-1914

14. Treat of the Reforms brought about in Great Britain during the period 1870-1914

"Progress is not an accident but a necessity"
— Herbert Spencer

Introduction

Britain, the strongest power in the world in 1870, was a constitutional monarchy. At its head was the King or Queen; real power, however, rested with Parliament. The two dominant political groupings were the Liberals and the Conservatives. Traditionally, the Liberals had been more concerned than the Conservatives with the task of reforming government and society, but realism dictated to the Conservatives also that some improvement in the conditions of the people was necessary. To that end, the period 1870-1914 witnessed degrees of progress on practically every front and a marked shift in the balance of power between classes. Within the parliamentary system, for example, it was necessary to inject a new democratic spirit into the House of Commons and to end, once and for all, the days of oligarchy or government by a privileged few. Universal suffrage, the payment of salaries to MPs and the development of a political voice for the working classes were just some of the necessary reforms. Other issues that needed to be tackled included those resulting from the Industrial Revolution and the accompanying shift of population from rural to urban - the development of large towns and cities, overcrowding, the emergence of slums and poor working conditions. In addition, there were the problems of unemployment, poor health services and too little education. The development of public services and changes in the army and civil service might be added to the list.

Parliamentary Reform

In 1870 Britain was still a long way from being a true democracy. Voting was open and this led to fear, intimidation and bribery. At the same time, millions of adult males and all women had yet to receive the vote. The Secret Ballot Act of 1872 provided for secret voting and was thereby a considerable step towards strengthening the democratic rights of ordinary people. Not surprisingly, this and the 1883 Corrupt Practices Act, which successfully eliminated bribery and corruption at elections, were resented by landlords and employers alike. Gladstone's Third Reform Act of 1884 gave the vote to the agricultural labourer and consequently increased the number of people eligible to vote from 3 million to 5 million. The Act also provided for the redrawing of electoral constituencies and established the principle of one MP per constituency. Then in 1888 the Local Government Act gave women the right to vote in local elections. In terms of constitutional reform, the Parliament Act of 1911 was of paramount importance in redistributing the balance of power from the House of Lords to the Commons. The Act removed the Lords' ultimate power of veto on money bills and gave them a two-year delaying power over other legislation. Another clause in the Act provided that henceforth the maximum duration between general elections should be reduced from seven years to five years.

Trade Unionism - Development of Labour

The working class represented a majority of the population in Britain. Reform for these necessitated the development of a trade union movement and of an independent labour representation in parliament. Up until 1870, trade unions were tolerated but not protected by law. By the Trade Union Act of 1871 they were given legal recognition. Then in 1875 trade unions were allowed to bargain collectively and to strike. Although not without their setbacks, the unions did increase thereafter and they were quite successful in improving the position of the ordinary worker. A major breakthrough for the workers was the Trade Disputes Act (1906) by which employers were not allowed to sue trade unions for damages, such as loss of earnings during a strike. Side by side with the trade union movement was the gradual emergence of a Labour Party. Keir Hardie, in fact, became the first Labour MP in parliament in 1892. Labour had its origins in socialist groups such as the Social Democratic Federation, The Fabian Society and the Independent Labour Party. These merged in 1900 to form the Labour Representation Committee (LRC). With the aim of establishing a distinct labour group in parliament, the LRC also proposed the nationalisation of key industries, votes for women and the payment of salaries to MPs. This latter proposal was taken in hand by the Liberals who passed a bill through parliament. In 1911, a sum of £400 a year was fixed as suitable payment. Meanwhile, the 1906 election returned 29 members of the LRC. Under the leadership of Ramsay MacDonald, the LRC adopted the name of the Labour Party and continued to increase in numbers. Thus it was that reform of the electoral and parliamentary system enabled the composition of parliament to change significantly.

Reform for Women

Women in 19th century Britain were little more than second class citizens, the property of their husbands and fit only for domestic duties. Their struggle for civil liberties and for their general emancipation is closely connected with the whole question of reform. Dominant among the *Suffragettes* was Emmeline Pankhurst who founded the Women's Franchise League in 1898 and then in 1903, the Women's Social and Political Union. Already by 1900 some considerable inroads had been made. In particular, women were allowed to retain their own property after marriage, they could claim custody of their children in a marriage break-up and they could no longer be detained by their husband in the domestic home. Yet women were unable to vote in parliamentary elections and thus the road to British democratisation remained incomplete. An intensification of the suffragette campaign in the early years of the 20th century meant that, in addition to public demonstrations, there was the harassment of government ministers, arson attacks and hunger strikes. Especially noteworthy in the history of the women's campaign was the force feeding of women prisoners, Black Friday (November 1910), The Cat and Mouse Act (1913) and the death of Emily Davidson in 1914. It was the war, however, which produced a climate of opinion favourable to the women's demands. Hence, the 1918 Representation of the People Act gave the vote to all men over 21 and to women over 30. Only in 1928 did women get the same voting rights as men.

Educational Reform

Britain, as an industrialised and urbanised society, needed some minimum of education if it was to function efficiently. But right up until the last decades of the 19th century the state believed that it had no role to play and consequently adopted a *laissez faire* attitude to education, leaving the issue to private enterprise and to religious voluntary societies. Only in 1870 with Forster's Elementary Education Act did real reform begin. The aim of the act was *"to fill the gaps, not to destroy the existing system"*. Accordingly, the government undertook to set up schools in areas where none already existed. The new schools were to be run by district boards and were of vital importance in bringing primary education within the reach of every child. As of yet, however, education was neither compulsory nor free. This was corrected in 1880 when education was made compulsory up to the age of 10 and in 1891 when fees were abolished. The system whereby teachers' salaries were based on the results of their students was abolished in 1897. Two years later, the school-leaving age was raised to 12. Reform in secondary level education was even slower to come about and even at the beginning of the 20th century, it continued to be enjoyed by the privileged few. Balfour's Education Act of 1902 sought to rectify this situation. It provided for the financing of secondary schools out of local rates with the help of government grants. Schools run by the religious were to receive grants. Further reform came in 1907 when a scholarship system enabled bright children of poor people to avail of secondary education. Teacher training was also improved. Thus by 1914, Britain had an efficient, organised and successful educational system.

Army Reform

That an overhaul of the British army was necessary became painfully obvious in the course of the 19th century. Particularly important in pointing to the need for improvement were the poor conditions under which British soldiers had served during the Crimean War (1853-1856), and the scandals which had emerged. Also of consequence was the inefficiency of the British army by comparison with other armies, most notably the Prussian one. In rapid succession, a number of reforms were implemented. The man most associated with making the army a more efficient and humane organisation was Edward Cardwell, Gladstone's Secretary for War between 1868 and 1874. Already in 1868, flogging during peacetime was abolished. It was not eliminated for active service until 1880. *'Bounty money'* which sought to entice young men into the army by a system of bribery, was got rid of. The Army Regulations Bill, 1871, did away with the purchase of commissions by the wealthy. Henceforth, the selection and promotion of officers was on merit. Ability rather than privilege became all important. Another reform came in the Army Enlistment Act which shortened the length of time spent by recruits in the army. Added to this was the improvement of weaponry. The new breech-loading rifle, the Martini-Henry, became the standard infantry weapon. Cardwell's plans to introduce a permanent general staff were not taken on board but he did succeed in ensuring that the Commander-in-Chief of the army would be subject to the Secretary for War. The result of such reforms was that the British army was enabled to take its place among the modern armies of the day.

Housing/Health/Children's Charter

As the 19th century progressed the state felt compelled to provide increasing protection for its weaker and disadvantaged members. Services in housing, health and general welfare expanded under various governments. Richard Cross, Disraeli's Home Secretary between 1874 and 1880, was one person to acknowledge that diseases were frequently caused by bad sewage, polluted water and poor housing. The 1874 Artisan's Dwelling Act witnessed the beginning of state involvement in public housing and paved the way for some considerable slum clearance and rebuilding. Then in 1875 the Public Health Act laid the groundwork for the development of sanitation services. The country was divided into health districts. These would be under the control of health authorities who, in turn, were made responsible for water, sewage, street lighting, and so on. A series of measures introduced between 1906 and 1912 became known as the Children's Charter. These included the provision of school meals for the needy in 1906, medical inspections of schools and free treatment to those that required it in 1907, the establishment of juvenile courts, corrective schools and a probation service in 1908. In that same year, infant welfare centres were set up. They provided advice to mothers, and free milk for babies.

Other Social Reforms - Conclusion

Some more measures were introduced to help ordinary people in the workplace. In 1906, for example, a Workman's Compensation Act and a Merchant Shipping Act were introduced. The former dealt with compensation for accidents at work, the latter sought to regulate conditions for ships' crews. The Coal Mines Act of 1908 introduced a maximum eight-hour working day for miners. Both the Trade Boards Act and the Minimum Wage Act, 1912, aimed to give people a somewhat reasonable standard of living. Other reforms that were called for concerned health insurance and pension rights. January 1909 saw the introduction of an Old Age Pensions Act. Pensions of 5 shillings per week were to be given to people over 70 years of age, a married couple received 7 shillings and six pence. And in 1911, the National Insurance Act provided insurance to the poor against sickness as well as giving assistance to unemployed workers. Reform also came in the areas of the civil service and the judiciary. In line with the liberal doctrine of *'equality of opportunity'*, from 1871 onwards, recruitment to the civil service was by examination. The administration of justice was simultaneously improved. The cumulative effect of these reforms was the attainment of basic minimum standards and while class distinctions remained, they were, at least, becoming less pronounced. Britain's reward for serving the interests and welfare of all classes and for admitting labour to some share of responsibility and power, was the emergence of a socialism that was in spirit largely co-operative and unrevolutionary. Though a lot had yet to be achieved, the foundations of a Welfare State had been laid.

15. Britain's Foreign Policy, 1870-1914

Unique Position - Policy of Splendid Isolation

Britain's position within Europe was a unique one. In terms of her geographical position, she was an island off the Continent of Europe. As such it was perhaps natural that she be less directly involved with, or affected by, her neighbours than might otherwise be the case. The English Channel alleviated, to some extent, the need for agreements or alliances. Economically, Britain, *'the workshop of the world'*, was almost completely self-sufficient. The home of the Industrial Revolution, she was well supplied with necessary raw materials. She also had a ready market for her goods, both at home and among the numerous colonies which she possessed, for Britain was at the centre of a far-flung and ever-growing empire. With a total population of some 235 million people, it was literally *'an empire upon which the sun never set'*. Added to this, Britain's navy *'ruled the waves'*. She had for many years assumed the right to adopt a two-power standard which ensured that the strength of her navy was greater than the combined strength of her two greatest rivals (traditionally France and Russia). At the same time, many British people regarded Europeans with a mixture of condescension and contempt. Queen Victoria, for example, maintained that *"we are the only honest people and therefore our task of dealing with others who are not so is dreadful"*. These factors, combined with Britain's lack of real territorial ambition in Europe enabled her to pursue a policy which one of her Prime Ministers, Lord Salisbury, described as *"splendid isolation"*. It was a policy of non-interference or non-commitment in the affairs of Europe. Britain was, however, prepared to collaborate or to intervene when she perceived her interests were in danger.

The 1870s

Abroad, the most notable event of 1870 was the Franco-Prussian war which transferred the reputed primacy of the Continent from France to Germany. Gladstone approached this war, and foreign affairs in general, with some caution. He sought to strike a balance between Britain's interests and the rights of others, believing it was best to *"avoid needless and entangling engagements"*. Not so with Disraeli who became Prime Minister in 1874 with the aim of pursuing a strong foreign policy and in engaging in active imperialism. His *'commanding policy'* led, in 1875, to the purchase of Suez Canal shares from Khedive Ismail, the Egyptian ruler. This allowed Britain to assume greater influence over Egypt and to gain increased control over the main route to India. Two years later, in 1877, Disraeli persuaded Parliament to grant Queen Victoria the new title of *'Empress of India'*. The policy of determination, insofar as it applied to Europe, originated in the Eastern crisis, 1875-1878. The crisis arose out of a rebellion by Turkey's Slav Christian subjects in protest at how they were being treated. Russia, swayed by powerful Slavophile influences and her own imperialistic ambitions, invaded and defeated Turkey, forcing her to accept the Treaty of San Stefano, 1878. This Treaty, through the creation of a puppet state of Bulgaria with access to the Aegean and Mediterranean Seas, threatened Britain's main trade route to India. Britain now sat up and took notice. A contingent of 7,000 Indian troops were sent to Malta, to be ready to seize Cyprus or Alexandria if necessary. Simultaneously, a revision of the San Stefano agreement was demanded.

The Congress of Berlin, 1878

Bismarck offered himself as an *'honest broker'* in the crisis and invited Russia, Austria-Hungary and Great Britain to a great European congress to be held in Berlin. It convened in June 1878. Britain was represented by Disraeli whose belief in the importance of the Eastern question was such that he sought to have policy directed by himself, and by Lord Salisbury, recently appointed Foreign Minister. Before the conference met, Britain had taken the precaution to prepare for it by making advance agreements with Russia, Austria-Hungary and Turkey. This now allowed for the replacement of the Treaty of San Stefano with the Treaty of Berlin. The idea of a big Bulgaria was dropped, Turkish influence in Europe re-emerged and Britain secured Cyprus as a compensation for Russian acquisitions in the Caucasus, and as a base from which to watch over the Straits and from which to put pressure on the Turks to introduce internal reforms. Thus it was that Disraeli, about whom Bismarck respectfully remarked *"The old Jew, that is the man"*, had exerted a decisive influence and achieved nearly everything that he had wanted for Britain. Returning home in triumph, he could well maintain that he had brought *"peace with honour"*. With regard to Britain's policy of isolation, the Congress of Berlin can be taken as a high point. Once her interests were threatened and she became involved, she found it impossible to fully disassociate herself from European affairs, although it must be said that she played a less active role than other powers.

Colonies - The Scramble for Africa

With the return of Gladstone to power in 1880, there was another shift in British foreign policy. Gladstone thought Disraeli's foreign policy to be *"the most selfish and least worthy"* he had ever known and sought, along with the Foreign Minister, Lord Granville, to undo some imperial matters. He withdrew from Afghanistan and reached a compromise with the Boers in the Transvaal. But this was the era of the so-called *'scramble for Africa'* and although Gladstone decried the widening of frontiers and wished for Britain to have no unwilling subjects, British imperialism could not be held back. In 1882, for example, trouble in Egypt as a result of a military coup under Colonel Arabi Pasha, necessitated a British presence there if her interests in the Suez Canal were to be protected. The suppression of the revolt was followed by British occupation. Regarded as temporary, it was, in fact, 1954 before the British left Egypt. A rebellion in the Sudan, to the south of Egypt, General Gordon's decision to make a stand at Khartoum and Gladstone's hesitation in sending him reinforcements, led to Gordon's death in January 1885 and contributed to the collapse of Gladstone's government in 1885. Meanwhile, the Second Congress of Berlin, 1884, aimed to avoid serious confrontation between European nations in their competition for colonial gain. Spheres of influence were drawn up and Britain again showed herself willing to abandon her policy of isolation when her interests were at stake. By then, her vast empire ranged from Egypt in the north of Africa to Cape Colony in the south. It continued to expand thereafter.

Deteriorating Anglo-German Relations

For most of the period between 1886 and 1906 foreign policy was in Conservative hands with Salisbury sometimes holding the position of Foreign Minister as well as Prime Minister. Up until the 1890s, Salisbury was inclined to favour the Triple Alliance of the central powers more than the Dual Alliance of France and Russia (1894), chiefly because of the hostile attitude of France on Egyptian and colonial questions. As early as 1887, for example, Salisbury signed the secret Mediterranean Agreements with Italy and Austria. These were concerned with the maintenance of the status quo and while Britain refused to turn the agreements into an alliance, or indeed to become a member of the Triple Alliance, they were reflective of where her sympathies lay. In 1890, Salisbury was also willing to do a deal with Germany. He ceded Heligoland to the Germans in return for Zanzibar. The fall of Bismarck in 1890, however, and Wilhelm II's interests in world politics brought Germany into conflict with Britain. Following the Jameson raid in the Transvaal in 1895, Wilhelm sent a telegram to President Kruger, congratulating him on having successfully repelled the British. Britain resented such blatant interference in the Transvaal which was within her sphere of influence and the incident gave rise to much anti-German feeling. Further hostility arose in 1899 when Germany financed the building of the Berlin-Baghdad railway for the Turks. Britain had only recently turned her back on Turkey as a result of the massacre of Armenian Christians around this time. Another issue which should be borne in mind was the growing commercial and industrial rivalry between Britain and Germany.

Naval Rivalry - Conflict in Sudan - Boer War

Insult was added to injury when Wilhelm backed Admiral Von Tirpitz's plans for German naval expansion and it was perhaps this, more than anything else, that decisively altered the whole tone of Anglo-German relations. The First German Naval Law of 1898 initiated a vast programme of shipbuilding in Germany, prompting the British to fear that *"the new German navy is being carefully built up from the point of view of war with us"*. Britain found herself driven to build in reply and so the naval race began. This was a competition which quickly and decisively aroused British popular emotions and drove the British not into amenability but into increasingly close relations with the French and Russians. Before this happened, Britain came dangerously close to open hostility with France when, in 1898, conflict over the Sudanese village of Fashoda arose between Captain Marchand, who claimed it for France, and General Kitchener, who insisted it was within the British sphere of influence. The matter was peacefully resolved when the respective governments decided that Marchand should leave. Especially important about the incident was that it proved the advantages of dialogue as opposed to isolationary aloofness. Once again, Britain was forced to become unpleasantly conscious of her isolation when she became involved in the Boer War, 1899-1902. This war between the British and Dutch settlers led to the defeat of the Boers and the Treaty of Vereeniging whereby the Boer republics were brought under British rule. It was an occasion when there was talk of a continental league against Great Britain and when Wilhelm II angered the British by his forthright support for the Boers.

Appeal of Allies

From 1895 Britain was the only major power not part of any alliance bloc. Salisbury was criticised by members of his cabinet for not adopting a more positive foreign policy. Britain's dangerous position and vulnerability to attack prompted Chamberlain to insist that *"as long as we have interests which at one time or another conflict with the interests of all, we are liable to be confronted at any moment with a combination of great powers"*. Increasingly necessary, therefore, for the protection of essential interests, the search for allies began in earnest in the early years of the 20th century, first under Foreign Secretary Lord Lansdowne and then under his Liberal successor, Sir Edward Grey. The Anglo-Japanese Alliance of 1902 allowed Britain's interests in the Pacific to be looked after by Japan in time of war, in return for British recognition of Japanese interests in Korea. Lansdowne's next step in foreign policy was the conclusion of the *Entente Cordiale* with France in 1904. This was a cordial understanding rather than a specific commitment to act, and its significance lay not in the character of its terms, but in the power with whom it was concluded and in the development in Great Britain's relationship to continental Europe which followed it. The British then came to terms with Russia through the Anglo-Russian convention and Triple Entente, 1907. The convention was concluded, in the main, for the sake of India and regardless of how tenuously Great Britain, France and Russia were now linked together. And by its political implications rather than by its content, the Entente undermined the basic German assumption of British hostility to France and Russia.

Preparations for War - Conclusion

Britain also reacted to possible threats to her peace and security by reforming her army and navy. Expenditure in these areas rose steadily in the pre-war years. R.B. Haldane, War Secretary from 1906-1912, played a very important role in updating the army while Lord Esher was an influential 'behind the scenes' figure. Measures taken included the creation of an Army Council and a General Staff. Simultaneously, officers and men were given a new sense of professional purpose and war preparations were extended over a wide range of matters such as food supply, censorship and espionage which were previously given little consideration. The War Book laid down the sequence of action to be followed when hostilities seemed imminent. The formation of an *'expeditionary force'*, which could be sent to France if the British government decided to intervene in a continental war, was a major step forward. Naval improvements, many of which took place under Sir John Fisher, included the building of dreadnoughts and the ruthless scrapping of 150 obsolescent ships. Yet, in spite of all the preparation for what might happen, the reality was that right up until the outbreak of World War I, none of Britain's allies felt sure of Britain's support, so reluctant was she about committing herself. What she had done was to leave the door open for such an eventuality if it suited her. Only in August 1914, with the invasion of Belgium, did Britain become convinced that to stay out of war would point to *"nothing but a miserable and ignoble future"* (Edward Grey).

Britain, 1870-1914: Past Exam Questions

1991

C1. The British Overseas Empire

Discuss developments in the British overseas Empire, 1870-1914.

1990

C1. Reform in Great Britain

Treat of the reforms brought about in Great Britain during the period 1870-1914.

1989

C2. Anglo-German Relations

Treat of relations between Germany and Great Britain during the period 1870-1914.

1988

C3. British Foreign Policy

Treat of British foreign policy during the period 1870-1914.

1987

C3. Britain, 1870-1914

Treat of social and political reform in Britain during the period 1870-1914.

1986

E4. Essay

(iii) The development of the welfare state in Great Britain, 1906-c.1950.

*Kaiser Wilhelm II, Emperor of
Germany, 1988-1918*

*Otto von Bismarck, Chancellor
of the German Empire,
1871-1890*

*Tsar Nicholas II of
Russia*

*Leon Gambetta,
French Republican leader*

*Adolphe Thiers, Head of the French
National Assembly, 1871*

General George Boulanger

THE AGE OF IMPERIALISM

16. European Expansion Overseas, 1870-1914

A. *Account for the rapid European expansion overseas during the period 1870-1914.*

Introduction - Technology

The outward expansion of European power over other parts of the earth dates back to the 15th and 16th century when countries like Spain, Portugal, Britain and France had sought to build huge empires. The years 1815-1870, however, witnessed a decline in colonial activity stemming from the belief that colonies were of little importance. In the period 1870 to 1914, countries again began to acquire, administer and establish control over the less materially advanced territories of the world. Because they did so with a new and stronger interest than ever before, the years after 1870 have come to be known as *'The Age of Imperialism'*. In particular, the hectic colonial scramble that took place concentrated upon the continents of Africa and Asia. These were the only two important areas of the globe still not brought under European influence. Such was the dramatic suddenness of overseas expansion and its pre-eminence in the policies of major European powers, that some extraordinary explanation seems to be called for. Whether of an ordinary or extraordinary nature, there can be no doubting that the timing of the expansion was linked to the technology available to Europeans in the late 19th century. Medical science, for example, had developed quinine which enabled white colonists to resist the malarial mosquito. Simultaneously, advances in railways, steamships and telegraph made exploration more feasible than ever before. And the invention of the *Gatling* and *Maxim* machine guns gave Europeans an obvious advantage over non-Europeans and allowed small European forces to overcome considerably larger forces of native people.

Economic Reasons

Economic reasons are considered by many historians to be a major driving force behind the new imperialism. This view was supported by the famous British economist, J.A. Hobson in his book *'Imperialism: A Study'*. Following him, V.I. Lenin attributed the colonial expansion of 1870 to 1914 to special new economic forces at work maintaining that *"If we are to give the briefest possible definition of imperialism we should say that imperialism is the monopoly stage of capitalism"*. There were three main economic reasons why the industrialised nations of Europe wished to acquire colonies. The first of these was for investment. The Industrial Revolution had produced a 'glut of capital'. Surplus capital needed lucrative, yet secure, investment. Because the rates of return for money invested by business people in Europe were falling, it was decided that the money might best be invested outside of Europe. Colonial enterprises in Africa and Asia offered ample opportunities for financiers. Of the annual investment of British capital between 1909 and 1913, 36% went into British overseas territories. At the same time and secondly, European industrialisation had produced a surplus of goods leading to a saturation of European markets. If industrial production was not to drop and unemployment and social unrest were to be avoided, a search for markets outside of Europe was necessary. A third reason for rapid European expansion was the desire to acquire raw materials and foodstuffs. Cotton, wood, rubber, gold, diamonds, copper, ivory, vegetable oils, tea, coffee, bananas all attracted European attention. Added to this was the lure of cheap labour which the new colonies could provide and the possibility of finding an escape route for some of the economic crises in Europe in the 1870s such as the crash of the Berlin Stock Exchange, 1873.

Nationalism

Important as economic factors were in explaining the rapid European expansion overseas, in some areas this theory falls short. France, one of the less industrialised of the north-western European nations, was heavily involved in colonisation. And even for industrialised nations, the possession of overseas territories sometimes proved overly costly and difficult to administer. Thus, other reasons need to be investigated. The link between the rise of nationalism and imperial expansion holds up to scrutiny. Colonies were regarded as a symbol of national power and glory. Pride in one's country was swelled by raising the flag over hitherto unknown and/or unpossessed areas of the world. The more colonies a country had, the more powerful it was thought to be. Accordingly, Leon Gambetta, the French statesman, believed that *"To remain a great nation or to become one, you must colonise"*. For France, her move into Africa and Asia showed that she had recovered from defeat against Germany in the Franco-Prussian war, and that she was, once more, a major power. Britain managed to acquire for herself *'an empire on which the sun never set'*. Her nationalistic pride and confidence in her empire was expressed by A.C. Benson in his song *'Land of Hope and Glory,'*

> *"Land of Hope and Glory, Mother of the Free,*
> *How shall we extol thee, who are born of thee?*
> *Wider still and wider shall thy bounds be set*
> *God who made thee mighty, make thee mightier yet"*

Italy's colonialism can perhaps be best regarded as an attempt to attain *'great power status'*. But even smaller countries like the Netherlands and Belgium made significant colonial gains. Germany was motivated to become involved in the *'rush for empires'* when it appeared that she alone of the *'Great Powers'* was failing to build an overseas empire. National pride dictated that she, too, should have *'a place in the sun'*.

Missionary/Humanitarian Reasons

Rudyard Kipling wrote a poem *'The White Man's Burden'* whose sentiments were shared, and indeed, taken up, by missionaries, humanitarians and others.

16. European Expansion Overseas

"Send forth the best ye breed,
Go, bid your sons to exile,
To serve your captives' need"

Christian missionaries launched a kind of crusade as they organised missions and sent them into *'darkest Africa'* to convert the heathens to Christianity. The religious motivation for imperialism was especially true in relation to France. She provided two-thirds (some 40,000) of all Catholic missionaries. Gambetta said of Cardinal Lavigerie, the founder of the Society of African Missionaries, the *'White Fathers'*, that *"His presence in Tunisia is worth an army for France"*. Dr. David Livingstone, a Scottish missionary, was one of the most famous of all African explorers. Belgian missionaries were active in the Congo from 1878. On the humanitarian level, many groups and individuals worked to stamp out the 'evils' of slave trade and barbaric punishment. They believed they knew what was right for the African and Asian peoples and sought to provide medical services and education. They also welcomed an opportunity to bring order and efficiency to a chaotic administration. But arrogance, aggression and exploitation were present on the part of still more explorers. They believed in their own God-given racial and social superiority. Applying Charles Darwin's *'survival of the fittest'* theory to society, they insisted that it was right and fitting that the more advanced societies should conquer and rule the weaker ones.

Security/Personalities/Adventure/Overpopulation

In addition to the aforementioned reasons for the rapid European overseas expansion during the period 1870-1914, there was a medley of other considerations which, in varying degrees, entered into the desire for colonies. One of these was the need for coaling stations and seaports to service a growing international trade. Nations also wanted to strengthen their national security by acquiring naval bases. They knew, in the prevailing climate of political tensions and rivalries, that if they did not take an advantage, it would be snatched by potential enemies. The role of explorers and adventurers in the new imperialism cannot go unrecognised. People of initiative and enterprise like the Frenchmen Du Chaillu and De Brazza, the Welshman Henry Stanley, the Germans Heinrich Barth and Karl Peters, the Englishman Cecil Rhodes and of course Dr. Livingstone all played a huge part in the whole story. They were prompted by adventure, the desire to explore into the unknown as well as devotion to scientific discovery and a buccaneering love of money and power. Politicians and monarchists, Joseph Chamberlain, Jules Ferry, Agostine Depretis, King Leopold and Wilhelm II deserve mention for it was they who, from their position of power, actively involved their own nations. The pressure of overpopulation in Europe is often cited as another reason for overseas expansion and while there is some veracity in this, it must be remembered that Europeans, for the most part, preferred the more temperate climate of the US and Australia to the new colonial areas. Nonetheless, opportunities for wealth, employment and advancement did attract ambitious young men.

B. *Estimate the extent to which European expansion overseas was responsible for the international tensions of the period 1870-1914.*

Colonisation as a Cause of Tension - Jameson Raid

By no means did European expansion overseas always lead to disputes between nations. The French conquest of Algeria and Annam or the British conquest of Nigeria and Ashati, for example, aroused little or no tension from other powers. And sometimes it was possible for one power to make gains with the encouragement or consent of others. To this end, the Berlin Conference of 1884 proposed to partition the *'spheres of influence'* in Africa as amicably as possible. But peaceful co-operation and tacit approval were the exception rather than the rule, and the age of imperialism showed itself to be a period when the realism, ruthlessness and rivalries of European national governments were especially great. Colonial collisions between national states in Africa and Asia, were all too common. As well as serving as a source of tension, these collisions often took the form of the projection of the interstate frictions and rivalries of Europe, onto an overseas 'screen'. The Jameson Raid, 1895 and its aftermath provides ample evidence of this. In December 1895, Dr. Jameson, an agent of Cecil Rhodes, led a force of about 500 men into the Transvaal. The force was easily defeated but Germany, posing as the *"grown-up power that would stop England from kicking the child republic"* sent a telegram to Paul Kruger, President of the Transvaal, congratulating him on successfully repulsing the invaders. The British were infuriated by the action and the incident served only to heighten growing tensions between the two countries.

Sudan/Boer War

The Sudan was another area of international tension, caused as a result of imperial ambitions. Trouble arose when the British and French competed for control of Fashoda, a Sudanese village. On 16th July, General Marchand of France reached Fashoda and claimed it for the French. About a fortnight later, General Kitchener, representing British ambitions in the Sudan, arrived with five gunboats and 2,000 men. Thus, while the French had won the race in time, Kitchener had superior strength. Rather than face war, the two men decided to refer the matter back to their respective governments. The situation was tense as the popular press in both countries adopted warlike attitudes. In the end, however, France decided not to risk war and Marchand withdrew. Although the conflict had represented an all-time low in Anglo-French relations, both countries thereafter moved towards more amiable co-operation. The Boer Republics of the Orange Free State and the Transvaal provided yet another area of tension, this time between the British and the Boers (Dutch settlers). As the British extended their influence in South Africa, relations between the two worsened, leading to the outbreak of war in October 1899. The British, with their superior numbers, weapons and military expertise finally won through and the Treaty of Vereeniging, 1902, brought the Transvaal and Orange Free State under British rule. A grant of £3m was given to the Boers. In addition to the tension caused between the British and the Boers, the Boer War was important in terms of how it was viewed by international powers. The Russians, for example, had proposed European intervention but Germany, though she sided with the Boers, opposed such a step. European nations were not yet ready to engage in international war.

Morocco - Conclusion

The imperial dispute between Germany and France about Morocco was a recurrent bone of contention between them in the 20 years before 1914. Although France claimed special interest in Morocco, Germany continually challenged the arrangement. In a visit to the Sultan at Tangier in March 1905, Wilhelm II promised to support the Sultan against France. He also demanded an international conference to discuss the position of Morocco. That conference, held at Algeciras in January 1906, showed widespread support for France and the country was allowed to continue to administer Morocco. The Algeciras conference strengthened relations between Britain, France and Russia. Germany, for her part, had received a blow to her prestige and because she was supported only by Austria-Hungary, she now felt compelled to draw closer to that country. A second Moroccan crisis occurred when French troops occupied Fez, the Moroccan capital, in 1911. Germany demanded the withdrawal of French troops but again she received a rebuff. The country was forced to recognise the French protectorate over Morocco in return for two strips of territory. This crisis not only increased suspicions towards Germany but convinced Germany that in the future there should be no backing down. To that extent, it might be argued that European expansion was responsible for serious international tensions. Also noteworthy is the fact that colonial events undoubtedly contributed to the system of international alliances. The *Entente Cordiale* and Triple Entente, for instance, were largely motivated by the need for security in the wake of colonial crises. But although the temper of the colonist has been described by British historian, David Thompson as *"uniquely masterful, and remorseless, brooking no obstacles and pushfully self assertive"*, in the final analysis, imperialism alone would not have caused a world war. Rather, it was a potent force, accumulatively accentuating international tensions and thereby acting as a contributory factor towards war.

17. Treat of European Involvement in Africa, 1870-1914

"The day of small nations has long passed away. The day of Empires has come".

— Joseph Chamberlain, 1904.

Introduction

Before 1870, the colonisation of Africa, *'the dark continent'*, was largely confined to coastal areas. The interior, because unexplored, was frightening and sinister, its people black and 'backward'. The period after 1870, however, witnessed a sudden burst of colonial activity and it was in Africa that the age of imperialism was most clearly visible. European influence and civilisation were expanded to all areas of the continent and her influence there, as in other areas of the earth's surface, ensured that in the period 1870-1914 Europe dominated the world more than at any other time before or since. The chief rivals in the *'scramble for Africa'* were Britain, France, Germany, Italy and Belgium; their reasons numerous and interacting. One such reason was the *'economic taproot of imperialism'*. In a world of increasing industrialisation and tariff barriers, colonies provided an outlet for capitalistic greed. Financiers and businessmen hoped to sell their surplus goods abroad, avail of the cheap raw materials that Africa possessed and make good investments. European involvement in Africa was also caused by superabundant nationalism. Colonies were associated with power and glory and the more colonies a country had, the more powerful it was thought to be. Added to these reasons was a claim that European countries needed a place for surplus population, a search for strategic bases, a missionary spirit and a sense of obligation towards 'inferior' people. The desire for adventure and a wish to divert public attention from home problems might be added to the list of diverse combinations which explain the 'why' of European involvement. Imperial control was made possible by improvements in the means of communication and transport, as well as a greater knowledge of tropical medicine.

Britain - Egypt/Sudan

Britain established a huge colonial empire in Africa. One area of special interest was Egypt. With the building of the 100 mile Suez Canal in 1869, Egypt had taken on a new significance for Britain, who regarded the canal as her lifeline to India. In 1875, when the Khedive of Egypt was unable to repay his loans on the canal, Britain purchased his shares. Along with France, the other country involved in the Suez Canal, a system of financial *'dual control'* was established. But many Egyptians resented the foreign intruders. Led by Arabi Pasha, these militant nationalists were on the point of seizing power in 1882. Riots in Alexandria led to the British bombardment of the town. By September 1882, Arabi's army was destroyed and Cairo captured. The French, who had refused to use force, were pushed out and while Egypt technically remained part of the Ottoman Empire until 1918, to all intents and purposes, it became a British colony. Fresh fields for Anglo-French competition appeared in the Sudan, to the south of Egypt. Fashoda, a Sudanese village, became the focal point of a great race to control the Nile waterway and its fertile valleys. On 16th July 1898, Captain

Marchand of France reached Fashoda and claimed it for the French. A fortnight after Marchand, Sir Herbert Kitchener arrived, claiming that the Sudan was within the British sphere of influence. With 5 gunboats and 2,000 men, Kitchener's forces were far superior to Marchand's. Both men decided to refer the matter to their respective governments. A wild and irresponsible public reaction meant that the two nations hovered on the brink of war. This was avoided when an agreement of March 1899 ordered Marchand to withdraw. The Nile valley was now firmly within British control.

Britain - South Africa

In 1814, Britain had taken over Cape Colony from the Boers (Dutch descendants). Thereafter, the Boers moved inland and established the Orange Free State and the Transvaal. This interfered with British dreams of controlling all areas from the Cape to Cairo. The situation became still more complicated by the discovery of gold in the Transvaal in 1886. The find attracted many people to the area. Known as *Uitlanders* (outsiders) they were denied equal rights with the Boers. Cecil Rhodes, Prime Minister of Cape Colony from 1890-1896, objected. In 1895, he encouraged his friend, Dr. Jameson, to lead a raid in the Transvaal in the hope that it would inspire a general revolt of the *Uitlanders*. The raid was a miserable failure. Relations continued to deteriorate between the British and the Boers and in 1899, President Kruger of the Transvaal issued an ultimatum to the British demanding they keep out of Transvaal affairs. The ultimatum was rejected and in October 1899, the Boer War began. The early initiatives lay with the Boers. The British then launched a counter-offensive. Under the command of Lord Roberts and General Kitchener, and with around 350,000 reinforcements, they now gained the upper hand. In May 1902 the Boers, unable to continue their guerilla warfare, accepted defeat and signed the Treaty of Vereeniging. This brought the Transvaal and Orange Free State under British rule and gave the Boers a grant of £3m to rebuild and restock farms burned during the war. In 1910 Cape Colony, Natal, the Orange Free State and the Transvaal joined together in the Union of Africa. This received dominion status in the British empire. In addition to her involvement in Egypt, the Sudan and South Africa, Britain established protectorates over or colonised a number of other areas of Africa - Somaliland, Bechuanaland, Zanzibar, Kenya, Uganda, Rhodesia, Nyasaland and Nigeria.

France - Tunisia

France's overseas possessions were second only to those of the British for, although she secured the largest share of area in the partition of Africa, in population and mineral wealth, hers was not the greatest. French interest in Africa was, in large measure, due to the need to regain lost prestige and recover from her low standing in the aftermath of her defeat in the Franco-Prussian War, 1870. Conquering foreign lands was her way of doing just that. There was also a considerable religious element attached to French imperialism and the country was responsible for two thirds (about 40,000) of all Catholic missionaries. Missionaries, in fact, often spread the faith in an area which the French government subsequently colonised, prompting historian Alfred Cobban to remark that *"the flag sometimes followed the cassock"*. Nor should the role of the army be ignored in the *'expansive urge'*. The French army often acted independently of the government. Its role was encouraged by men like Marshal

Lyautey, *"The army should be a school of citizenship and the officer an educator"*. The politicians chiefly responsible for colonisation were Leon Gambetta and Jules Ferry. They were encouraged to some extent by Bismarck who saw French ambitions in Africa as a means of diverting attention away from Germany and from a French war of revenge. Already in 1830, France had acquired Algeria in North Africa. She knew that the next logical step was to take Tunisia, Algeria's neighbour. France had hesitated about doing just that but when Italy showed an interest, France made her move. After a short war, involving 40,000 troops, Tunisia became a French protectorate in 1881.

France - Acquisitions and Conflicts

By pressing inland from Tunisia, Algeria, Senegal, Guinea and the Ivory Coast, France linked up her African territories into one vast bloc of French West Africa. From there she proceeded to drive inland along the north bank of the Congo to consolidate French Equatorial Africa. The French Congo was claimed by the explorer, Savorgnau de Brazza. On the east coast, France established her claim to part of Somaliland in 1885 and by 1896, she conquered Madagascar, the third largest island in the world. The French sought to treat colonies and their inhabitants as provinces and citizens of France. But French colonisation of Africa was not without its setbacks. In particular was the conflict with Britain over Egypt and the Sudan and later, conflict with Germany over Morocco. Although technically independent, Morocco was recognised as within the French sphere of influence. Following her entente with Britain in 1904, France sought to extend her interests. Germany became alarmed, however, and not only promised support for Morocco against France but also demanded an international conference to discuss the position of Morocco. The conference, which met at Algeciras in 1906, was a rebuff to Germany. Again in 1911, when French troops occupied the Moroccan town of Fez, Germany was forced to back down and recognise a French protectorate of Morocco. Further problems concerning French ambitions in Africa included the fact that her colonial commerce remained negligible and that the policy was attacked by the Left and Right alike and frequently led to the fall of ministers and governments.

Germany

Germany was a late starter in the scramble for Africa. This was because Bismarck, throughout the 1870s had consistently maintained that he was *"no man for colonies"*. He believed that colonies were little more than *'expensive luxuries'* and concentrated, instead, on domestic affairs and building up the economy. Nonetheless, industrialists, merchants, missionaries and adventurers favoured involvement and in 1882 the German Colonial Society was founded. Under pressure from this society and perhaps hoping to divert attention away from problems at home, Bismarck, became involved for a brief period. He proposed a conference of the major powers to draw up spheres of influence. In the event, the Berlin Conference, 1884-1885, witnessed a pledge by these powers to pursue the further partition of Africa as amicably as possible. In the absence of any formal body to legislate on or to oversee the pursuit of colonies, the Berlin Conference did, in the short term, ease tensions. Nevertheless conflicts and collisions were not long resurfacing. Meanwhile, Germany acquired Namibia, Togoland, the Cameroons and Tanzania. Under Wilhelm II, Germany took a much greater interest in colonial acquisition. Wilhelm determined to gain for Germany *"her rightful place in the sun"*. His policy of *Weltpolitik* increased Germany's share of the earth's landmass but it brought Germany into conflict with other powers. Interference in the aftermath of the Jameson Raid, support for the Dutch in the Boer War and an increase in the size of her navy brought relations with Britain to an all-time low. With France, there was conflict and bitterness over Morocco. And for all that, the German experience in Africa was generally disappointing. There was little German emigration and the colonies were all too often run at a loss.

Italy/Belgium

Hoping to establish herself as a major European power, Italy attempted, with limited success, to create an empire in North Africa. Her aspiration towards Tunisia was thwarted by the French in 1881. Italy, however, went on to acquire Eritrea, on the Red Sea. She sought also to occupy Abyssinia and consequently moved against her in 1895. The Abyssinians fiercely resisted the Italians and at the Battle of Adowa, March 1896, Italy was decisively beaten. 5,000 Italians were killed, 2,000 prisoners taken and the country humiliated. In 1905, Somalia became an Italian colony and in September 1911, the Italian invasion of Libya began. Although technically a triumph for Italy, the *'conquest'* brought no real benefits. A guerilla war with local tribesmen continued until 1931 and with 50,000 Italian troops in North Africa, there was a considerable drain on the country's already limited resources. Belgian interests in Africa were closely associated with King Leopold II. In 1876 he formed the International African Association. In 1882, Belgium established control over the Congo, and the Berlin Conference in 1885 recognised Leopold's personal authority over the area. The Congo had enormous mineral wealth but Leopold's regime engaged in extreme exploitation of the natives, subjecting them to inhuman slave labour. Growing international concern led to a takeover of the Congo by the Belgian government. In return for the *'blood-stained gift'*, eighty times the size of Belgium, Leopold received compensation.

Conclusion

Africa, the second largest continent in the world, had less than one tenth of its surface colonised by Europeans in 1875. Just over twenty years later, only one tenth remained unappropriated. France acquired some 11 million square kilometres of the continent, Britain obtained 9 million and Germany, Belgium and Italy got approximately 2 million square kilometres. No real control or regulation over the scramble took place and the result was that several clashes of interest occurred and tensions were heightened. Yet European expansion in Africa between 1870 and 1914 was accomplished without recourse to major war for, however much Europeans snorted and hinted at hostilities, they were generally apt to draw back from war among themselves about colonial disputes. Nonetheless, the colonisation of Africa must be seen as one of the contributory factors in the outbreak of war in 1914. It increased suspicion, envy and jealousy and strengthened the system of alliances. And once hostilities did commence, the imperial issue ensured that what started as a European war became a world war. In terms of the effects of imperialism, it is generally recognised that the disadvantages and burdens outweigh the alleged benefits. On the credit side, imperialism brought wealth for some. It also opened up areas previously inaccessible, developed natural resources, was responsible for building schools and hospitals, generally abolishing slavery and *'barbaric practices'* and spreading Christianity. The abuse of natives, the suppression of their traditions and cultures and the spread of European diseases are among the negative effects of the new imperialism. In time, the colonies were inspired by European ideas on nationalism and democracy and so developed movements for decolonisation.

The Age of Imperialism: Past Exam Questions

1995
E4. Essay
(i) European involvement in Africa, 1870-1914.

1994
C3. Imperialism, 1870-1914
Discuss the causes of imperialism (the creation of colonial empires overseas by European powers) during the period 1870-1914.

1992
C1. European Expansion Overseas
(a) Account for the rapid European expansion overseas during the period 1870-1914.
(b) Estimate the extent to which this European expansion overseas was responsible for the international tensions of the period 1870-1914.

1991
C1. The British Overseas Empire
Discuss developments in the British overseas Empire, 1870-1914.

1990
C3. European Involvement in Africa
Treat of European involvement in Africa, 1870-1914

1988
C2. European Expansion Overseas
(i) Account for the rapid rate of European expansion overseas in the period 1870-1914.
(ii) Assess the impact of that expansion on Europe.

18. The Causes of World War I

Introduction

There can be no doubting that in August 1914 the *'vials of wrath were full'* and that there existed a powerful current of explosive situations which were so strongly set that they refused to subside. The outbreak of the First World War contained many of the qualities of a Frankenstein monster, once begun it became almost an end in itself, its original objectives becoming swamped with many others which had scarcely been considered when it started. While there had been longer wars in the past, never before had the world experienced such total war, a war which demanded that the countries involved commit all their resources to the achievement of victory, a war fought on four continents and on land, sea and air. The havoc and destruction caused ensured that war could no longer be considered to be glamourous or indeed glorious. Nor could the manliness of war be extolled. Rather, people became convinced that such a catastrophe must never occur again. There was a general belief that if the causes - the 'why' of the conflict - could be discovered, remedies could be applied and such a widespread war could not happen again. Article 231 of the Versailles treaty of 1919 blamed Germany for causing the war and demanded her admission of war guilt. This was unfair to Germany, however, and failed to understand the complexity of events which brought about war, the factors which in one way or another went to make up the history of Europe during the previous 50 years. The truth is that all the participants of war were either directly or indirectly involved. Thus, while Germany does shoulder some of the responsibility for war, other countries must also bear the blame. So too must the question of nationalism, the alliance system, different forms of rivalry, attitudes to war, the assassination at Sarajevo and the Austrian ultimatum.

Germany

German unification, which was completed in 1870, upset the balance of power in Europe and must therefore be considered as one of the various background issues leading to war. But Bismarck, the man chiefly responsible for unification, thereafter sought to maintain the status quo and to keep the peace in Europe. As long as he was at the helm, European peace was reasonably secure. Yet with the ascension of Wilhelm II to the throne in 1888 and his *'bull in a china shop'* mentality, international relations were profoundly affected. Under Wilhelm, Germany was brought into conflict with many other states. In 1895, for example, Wilhelm angered the British by sending a telegram to President Kruger of the Transvaal congratulating him on his actions against the British in the Jameson Raid. During the Boer War, Wilhelm sent aid directly to the Boers. Germany's acquisition of Kiao-Chow in China irked both the British and the Russians. Another act of provocation of the British came in 1899 when

Germany financed the Berlin-Baghdad railway in return for trade concessions. Wilhelm's aggressiveness antagonised the French when in 1906 and 1911 he tried to curb French influence over Morocco. Wilhelm was prevented from going to war in 1911 over the Agadir incident only because he knew that Germany was not ready. Nonetheless, these and other incidents accelerated tensions and increased the likelihood of war. Meanwhile, German preparations for war went ahead in earnest. The development of the Schlieffen Plan, which would ensure that Germany did not have to fight a two-front war, meant that the likelihood of war became ever more real.

Nationalism

Part of Wilhelm's, and indeed Germany's, aggressiveness stemmed from the issue of nationalism. Like so many European powers in the late nineteenth and early twentieth century, prevailing national pride was linked with the urge for national expansion. Powers like Britain, France, Germany, Austria-Hungary, Russia and others had an exaggerated view of their own country, sometimes leading to an excessive, even hysterical patriotism. Their jingoism, or *'sabre-rattling'* tendencies, was such that they sought to expand the area under their influence, no matter what the cost. The lure of world power, which made itself felt directly in the *'scramble for Africa'*, meant that many of these countries came into conflict with one another, as they all too often overreached themselves. Germany, a late starter in the race, showed little sensitivity as she too sought *"her rightful place in the sun"*. But the growth of nationalism in the period prior to the world war could also be seen in a different form. This came in the belief by many national groups that people of the same language, culture, heritage and religion should form self-governing states. The existence of races of people who wished to be independent of those who ruled them posed a direct threat to peace in Europe. The western part of Russia, for instance, consisted of many non-Russian peoples, most notably the Poles and Finns. The province of Alsace-Lorraine created further tensions. Controlled by Germany since 1871, Alsace-Lorraine contained a French population. French people there and elsewhere harboured bitter thoughts towards Germany, some of them looking forward to the day when a war of revenge might be possible. It was not here but in the Austro-Hungarian empire, however, where the problem of nationalism was most acute.

Austria-Hungary/The Balkans

Austria-Hungary was a multi-racial empire. The different races of people living there included Magyars, Czechs, Slovaks and Slavs. Many of these groups were looking for independence but the Hapsburgs realised that nationalism, if successful, could lead to the break-up of the empire. Consequently, they tried to stamp it out. The situation was complicated still further by the collapse of the Turkish empire and the resulting power vacuum created in the Balkans. Both Austria-Hungary and Russia sought to fill the vacuum. This created a state of permanent tension and hostility between the two empires. The first Balkan crisis, 1875-'78, for example, leading to the Congress of Berlin and to the overthrow of the San Stefano treaty, sowed seeds of war because, in effect, the Congress inflicted defeat on Russia and led to closer links between Austria-Hungary and Germany. Austria-Hungary was thereby given necessary backing for her aggressiveness. Austria's expansion in the Balkans also ensured that she made a bitter enemy of Serbia, an independent Serb state that bordered the empire. The Serbs hoped to unite the Slav people into a new independent state called Yugoslavia. Bosnia and Herzegovina, taken over by Austria-Hungary in 1908, should form part of the new state. The Serbs thus encouraged Bosnia to rebel. This, coupled with Russia's support for the Slavs, made Austria-Hungary determined to crush Serbia and end, once and for all, her disruptive force. The opportunity to do just that came in 1914.

The System of Alliances

The system of alliances was undoubtedly Bismarckian in origin. It was seen as the best method of preserving the balance of power in Europe. A constant feature of alliances between 1871 and 1914 was the enduring hostility between France and Germany and the cynical political realism of the time. By 1907, the greater European powers had grouped themselves into two blocks - the Triple Alliance consisting of Germany, Austria-Hungary and Italy, and the Triple Entente comprising France, Russia and Great Britain. Neither alliance was constructed as a preparation for war. Rather, both alliances were attempts to prevent war by appearing so strongly supported by allies that the other would not dare to launch an attack. Yet the alliances, whatever their purpose, did become a cause of war. Surrounded by diplomacy and secrecy, the alliances aggravated suspicion and fear. They also ensured that any crisis which took place did so in the context of a Europe divided into two armed camps. Even a latent threat to the security of the great powers strengthened the ties within each group. A further contributing factor to war was that the alliances allowed a given country to be more aggressive than she might normally be, secure in the knowledge of back-up should war begin. On the subject of the alliance systems, it is worth noting that Britain refused to commit herself wholeheartedly, preferring to retain a certain amount of freedom right up to the outbreak of war. It might therefore be argued that she weakened the Triple Entente by this attitude. Had Germany been sure that Britain would fight, she might have moved with more caution.

Rivalry - Naval/Armed/Economic

Rivalry between nations took many forms in the pre-war period. Naval rivalry existed between Germany and Britain and it too accelerated international tensions. Britain traditionally adopted a two-power standard, believing that the Royal Navy should possess more battleships and cruisers than the next two largest navies in the world. In the late nineteenth century, Germany, under the influence of Admiral von Tirpitz, challenged British supremacy of the water. Competition between the two powers led to a naval power race which continued through to 1914. The launching by the British of the Dreadnought *"a new type of floating gun carriage"* in 1906, made all previous battleships obsolete and increased the danger, leaving observers free to speculate about a prospective war between the two countries. But the naval race, dangerous as it was in its own right, was nothing more than the edge of a larger arms race in which all the great powers were involved. From the late nineteenth century, European armies grew enormously. Especially noticeable were the huge reserves of trained men. Governments widened their military budgets and, as new weapons were invented, nations were driven into an ever spiralling arms race where cost was not a factor. War preparations became even more feverish after 1910 and room for manoeuvre dwindled. Whether or not economic interests, and particularly the economic rivalry between Great Britain and Germany, compounded the situation and that war was the inevitable outcome of competition among the great powers, is unclear. Certainly business profited from the arms race and was not anxious to limit arms manufacture. Then again, war could do untold damage to the economic well-being of participating nations.

Sarajevo - Austrian Ultimatum

On 28th June 1914, Franz Joseph, heir to the Austrian throne, and his wife, Sophie, visited Sarajevo, the Bosnian capital. It was Serbia's national day and although Franz Joseph intended the mission to be one of goodwill, warnings about the visit had come from many quarters. In spite of the explosive situation, security precautions were almost non-existent. Within such a context, Gavrilo Princip, a member of the Serbian terrorist organisation, the Black Hand, assassinated the archduke and his wife. Although no connection between Princip and the Serbian government could be proven, Austria decided that the opportunity was too good to be let pass. Serbia, the sorest of thorns in Hapsburg flesh, would be taught a lesson. Thus Leopold Berchtold, the Austrian Foreign Minister, claimed that the Serbian government had planned everything. Having on 5th July received a 'blank cheque' by way of support from Germany, Austria, on 23rd July, delivered a ten point ultimatum to the Serbians. Serbia was given 48 hours to reply to the strongly worded document. Serbia's reply was conciliatory. She showed herself prepared to accede to all points of demand save one i.e. that Austrian officials be allowed to enter Serbia and participate in the investigation of the assassination. Serbia felt this point compromised her independence. She was, however, prepared to hand over the matter to the International Court of Justice in the Hague. The Austrians, bent on war, rejected the Serbian request. On 28th July they broke off diplomatic relations with Serbia and declared war.

Outbreak of War - Conclusion

The alliance system now came into play. Russia, who had an alliance with Serbia, ordered full mobilisation on 30th July 1914. In spite of German demands that mobilisation cease, the Russians continued. On 1st August Germany declared war on Russia. Within days Britain and France were involved. As more countries *'stumbled and staggered'* into war, it became clear that *"by 1914 the sick man of Europe was not just Turkey, it was Europe itself, feverish and turbulent and with strong suicidal tendencies"* Any explanation of this drift towards the abyss would be incomplete, however, without some understanding of prevailing attitudes to war. War was associated with national pride and patriotism. It contained glory, colour, honour and comradeship. One German soldier likened war to Christmas. At the same time, there was the belief that the war would soon be over. Many soldiers welcomed war as an adventure. The Kaiser told his troops they'd be *"home before the leaves fall"*, others believed that the war would be over before the end of the year. More accurate was the British Foreign Secretary, Sir Edward Gray, when he stated that *"The lamps are going out over Europe and we will not see them lit again in our lifetime"*.

19. Account for the Early Successes but Final Defeat for Germany during World War I

Schlieffen Plan - Early Successes

"Lunch in Paris, dinner in St. Petersburg". Thus spoke Kaiser Wilhelm II of the Schlieffen Plan, a scheme by which the Germans planned total victory in the First World War. The Plan sought to avoid a two-front war. It worked on the principle that Russia would be slow to mobilise and that if the Germans concentrated their energies on speed of attack and rapid mobilisation in the West, a swift victory there would enable a massive transfer of troops to the Eastern Front to take the Russians. The Plan was brilliant in its daring, but it soon became clear that it was based on a number of misconceptions. These, combined with alterations in the Plan such as the decision by Germany's supreme commander, von Moltke, to strengthen the wing defending Germany from French attack along the frontier of the Rhine, would ultimately prove to be Germany's undoing. In the meantime, however, Germany, with the outbreak of World War I in August 1914, took the strategic initiative. The country's mobilisation went according to plan and vast numbers of men were transported to Belgium from where it was hoped that they would sweep into northern France and form a pincer movement from which to surround Paris. Although the Germans met with unexpectedly tough resistance in Belgium, particularly at Liège and Namur, and had to cope with the unexpected entry of Britain into the war as well as the appearance of the British Expeditionary Force (BEF), their advance could not be stopped. The Belgian army was forced to take refuge in the fortress of Antwerp while German soldiers proceeded to make their way through France, having successfully fought off the French offensive in Lorraine.

German Setbacks - Marne/Ypres

By early September 1914, the Germans were within 30 km of Paris and many believed the country to be on the point of victory. This belief was reinforced by the decision of the French government to flee Paris to Bordeaux. Yet, in spite of apparent victory, many German setbacks had already been suffered. Belgian resistance had guaranteed delay in Germany's advance. The 'hammer head' of the Schlieffen Plan was further weakened by von Moltke's decision to transfer two divisions to take Antwerp. Another blow came from the Eastern Front where the Russian armies were advancing more quickly than anticipated. This necessitated the transfer of four more divisions to the East. Nearing Paris, German generals Kluck and Bülow decided to change the Schlieffen Plan even further. Possessing an army reduced in strength they opted to avoid making the difficult pass to the west of Paris but rather to pursue the retreating French to the east of the city, along the river Marne. From 6th-9th September, the Battle of the Marne, one of the most dramatic and decisive conflicts of the whole war, took place. The French, assisted by the BEF, and using all available reinforcements, attacked the Germans. After some very heavy fighting, the Germans were pushed back along the river Aisne where they commenced to 'dig in'. Failure to capture Paris destroyed the German goals of a rapid victory and avoidance of a two-front war. It led to the dismissal of von Moltke and his replacement by von Falkenhayn. Thereafter, the Germans took Antwerp in early October but missed the chance to occupy the Channel ports. In the First Battle of Ypres, 14th October to 20th November 1914, Falkenhayn failed to outflank the BEF and while the Germans continued to hold most of the Belgian coast, the Allies retained the vital ports of Dunkirk, Calais and Boulogne, through which they received a continual supply of food and war materials from Britain.

Trenches - War in the East

As winter set in, the last major piece of mobile warfare had come to an end in the West. Both sides had by now dug trenches and strengthened their defences. The building of a vast network of trenches stretching from the English Channel to the Swiss border and across Belgium and France set the pattern for the First World War. It was a war of deadlock and prolonged battering, a war which seemed as if it might go on indefinitely. German successes to date consisted of the taking of nearly all of Belgium and of north-eastern France, including its heavy industry, coal supplies and iron fields. While these successes were real, overall success remained limited. Insofar as the war in the East was concerned, the Russian army, under General Samsonov, advanced into East Prussia as early as 17th August 1914. Although this quick advance possibly saved Paris, it was to cost the Russians heavily. After some initial setbacks, the Germans, under Generals Hindenburg and Ludendorff, hit back. Spectacular successes were achieved in the Battle of Tannenberg, August 1914, which resulted in the almost complete disintegration of Samsonov's army, and in the Masurian Lakes, September 1914, where the demoralised Russian forces suffered still more losses. Thereafter, much of the German Eastern Army had to be withdrawn to help their Austrian allies further south. This, coupled with Russian toughness *"The more you strike the Russian bear, the worse he hits back"* meant that by the end of 1914 the situation was inconclusive and paralysis had set in.

1915 - Stalemate

Although Germany did have some successes, 1915 was a year that produced no decisive victory for either side. It continued rather to witness stalemate and futile attacks. Between 8th January and 5th February, for example, heavy fighting in the Soissons and La Bassée Canal sections of the Champagne resulted in the Germans making only slight gains. From February to April the Allies mounted offensives against German lines in eastern Champagne, the Artois region and at St. Mihiel. While heavy losses were incurred, no tangible results emerged. The Second Battle of Ypres, April to May 1915 saw the introduction of poison gas by the Germans. While the British offensive was frustrated, Germany failed to take full advantage of her new, deadly weapon. Thereafter, the Second and Third Battles of Artois and the Second Battle of Champagne made little more than insignificant gains. By now, 400,000 large shells were fired every month on the Western Front and a desperate race for new and better weaponry was on. The development of the German *Howitzer* and *Mauser* played a part in the story and certainly German inventions were sufficiently good to ensure that she was, at least, capable of sustaining a two-front campaign for a prolonged period of time. Germany's campaign on the Eastern Front was more obviously successful. Russia lost Galicia and as Austro-German armies advanced further, the Russians were forced into major retreat. Incapable of winning the war, the Russians were still more incapable of escaping from it. And while Italy's entry into the war in 1915 on the side of the Allies was a blow to the Axis Powers, the Allied expedition to the Dardanelles augured well for Germany. It forced the Allies to open up a second front and ultimately it proved a costly failure.

Verdun/The Somme - Brusilov Offensive

In 1916 the *'war of attrition'* continued on a larger, fiercer and more intensified scale. The major battles on the Western Front were fought at Verdun and the Somme. As far as Verdun was concerned, General Falkenhayn believed that to attack the famous fortress, a symbol of French national pride, would be the means of *'bleeding the French white'*. On 21st February, the Germans opened the offensive with bombardment from 1,400 guns. Command of the defence of Verdun was given to General Pétain who brought in reinforcements and a renewed will to resist; *"They shall not pass"*. A series of attacks and counter-attacks took place over the following months, during which time the fortress was kept supplied by means of the *'sacred way'*, the only link road to Verdun. Eventually, French stubbornness and bravery prevailed and, in June, Falkenhayn abandoned the attack. By then, over 280,000 Germans and 315,000 French had been killed. The Battle of the Somme tells a similar story. This was a British offensive on the heavily fortified German lines at the Somme. It began on 1st July but while the Germans were greatly outnumbered, the Allies gained no more than 10km of ground before they called off the attack in November. Even the introduction by the British of the surprise weapon, the tank, in September 1916 failed to change the picture. Loss of life in this battle amounted to 620,000 deaths on the Allied side and 450,000 on the German side. Things were likely to have been worse for the Allies on the Western Front had it not been for General Brusilov's great Russian offensive in June 1916. His advance was only halted when the Austrians were joined by German soldiers.

Romania - War at Sea

The failure to achieve real success at Verdun and the Somme led to the replacement of Falkenhayn by Ludendorff as supreme commander. Shortly afterwards, German morale was damaged when, on 27th August 1916, Romania entered the war on the side of the Allies. But the Germans were no easy target and by the end of 1916 practically all of Romania had been taken by them. Gains there were restricted, however, by the destruction of Romanian oil wells which ensured that the German need for oil would not be met. War at sea was being waged concurrently. In May 1916 the German and British fleets met at Jutland off the Danish coast in the only major sea battle of the war. Admiral Scheer of the German High Sea Fleet devised a scheme to lure out part of the British Grand Fleet, and to destroy it. The battle which resulted from the 'baiting' of the British was indecisive, both sides claiming victory. German losses, nonetheless, were less severe than British ones. In any case, Germany now returned in earnest to her policy of seriously disrupting British merchant shipping. This was in response to the British economic blockade of Germany and it involved considerable submarine activity. Attacks on Allied and neutral ships alike had already, in 1915, led to the sinking of the *Lusitania* and nearly 1,200 deaths, of whom over a 100 were American. While opposition from the US led to a calling-off of all-out submarine warfare, it continued on Allied ships to such an extent that by 1916 the German U-boats were destroying 109,000 tons of Allied shipping, a figure that increased to 368,000 tons in January 1917.

1917

In 1917 the Germans took the decision to reintroduce unrestricted submarine warfare. They knew that by so doing they were running the risk of bringing America into the war but it was hoped that the Germans would win the war before the US could effectively change its course. The U-boat campaign reached a peak in April 1917 when 852,000 tons of Allied shipping were destroyed. The prospect of Germany delivering a knock-out blow to Britain and her Allies became ever more real. But April 1917 also saw the entry of the US into the war on the side of the Allied Powers. Her final prompting to do so came with the Zimmermann telegram, a telegram sent by the German Foreign Minister to an agent in Mexico suggesting an alliance between Mexico and Germany and a future Mexican attack on the US. America's entry into the war had a tremendous psychological effect, giving new heart to the Allies. This, combined with a guarantee of fresh men and materials, undoubtedly tipped the balance of war in favour of the Allies. Even the withdrawal of Russia from the war by the Treaty of Brest-Litovsk in March 1918, and the freeing of German troops to fight on the Western Front only, did not quite even the sides. The Allied position was further helped by the British increasing their number of submarine chasers and destroyers as well as their building of still more ships. On the Western Front, however, it was not quite so obvious that the course of war was changing. There the French offensive launched by General Nivelle and the British offensive, resulting in the Battle of Passchendaele, 1917, failed to produce decisive victories. Only against the Italians was a breakthrough achieved by the Austro-German forces when that country received a crushing defeat at Caporetto in October 1917.

German Defeat - Conclusion

In March 1918 Ludendorff decided to launch an all-out offensive. Such was the success of the March offensive that the Germans were able to take Armetières and Soissons as well as to cross the river Marne. It was as if the stalemate of trench warfare was at an end and Paris was once more an objective. Yet the Allies were not to be defeated. Rather, they sought to place all their armies under the control of Marshal Foch, and not only to stop the German advance but to launch a counter-attack. On 8th August, *'the black day of the German army'*, the German lines near Amiens were broken. Thereafter, the Hindenburg line was broken and Allied progress became more rapid. Germany's condition was one of shortages of food and materials, considerable social unrest and huge losses in manpower. Mutinies of German sailors at Wilhelmshaven and Kiel further upset the balance. As far as Germany's allies were concerned, Bulgaria, in September 1918, was the first of the central powers to admit defeat. Turkey's turn came next in October 1918 and, following the decisive Italian victory at Vittoria Veneto, the Austrians signed an armistice early in November 1918. The faith in victory which for so long had carried the German soldiers forward, was shattered. They wanted only to end the war. Germany's unconditional surrender came in November 1918. Thus it was that the country which for so long had seemed invincible, was plunged into defeat and humiliation. While the exact moment and reasons for defeat cannot be pinpointed precisely, what is clear is that Germany, with perhaps incomparable skill and endurance, more than held her own for four years against superior numbers. Her nightmare of militarism is also an epic of military achievement.

20. Treat of the Main Developments in Warfare during World War I, 1914-1918

Introduction - Importance of Warfare

The outbreak of war in August 1914 was accompanied by a mood of high excitement, even of exultation. It was as if after long months of waiting, war had come at last and the moment had to be savoured to the full. Yet the reality was that people had no conception of what this war would be like. The idea of a short war that would be over by Christmas proved to be nothing more than an illusion. So too the notion that war would be an affair of great marches and battles, and of rapid movement. After a month or so of manoeuvre, the initial impetus for war faded and there followed long periods of deadlock, or *immobilisme*. There were technical reasons for this because parallel to the actual war came technological development. And although the extent of the involvement of nations made it difficult to speak of 'typical conditions' for warfare, World War I was the first major struggle in which all three modes of warfare - land, sea and air - were significant. It was a contest which increasingly hinged upon scientific discovery and application, upon industrial capacity and upon intelligent use of manpower. The *'home front'* thus became almost as important as the scenes of actual battle and people became increasingly aware that wars were lost by men (scientists, chemists, inventors, technicians) other than great generals and captains. No warring nation could afford to show serious shortcomings in any major development of warfare. Instead they engaged in a continual race to perfect both new weapons and countermeasures that would neutralise their importance. War became a great industry in which the balance of advantage was constantly shifting.

Land Warfare - Trenches

Trench warfare was to dominate military strategy for much of the war. It had its own rules, rhythms and customs and, perhaps more than anything else, it showed how much defence had caught up with offence. A vast network of trenches was dug. One line stretched about 750km from Belgium through northern France to Switzerland. The Germans set the example with the systems of trenches. The British followed suit, as did other countries to a lesser or greater extent. Gradually the trenches became more elaborate. A 'typical' trench was over two metres deep and just under two metres wide. Three lines of trenches, all interconnected, existed. These consisted of a front line trench, a support or centre line trench and a reserve. The sides of the trenches were supported by sandbags. These were piled up to give protection from splinters and became a very important materiel of war. Parapets, for observers, had to be constructed. Trenches also contained saps, dugouts and listening posts. The ground between the opposing sides' trenches was called *'no man's land'*, within which concealed mines made it particularly difficult to cross. Weaponry of trench warfare included the development by the Germans of a steel-cored bullet to pierce parapets and sandbags. Camouflage, particularly for guns, became another novelty of this type of warfare. The barbed wire laid between trenches presented some difficulty and terrified the soldiers -

20. Developments in Warfare during WWI

"Wire, barbed wire - a dour
and monstrous serpent round our lives ....
...it glares at us, all day, malignant, sour".

— R. H. Sauter

Various efforts were made to overcome the problems presented by it. Cutters were effective but there were insufficient numbers. The development of a bomb cradle supposed to explode on impact with the wire as well as the invention of oxyhydric pipes proved unsuccessful. In the end, machine guns were used. At a huge cost in ammunition, they could cut the wooden staves upholding the wire.

Guns - Life in the Trenches

The weapons used in World War I were unlike those in previous conflicts. The most important development was in the use of artillery barrage. At the onset of the war, infantry attacks were preceded by artillery bombardment which came to a halt when the foot soldiers advanced. This proved too costly, in terms of the number of casualties, and a rolling barrage was developed to move just ahead of the advancing troops. Thereafter, the sound of gunfire scarcely ever ceased and although there was probably nothing more frightening than a sustained artillery barrage, by 1917 the technique was used by all armies. Engineers worked frantically to improve the performance of guns, and the gunners, in their turn, mastered new techniques in their use. Consequently, while the French 75mm gun proved superior to the German 77mm, that advantage was offset by the devastating impact of the German *Howitzer* which had a range of over 13km and was capable of delivering shells that caused huge craters or exploded into flying shrapnel. Other guns included the Vickers and Lewis machine guns, with the ability to fire up to 600 rounds per minute, and the British Lee-Enfield rifle as well as the German *Mausers*. These had a range of just over a kilometre and could fire about 25 rounds a minute. Such was the nature of trench warfare that much of this equipment sat in the same place for very long periods of time. Slight gains were made at huge cost. The lack of conventional warfare also necessitated the development of hand grenades and mortars on a large scale. Meanwhile, life in the trenches was all too often horrific. Appalling living conditions, the presence of lice, fleas and rats, unappealing foodstuffs, continual noise and cold and damp were part and parcel of the demoralising life of the soldier.

Poison Gas - Tanks

Because chemical warfare seemed to offer endless possibilities, physicists and chemists were recruited and put to work. The chemist, Fritz Haber, first urged the German High Command to use chlorine gas to incapacitate the defenders of the trench line. Condemned by world opinion as a *'breach of the laws of war'*, the first occasion of the employment of the new weapon was at Ypres on 22nd April 1915. Although its effect was immediate and shattering, the Germans failed to exploit it. Not only was there no reserve of troops made available to take advantage of the element of surprise, but there was the danger that the wind could blow the gas back on their own lines. Nonetheless, once used, gas became a weapon employed by all belligerents. In time, new and more deadly forms were introduced, such as phosgene and mustard gas. Face masks, however, reduced its overall effectiveness. The tank was another important innovation. Separately, the British and French experimented with various types of bullet-proof machines, armed with cannons and machine guns and capable of crossing the shell holes and wire entanglements of *'no-man's land'*. The British were first and in September 1916, at the Battle of Somme, the tanks were introduced. There were too few tanks and they were so heavy, slow moving and ungainly that they failed to alter the course of that battle. Later, light *Renault, Berleit* and *Schneider* tanks were preferred. These were more successful. Both the British and French produced tanks in large numbers. German tanks, for their part, were a failure and the country was more inclined to rely on anti-tank tactics.

War At Sea - Submarine Warfare

In the years before the war, European powers were enthusiastically building or rebuilding their navies. The domineering sea power in 1914 was still Britain, although Germany was a close second in the building of mighty vessels and dreadnoughts. But during the entire course of the war, the two major fleets met only once, in the Battle of Jutland, May 1916, an indecisive battle in which British losses were greater than German. It became necessary therefore to achieve victory at sea by other means. It was in such a context that submarine warfare made its mark in a way which few anticipated in 1914. In September of that year, for example, a single U-boat, the U-9, sank three British cruisers (*'Aboukir', 'Cressy'* and *'Hogue'*) within an hour, costing the lives of 1,400 British sailors. It was the British implementation of an economic blockade of Germany, however, that was to lead to more widespread submarine warfare as the Germans sought to seriously disrupt British merchant shipping. In June 1916 the German U-boats were destroying 109,000 tons of Allied shipping per month, by January 1917 this had increased to 368,000 tons and with the declaration of unrestricted submarine war in February 1917, the figure reached a peak of 852,000 tons in April 1917. It now looked as if the Germans would deliver that knock-out blow to Britain and her allies. That this did not happen can be attributed to the extensive anti-submarine measures that were taken, to the long-term hostility of neutrals to the campaign which precipitated to some extent the entry of the US into the war and to the continuance of the British blockade against Germany.

Anti-Submarine Warfare

A variety of anti-submarine measures were put into effect. Indicator nets, with glass buoys attached, were laid in various places. When a U-boat ran into the nets, it caused the buoys to bob like fishermen's floats. Hydrophones located the noise of a submarine's engine while depth bombs destroyed it under water. The Q-ships posed as innocent trading vessels but on the approach of a submarine they could uncover a bristling array of guns to engage it in surface combat. The war years also witnessed extensive mine laying which, with technical development, made conspicuous improvements in the later stages of war. In 1916 a line of mines had been laid from the Flanders Coast to curb the activities of the U-boats working from Belgian bases. Then in 1917 thousands of mines were laid in the Heligoland Bight. 1918 witnessed an even more ambitious scheme. A mine barrage was laid across the entire North Sea from Scotland to Norway. Another novel idea was the introduction of the convoy system which changed the circumstances in which vessels went to sea. Instead of sailing independently, merchant ships, after 1917, left in convoys, perhaps of 20 ships. This had immediate gains as the U-boats were unable to tackle a whole system. Collectively, these innovations led to the gradual containment and ultimate defeat of the German U-boat campaign.

Air Warfare

Aeroplanes were a relatively new invention and were not widespread at the outbreak of war in 1914. Britain, for example, had only 37 planes, France 131 and Germany 180. These planes were, as of yet, unstable and mechanically unreliable. The initial view of the role of aeroplanes was that they were suitable for scouting or reconnaissance. Pilots could spy an enemy trenches, observe where artillery was sited, make photographs of targets, report troop movements. Accordingly, in the first months of war, aeroplanes were used along these lines. After December 1914, air battles or *'dog fights'* became more and more frequent. An early problem for fighter planes was the propeller which got in the way when the pilot fired his gun. The French overcame this by installing steel deflectors on the edge of each blade and the procedure was subsequently taken on board by the Germans. Their *Fokker* planes, which allowed them to enjoy marked superiority in the air, carried machine guns whose rate of fire was itself controlled by the propeller. Aeroplanes could also bombard troops with the help of steel pellets, moving at the rate of 100 metres per second. Great *'knights of the air'* included the Germans, Richthofen (the *'Red Baron'*) and Udet; the Frenchman, Fonck; the Canadian, Bishop; the Englishman, Monnoch and the Italian, Caproni. Speed, range and rate of climb had all to be worked on, giving the advantage to one side or another as the war progressed. Radio installation in planes was a further feature of these war years.

Air Warfare - Conclusion

Although the Germans were still maintaining their spectacular lead right up to 1916, the Allies were competing well by the summer of that year. Bréquet, Nieuport, Spad and British fighters became, more than ever, equal to the German ones. The *Fokker* triplane restored Germany's lead thereafter, but once again the Allies fought back. Bombing campaigns on British towns and cities were generally carried out by the German *Zeppelins*, or airships. Over 50 raids took place but they were responsible for less than 2,000 casualties. British raids on German cities were even less effective. Bomber aircraft such as the *Gotha* and *Handley Page* proved to be more destructive, but, notwithstanding the astonishing developments that did take place, aerial warfare in World War I was far less decisive than in the Second World War. Constant saturation bombing was a dream or promise left to the future. Another great German innovation of 1918 was the use of air squadrons for covering fighter planes which, flying low, could support the infantry. Yet while air superiority in the final stages of the war rested with the Allies, the outcome of war was not decided in the air. Nonetheless, in so far as technological and scientific development is concerned, any conclusion or evaluation of the facts thus far must surely point to the fact that *"one does not fight with men against materiel, it is with materiel served by men that one makes war"* (Marshal Pétain). Consequently, while war is experienced at each stage by the combatants, it is often won or lost by inventors. Their works are sometimes known in a way that their names are not.

21.   The Treaty of Versailles

"Yet when we achieved and the new world dawned, the old men came out again and took our victory to remake in the likeness of the former world they knew".

— T.E. Lawrence

Background

Germany's defeat in World War I led to the armistice of 11th November 1918. The Allies now made arrangements to hold a peace conference in Paris on 18th January 1919. The conference was attended by representatives of 32 powers but it was dominated by the *'Big Three'* (America, France and Britain) and, to a lesser extent, by Italy. In terms of achieving an acceptable and enduring peace, many problems got in the way. In particular, there was the difficulty of reconciling all the differing views as to what the settlement should constitute. This was further aggravated by the pressure of public opinion. President Wilson wished especially that the Great War would be *"a war to end all wars"* and that a new era of co-operation would begin. However, Wilson was very self-righteous and intolerant of other people's views, and that made him unpopular. Added to that, Wilson was handicapped by his lack of understanding of European politics and geography and by the fact that Europe in 1919 was not the best of all possible worlds. The French, who had borne the brunt of the war effort, worked on the principle *"reward the victor, punish the defeated"*. Clemenceau, the French Premier, had lived through two German invasions (1870 and 1914) and symbolised the determination of Frenchmen to cripple Germany and *"never to let it happen again"*. Known as *'The Tiger'*, Clemenceau had little time for Wilson's fair-mindedness, maintaining that *"Mr. Wilson bores me with his Fourteen Points, the Good God had only ten"*. Britain was also eager *"to make Germany pay"*, popular opinion calling for Germany to be *"squeezed until the pips squeaked"*. Lloyd George, the British Prime Minister, was, nonetheless, not quite so committed to revenge as the French. Italy, whose concerns focused on the Austro-Hungarian empire, played little part in the debate about what to do with Germany.

Paris - A Dictated Settlement

The venue for the peace conference had some significance. Paris had been the choice of President Wilson because American forces were in plentiful supply there. At the same time, Paris was recognised as the centre of the Western liberal democratic powers. The city's variety of palaces meant that separate treaties could be given suitable, even symbolic, names while the choice of location also ensured that the aged Clemenceau, by courtesy, should become President of the conference. Yet Paris was, in many ways, an unfortunate choice. Above all, it proved to be too close to the misery and bitterness of war, a place where atmosphere could not but influence events to some extent. In any event, the treaty dealing with Germany was signed in the Hall of Mirrors in the Palace of Versailles, where the German empire had first been proclaimed in January 1871. The date was 28th June 1919, the fifth anniversary of Sarajevo. The treaty quickly dashed any German hopes of an equitable settlement, one which was guided by a spirit of reconciliation such as that expressed by Wilson. Perhaps such hopes were nothing more than extraordinary feats of wishful thinking on the part of the Germans. But even those who had expected the treaty to be severe were horrified. The treaty was not a negotiated settlement. Rather, it was one decided by the victors for the vanquished, which was imposed on Germany in the form of a *Diktat*. The Germans, threatened with a renewal of war, had no real choice but to accept. Acceptance aggravated German national outrage and humiliated the Republican government, whose career thereafter was blackened. And because the terms were 'imposed', many Germans repudiated responsibility for the implementation of the treaty's provisions.

Territorial Settlement [I]

The Treaty of Versailles restored to France the lost provinces of Alsace-Lorraine. To Belgium, Germany surrendered Eupen, Moresnet and Malmédy. Plebiscites were to be held in Schleswig to determine her frontier with Denmark. These resulted in the northern parts going to Denmark, the central and southern parts to Germany. The newly constructed state of Poland was to create many problems for Germany. The *'Polish Corridor'* which gave Poland access to the Baltic Sea, was created by splitting East Prussia from the rest of Germany. The loss of East Prussia which created this division was greatly resented by the Germans. Germany also lost most of Posen. The port of Danzig was initially claimed by Poland but because half of the population was German, protests were made. A compromise solution created Danzig as a Free City to be administered by the League of Nations. Further territorial adjustments forced Germany to revoke the Treaty of Brest-Litovsk which she signed with Russia in March 1918. Thus it was that the former Russian territories of Finland, Estonia, Latvia and Lithuania were made independent sovereign states. To Czechoslovakia, Germany ceded a small area near Troppau. The port of Memel in East Prussia was placed under international control to guarantee Lithuania's access to the sea. In 1923, Lithuania seized complete control of Memel.

Territorial Settlement [II]

The Saar, a German district with valuable coal deposits, was to be administered by the League of Nations for a period of 15 years. During that time the French were to control the Saar's mines in compensation for the destruction of her own coalfields by German troops during the war. After the 15 years, a plebiscite of the inhabitants would determine its future status. The Saar plebiscite was duly held in 1935, whereupon an overwhelming majority voted in favour of union with Germany. The future position of the Rhineland created many problems for the Paris delegates. Clemenceau argued that France's only security against a future German attack lay in taking the Rhineland from Germany altogether. Consequently, he demanded infinite control of the area. Wilson and Lloyd George refused to agree to the permanent detachment of the Rhineland. This, they believed, would create a new Alsace-Lorraine in reverse and sow the seeds of future Franco-German conflict. Instead it was agreed - reluctantly by France - that Germany would have to undertake not to fortify the left bank of the Rhine or a zone of 50 kilometres wide along the right bank. The guarantee of joint Anglo-American support for France in the case of a German attack came to nothing when the Americans refused to ratify the treaty. On the issue of Germany's colonies, Germany was forced to renounce *"all her rights and titles"* on the grounds that she was not fit to govern *"backward people"*. This meant for Germany a loss of a colonial empire of some million square miles. These colonies were given as mandated territories to the victors.

Military Clauses

The Paris peacemakers believed that it was necessary to disarm Germany. They did so on the principle that if they wanted a guarantee against war they had to remove the means of waging it. It was also felt that, at some stage in the future, all powers would disarm. The German armed forces were thus severely limited. No conscription was allowed, while the army was reduced to 100,000 men. Soldiers were recruited by voluntary service for a 12-year period of service. This clause was believed to be necessary in order to prevent a build up of reserves by short periods of service thereby circumventing the limitation of size. Germany's General Staff was dissolved. The navy, for its part, was not to exceed 15,000 sailors. Nor could the navy have more than six battleships of 10,000 tons, six light cruisers, twelve torpedo boats and twelve destroyers. The naval base of Heligoland in the North Sea was to be demolished. The treaty further stipulated that no military air force was permissible and that all aircraft and submarines were to be surrendered to the Allies. In addition to the limitations placed on the Rhineland, the Versailles settlement forbade universities and sporting clubs to *"occupy themselves with any military matters"*. They were, in particular, forbidden to instruct or exercise their members *"in the profession or use of arms"*. And in order to supervise the carrying out of these military clauses, an Allied Commission of Control was set up. A Conference of Ambassadors would, in turn, receive reports of the Control Commission and act as executors of the treaty.

War Guilt Clause - Reparations

Article 231 of the Versailles treaty stated that *"the Allied and Associated Governments affirm, and Germany accepts, the responsibility of Germany and her allies for causing all the loss and damage to which the Allied and Associated Governments and their nationals have been subjected as a consequence of the war imposed upon them by the aggression of Germany and her allies"*. This clause was bitterly resented by the Germans and became the infamous *'War Guilt Clause'*. In addition to accepting general responsibility for the war, it meant admitting that all Germans who had died in the war had done so for an unjust cause. Not surprisingly, it became the subject of tremendous propaganda in Germany over the following years. The clause led directly to Article 232 of the treaty: *"Compensation will be made by Germany for all damage done to the civilian population of the Allies and their property"*. Service pensions and allowances for the Allied soldiers and their families were also demanded. No sum was agreed upon by the Allies before the treaty was signed, however. Rather, Germany was required to sign 'a blank cheque'. A Reparations Commission was thereafter set up to determine the amount that Germany should be required to pay and to supervise its collection on behalf of the Allied governments. The issue was beset with difficulties. France and Belgium wanted to claim the maximum. As well as providing compensation, this would be a means of keeping Germany weak and delaying her economic recovery. Britain was not as adamant - while Germany should be made to pay, too heavy reparations got in the way of viewing Germany as a potential customer in international trade. In any event, and after prolonged wrangles, the Reparations Commission presented its bill in April 1921. Germany's liability was fixed at £6,600 million, to be paid in regular instalments. This huge bill was a further cause of resentment and exacerbated political and economic tensions. Hitler was later to argue that it placed Germany *"under permanent interest slavery"*.

Other Aspects of the Treaty Settlement

The union of Austria and Germany, known as the *Anschluss*, was forbidden under Article 80 of the treaty. Such a clause clearly denied Germany the principle of self determination on which the new Europe was supposedly being constructed. Yet it was believed that this would be another means of preventing Germany from re-emerging as too strong and aggressive a power, capable of inflicting harm and defeat on others. Another aspect of the treaty settlement was the opening of the Kiel Canal to international shipping. The Rhine and other German rivers were to be internationalised. Article 227 provided for the trial of the former Kaiser, Wilhelm II, as well as *"other persons accused of having committed acts in violation of the laws and customs of war"*. The Kaiser was to be tried by five judges, one each from France, Britain, Italy, America and Japan. Upon those would rest the task of fixing an appropriate punishment. But this article was never realised. Wilhelm II had sought asylum in the Netherlands after the war and the Dutch now refused to hand him over. It was eventually decided to let the matter drop. One final term of the Treaty of Versailles was that it provided for the establishment of a League of Nations whose duty it would be to establish peace and harmony. Germany was not, however, permitted to join the League until 1926.

An Evaluation

In conclusion, it must be acknowledged that the treaty was a moral condemnation of Germany and her people. It was very much an 'act of the moment', a document which reflected the heavy clouds of hatred and bitterness aroused by war. Reparations, the War Guilt Clause, the failure to apply the right of self-determination fairly, the fact that it was not a negotiated settlement but one in which the human emotions of vindictiveness and vengeance were all too apparent, are just some of the treaty's faults. Collectively, they helped to cause the Second World War, only 20 years later. To that extent, the treaty was a conspicuous failure, one which proved beyond all doubt that 'two wrongs don't make a right' and one which was unable to endure the test of time.

> *"But the Freedom that you kill*
> *Will not halt its progress.*
> *Even tomorrow, scoffing at its executioners,*
> *It will arise triumphantly from its graves."*
>
> —Max Kegel

Nonetheless, the passions of the time, fired by the huge casualties, the massive devastation caused by the Germans even as they prepared for an armistice and Germany's deplorable treatment of the Russians in the Treaty of Brest-Litovsk must also be recalled, as one passes a final verdict on the Versailles settlement. Any consideration of them shows that an equitable peace would have been too much to have expected and that the treaty was essentially a compromise settlement between Clemenceau's desire for punishment and the idealism of Wilson.

22. The League of Nations

Foundation - Aims

The immediate post-war mood of revulsion against slaughter and destruction, as well as the widespread rejection of pre-war diplomacy and a general anxiety to evolve new habits of inter-state relations, helped to bring about a situation conducive to the setting up of a League of Nations. The scheme for the League was largely the brainchild of President Woodrow Wilson who believed that *"merely to win the war was not enough. It must be won in such a way as to ensure the future peace of the world"*. When putting forward his Fourteen Points, Wilson thus spoke in terms of the creation of *"a general association of nations"*. The idea was taken up and developed by Jan Smuts, Prime Minister of South Africa, who published a book '*The League of Nations: A Practical Suggestion*'. The Paris Peace Conference, January 1919, agreed to set up such an organisation. But any assessment of Europe in the period prior to the Great War shows that the idea for the League was not unique. Rather, it was the revival and elaboration of the idea of a concert of Europe into a concert of the world. In another light, however, the League was new and different. It was a multilateral treaty dedicated to seeking world peace through the process of collective security. Because *"an attack upon one is an attack upon all"*, every member of the League was expected to shoulder responsibility for defending every other signatory against aggression. And in addition to its foremost aim of preserving world peace, the League also sought to promote international co-operation and human welfare. It was formally established in January 1920 with its headquarters in Geneva, Switzerland. Switzerland was chosen because of its traditionally neutral stance.

Structure of the League

At the heart of the League was the Covenant. This was similar to a constitution and provided, through its 26 articles, the framework or guidelines by which the League was run. The League's basic machinery consisted of two chambers, the Assembly and the Council. The Assembly was represented by all member states, each of which had one vote. Complete unanimity of all members was required. The Assembly took the form of a debating chamber for its members and to that extent, it provided a forum for world opinion. It had no real powers of decision other than to vote on the League's budget, to admit new members and to elect non-permanent members of the Council. It met every September in Geneva or more often if required. Much of its work was done by committees. Real power rested with the Council. Its primary function was to hear and consider disputes referred to it, and to report and give advice about what the Assembly should do. As with the Assembly, decisions had to be unanimous. The Council met three times a year and whenever emergencies arose. It consisted of permanent and non-permanent members. There were four permanent members in 1921 - Britain, France, Italy and Japan. They were joined by Germany in 1930. The non-permanent members initially also numbered four, but this figure was later increased. They worked on a rotation basis, each temporary member being elected for a three-year period. The existence of the permanent and non-permanent members worked as a compromise between the reality of recognising the most powerful states and the ideal of democracy.

Secretariat - International Court of Justice

Another body known as the Secretariat was run behind the Assembly and the Council. This was an international civil service consisting of a permanent body of officials drawn from all member states. With a staff of about 500, it was responsible for the administration or day-to-day running of the League. It prepared data for conferences, kept records, organised meetings, registered treaties between member states and provided a link between the League and national governments. It also liaised with other bodies affiliated to the League. The first Secretary-General of the League was an Englishman, Sir Eric Drummond, who held the position until 1933. The International Court of Justice, referred to as the World Court, was set up in 1922 at the Hague in the Netherlands. It was a permanent court and comprised 15 judges appointed by the Assembly and the Council. Because they were drawn from many different nationalities, the judges reflected the world's different legal systems. The International Court was set up to settle legal disputes between nations, such as those relating to breaches of treaties or interpretations of international law. It also advised the Council and the Assembly. Those states that submitted cases to the court had to agree in advance that they would accept the verdict. This was necessary as the power of the court was limited, it could neither compel a state to appear before it, nor enforce its verdict.

Subsidiary Bodies

A number of subsidiary bodies helped to carry out the aims of the League. The International Labour Organisation (ILO), though distinct from the League, worked in close association with it. The ILO was based in Geneva and its first director was a French socialist, Albert Thomas. Resting on the sound beliefs that economic privation and social injustice were themselves a threat to peace, the ILO aimed to improve workers' conditions around the world. Matters such as rates of pay, workers' compensation, industrial safety, child labour and unemployment were debated by representatives of governments, employers and workers. Although the recommendations of the ILO were not binding, its impact was worldwide. The Disarmament Commission was established to help control the manufacture and sale of arms. It was hoped that there would be a general reduction of armaments throughout the world. Such an aspiration proved difficult to implement, however. Nations constantly argued against disarmament on the grounds that they needed national security. The Mandates Commission, for its part, supervised 16 mandated territories - former German colonies or provinces of the Turkish empire. It was based on the principle that mandated territories would be held 'in trust' (mainly by Britain and France) as the territories worked towards self government. The Minorities Commission sought to protect minority rights such as those of language and religion while the Refugees Commission helped in a practical way with refugees and prisoners of war. The Health Organisation collected and disseminated information on diseases, drugs and standards of nutrition. Other bodies dealt with matters of transport, communication and intellectual co-operation. All of the new institutions reflected a faith in the ideology of *'internationalism'*.

Problems of Membership, Finance, Peacekeeping

From the beginning, there were serious problems and shortcomings in the League. One failure stems from the fact that it was never truly a 'league of nations'. The original membership of the League was 42 states. These comprised the Allies who signed the peace treaties and 13 other states that had been neutral in World War I. By 1924, membership had grown to 54, by which time some of the defeated powers had become members. But the US, the world's greatest power, never joined the League, preferring, as it now did, to fall back on its traditional isolationism and leave Europe to the Europeans. Germany was not admitted until 1926, nor the Soviet Union until 1934. Japan was lukewarm in her attitude to the League and left it, as did Germany and Italy in the 1930s. Consequently, there was no moment in the League's history when more than five of the great powers belonged to it or when at least two of the great powers did not belong to it. Any pretension that the League was a world organisation must thus collapse. The League also suffered from a lack of strong financial resources. Although it was supposed to receive an annual budget, amassed from monies contributed by member states, few countries seemed willing to pay on time or, in the context of the world depression, to make national economic sacrifice for international concern. As well as arguments over payment, it was not unusual to see quarrels flare up over the distribution of funds. An even greater obstacle to the success of the League was its lack of power to enforce decisions. The organisation had no army. Rather, it relied on the trust and co-operation of member states to ensure that war did not break out. If moral persuasion was not enough, the League could apply economic sanctions but these were impractical and damaged the economies of those applying the sanctions as much as the economy against which they were directed.

Successes and Failures

In spite of its drawbacks, the League did manage to establish itself as an organisation capable of dealing with economic and humanitarian issues. It also managed to solve disputes between minor states. The League, for example, secured co-operation between Germany and Poland over the question of Silesia. A League plebiscite allowed for the area to be partitioned between the two countries. The League's appointment of a commissioner for the city of Danzig helped to alleviate further possible trouble between Poland and Germany. An argument between Poland and Lithuania about Vilna was resolved in 1920 by the League's recognition of Polish possession. Then in 1921 a dispute between Finland and Sweden concerning the Aaland Islands was settled. The League decided in favour of Finland, although the Swedish speaking inhabitants of Aaland did receive home rule. When in 1924 Turkey and Iraq clashed over Mosul, the League assigned nearly the whole of the disputed area to Iraq. In South America in 1932 the League played a major role in settling two international disputes over territories involving Bolivia and Paraguay, and Peru and Colombia. Yet the League's success was not always so apparent, particularly when more powerful nations were involved. As Mussolini insisted *"The League is all right when sparrows quarrel. It fails when eagles fall out"*. This could be seen in 1923 when four Italians were killed on Greek territory, leading to Italian occupation of the Greek island of Corfu. Mussolini refused to have the matter submitted to the League or to allow for League intervention. The matter was eventually satisfactorily resolved by the

Conference of Ambassadors (Britain, France, Italy, Japan) at Paris. Again in 1928 when Italy was involved in illegal arms shipments to Hungary, the League could do little more than mildly reprimand Italy.

Open Acts of Defiance

The inadequacies of the League became more painfully obvious as the League entered its second decade. In September 1931, Japan invaded Manchuria, a province of China which she had long coveted because of its vast resources of coal and other raw materials. By 1932, the Japanese conquest of Manchuria was effectively complete and the birth of a new state, Manchukuo, was announced. This was a mere puppet of Japan. China meanwhile appealed to the League, which appointed a commission under Britain's Lord Lytton to enquire into the matter. Lytton recommended home rule for Manchuria under China but the Japanese refused to accept the findings. Japan, who was condemned as an aggressor, left the League in March 1933. She continued to occupy Manchuria. In October 1933, Hitler made the decision to withdraw Germany from the League when the other powers refused to disarm as Germany had done. Worse was to follow. In October 1935, Italy invaded Abyssinia, a League member. Haile Selaisse, the emperor of Abyssinia, appealed to the League for help. The League condemned Italy's action and imposed economic sanctions. However, oil, coal and steel were excluded as League members showed themselves to be more concerned with not antagonising Mussolini than with the principles of collective security. When in 1936 King Victor Emmanuel III of Italy was proclaimed the new emperor of Abyssinia, Haile Selaisse went into exile. Two months later, sanctions were withdrawn. Another act of aggression took place in March 1936 when Hitler, in open defiance of the Treaty of Versailles, marched his troops into the Rhineland. The League merely condemned the invasion. Later in that same year, when the Spanish civil war broke out, the League adopted a policy of neutrality or non-intervention. This did not deter Hitler, Mussolini or Stalin from becoming involved.

The End of the League - Conclusion

Such failures dealt serious blows to the moral authority of the League as an instrument of peace. Disparity between purpose and achievement meant that by 1937 the organisation, a *"League of Some Nations"*, had slipped into the background of world affairs. Thus while international crises continued and indeed, worsened, the League's useful life was over. During the Nazi invasions of Austria, Czechoslovakia and Poland, 1938-'39, the League's covenant was not invoked. Even when war broke out in September 1939, as a result of the German invasion of Poland, Britain and France became involved, not to uphold the principle of collective security but because of treaty obligations to Poland. The League's final act, one which was largely token, was to expel the Soviet Union following her attack on Finland in November 1939. Only on the 8th April 1945, however, did the League officially cease to exist. Yet the League of Nations, which clearly failed to achieve its primary objective, that of keeping world peace, was not a complete fiasco. Rather it left behind a permanent legacy. Its valuable lessons and assets were passed on to the United Nations, through which the League's *'soul goes marching on'*. And, as Lord David Cecil suggested, perhaps it was not the League but the nations in it which failed to keep peace, *"The League of Nations has not been tried and found wanting. It has been found inconvenient and not tried"*.

War and Peace: Past Exam Questions

1995

C5. World War I, 1914-1918

Account for the early success but final defeat of the Central Powers during World War I.

E4. Essay

(iii) Naval warfare in World Wars I and II.

1994, 1991, 1988
E4. Essay

The League of Nations

1993
C5. World War I

"The causes of World War I were many and complex". Discuss.

1991

C4. Warfare, 1914-1918

Treat of the main developments in warfare during World War I, 1914-1918.

1989

C4. World War I

"World War I lasted longer and was far more destructive than was anticipated at its outset". Discuss.

C5. The Versailles Settlement

(i) Discuss the treatment of Germany in the Versailles Settlement, 1919.

(ii) How did the Versailles Settlement contribute to the rise of Hitler?

1986
C5. World War I

"World War I revealed the horror of total war in the industrial age". Discuss.

D2. The League of Nations

(i) Treat of the origins and aims of the League of Nations.

(ii) Estimate the extent to which the League of Nations achieved its aims.

1985
C5. International Relations

"International relations, in the decade before 1914, deteriorated". Discuss.

23. The Weimar Republic, 1919-1933

Birth of the Republic

In 1918 it was clear that the war was going against the Germans. In the wake of defeat, the Second Reich was in danger of tumbling as strikes and demonstrations took place in many towns. They were accompanied by the eruption of violence. Not surprisingly, Germany was declared to be in a *'state of siege'*. Phrases such as *"The Kaiser is a scoundrel"* and *"Up with the German Republic"* became all too common. A mutiny at Kiel began in October 1918. Within days it had spread to most of the ports of northern Germany. A further crisis occurred when revolutionaries took to the streets in Berlin. Prince Max of Baden, the last Chancellor of the German empire, was unable to cope and on the morning of 9th November, he resigned. Friedrich Ebert, the leader of the Social Democratic Party, became acting Chancellor. He was charged with the task of calling a Constituent Assembly to determine the form which the new state should take. At 2pm on the 9th November, Philip Scheidemann, another leader of the Social Democrats, was pressed to take the initiative when a mass demonstration took place in the *Reichstag* square. He declared that *"The Hohenzollerns have abdicated. Long live the German Republic"*. It was only then that Wilhelm resigned himself to the inevitable by abdicating and fleeing across the border into the Netherlands. Thus was Germany's first republic born. Germany's experiment in parliamentary democracy was taken a step further on the 19th January 1919 when elections for the National Assembly were held. These resulted in a clear majority for those parties supporting the Republic. Between them, the Social Democrats, the Centre Party and the Democrats took 75% of the poll.

The Constitution of the Weimar Republic

In February 1919 the Assembly met for the first time at Weimar in south-east Germany. Weimar was chosen as the new seat of government because it represented a break with the past and the town, once the home of Goethe and Schiller, symbolised all that was best in German culture. Weimar also represented a psychological break with the old military authoritarianism of Berlin. Thereafter, a constitution was framed. Mainly the work of Hugo Preuss, an academic lawyer, the constitution was liberal and democratic and found the approval of the National Assembly in July 1919. Germany remained a federal state but the central government enjoyed more complete national power than that of the old Reich - it controlled foreign affairs, communications and finance. Parliament consisted of two houses, the *Reichstag* and the *Reichsrat*. The *Reichstag* was to be elected for a period of four years by secret ballot of all persons over 20 years by a proportional representation system. The *Reichsrat* was the upper house and was to represent the seventeen provinces which comprised the Republic. Bills passed by the *Reichstag* were to be sent to the *Reichsrat* for approval. At the head of the Republic was a President, elected by universal suffrage for a seven-year term of office. The first President was Ebert. He could appoint the Chancellor, was head of the armed forces and was responsible for the conduct of diplomacy. In time of national emergency, the President could assume special powers and suspend civil liberties. The fundamental rights and freedoms associated with other western democracies, such as freedom of speech, religion, association and the press, were guaranteed under the new constitution.

The Spartacist Uprising, 1919

Post-war politics in Germany got off to a bloody and difficult start. The German *Spartacists* were led by Rosa Luxemburg and Karl Liebknecht. They had broken away from the Social Democratic Party as early as 1915. Having taken their name from Spartacus, the man who led a great revolt of the slaves in ancient Rome, the Spartacists denounced war as an imperialist conflict. They believed that the opportunity presented by war should be used to instigate a socialist revolution. Such was their aversion to a parliamentary democracy that this remained their goal even after war officially ended. In December 1918 the Spartacists and some left-wing independent socialists formed themselves into the German Communist Party. Shortly afterwards, on the 6th January 1919 - even before the first democratic elections had taken place - the Spartacists attempted a communist revolution in Berlin. A series of strikes were organised, a number of public buildings were occupied and barricades were erected. Many demonstrators carried weapons, and riots and street fighting threatened the very existence of the government. Gustav Noske, Ebert's Minister of Defence, acted quickly. He employed the *Freikorps* (Free Corps), volunteer army units committed to right-wing policies and law and order at any cost, to deal with the rebels. Within days the revolt was ruthlessly crushed, for the Spartacist action had been ill-prepared and badly supported. The dead numbered about 100 Spartacists and 13 *Freikorps* men. Among the communist dead were Karl Liebknecht and Rosa Luxemburg. Other minor Spartacist uprisings occurred in Bavaria, Bremen and Düsseldorf but these too were brutally suppressed by the *Freikorps*. Thus it was that democracy in Germany had withstood its first major test, an attack from the undemocratic Left.

The Kapp and Hitler Putsch

The signing of the Treaty of Versailles had turned many right-wing officers against the Republic. They resented its harsh terms and were opposed to the limitations placed on the German army and the insistence that bands of irregular troops, such as the *Freikorps*, be disbanded. Calling Ebert's government the *'November Criminals'*, one Freikorps group attempted a coup d'état in Berlin in March 1920 as members sought to overthrow Weimar democracy. Led by Wolfgang Kapp, the group had the support of army generals, Lüttwitz and Ludendorff. The putsch began on 11th May when Captain Ehrhardt marched 5,000 *Freikorps* into Berlin. The National Assembly was proclaimed to be dissolved, the Weimar Constitution void and the government deposed. Ebert and his followers fled to Dresden and then to Stuttgart. Meanwhile Kapp and his associates set up their own government in Berlin. Noske's call on the regular army to act against the mutineers complicated the situation still further, for the army refused to comply, *"The Reichswehr (German army) does not fire on the Reichswehr"*. The situation was potentially very dangerous, capable of getting completely out of control. It was then that Ebert and Noske turned to the working class to defend the Republic. A general strike was called and, as commercial life and public services ceased, Berlin became paralysed. The workers had united in a resolve to defeat counter-revolution and Kapp and his followers found themselves isolated. Within a week the putsch had petered out. A second right-wing revolt came in the form of the Munich Putsch, March 1923. The Nazis, led by Adolf Hitler, fired shots in the air and declared that they were about to set up a new government. By then the government was more confident and the army remained loyal. The insurgents were soon dispersed, Hitler was himself arrested. The real importance of this revolt lies in the fact that here was the basis of the party which, 10 years later, would overthrow the Weimar Republic.

The German Economy

The crises affecting the Weimar government were aggravated by the state of the German economy. Germany was already in debt from her own financing of the war but the Versailles treaty imposed further crippling terms. Valuable territories such as the coal deposits of Silesia were taken away, the Saar was placed under international control while a reparations bill of £6,600m posed a further drain to the economy, making the situation hopeless. In August 1921, the government made its first large cash payment of £50m to the Allies but thereafter it found itself unable to pay any further instalments. This was due to the Republic's inability to raise enough money through taxation and to the rapid inflation which was already making itself felt. The Foreign Minister, Walter Rathenau, had opted for a policy of fulfilment of the Versailles treaty and made some effort to face up to the economic crisis, but he was branded a traitor and assassinated in June 1922. Ebert then asked William Cuno to form a cabinet. Under him, things went from bad to worse. Germany's request for a moratorium, or suspension of payments, was not granted and her subsequent failure to meet obligations led to French and Belgian troops occupying the Ruhr in January 1923. The industrialists and workers of the Ruhr were encouraged by the German government to offer passive resistance and to boycott the invaders by refusing to work. Clashes between the two sides led to 132 deaths. Meanwhile, massive or hyper-inflation meant that while in 1920 one dollar was worth 64.8 Marks, by August 1923, the dollar was valued at more than 4 million Marks! The currency crash hit the whole economy and ensured that confidence in the Republic was badly shaken, forcing people to comment that *"Under the Kaiser things were better"*.

The Stresemann Years [I]

The dominant politician of the Weimar era was undoubtedly Gustav Stresemann. He served as Chancellor from August-November 1923 but it was as Foreign Minister, 1923-'29, that Stresemann is best remembered. Stresemann believed that it was necessary to make Germany *"acceptable and respectable"* in the eyes of the world. Consequently, he followed a policy of fulfilment as he announced that Germany would resume reparations payments. At the same time, Stresemann ordered an end to passive resistance in the Ruhr, introduced tax reforms, reduced government expenditure and called in old inflated banknotes. In place of the old Mark a new currency, the *Rentenmark,* was introduced. This was strictly controlled and backed up by a *Rentenbank.* The revival of the economy was aided by the Dawes Plan of September 1924. The plan proposed that the invading forces would be withdrawn from the Ruhr, that there would be a two-year moratorium of reparations payments and that Germany was to receive a loan of 800 million dollars. The influx of foreign capital, mainly from America, helped to create an air of tranquillity and prosperity after the catastrophic collapse of 1923. Industries were re-equipped and new schools, hospitals and public works were built. By the Young Plan, the total amount of reparations was reduced to £2,000m and payments were to be made over 59 years. Yet when looking at the economic recovery of the years 1924-'29, one must remember that it was largely a superficial prosperity and that Germany was living dangerously on foreign loans; *"dancing on a volcano"* as Stresemann warned.

The Stresemann Years [II]

Although at heart an ardent nationalist, Stresemann was also a realist. He knew that in order to bring Germany *"back into the family of nations"*, he would have to co-operate with the Allies. Stresemann was especially eager to end the isolation of Germany. Already in 1922 Germany had signed with Russia the Treaty of Rapallo, re-establishing diplomatic links. But the Locarno Pact of 1925 proved to be a much greater international triumph for Stresemann and showed his superb gifts as a negotiator. Its five signatory states were Germany, Britain, France, Belgium and Italy. The terms of Locarno included Germany's acceptance of existing frontiers between Germany, France and Belgium. In the east, there was a guarantee that frontiers would not be altered by force. The demilitarized Rhineland was recognised and Allied troops were to be gradually withdrawn. 1926 witnessed Germany's entry to the League of Nations. Germany was subsequently given a permanent seat on the League's Council. Appreciation that old enmities seemed to be disappearing came when in 1926 Stresemann shared the Nobel Peace Prize with Aristide Briand. Further stabilisation of European affairs came in 1928 with the Kellogg-Briand Pact, which outlawed war as an instrument for solving political differences between countries. This, too, was signed by Germany. Behind all the goodwill, there was, however, a darker side to Weimar foreign policy. The Treaty of Rapallo with Russia was renewed in 1926 and Germany frequently used that treaty to get around the military clauses of the Versailles settlement by using Russia as the base for military development and experimentation. In any event, Stresemann died suddenly from a heart attack on the 30th October 1929. His death left a vacuum in German politics that was not easily filled.

The Collapse of the Weimar Republic

Three main reasons have been accredited for the collapse of the Weimar Republic. The first of these concerns the inherent weaknesses or flaws within the democratic system. The constitution of Weimar had assumed a desire for a democracy. However, there were many people who, for one reason or another, were opposed to the democratic system. These awaited the opportunity to destroy the Republic. Meanwhile, the electoral system resulted in the emergence of a multiplicity of parties who engaged in a continuous game of musical chairs. Weak coalition governments were no match for the powerful forces ranging against them. Then, in October 1929, only three weeks after the death of Stresemann, came the Wall Street Crash. Followed, in turn, by the Great Depression, it hit Germany with devastating force and was to prove a further nail in the coffin of the Republic. American money flowing into Germany stopped, while short-term loans were recalled. The economic system broke down and unemployment soared, reaching a figure of 6 million in 1932. The poverty, depression and despair of these years allowed reactionary forces to come to the fore. One such force was that of Hitler and the Nazis, and it proved to be the final undoing of Weimar Germany. With an uncanny political instinct and great determination, Hitler outlined policies that appealed to the German people. Above all, he offered hope. As a succession of unstable ministries failed to overcome the drift to economic collapse, the Nazis were enabled to secure the largest number of seats in the Reichstag in 1932. In January 1933, Hitler was appointed Chancellor by President Hindenburg. He now used the Weimar constitution to establish his dictatorship and undo republicanism. So much for the belief of von Papen and his friends, *"We have him framed in!"*

24. Gustav Stresemann, 1878-1929

Background, 1878-1923

Gustav Stresemann was born on 10th May 1878 in Berlin. Educated in economics and political science in the universities of Berlin and Leipzig, Stresemann emerged with a doctorate in 1900. In 1902 he founded the Saxon Manufacturers Association. Success in commerce gave him the springboard into politics and in 1903 Stresemann joined the right-wing National Liberal Party, eventually emerging as its chairman in 1917. Stresemann was first elected to the *Reichstag* in 1907 when, at 28 years of age, he became the youngest deputy. Having lost his seat in the *Reichstag* elections of 1912, Stresemann was a staunch supporter of the monarchy and of *Weltpolitik*. He was also an uncritical admirer of the military. The defeat of Germany in World War I, the collapse of the monarchy and Kaiser Wilhelm's flight to the Netherlands were cruel blows to Stresemann. Although in 1918 he founded his own party, The German People's Party, which was a right-wing grouping of educated and propertied elements, Stresemann's hopes for a restoration of the monarchy were abandoned only slowly and reluctantly. The impetus to do so came from the failure of the Kapp Putsch, March 1920, and the occurrence of political murders such as the assassination of Walther Rathenau in June 1922. Increasingly, Stresemann became convinced that the alternative to the Republic and German democracy was a dictatorship. Consequently he decided to throw himself wholeheartedly into the struggle to save constitutional government. Stresemann earned a reputation for himself for his bitter attack on the French and Belgian occupation of the Ruhr and for his condemnation of businesses who were using inflation for their own benefit. In August 1923 he became Chancellor of the *Reich* at the head of a *'Great Coalition'* composed of representatives of the Social Democrats, the Centre and the German Democrats, as well as his People's Party.

Stresemann's Chancellorship

From August to November 1923, Stresemann served as Chancellor. When he came to power, Germany was experiencing widespread difficulties, including the problem of runaway inflation. This was definitely not helped by the policy of passive resistance that German workers in the Ruhr had adopted since its occupation in January 1923 when the German government had failed to make good a reparations payment. Stresemann now decided to abandon this policy of resistance which he argued was accelerating inflation and precipitating a financial collapse. Although it was a move that was bitterly attacked, Stresemann defended his position, *"Giving up passive resistance is perhaps more patriotic than the phrases used to combat it... I knew when I did it...... that I was putting my own political position in my party - yes, and even my life in jeopardy. But what is it we Germans lack? We lack the courage to take responsibility"*. Stresemann realised that bitter medicine had to be swallowed before the cure could take root. Meanwhile, Stresemann's government had to contend with various threats from the Left and Right. In Saxony, for example, the Socialist government led by Zeigner, insisted on having members of the Communist Party

(KPD), who appeared to be on the verge of staging a revolution, in the cabinet. On 27th October, Stresemann ordered Zeigner to expel his Communist ministers, maintaining that their presence was *"incompatible with constitutional conditions"*. When Zeigner refused to expel the members, Stresemann sought his deposition. Similar measures followed in Thuringia. A revolutionary attempt from the radical Right came in the form of Hitler's Munich Putsch, 8-9th November 1923. This too was put down. Before relinquishing the Chancellorship, Stresemann had put in train the measures that finally led to the stabilisation of the currency and the end of inflation. With the help of his able Minister of Finance, Hans Luther, the old *Mark* was replaced by the *Rentenmark*. This was backed up by a *Rentenbank* and was strictly controlled. Simultaneously, tax reforms and a cut-back in government expenditure took place. The budget was balanced, inflation steadied and this, in turn, helped to restore national confidence and morale.

Foreign Minister - Dawes Plan

As was typical of unstable Weimar governments, inter-party disputes and a vote of no confidence led to the resignation of Stresemann's government in November 1923. Stresemann took over the post of Foreign Minister in the new government and held it, unchallenged until his death, in coalition governments of varying composition under three Chancellors ranging from the Left to the Centre. An ardent nationalist at heart, Stresemann had as his enduring aim a desire to regain full sovereignty and independence for his country. More specifically, his goals included

1. the reduction and eventual removal of the financial burdens imposed by the Treaty of Versailles,
2. the evacuation of foreign troops from German soil,
3. the attainment of equal rights with other powers,
4. a revision of Germany's eastern borders of 1919, as well as the annexation of Austria.

Stresemann's realism was such that he believed the revision of the hated Versailles settlement could best be achieved through co-operation with other powers. Diplomacy would be the means through which Germany would become *"acceptable and respectable"*. Such a policy was essentially long term and very often misunderstood by Germans who interpreted it as a surrender, a form of cowardice. But Stresemann pressed ahead. He realised that arrangements on the international level were necessary to further stabilise the economy. The Dawes Plan, which came into force on 1st September 1924, ended the French and Belgian occupation of the Ruhr and determined that sanctions could be applied in the future only in case of a flagrant default that had been declared as such by a board of arbitration. The country was to have a two-year moratorium after which reparations of a more modest level would commence. An American loan of $800 million was also granted to Germany. The influx of foreign capital helped Germany to re-equip her industries and to initiate a more general economic recovery programme.

The Locarno Pact, 1925

One of the great post-war achievements in the area of international affairs and an undoubted triumph for Stresemann was the Locarno Pact of 1925. It has been said of Stresemann that in negotiating Locarno he was *"forced to manoeuvre like a dog moving through a thick wood with a long stick in his jaws"*. This refers to the difficulties Stresemann encountered both at home and abroad, his need for patience, for superb timing, and his ability to exploit circumstances. Locarno was signed by Germany, France, Belgium, Britain and Italy, the latter two countries acting as guarantors. By its terms, Germany promised to accept her western frontiers i.e. the borders between Germany and France, and Germany and Belgium. Although the French wanted Germany to give the same guarantees with regard to her eastern borders, Germany refused. She agreed, however, not to alter her eastern frontiers by force, opting instead for peaceful negotiation and arbitration. Locarno gave confirmation to the clause within the Versailles settlement which stated that the Rhineland would be permanently demilitarised but the Allied troops in the Rhineland were to be gradually withdrawn so that by 1930 the area would be completely evacuated. Locarno has been described as *"a victory for confidence in the future over the suspicions of the past"*. Certainly it ended Germany's isolation while at the same time it did much to ease tensions in Europe. Stresemann, together with the French Foreign Minister, Aristide Briand, was awarded the Nobel Peace Prize in 1926. The prize was in recognition of their courage and efforts with regard to reconciliation and negotiation.

The League of Nations - Some Difficulties

It was agreed in negotiations concerning the Locarno Pact that Germany should join the League of Nations. In September 1926 Germany duly became a member. Because Germany had now been brought back into the magic circle of great powers, it was understood that she would become a permanent member of its Council alongside Great Britain, France, Italy and Japan. Deadlock developed when the governments of Poland, Spain, and Brazil reacted to the prospect of Germany receiving a permanent seat by demanding equal treatment. Stresemann and Luther, the then Chancellor, had gone to Geneva to be present at Germany's induction. They had to return home, irritated and embarrassed, to face a hostile Press that made much of the *"national humiliation"*. This unforeseen hitch was overcome, in part, by the creation of a new category of semi-permanent League members. In any event, Germany was finally admitted to the Council in 1930. In other ways, too, the mood of optimism and relaxation found at Locarno ran into difficulties. In 1926 Briand and Stresemann negotiated an agreement at Thiory which aimed at resolving all outstanding differences between France and Germany. There had even been talk of a reunion of the Saar with Germany without the plebiscite stipulated in the Versailles treaty, in return for a sizeable reparations payment in advance of the Dawes schedule. The agreement failed to survive the pressure of growing national opposition in both countries. The process of international pacification was, however, carried a stage further in 1928 with the Kellogg-Briand Pact, the initiative for which came from Briand and the American Secretary of State, Frank P. Kellogg.

Kellogg-Briand Pact - Young Plan

In August 1928 representatives of about fifteen states, including Germany, met at Paris and signed the Kellogg-Briand Pact. By virtue of the Pact, signatories condemned *"recourse to war for the solution of international controversies and renounce[d] it as an instrument of national policy in relations with one another"*. In addition to the countries represented at Paris, an invitation was extended to every other state to accede to it. In all, sixty five states signed. The agreement was thus a high point of inter-war pacifism. Stresemann's last political or diplomatic success came in 1929 when he persuaded the French and other nations to agree to a review of the reparations obligation. What they sought was a *"new and final settlement"*. The initiative took root in February 1929 when an international board, headed by the American banker Owen D. Young, began this assessment which was completed in June and submitted to a conference of the interested powers at the Hague. Stresemann led the German delegation to the Netherlands and pursued exhausting, often acrimonious, debate before accepting the Plan. In the final analysis, the Young Plan recommended that the amount Germany owed should be reduced to £2,000m and that the period of repayment should be extended to 59 years. Stresemann was now obliged to put the plan to referendum. He used all his diplomatic gifts to persuade his colleagues not to jeopardize what had been gained at the Hague but died before full approval had been given.

Relations with the East

When Stresemann came to power, Germany and the USSR were 'outcast' nations, the 'black sheep' of Europe. The Treaty of Rapallo, 1922, had established formal relations between the two countries. Germany and Russia renounced financial claims on each other and pledged co-operation. In reality, Rapallo was used by the Germans to circumvent the military clause of the Treaty of Versailles by building up her forces in the Soviet Union. Secret army units, for example, were disguised as labour battalions and heavy industry used to produce arms. The USSR, for her part, gained from German knowledge and expertise. Although Stresemann never forgot that Moscow was the home of the Comintern and the source of some of his internal problems, he saw no point in sacrificing the balance that Rapallo had brought to German foreign relations. Consequently, he continued to build on the Rapallo Treaty during the 1920s. In 1926, at the height of the controversy surrounding Germany's membership of the League of Nations' Council, Stresemann negotiated a new agreement with the Soviet Union, the Treaty of Berlin. Essentially this was a reaffirmation of the Treaty of Rapallo and underlined the intent of the signatories to consult in time of crisis and the obligation of each to remain neutral in the case of an attack upon the other. Such a seesaw policy between the East and West was strongly condemned by many contemporary critics but there is some evidence to suggest that Germany's relations with Russia actually improved her bargaining position with other powers. As Chamberlain insisted to Briand *"We are battling with Soviet Russia for the soul of Germany....the more difficult our relations with Soviet Russia became, the more important was it that we should attach Germany solidly to the Western powers"*.

Death - An Evaluation

The last two years of Stresemann's life were marked by illness. Having suffered two strokes, he died of a heart attack on 3rd October 1929, aged just 51 years. Stresemann's ill health was undoubtedly aggravated by the years of hard work and the strong domestic opposition which often arose and to which he had to devote an extraordinary amount of effort to combating. In general, Stresemann's foreign policy received the support of the parties of the moderate Left and the Middle, while being consistently opposed by the Nationalists, the Nazis, the Communists and the right wing of his own party. Frequently branding him as a traitor, opponents of Stresemann described him as *"the essence of all the dangerous tendencies of our nation [whose] psychic degeneracy is clearly derived from his political decadence"*. By the time of his death, the radicalisation of German politics and the beginning of attempts to mobilize the masses against the parliamentary system were already in swing. There is some doubt as to whether even Stresemann, had he survived, could have held such forces in check and saved the Weimar Republic from the fate of Nazi totalitarianism that awaited it. Nonetheless, Stresemann made an essential contribution to securing the Weimar Republic's stability and survival during the last months of 1923 through to 1929. His diplomacy effected the removal of many of the restrictions placed by the Versailles treaty upon Germany and brought the community of nations on terms of equality with other powers in most respects, save that of armaments. Yet Stresemann as a pragmatic conservative also knew that Germany, by relying too heavily on foreign loans, was *"dancing on a volcano. If the short term credits are called in, a large section of our economy will collapse"*. This very situation occurred only weeks after his death, a death which deprived Germany of one of its few statesmen, thereby leaving a vacuum in German politics at the very time when a strong hand was needed. *The Times* newspaper reporting on his death maintained *"Herr Stresemann's death … is freely admitted to be a disaster not only for Germany but for the world"*.

25. Weimar Culture

Introduction

In the richness and variety of its cultural achievements, the Weimar period 1919-1933, is a glorious period, second to none in German history. Germany now became the cultural centre of Europe, just as France had been before 1914. The old restrictions associated with the authoritarian regime of Wilhelm II - art should not venture *"beyond the laws and limits imposed by myself"* - were swept away. War ensured that alongside the demise of former institutions was the abolition of many traditions and values. One German, Paul Ernst, expressed his understanding of the change by exclaiming *"Our age is over! Thank God, it is over! A new age dawns that will be different!"*. Weimar culture thus had a sense of beginning anew, it became a cradle of modernity, as old restrictions fell away and everything had to be created afresh. Yet, at the same time, it is important to bear in mind that many of the new artistic and literary trends associated with Weimar culture, actually had their origins before the war. They failed, however, to enter popular consciousness, to affect people's attitudes about themselves and the world they lived in, to reach their full flowering until the 1920s. This was largely because the Weimar regime had no censorship, it allowed for freedom of expression in whatever form, actively encouraging works of the spirit and imagination. Special exhibitions were arranged for modern artists, and visitors to museums became used to seeing paintings that broke with the formalistic canons of the past. While, on the one hand, the achievements are all the more remarkable in light of the difficult economic and political circumstances of the day, on the other, these same difficulties helped to create the spirit of revolt and emancipation.

> *"Our remarkable times, this period*
> *Since the war, troubled and confused*
> *but yet so fertile."*
> — Hermann Hesse

Bauhaus [I]

A movement that did more to change the appearance of the modern world than any other force that was active in the 1920s was the *Bauhaus*. This was a new school of art, architecture and design that was founded in 1919 by Walter Gropius (1883-1969). Announcing the establishment of his new school at Weimar, Gropius defined its purpose as *"to break down the arrogant barrier between craftsmen and artist, in order to conceive and create the new building of the future"*. Gropius disliked and consequently abandoned, the old decorative and ornamental style of imperial days. Students at his school were required to learn various crafts, which Gropius believed to be allied to architecture, the matrix of the arts. Although richly diverse, designs were noted for their clarity, their straight lines and their functional suitability. Steel frameworks, austere pillars and the use of glass were features of the *Bauhaus* school. The result was both severe and elegant, and carried out with great economy of means. Such a building would be *"a crystalline symbol of a new and rising faith"*. But architecture and design, Gropius insisted, should be forever changing, always related to the contemporary world. Realising that machine production had to be the precondition of design if that effort was to have an impact in the 20th century, Gropius directed the school's design efforts towards mass production. Gropius also emphasised housing and city planning, the usefulness of sociology and the necessity of using teams of specialists.

Bauhaus [II]

In the summer of 1923, the *Bauhaus* held its first exhibition. This was a week-long festival which attracted 15,000 visitors. Its highpoint was a stunning display of varied products that illustrated the exhibition's theme *'Art and Technics : a new unity'* and the showing of a modern house. In spite of such landmark exhibitions, however, the *Bauhaus* came under fire from various right-wing groups who were outraged by the movement's flaunting of their disregard for tradition. They accused it of having wicked political purposes. Financial pressures resulting from this prompted a move from Weimar to Dessau in 1924 and then, in 1932, to Berlin. During that time, the *Bauhaus* had a far-reaching influence, not just in the world of architecture and industrial design but in sculpture, painting, textiles and pottery. It demonstrated that objects of everyday living like furniture, cutlery, china and lamps could be made to combine simplicity, strength and beauty. The Nazi regime, seeking, as it did, to recapture the old days of German glory, failed to appreciate the achievements of the *Bauhaus*. Having been condemned as decadent, in April 1933 its schools were closed down. Thereafter, Gropius, himself unsympathetic to the Third Reich, left Germany and went to live in the United States. There he was greeted with open arms and continued to meet with great success. Arguably the greatest architectural genius of the 20th century, Gropius' works included the school building and faculty house at the *Bauhaus*, the Harvard University Graduate Centre, the Pan-Am skyscraper in New York, and the United States Embassy in Athens.

Literature [I]

The new freedom from censorship gave a marked impetus to the literary works of the Weimar period. The writings of Thomas Mann (1875-1955) acquired the status of classics both within and outside Germany and ensured that he won the Nobel Prize for Literature in 1929. His subtly structured novels and short stories constitute an imaginative enquiry into the nature of western bourgeois culture. In his great work, *'The Magic Mountain',* Mann formulates with remarkable insight the fateful choices facing Europe. The allegorical tale, *'Dr. Faustus'*, is the most directly political of Mann's novels. It is the lifestory of a German composer, Adrian Leverhühn. A solitary, estranged figure, he 'speaks' the experience of his times in his music. The story of Leverhühn's compositions is that of German culture in the two decades before 1930. Mann's influence was such that he too became a victim of Nazism. His books were condemned while he himself found residence in Switzerland and later, the United States. Another 'un-German' writer who actually witnessed his own works committed to the flames in 1933 along with other subversive books, was Erich Kästner. His novel of the depression years, *'Fabian'* (1931) took a very gloomy view of contemporary society, *"we are perishing because of the spiritual ease of all concerned. We want things to change, but we don't want a change in ourselves... The bloodstream is poisoned"*. Kästner also found success as a writer of books for children. *'Emil und die Detektive'* is a classic in children's literature and has been translated into 28 languages.

Literature [II]

The ability to depict the horror of war was part of the freedom enjoyed from 1919-1933. Eric Remarque (1898-1970) is chiefly remembered as the author of *'All Quiet on the Western Front'* (1929), a remarkable novel dealing with World War I. The events of the novel are those in the daily routine of soldiers who seem to have no past or future apart from their lives in the trenches. Its casual amorality was in shocking contrast to patriotic rhetoric. The book was an immediate international success and sold 3.5 million copies in 25 languages in the first 18 months of its publication. It was followed by a sequel, *'The Road Back'* (1931), dealing with the collapse of Germany in 1918. As might be expected, Remarque's works fell victim to the Nazi purge. The extreme pessimism of Oswald Spengler is particularly obvious in the first volume of *'Decline of the West'*, a work based on a loose comparison between his own time and the later centuries of the ancient world. Although closely associated with French writers such as Sartre, the philosophy of Existentialism was a predominantly German phenomenon which had its roots in Weimar culture and society. Martin Heidegger, for example, emphasised the importance of the subjective and personal. He believed it was necessary that man should not attempt to flee from the reality of life.

Art/Music

German artists explored the emotional unrest and turmoil that many were experiencing in Weimar society. Max Beckmann (1884-1950) was an Expressionist painter and printmaker whose works are notable for the violence with which they reflect the tragic events of the 20th century. The shock of exposure to dead and maimed soldiers during his experience as a medical corpsman in World War I, filled his art with sordid, often horrifying, imagery. In *'The Night'* (1918-1919), a scene of nightmarish sadism, the deliberately repulsive colours and the erratic forms convey Beckmann's horror of man's bestiality. The painter and engraver, Otto Dix (1891-1968) mixed compassion and expressionist despair to create works harshly critical of society. *'War Wounded Playing Cards'*, *'Large Towns'*, *'Pimp and Girls'* and *'Two Sacrifices of Capitalism'* show his horrified vision of contemporary social reality. The 'two sacrifices' for instance, are a grotesque prostitute and a defaced former soldier. The works of these artists were later condemned as *'degenerate'*. Germany's contributions to modern music during the Weimar period, though somewhat less impressive, are nonetheless notable. The new forces were Hindemith and Schönberg. A remarkably versatile composer with considerable influence both in Germany and abroad, Hindemith wrote string quartets, song cycles, jazz music and operas. Less prolific but more revolutionary in his technique, Schönberg was the creator of the twelve tone scale and of atonal music. The fact that performances of the new music were not restricted to the largest cities was symptomatic of the openness of Weimar.

Theatre

Theatre thrived in Weimar Germany, especially in Berlin. A new approach called for the doing away with the old-fashioned overcrowded stage. Producers now experimented with new techniques and settings, and the audience was encouraged to use its imagination. Leopold Jessner (1878-1945) was a pioneer of such bold innovations. As director in the Berlin State Theatre, he produced classic and contemporary plays on a bare, denaturalised stage on which graduated levels and flights of steps served in the place of scene changes as platforms for different actions. Memorable performances were Schiller's *'William Tell'*, Shakespeare's *'Richard III'* and a *'Hamlet'* in modern dress slanted to be a criticism of Germany in the 1920s. Erwin Piscator (1893-1966) was another great name in the theatre. Piscator used the theatre to convey radical political instruction. A bold innovator, he used films, newsreels, puppets, newspaper montage and wooden props. Optical, acoustical and mechanical devices were used to great effect. One of the most famous playwrights of the period, Bertolt Brecht (1898-1956), emphasised the shortcomings of western bourgeois life and orthodox morality. He argued that the cruelty of the social system was responsible for freezing all human feeling. Thus capitalism was denounced and the ideals of communism praised in such works as *'Mother Courage'* and *'The Beggar's Opera'*. The leading character or hero in Brecht's works was generally a shabby, down-to-earth figure, the outcast or disillusioned tough. Other notable playwrights include Heinrich Mann and Hermann Sudermann. Together these men sought to use the theatre as a means of teaching and transforming society.

Cinema - Conclusion

The cinema was one of the new forms of popular entertainment and although Hollywood continued to dominate commercial films, there is little doubt that the Weimar period was a golden age for German cinema. It was a time of great directors like Carl Mayer, G.W. Pabst, F.W. Murnau, Joseph von Sternberg, of artists whose fame spread beyond Germany, like Asta Nielsen, Conrad Veidt, Emil Jannings and Marlene Dietrich, and of film masterpieces. *'The Blue Angel'* was a film of sex and outright sadism which tells the story of the decline and fall of a high school professor who succumbs to the charms of Lola Lola, a night club singer. It proved to be a very strong statement on the psychological situation of the time. *'The Cabinet of Dr. Caligari'* was an outspoken revolutionary story. In it the omnipotence of a state authority manifesting itself in universal conscription and declarations of war is stigmatized. *'Western Front'*, *'M'*, *'Comradeship'* were other films of the period. Theatre and cinema, like other art forms, suffered from Hitler's condemnation of Weimar culture, *"fourteen years a junkyard"*. The policy of general denegration adopted by the Nazis cannot, however, cloud or detract from these years of achievement. Worth noting is that in spite of the support given by the Weimar Republic to artists, writers and musicians, few of them seemed to feel any reciprocal obligations or any inclination to come to the Republic's defence. Too many of them remained *'angry young men'*, crying out through their artistic endeavours.

"Change the world, she needs it"

—B. Brecht

Weimar Germany: Past Exam Questions

1993

E4. Essay

(iii) Culture and arts in Weimar Germany.

1992

C5. The Weimar Republic

Treat of the strengths and weaknesses of the Weimar Republic.

1998

C5. Weimar Germany

"The period 1919-1933 was, for Weimar Germany, a period of political instability and cultural achievement". Discuss.

1987

D1. The Arts in Europe, 1900-1950

Treat of experiments and movements in the arts in Europe during the period 1900-1950. Refer in your answer to one or more of the following: painting, sculpture, architecture, music, literature, theatre, cinema.

1985

E4. Essay

(ii) Cultural and intellectual developments in Weimar Germany.

MUSSOLINI'S ITALY

26. Benito Mussolini, 1883-1945

Early Years - Post War Italy

Mussolini was born on 29th July 1883 in the village of Doria in Romogna, central Italy. His father was a socialist blacksmith, his mother a school teacher. The young Mussolini was never a diligent student but was rather unruly, managing to secure expulsion from two schools. Although Mussolini did manage to qualify as a teacher in 1901, he was to practise the profession very little. Having spent some time in Switzerland, the years 1904-1906 were given over to military service. Mussolini had by this time become involved in politics and journalism. In 1912 he was appointed editor of the socialist newspaper, *Avanti*. Shortly after war broke out in 1914, Mussolini broke with the Socialist Party when he began to call for Italy's involvement. In November 1914, Mussolini started his own newspaper, *Il Popola d'Italia,* which was subsidised by fellow interventionists and the Allies. Italy's entry into the war in 1915 led Mussolini to join the army. Released in 1917 when he suffered an injury in grenade practice, Mussolini returned to journalism. In spite of the fact that Italy was one of the victorious powers in 1918, Italy had played a minor, largely unsatisfactory role in the war. In 1919, she performed badly at the Peace Conference in Paris. She failed, for example, to exact all the benefits of the Treaty of London, 1915. Italians were particularly resentful about their failure to gain Fiume. The abortive attempt by the nationalistic poet, Gabriele D'Annunzio, to establish a dictatorship in Fiume, 1919-1920 was important in that it demonstrated the depth of Italian resentment and the weakness of her government. Post-war instability, indecisiveness, the existence of a multiplicity of parties and corrupt politicians created a variety of short-lived governments. To compound Italy's problems, the country faced economic stagnation and social unrest. It was within such a context that Mussolini and his Fascists managed to secure power.

Fascist Party - March On Rome

On 23rd March 1919, Mussolini summoned a meeting of like-minded followers in Milan, and announced the birth of *Fascio di Combattimento* (Groups for Combat). The term *'fasces'* had its origins in ancient Rome when law enforcement officers there carried bundles of rods bound tightly together with an axe in the middle. The Fascists used them as symbols of authority and strength, so necessary if the Fascists were to end disorder and allow Italy to regain her pride of place in Europe. Mussolini's followers wore black shirts. Over the following months, a violent speech-making campaign did nothing to endear the Fascists to the electorate and in the November 1919 election they failed to get any seats. Mussolini decided to moderate his programme. The party also became increasingly right wing. The growth of the party thereafter was helped by the climate of disorder, the fact that the Fascists were seen as a potential block against Socialists and Communists, the support it received from a variety of backgrounds, including rich industrialists, and the government's reluctance to deal with illegal Fascist activity, fearing, as it did, the possiblility of creating still more disarray. The general election of May 1921 secured the Fascists 35 seats. But the unstable political situation meant that governments continued to come and go. In August 1922 the showdown between Left and Right took place when the Socialists called for a general strike. Mussolini, posing as the champion of law and order, got his Blackshirt squads to break up the strike. He then intimated to the papacy and the monarchy that he was supportive of them both. In October 1922, Mussolini presented his ultimatum, *"Either we are allowed to govern or we will seize power by marching on Rome"*. Failing to get King Victor Emmanuel III's agreement to impose martial law and to call upon the army, Prime Minister Luigi Facta resigned. Mussolini was invited to take his place. The Blackshirts, who had been ordered to *'March on Rome'*, were in readiness. On 31st October 25,000 Blackshirts held a victory parade.

Consolidation of Power - Dictatorship

Mussolini did not gain complete power in 1922. He was head of a moderate coalition, containing only four Fascist ministers. Out of a total of 535 deputies in parliament, the Fascists numbered only 35. Although Mussolini aspired to dictatorship, in the early days he moved carefully, achieving his goal by constitutional means. In 1923 the Acerbo Law was passed. This entitled the party which won the biggest vote in elections to claim two-thirds of the seats in chamber. Early in 1924 the Blackshirts were transformed into an official Fascist Militia with state salaries. Known as the Volunteer Militia for National Security (MVSN), members swore allegiance to Mussolini rather than to the King. The Fascist Grand Council was a consultative body which in time became the decisive element in Italian life. In the election of April 1924 the Fascists gained 64% of the poll and could claim two-thirds of the chamber. On 10th June 1924, Giacoma Matteotti, an outspoken critic of fascism who had written a book, *'The Fascists Exposed'*, was abducted. When his dead body was found in August 1924 and the Fascists were implicated, over 100 deputies withdrew from the chamber in opposition. Dubbed the *'Aventine Secession'*, deputies had hoped to isolate Mussolini by their action. Mussolini rode the storm, however. In a daring speech on 3rd January 1925, Mussolini assumed responsibility for what happened *"Italy wants peace ...... we will give her this by means of love if possible, but by force if necessary"*. Thereafter, political parties and their papers were suppressed. Italy became a one-party state with the Fascists as the only 'legitimate' party. The cult of Mussolini was fostered and he became known simply as *'Il Duce'* (the leader). In January 1926, Mussolini was given the power to govern by decree, a power which he used over 100,000 times. The strong arm tactics of Mussolini's rule could again be seen in 1927 when a secret police force, the OVRA, was set up. Individual rights and liberties were now largely ignored.

The Fascist State

Trade unions were abolished and the economy was brought under Fascist control through the establishment of corporations representing employers and workers. Strikes and lock-outs were forbidden, and wages, prices and conditions of work were set. In terms of economic well being, the early years 1922-1925 under Finance Minister, De Stefani, were the most successful. Foreign investment was encouraged, government expenditure reduced, the tax system simplified and the budget balanced. Unemployment fell. The mid-to-late 1920s, by comparison, witnessed an increase in inflation, a fall in the value of the lira and a balance of payments deficit. Unemployment exceeded 1 million in 1932. More enduring was the large-scale public works including the building of new motorways (the *autostrada*), railways, hospitals and electric trams. The draining of the Pontine marshes, near Rome, transformed 60,000 hectares of land. The *'Battle for Grain'*, launched in 1925, was only partially successful and Italy, under Mussolini, never became self-sufficient. However, Fascist propaganda, which penetrated every area of life, played a significant role in ensuring that only success stories were fed to the masses. The 'herd' instinct was exploited at every opportunity and slogans such as *"Believe, Obey, Fight"*, *"The Leader is always right"* and *"I believe in the genius of Mussolini"* were commonplace. After 1931, it was obligatory for public servants to be party members. Schools, for their part, were required to teach Fascist doctrine and new compulsory textbooks emphasised Italian greatness. Children from the age of eight were expected to join the *Balilla*, the Fascist youth movement. A major Fascist coup, one which guaranteed that Mussolini would be hailed as a statesman of respectability and renown, was the signing of the Lateran Treaty and Concordat with Pope Pius XI in 1929. This agreement ended the poor relationship which had existed between the Vatican and the Italian state. It recognised the Pope as head of the tiny Vatican state and gave £10m by way of compensation for the loss of the Papal states in 1870. Catholicism was declared the official religion of Italy.

Foreign Policy to 1935

For most of the period up to 1936, Mussolini acted as his own Foreign Minister. The position was then held by his son-in-law, Ciano, through whom Mussolini retained control. Mussolini's aims were essentially aggressive and expansionist. Phrases such as *"A minute on the battlefield is worth a lifetime of peace"* or *"Peace was just a pause between wars"* and *"Better to live one day as a lion than a thousand years as a lamb"* give credence to this outlook. The three main areas of Fascist expansion were the states of southern Europe, the Balkans and Africa. The world was given its first taste of Mussolini's Fascist spirit in 1923 when, following the assassination of four Italians and an Albanian on Greek territory, Mussolini demanded high compensation to the tune of 5 million lire. The Greeks refused to pay so Mussolini used the opportunity to occupy the Greek island of Corfu. His army remained there until the money was paid. Later in 1923, Mussolini sent a military officer to govern the city of Fiume which, he claimed, was falling into anarchy. In 1924, he successfully negotiated for the return of Fiume to Italy. That Mussolini, during his first decade of rule, also recognised the attraction of diplomacy is obvious from the number of peace pacts he signed. In 1925, he signed the Locarno Pact, recognising Germany's borders. The following year he established a protectorate over Albania. A treaty was signed with Hungary in 1927. By the Kellog-Briand Pact of 1928, Mussolini committed Italy to renounce war as an instrument of policy. Mussolini's reluctance to being bound by such agreements became more apparent in the 1930s. For the moment, however, he remained worried about Hitler's aggression. Mussolini was opposed to the Union of Austria and Germany. An Italian show of force in 1934 forced Hitler to postpone the *Anschluss*. The Stresa Front of Britain, France and Italy, 1935, condemned Hitler's rearmament and pledged *"close and cordial collaboration in European affairs"*. Mussolini thereupon sought to satisfy his territorial ambition in Africa by launching a surprise attack on Abyssinia in October 1935.

Foreign Policy, 1935-39

Italian forces, backed up by aeroplanes, bombs, poison gas, machine guns and artillery had little difficulty in overcoming the primitive resources of Abyssinian resistance. The League of Nations condemned the action and made the decision to impose economic sanctions on Italy. The sanctions were only partially applied, however, and did not affect the course of the war. In May 1936, the Italians captured Addis Ababa, the capital of Abyssinia. Haile Selaisse, the emperor, went into exile and Victor Emmanuel III was proclaimed leader in his place. Hitler's non-interference and general support of Italian action during the Abyssinian war brought the two leaders closer together and destroyed the unity of the Stresa Front. When the Spanish Civil War broke out in July 1936, Italy and Germany jointly aided Franco and the Nationalists. Mussolini committed Italy heavily to the war so that in 1937-1938 there were over 70,000 Italian troops in Spain. Large quantities of Italian planes, weapons and ammunition were also used. Meanwhile, Italian newspapers were ordered to be pro-German. The Rome-Berlin Axis of 1936 was a mark of improving relations as was the Anti-Comintern Pact, November 1936. The bond was further strengthened in 1938 by Mussolini's declaration of neutrality over the *Anschluss* and his role of peacemaker in the Czech crisis, leading to the Munich conference. In March 1939, the Axis was converted into a formal military alliance, the Pact of Steel. This provided for automatic mutual help *"if it should happen ... that one of them becomes involved in warlike complications with another power or powers"*. Effectively Mussolini had given Hitler a free hand to attack Poland. Such an attack occurred on 1st September 1939 and led to the outbreak of World War II.

World War II

By the time World War II began, Italy was already economically and militarily exhausted. This resulted from imprudent decisions and from involvement in a succession of wars, including those in Libya, Abyssinia and Spain. Thus in September 1939 Mussolini was forced to break his Pact of Steel Agreement and declared Italy's non-belligerence. Italy, fearful of a German invasion, subsequently built costly fortifications on her northern frontier with Germany. The money and time might have been better used re-arming. In March 1940, the conflict in Mussolini's mind between fear and the desire to play a historic role in events, was skilfully played upon by Hitler at a famous meeting held in a train at the Brenner Pass. Hitler overwhelmed Mussolini with a flood of positive talk. Confident of a German victory and fearful of being left out of the division of the spoils, Mussolini, on 10th June 1940, announced Italy's involvement in the war. By then he had already assumed for himself the position of Commander-in-Chief of the armed forces. This decision, ill-researched military campaigns and the appointment of Fascist ministers without military experience to senior army positions all contributed to Italy's failure in the war. An invasion of southern France in June 1940 gained little for the Italians. In September 1940, the North Africa campaign started. After some early Italian successes, the story of North Africa became largely one of shambles, defeat and collapse. The splitting of Italian forces with the attack on Greece on 28th October 1940 emphatically did not help Mussolini's cause. The Greeks fought back. Having successfully repulsed their Italian invaders, they began occupation of Albania. Defeat in Greece and in Egypt in December 1940 forced German intervention. This allowed German influence over Italy to increase as the war went on. Yet the Italian empire was not saved. In 1941, Italy lost Abyssinia and Italian East Africa. Further defeats, such as that at El Alamein in 1942, left the Italian North Africa army with no choice but to surrender which it duly did at Tunis in May 1943. Continued Allied success led to the invasion of Sicily in July 1943. Mussolini's days were now well and truly numbered.

Final Years - An Evaluation

By 1943, Mussolini's support was dwindling even among prominent Fascist members. Ciano, Bottai, Grandi were just some of those who had been demoted by Mussolini, and who were now seeking revenge. Their cause was helped by the Fascist Grand Council's decision to ask for Mussolini's removal. On 25th July 1943, Victor Emmanuel III dismissed Mussolini, who must surely have been regretful that he had not *"rubbed out the King"*. The new Prime Minister, Marshal Badoglio, surrendered to the advancing Allies in September 1943, and declared war on Germany. The Germans remained in control of northern Italy, however, and Mussolini, who had been arrested in July was rescued on 12th September by a German Commando unit. He was now made head of a puppet government, called the Salo Republic, in northern Italy. Mussolini was by then a much changed, shrunken and ageing man. His Salo government followed a squalid and undistinguished career. With the fall of Rome in June 1944 and the advance of the Allies towards the Lombardy Plain, self preservation became Mussolini's primary concern. Disguised as a German soldier, he attempted to flee the country. Captured by Italian partisans at Dongo on Lake Como, Mussolini, together with his mistress, Clara Petacci, was shot on 18th April 1945. Their bodies were hung upside down in Milan for all to see. Mussolini, the man who had introduced to the world the concepts of Fascism and Totalitarianism, faced what could only be described as an ignominious and an inglorious end. With his death, Fascism and all it stood for, came tumbling down. The myth of the invincible leader was well and truly shattered. But Fascism in Italy, for all its aspirations of totalitarianism, was never really a reality. The monarchy was retained and the church maintained a degree of independence. Perhaps Hitler's assessment is not too far off the mark *"He is not a revolutionary like the Führer or Stalin. He is so bound to his own Italian people that he lacks the broad qualities of a world-wide revolutionary and insurrectionist"*. Mussolini's Fascist state was, in the final analysis, a failure, one which for far too long fed off its own propaganda.

27. Account for the Rise of Fascism in Italy under Mussolini

Introduction - Defeat in War

Benito Mussolini came to power in Italy with the aim of securing complete power for himself in a fascist state. The ambitious young agitator was, for over twenty years, to provide Italy with the mixed blessings of one of the earliest and longest of the European dictatorships. Yet it took Mussolini only three years to achieve power. The question must therefore be asked - what enabled Mussolini to come to power with such relative ease? The answer lies in a look at Italy's experiences during the war years, the post-war climate of disillusionment, the fear of communism and in Mussolini's own determination. Italy entered the war in May 1915, having earlier failed to fulfil the terms of her Triple Alliance. The Treaty of London, signed on 26th April 1915, and allying Italy to the British and the French, had promised Italy considerable gains in return for her involvement. But the war went none too well for Italy. Her army was badly armed and quite unready for war and from early on, morale was low. Defeat at Caporetto in October 1917 was such that the entire Italian front collapsed. So immense and unexpected was the shock that Mussolini wrote with typical exaggeration that 24th October 1917 witnessed the greatest defeat in world history, adding that nothing in his life caused him greater humiliation. Even the success at Vittorio Veneto later that month failed to compensate for the many hardships imposed by war. In 1918 when the war ended, of the 5 million men that had been mobilised, 650,000 were dead and huge numbers, estimated as between 150,000 and 500,000, were in hiding as deserters, most of them living as bandits. Thus, while Italy was one of the victorious powers, time would show that her disillusionment was as great as that of the defeated powers.

Post-War Disillusionment

At the Paris Peace Conference, Prime Minister Vittorio Orlando was responsible for pressing Italy's position, particularly the territorial gains promised her under the Treaty of London. Orlando, however, lacked political skill on the international level. His position was further complicated by the fact that many of his claims could not be justified on the grounds of race or the principle of self-determination and by the fact that President Woodrow Wilson, who was not a signatory of the Treaty of London, had little sympathy with Italy. Orlando had no real interest in other aspects under discussion and when his demands were not met, he withdrew his delegation from the discussions for a time. When, thereafter, the treaties were concluded, Italy received Trentino, Istria and Trieste. The failure to gain Dalmatia and the city of Fiume caused considerable disillusionment. Italians also grumbled that they were not given a German colony as a mandate and that they were not allowed to expand their African colonies. Not surprisingly, the Italians spoke in terms of a *"mutilated victory"*, Mussolini insisting that although Italy *"had won the war, we were utterly defeated in the diplomatic battle"*. Fiume, a city placed under international control, was primarily peopled by Italians and Slavs. Before too long, it was awarded to the newly created state of Yugoslavia. Italian resentment at the failure to secure this important port city led Gabriele D'Annunzio, a colourful soldier poet with strong nationalistic leanings to seize Fiume in September 1919. For over a year, he and about 2,600 ex-soldiers held the city. Although D'Annunzio was eventually forced to relinquish control over Fiume, the incident gave Italy its first taste of dictatorship as well as highlighting the weakness of the Italian government. Mussolini, who learned a great deal from the incident, looked upon it as a dress rehearsal for a fascist coup.

Economy

The Italian economy which had experienced a boom during the war years was badly disrupted and insecure in the post-war period. War had strained the government's limited finances and the public debt had risen by almost 100%. The production of armaments stopped and inflation increased. This wiped out many people's savings and ensured that the price of goods rose steadily. The cost of living rose by over 500% between 1914 and 1920 so that while five lire equalled one US dollar in 1914, by 1920 the figure was twenty eight lire. Italian imports, which ranged from such essentials as coal to wheat, became very expensive and for some impossible to come by. Meanwhile, the government sought to increase state revenue by a system of high taxation. The middle class, in particular, suffered as a result of this. Coinciding with these problems was a marked increase in unemployment. The demobilisation of 2 million soldiers, who could not be absorbed into the workforce, worsened the situation. Emigration, traditionally providing some sort of release for the poorest and most dissatisfied groups, was slowed down when, in 1921, the US restricted the number of immigrants it would admit from each country. The result was considerable social unrest. This took the form of strikes, lock-outs and worker sit-ins. The number of labour disputes between 1918 and 1920 was so great that the period became known as *'biennio rosso'* (two red years). Discontent spread to the countryside. The peasants, particularly abundant in the south, seized land from the large landowners. A communist revolution seemed imminent and people began to compare conditions in Italy to those in Russia in 1917.

The Weakness of Italian Politics

In the face of all these difficulties, Italy's government proved weak and ineffective; so much so that in 1919 Mussolini was fairly sure that the parliamentary regime was drifting to an end and *"the succession was now open"*. At that time, Italy was a constitutional monarchy, containing as it did a King and a parliament. Its parliamentary system allowed for a uniquely Italian technique called *Transformismo*. This was concerned with the art of maintaining a majority by bribes and other opportunist devices which brought enough support from opponents to pass measures deemed essential. Coalition governments and frequent changes of ministries became the norm. The introduction of a system of proportional representation served only to compound problems and workable conditions became increasingly difficult to maintain. The two main parties, the Socialist Party and the Catholic Popular Party, for example, were not only opposed to each other but were divided within themselves. In the four years after the war, 1918 to 1922, there were no less than five changes of government. Prime Ministers included Francesco Nitti, Giovannia Giolitti, Ivanoe Bonomi and Luigi Facta. None of them proved capable of providing stable government. The King, Victor Emmanuel III, was a timid figure who had to admit that the liberal leaders had no answer to anarchy and parliamentary stalemate. Temperamentally he was drawn to anyone who could take firm decisions and control domestic unrest as well as standing up for Italian interests with the world at large. Such a leader emerged in the person of Benito Mussolini. He was the one strong and ruthless personality to emerge who was prepared to exploit the vacuum that existed.

The Fascist Party

On 23rd March 1919, Mussolini launched his Fascist movement. The first meeting took place in a hall provided by Milanese businessmen in the Piazza San Sepolcro and about 50 people were present. The party was composed of units known individually as *Fascio di Combattimento* or 'Groups for Combat'. The Fascists adopted a uniform of black shirts, used the straight arm Roman salute and suggested their authority and strength by using the symbol of a bundle of rods with an axe in the middle. Originally intended as a strong composite movement, the Fascists approached the election of November 1919 in some disarray, with each local group deciding its own programme. The result was an electoral catastrophe in so far as no Fascist gained a seat. Many Fascists now abandoned the movement and by the end of the year fewer than 4,000 committed adherents were left in the whole of Italy. But Mussolini showed talent and resilience of an exceptional order. He had an instinctive political cunning, grasping political opportunities as they presented themselves. He demanded a new deal for the poor, a share in company profits for industrial workers, an eight-hour day for everyone and small holdings for landless peasants. Big businesses supported Mussolini when he condemned Marxism as a *"heap of ruins"* containing obsolete doctrines such as class war, economic determinism and the dictatorship of the proletariat. To endear himself to the ex-servicemen he adopted an odd mixture of nationalist and revolutionary ideas overlaid with a populist appeal to national grandeur and individual prosperity. He was a man for all seasons, *'an adventurer for all roads'*. Thus did Fascism begin to grow over the next few years.

From Illegality to 'Champions of Law and Order'

Because the Fascists were armed and willing to use force, illegal Fascist activities were common. Sometimes they terrorised their opponents by forcing them to drink whole bottles of castor oil. Sometimes they beat them. Occasionally they murdered them. The authorities, by adopting a largely passive attitude, undoubtedly helped Mussolini's rise to power. Mussolini was also helped by the split in the Socialist movement which led to the formation of the Italian Communist Party in January 1921. So alarmed were the monied and propertied classes that they prepared to place almost unlimited funds at Mussolini's disposal. The elections of May 1921 took place in conditions of unusual violence with as many as 100 people being killed. Mussolini's Fascists gained 35 seats, about 7% of the total. Although he had hoped for greater success, Mussolini's entry into parliament gained him a new authority and a new respectability. For a time, Mussolini decided to quieten the physical force tradition and this won him more support from the respectable sections of society. Meanwhile, as the economy continued to stagnate, the Socialists called for a general strike in August 1922. The government, then under the leadership of Facta, a negligible politician, was afraid to take action. Mussolini stepped in and offered to break up the strike.

Blackshirt squads moved into the affected areas and ensured that public utilities continued to function. Strike headquarters were attacked, labour demonstrations broken and terrorised workers were soon forced to end the strike. Posing as the defender or champion of law and order, Mussolini had used the opportunity of the strike to burn down the offices and printing presses of the socialist agitators. Their morale was now damaged and the incompetence of the government all too clear.

March on Rome

Mussolini continued, thereafter, to play a double game saying that he was ready to seek power inside the parliamentary system but also hinting that he might be ready for a coup d'état. He knew, however, that it was necessary to work out tactics for dealing with possible opponents. He needed, in particular, to sound out, and if possible neutralise, both the Vatican and the King. Accordingly, in September 1922, Mussolini declared that he was a friend of the Church and ready to renounce his Republican ideas. Having indicated his support for the papacy and the monarchy, Mussolini became more confident. On 24th October, at a mass meeting of Fascists in Naples, the plan for an insurrection crystallised. Mussolini maintained that *"either we are allowed to govern, or we will seize power by marching on Rome"*, that he would *"take by the throat the miserable political class that governs us"*. The march of all Fascist groups would take place from three separate points to arrive in the capital on 28th October. Mussolini, by then, had established his headquarters in Milan from where he could easily slip into exile in Switzerland should plans backfire. When on 27th of the month, the Fascists began to mobilise, Prime Minister Facta, fearful of confrontation and civil war, asked the King to impose martial law and to prepare to use armed troops against the Fascists. Victor Emanuel III agreed at first but, lacking confidence in Facta's ability to control events, he soon changed his mind. Facta resigned and on 29th October, Mussolini was asked to become Prime Minister. The following morning, Mussolini arrived by train to the capital. On 31st October, the *'March on Rome'* took place. It was nothing more than a victory parade of about 25,000 Blackshirts although Mussolini, not satisfied with anything so unspectacular as a royal appointment, developed the myth of a forceful seizure of power.

The Drive towards Totalitarianism

Having come to power at a time of depression, hopelessness and fear, Mussolini was regarded as a lesser evil, the one person who might be capable of averting civil war and restoring law and order. In office, Mussolini moved carefully, using constitutional means to become a dictator. The Acerbo law of 1923, for example, ingeniously provided that the party gaining the largest number of votes in a national election should have two-thirds of the seats in the chamber. Around the same time, the legalised Blackshirts, renamed the Volunteer Militia for National Security, swore an allegiance to Mussolini rather than to the King. In the 1924 elections the Fascists used violence and intimidation, and won a majority of seats. Mussolini now showed increasing ruthlessness. Giacoma Matteotti, an outspoken Socialist deputy, was found murdered in June 1924. This, along with further repressive measures, led some members of parliament to secede in protest. The Aventine Secession, in fact, made Mussolini's power all the stronger so that throughout 1925 and 1926 the dictatorial regime grew more flagrant. Political parties, other than the Fascist Party, were dissolved, non-Fascists were removed from government posts, labour was placed under severe restrictions and the press was rigidly controlled so that all anti-Fascist propaganda was effectively muzzled. Mussolini became known as *'Il Duce'* (The Leader) and the cult of Mussolini was fostered openly. Before long, Mussolini had claimed the right to govern by decree, a privilege he used over 100,000 times during his years in office. Mussolini also established his own secret police, the *OVRA*, to root out opposition. Control over youth, education and culture increased Mussolini's power. By 1929, his dictatorship was fully intact, he demanded only applause and obedience, appreciated only servility. As he aspired towards the creation of a totalitarian state, Fascism had become a vehicle for Mussolini's own power.

28. Mussolini's Domestic Policy

Mussolini in Power

Having first threatened to seize power by means of the *'March on Rome'*, Mussolini was invited by King Victor Emmanuel III in October 1922 to become Prime Minister. He headed a broad coalition government which included the Catholic *Popolari* (Italian Catholic Popular Party), the Nationalist Party and representatives of most of the Liberal factions. Only four Fascist ministers served in the cabinet, Mussolini retaining the posts of Foreign Minister and Minister of the Interior for himself. At 39 years of age, Mussolini had the immediate problem of persuading everyone to accept the situation and of increasing the number of Fascist deputies which then stood at 35 out of a total of 353. He knew that he would have to proceed cautiously. Although intent on becoming a dictator, he temporarily observed existing constitutional forms. In December 1922 Mussolini established the Grand Council of Fascism which helped to develop his personal primacy. Mussolini was also responsible for the fusion of the Fascist and Nationalist parties in 'a marriage of convenience'. The legal pretence continued when in July 1923 a new electoral law known as the Acerbo Law was passed by a huge majority. This gave two thirds of the seats in the chamber to the party that gained the largest number of seats. At the time it was not obvious that the Fascists would be the first to benefit from the law, most deputies believing that it would help to stabilise government. Mussolini's next move was to transform the legalised Blackshirts into the Volunteer Militia for National Security (MVSN). Its members swore allegiance to Mussolini, not to the King. In the lead up to the April 1924 elections the MVSN used violence and intimidation, prompting one observer to remark that *"the Fascists are, in their methods, as barbarous as the Bolsheviks"*. Fraud in the form of rigging of votes was also used. This ensured a substantial victory for the Fascists who secured 64% of the votes and could therefore claim two thirds of all seats.

Murder of Matteotti - Aventine Secession

It is generally agreed by historians that until 1924 it was still possible to moderate, perhaps even stop, Mussolini. One politician brave enough to condemn Mussolini at that time was Giacoma Matteotti, a leading Socialist deputy. Matteotti spelled out in detail how the April 1924 election had been won by fraud and violence and how only a minority of electors had been able to vote freely. His book *'The Fascists Exposed'* was a large dossier of Fascist crimes. But Mussolini could never allow a single deputy to stand in his way. On 10th June 1924, Matteotti was murdered by leading Blackshirts. Mussolini sought to deny all knowledge of the crime and failed to arrest those he knew to be the culprits. The attempted cover-up aroused much fury and indignation throughout the country, however, and Mussolini, who confessed that the days after the murder were among the most terrible of his life, realised that Fascism was in danger of being swept away. Over 100 deputies from the Catholic and Socialist parties withdrew from parliament in protest. Dubbed the *'Aventine Secession'*, the deputies hoped to isolate Mussolini by their move. They also thought that the King would censure Mussolini. The King refused to do this and in time, Mussolini, having temporarily arrested the murderers, was allowed to recover his position. The Aventine Secession greatly reduced opposition to Mussolini and while Fascist membership may have dropped and moderates turned away in the wake of the Matteotti murder, Mussolini was thereafter enabled to create the machinery of dictatorship. In a daring speech on 3rd January 1923, he assumed full responsibility for what happened and asserted that he would now put the country to rights.

Dictatorship

In 1925 all other political parties in Italy were suppressed and the Fascist Party became the only 'legitimate' party in the state. Around the same time, the press was effectively muzzled. New press laws of June 1925 ensured that the people heard only what Mussolini wanted them to hear. Newspapers contained an exaggerated worship of Mussolini, Italy's man of destiny who was known simply as *Il Duce* (The Leader). The cult of Mussolini was especially fostered in *Il Popola d'Italia*, a newspaper edited by his brother, Arnaldo. *"Mussolini is always right"* and *"Believe, Obey, Fight"* were common catchphrases. In 1926, Mussolini's personal rule was further strengthened when he was given the power to by-pass parliament and to govern by decree, a privilege he used over 100,000 times during his dictatorship. The bureaucracy and the judiciary were brought within the system. In 1928, the Grand Council was given the authority to choose 400 names from lists provided by unions of employers and employees and present them to the electorate for approval. In that same year, the right to vote became dependent on membership of a Fascist syndicate. Simultaneously, Mussolini and his henchmen maintained loyalty and devotion through a system of terror. Fascist thugs were given a free hand and in 1927 a secret police force called the *OVRA* was set up. The *OVRA* dealt with those who opposed the regime. In so doing, it was helped by the existence of special courts which tried enemies of the state. Those accused of crimes were allowed no witnesses, no jury and no right of appeal. The tribunals had the power to sentence people to death. Prisons, which were nothing more than concentration camps or penal settlements were built on islands off the coast of Italy. Such strong-armed tactics were responsible for spreading fear and terror throughout Italy. They were the price of dictatorship.

The Corporate State

One of Fascism's most interesting contributions to economic history was the Corporation system by which it was intended to replace or transcend the out-of-date ideas of liberalism and socialism. Trade unions were abolished, and strikes and lock-outs forbidden as each company and profession formed its own corporation. These consisted of employer delegates, employee delegates and three Fascist members. In July 1926, a Ministry of Corporations was set up. This sought to regulate and co-ordinate the activities of corporations. The General Assembly of Corporations was later formed. Presided over by Mussolini himself, it decided on important industrial policy, such as wages and prices. The *'Charter of Labour'* of April 1927 made work *'a social duty'* and voluntary withdrawal of labour a punishable offence. Hailed as the Magna Carta of the Fascist revolution and even *"the greatest document in the whole of history"*, Mussolini envisaged a situation where one day the corporations would effect what would amount to compulsory recruitment of all Italian civilians for civilian work.

28. Mussolini's Domestic Policy

In 1929, Mussolini optimistically announced that the former antagonism between capital and labour was at an end and that both sides of industry were working together with complete parity of rights and duties. Yet, for all the rhetoric about the corporations being *"Fascist institutions par excellence"* and the *"corner stone of the Fascist state"*, the directing force for the whole economy and the most original creation of the regime, they were, in practice, responsible for much bureaucratic bungling and bribery. The Corporation State never lived up to its claims of bringing social justice for it showed a bias towards the interests and purposes of the wealthier classes.

The Economy [I]

With the economy, as elsewhere, Mussolini wanted people to think his intuition *"was almost infallible"* - hence he gave an impression of confidence and certainty as he manipulated economic facts. Mussolini aimed first and foremost to obtain self-sufficiency, especially in food production. This policy of autarky went hand in hand with *Il Duce*'s desire to keep Italy agricultural, for Mussolini believed that urbanisation was threatening to endanger the food supply of a rapidly growing community. Another hazard of urbanisation was that as people moved to the towns they began to think and talk too much. Peasants, Mussolini believed, were more necessary to Fascism than intellectuals or town artisans. Consequently, cities were condemned as *'pernicious and parasitic'* and attempts were made to stop any move away from the land, by force if necessary. But this was a battle that Mussolini couldn't win and towns went on expanding as before. On the surface, the *'Battle for Grain'*, launched in June 1925, was more successful. This battle, which was close to Mussolini's heart, attempted to *"free the people from the slavery of foreign bread"*. High import taxes were imposed on all cereals. The result was that while cereal production did increase substantially it did so at a great cost. The Italian climate was not particularly suitable for cereal growing so that the yield per hectare was relatively low. There was also the loss of export markets for other produce no longer produced on land that had been converted to cereal growing. The *'Battle for Land Reclamation'* was more genuinely successful. A great deal of money was allocated by the government to drainage, irrigation, reafforestation and farm building. The draining of 60,000 hectares of malarial infested marshes at Pontine, near Rome, transformed the land and allowed for the resettlement there of 75,000 families from the poor south.

The Economy [II]

A further and undoubtedly more unusual battle was the *'Battle for Births'*. Mussolini, in order to encourage marriage and parenthood, imposed taxes on bachelorhood from 1926 onwards. Yet legislation and propaganda failed to bring about an increase in Italy's birthrate. Meanwhile, efforts were made to cure the worse excesses of unemployment by introducing a public works programme. New motorways *(autostrada)* were built, as were railways, hospitals and hydro-electric dams. For the first time in the history of Italian transport, trains ran on time. Impressive public buildings were erected, while ancient monuments were reconstructed. Improved schemes of insurance, covering accident, sickness and unemployment bettered the position of some Italian workers. Any evaluation of the economic life of Italy in the post-war years, however, show that other than in the few years prior to 1925, real growth was small. The Minister of Finance, De Stefani, had in those years succeeded in balancing the books and attracting considerable foreign investment. Unemployment fell to an all time low of 100,000. De Stefani's dismissal in 1925 saw some change in economic policy. Mussolini became more directly involved and he insisted that national prestige should take priority. The lira was revalued in 1926 by 10%. This caused great hardship as Italian exports became relatively more expensive. Problems were further aggravated by the depression and in 1932 unemployment exceeded 1 million. Only in 1936 did Mussolini devalue the lira. Grants and government orders added to the burden on state resources. Perhaps more than anything else, the speed with which the economy collapsed during the war demonstrated the superficiality of the economic progress of these years. Under all the show, the problems of poverty and shortages of raw materials remained.

The Catholic Church

Since boyhood, Mussolini had not been a churchgoer and his anti-clericalism, which was never far beneath the surface, was such that he scorned the rites and dogmas of the Church. Italy, however, was a Catholic country and history had taught him that he would hardly emerge unscathed from a head-on struggle with the Church. Thus, when Mussolini founded the Fascist movement he realised that *"the papacy was an ally he was unwilling to lose; it was an enemy he could not afford to make"*. Mussolini decided that the Church and Fascism could help each other. Accordingly, Mussolini moved towards friendlier relations with the Church. He publicly proclaimed that he had once more converted to Christianity and was now a good Catholic. Mussolini had his children baptised in 1923 and then regularised his family status when he had his civil marriage blessed by a Catholic ceremony in 1925. Crucifixes were restored, not just in schools, but also in courthouses. The Church, for its part, was greatly pleased by the anti-communism of Fascism. The Church also approved of Fascists' opposition to birth control, divorce and abortion. Nightlife was severely restricted and a Press campaign was launched against alcoholism as Fascism assumed an austere and strait-laced appearance for the outside world. Mussolini's attempts to deliver Italy from the heresies of liberalism was such that Pope Pius XI referred to him in the 1920s as *"a man sent by Providence"*. The most tangible evidence of the improved relations between church and state came in 1929 when the Lateran Treaty and Concordat was signed. This brought the church-state conflict - which had existed since 1870 - to an end. Under the terms of the treaty the Pope was recognised as head of the tiny Vatican City state and was heavily compensated (£10m) for the loss of the papal states. Catholicism was recognised as the state religion in Italy. Mussolini gained increased national and international recognition as a result of the treaty and although good relations between the Pope and Mussolini did not last, it was to prove one of the most enduring legacies of the Fascist regime.

Education - Youth - Totalitarianism

Mussolini was well aware of the need to achieve total control of education. Educational reform began in 1923. School teachers were forced to take an oath of loyalty to the Fascist regime. Those that did not toe the party line were dismissed.

28. Mussolini's Domestic Policy

History was rewritten: *"It was Italy's entry that decided the fate of the war... it was Italy that won the war at the Battle of Vittorio Veneto"*. New compulsory textbooks emphasised Italian greatness. Sport was also stressed. The need to control every aspect of arts, learning and culture was evident in the setting up of an Italian Academy in 1926 to *"co-ordinate and direct"* Italian culture. In that same year, the *Balilla* Youth Organisation was created. Children were expected to join at the age of 8 years. At 14 they graduated into the Avanti-Guardisti Corps and at 18 they were compulsorily recruited into the Fascist Party. The motto of the *Balilla* was *"live dangerously"*, its symbols the rifle and book. All organisations aimed to produce good Fascists and to further the one-party totalitarian state *"everything within the state, nothing outside the state, nothing against the state"*. Yet for all that, Italy was never fully totalitarian, particularly if compared with Nazi Germany or Soviet Russia. Francis T. Holohan concludes that *"Rather, it was a unique type of nationalist dictatorship which perfected the cult of the leader, fed off its own propaganda, and was eventually brought to ruin when it fell under the spell of Nazi totalitarianism"*.

29. Mussolini's Foreign Policy

Importance of Foreign Policy - Aims

Such was Mussolini's belief in the importance of foreign policy that, apart from a brief interlude during the period 1922-1936, he acted as his own Foreign Minister. Thereafter, his son-in-law, Count Galeazzo Ciano, held the office. Through him, Mussolini retained control. In the pursuit of a successful expansionist foreign policy, Mussolini acted with an eye on the domestic front. Frequently he sought to distract attention from internal problems while simultaneously wishing to impress Italians with successes abroad even if these successes were ephemeral or illusory and won him few foreign friends. Certainly, Mussolini tended to be the bully rather than the negotiator, believing that it was more advantageous to be feared than liked. Aggressive and outrageous statements, *"It is a crime not to be strong"*, *"peacemongering is folly"*, *"a minute on the battlefield is worth a lifetime of peace"* underline his military-style policy. Mussolini insisted again and again that Italians must learn to feel themselves *"in a permanent state of war"* as they moved towards making this *"the century of Italian power"*. The three main areas of planned Fascist expansion were to be the Balkans, Southern Europe and North Africa, while the Mediterranean was to be an Italian lake, *'Mare nostrum'* (our sea). Yet Mussolini was all too often erratic in the methods that he used to win glory and power for Italy. At the same time as he told Italians that his aim was national grandeur, he told foreigners that his policy was one of peace and co-operation. Inconsistency in foreign policy, as in other matters, cannot go undetected.

The Corfu Incident - League Membership

During its first year of rule, Fascism gave the world opportunity to judge its ideas on world policy, not only by official declarations but by actual proof. In August 1923, four Italians and an Albanian were murdered on Greek territory while drawing up a border for the League of Nations between Greece and Albania. The event provided Mussolini with a welcome opportunity for imperialist expansion. Two days after the murders, the Italian government presented an ultimatum to the Greek government which demanded an official apology and the payment of an indemnity of 50 million lire within five days. Mussolini had deliberately made the demands impossible for Greece to accept. On the pretext of an unsatisfactory answer, he had the Greek island of Corfu bombarded and occupied. Mussolini refused to allow the League of Nations to settle the matter under dispute, threatening to secede from the League if necessary. The Conference of Ambassadors of Allied Powers thus dealt with the issue. Mussolini was ordered to evacuate Corfu while the Greek government was forced to pay the 50 million lire. The Corfu incident appeared to suggest that aggression did pay and was seen as a triumph by Italian nationalists. However there were some elements of defeat in the affair. The costs of occupation had reached the considerable sum of 80 million lire while England and France drew closer together as they made common cause against Mussolini. The Italo-Greek incident also brought home Italy's difficult position within the League of Nations. Italy remained a member of the organisation in that it suited her purposes to do so but her membership was insincere. While on the one hand

Mussolini pledged that *"Fascism accepts as highest postulate the League of Nations"*, on the other, Mussolini claimed that *"Fascism does not believe in the vitality and the principles which inspire the so-called League of Nations"*. It seemed that Italy wished to remain in the League to exploit it in her own interest until such time as her resignation *"would signal the end or at least the certain beginning of the end"* of the League of Nations.

Fiume - Albania - Libya

Only weeks after the Corfu incident, Mussolini sent a military officer to govern the city of Fiume, which he claimed was falling into anarchy. Since Yugoslavia's ally, France, was preoccupied with the Ruhr and King Alexander of Yugoslavia was an admirer, Mussolini managed to secure an agreement with Yugoslavia in January 1924 by which Fiume was finally annexed to the Italian state. This was a major triumph for Mussolini and proved that he could use traditional methods of diplomacy when it was really necessary. Another diplomatic success was the recognition of Soviet Russia in 1924. Mussolini was anxious to maintain that his was the first Western government to give formal recognition to the Russians. When the British preceded him by a few days, Mussolini sent protests to both London and Moscow at the *"impudence of such a blow to Italian prestige"*. In the 1920s Mussolini also showed himself anxious to win a predominant position in Albania, across the Adriatic Sea. He sought to turn Albania into an Italian puppet by lavishing money and arms. The result was the establishment of a protectorate in Albania in 1926. Libya, an Italian colony since 1912, was an area where Mussolini ordered a 'hard-hitting' policy. Free speech and other liberties were withdrawn and in 1926, on a personal visit to Libya, Mussolini made a grand theatrical gesture when he arrived with two battleships and 15 other naval vessels. The visit sparked off a protracted and expensive war with Libyan 'rebels' which came to an end in 1932 with an uneasy peace.

Mussolini as a Man of Peace

Mussolini knew that he could not afford to be isolated in the councils of Europe. This prompted him to ask other countries not to take too seriously his bellicose outbursts *"we shall all make ugly faces at each other but nobody means to fight"*, and to attend many international conferences in the 1920s as well as signing a number of treaties. These were chiefly a matter of the publicity he could extract from them, for Mussolini was ready to sign a treaty just for the effect on the public and without bothering too much about the details of what it contained. Treaties were mere pieces of paper with no binding force if circumstances changed. Consequently, Mussolini attended the Locarno Conference in 1925. Although he briefly attended only one session, *'Il Popola d'Italia'* described how a large audience was deeply impressed by what he had to say. No mention was made of the fact that 100 journalists boycotted his appearance in protest against Fascist brutality. In any case, Mussolini's signing of the Locarno Treaty which agreed to honour existing borders between Germany and her Western neighbours, France and Belgium, allowed Mussolini to adopt the role of statesman. In 1928, Mussolini signed the Kellogg-Briand Pact outlawing war as an instrument of national policy. Privately, Mussolini hoped that the Pact would fail, jocularly remarking that he had already agreed to 134 different international conventions in two years and that he could hardly be upset by one more. Thereafter, the two-faced posture of aggression and pacifism continued. As Mussolini spoke to the outside world of disarmament he thought of *"adorable"* machine guns, bomber aircraft and war. Meanwhile, the rise of Hitler and the Nazis worried Mussolini and in 1934 he made clear his opposition to a union between Germany and Austria. In January 1935 a formal treaty was signed with France. Then at Stresa in April, Italy, France and Britain jointly condemned Hitler's re-armament plans and committed themselves *"to close and cordial collaboration to maintain the status quo in Europe"*.

Invasion of Abyssinia

Believing that France and Britain would curtail Hitler's aggressiveness, Mussolini turned his attention to North Africa in 1935, and, in particular, to Abyssinia. Abyssinia bordered on two existing Italian colonies, Eritrea and Italian Somaliland, so could be attacked simultaneously from north and south. Its resources were said to include great riches ranging from pineapples to platinum. Using the Italian defeat of Adowa in 1896 and Italy's subsequent expulsion from Abyssinia as well as the death of 30 Italian soldiers at Walwal in 1934, Mussolini, on 3rd October 1935, launched his attack, without first declaring war. By employing aeroplane bombs, machine guns, artillery and poison gas on a large scale, the Italians had little difficulty in overcoming Abyssinian resistance. But Abyssinia was a League of Nations member and its emperor, Haile Selaisse, applied to the organisation for help. Italy was condemned as an aggressor and economic sanctions were imposed. In practice, the sanctions proved of little use. As there were no precedents, it was a slow job devising the mechanism for their application. A further difficulty was that sanctions were only partial, oil and coal being excluded. There were also a few states that refused to apply the penalty. The sanctions thus failed to affect the outcome of the war. In May 1936, Marshal Badoglio led the capture of the Abyssinian capital, Addis Ababa. Mussolini triumphantly declared the creation of an Italian empire with Victor Emmanuel III as emperor. The attack on Abyssinia, while successful, was not without a number of important repercussions. These included the break up of the Stresa Front and the withdrawal of Italy from the League of Nations in December 1937.

Relations with Hitler

A further consequence of the Abyssinian attack was that it drove Mussolini to have closer ties with Hitler's Germany. Hitler was the only major leader not to have criticised Italian aggression and relations between the two now started to improve. Italian newspapers were ordered to be pro-German and in October 1936, Foreign Minister Ciano signed the Rome-Berlin Axis around which, it was believed, the affairs of Europe should revolve. On this rather loose agreement of friendship between Germany and Italy Mussolini declared *"we shall march together to the very end"*. In 1937, Italy joined the Anti-Comintern Pact of Germany and Japan, by which she pledged her opposition to Communism. In joining the Pact, Italy had unexpectedly changed sides because hitherto Fascists had been strongly against the Japanese and in favour of the Chinese. Already Mussolini, even as he spoke of a partnership of equals, was starting to conform to Germany policy. The price of friendship with Hitler was also such that when Hitler annexed Austria in March 1938, Mussolini made no effort to stop him. Hitler next provoked the *'Czech crisis'* over the Sudetenland, and Mussolini was among those leaders who mediated with Hitler at the Munich Conference of September 1938. The Munich Agreement appeared to be Mussolini's idea. Certainly Mussolini gloried in the role of peacemaker, believing himself to have saved Europe. In reality, however, what took place in Munich was much more likely to be German in origin. In any event, the agreement left non-German Czechoslovakia helpless and isolated. Meanwhile, Germany continued to push for a full military alliance with Italy. The alliance came in the form of the Pact of Steel, May 1939. Both parties agreed *"to act side by side"* in the task of safeguarding the foundations of civilisation.

From Spain to Albania 1936-1939

Mussolini's first military venture with Hitler was support for Franco and the Nationalist forces in the Spanish Civil War, 1936-1939. A common meeting ground for the three Fascist leaders, Mussolini, Hitler and Franco, was found in this war against Communism. During the 1937-1938 period, Mussolini had over 70,000 troops in Spain. Large quantities of planes, weapons and ammunition were also supplied. Italy's intervention in the Spanish Civil War, however, was an expensive commitment which brought little reward. Along with the other wars that Mussolini had fought since 1926, Spain ensured that Italy was militarily and economically exhausted before World War II even started. And yet Italy continued to doctor statistics and to give the impression that a substantial army could be mobilised in a matter of hours. Experience of war thus far stimulated, rather than reduced, Mussolini's instinctive delight in *"punitive action"*. Nonetheless, when news broke of Hitler's invasion of Czechoslovakia (March 1939), Mussolini, caught unawares, was perturbed by the blow to his personal prestige, and feared he would be laughed at for his gullibility in believing Hitler's promises of no further aggression at Munich. While he thought of changing sides and renouncing the German friendship, Mussolini upon further contemplation, pretended to approve of what Hitler was doing and to seek for himself a compensatory conquest in Albania. In April 1939 Italian troops overran the country. King Zog fled to France while another crown, that of Albania, was handed to Victor Emmanuel. Although the annexation of Albania had cost a lot of money and the economic potential of the country was negligible, Mussolini believed that the Italians by their action there and elsewhere, had proved that their destiny was to dominate other countries. At once he started to use his new Albanian base for an attack at some future date on Greece and Yugoslavia.

Outbreak of War - Conclusion

Some recognition of Italy's real military strength was necessary when in September 1939 World War II broke out as a result of Hitler's invasion of Poland. This showed a marked difference between Italy's theoretical and practical position. Mussolini's appreciation of this fact was such that he insisted he was ready to join Germany only on condition that 17,000 train loads of materials were sent to help his re-armament. This was, as he well knew and intended, an impossible demand, designed as an excuse not to fight. Hitler reproached Mussolini with taunts of cowardice and bad faith but Mussolini persisted, maintaining that he had not expected war to come so soon and that Germany's sudden attack on Poland exonerated Italy from the Pact of Steel obligation. Since the word *'neutral'* was considered un-Fascist, Mussolini coined the term *'non-belligerent'* to describe Italy's position. Meanwhile, Italy sought to fortify her northern frontiers with Germany for fear of a possible attack. As hostilities continued, Mussolini fluctuated between readiness to intervene on one side or another and the fear that Italy was not yet in a position to fight. But by June 1940, Mussolini was convinced that Germany would win and unless he took the plunge, the Germans might get *'all the booty'* for themselves. Hence his decision to bring his country into war. This was a decision that ultimately was to prove to be Mussolini's undoing and to lead to the collapse of his Fascist state. Any examination of Mussolini's foreign policy shows that his was a complex and contradictory personality, all too willing to believe in the myth of his own infallibility. He proved, however, to be less of a 'leader' than might appear from his myth. He had little capacity for long-range planning, and for all his brilliance as a political tactician in the really serious crisis of his political career, he often proved himself hesitant and vacillating. Mussolini himself drew the conclusion that *"no dictator could ever calculate with prudence, because all dictators in the end lose any sense of balance as they pursue their obsessive ambitions into a world of unreality"*.

Mussolini's Italy: Past Exam Questions

1994

D2. Mussolini

   Describe the part played by Mussolini in Italian affairs during the period 1922-1940.

1989

D2. Mussolini

   Analyse the part played by Benito Mussolini in the history of Italy.

1986

E4. Essay

   (v) Fascism in Italy

Congress of Berlin, 1878 - Bismarck, Disraeli and other European statesmen discuss the colonisation of Africa

Lenin in 1918

Leon Trotsky

The German war leadership: Ludendorff, the Kaiser, Hindenburg.

The 1914-1918 war saw a new form of fighting: trench warfare. British troops go over the top under a German barrage in Flanders.

The Bauhaus, the highly influential school of architecture and design founded by Walter Gropius in 1919. The headquarters at Dessau was designed by Gropius (1925-1926)

Heads of state of the victorious powers at the 1919 Versailles peace conference: Vittorio Orlando, David Lloyd George, Georges Clemenceau, Woodrow Wilson.

HITLER'S GERMANY

30. Adolf Hitler, 1889-1945

Background - Early Influences and Involvements

Hitler was born on 20th April 1889 in the Austrian town of Brannau. His father was a customs official for the Austrian government. At school, Hitler proved to be a lazy, bad tempered student. He developed a loathing for teachers whom he described as *"erudite apes"*. In spite of a keen interest in art, Hitler failed to gain entry into the Vienna Academy of Fine Arts. Nonetheless, he moved to Vienna when he was 18 years. There he eked out a living as an artist. The years in Vienna were subsequently recalled as the unhappiest of Hitler's life. Yet they were formative years when Hitler, influenced by Lanz von Libenfels and Schönerer, developed very strong nationalistic and anti-semitic views. In May 1913, Hitler left Vienna for Munich. With the outbreak of the First World War in August 1914, Hitler enlisted in the German army. He fought on the Western Front for four years and was decorated with the Iron Cross for bravery. Promoted to the rank of corporal, Hitler bitterly resented the German surrender in 1918 which he described as *"the most terrible certainty of my life"*. After the war, Hitler remained in the army and was stationed in Munich where he was given the task of spying on the newly developing political parties. One such party was the German Workers' Party, founded by Anton Drexter in January 1919. Hitler attended his first meeting of the party on 12th September 1919 and soon afterwards joined the party's organising committee. Hitler's oratorical gifts proved indispensable to the party which in 1920 was renamed the National Socialist German Workers' Party. In 1921, Hitler became its leader. In spirit, the Nazi party was anti-semitic, anti-communist and anti-parliamentary. Weimar politicians were condemned as *'The November Criminals'* because through surrender and acceptance of the Versailles settlement, they had proved themselves *"miserable and degenerate traitors"*. Early recruits to the party included Josef Goebbels, Heinrich Himmler, Hermann Göring, Rudolf Hess, Ernst Röhm and Julius Streicher.

Vacillating Fortunes

With the Weimar government facing economic and political crisis in 1923, Hitler decided to make a bid for power. This came in the form of the Munich Putsch. On 8th November, the Nazis took over a beer hall in Munich and declared that *"the national revolution had begun"*. The following day, Hitler, Ludendorff* and about 2,000 brown-shirted Nazi stormtroopers marched through Munich where they were confronted by a large force of armed police. When firing started, the Nazi supporters fled in disorder. 14 Nazis and three policemen were killed. Two days later, Hitler was arrested. He used his trial to gain much publicity by making defiant political speeches

---

* Heroic World War I leader of the German army.

from the dock. Hitler was given a minimum sentence of 5 years. During his imprisonment in Landsberg, Hitler wrote the first volume of his autobiography, *'Mein Kampf'* (My Struggle). Released early from prison, in December 1924, Hitler found a more stable and prosperous country awaiting him. Determined to outvote rather than outshoot his opponents, Hitler used the *"Golden Age of the Weimar Republic"*, 1924-29, to rebuild his party and give it organisational structure. The stormtroopers, or SA, were placed under the care of Captain Ernst Röhm while Hitler's own paramilitary bodyguard, the SS, was controlled by Heinrich Himmler. Party membership rose from 27,000 members in 1925 to 178,000 in 1928. Yet the Nazis gained only 12 seats in the *Reichstag* in the general election of 1928. The breakthrough came in October 1929 with the death of Stresemann and the Wall Street Crash. The world depression which followed hit Germany with devastating force. American loans were recalled and hardship, hunger and discontent became all too common. In 1932 unemployment soared to 6 million. A succession of unstable ministries under Herman Müller, Henrich Brüning, von Papen and von Schleicher proved unable to cope. Hitler, meanwhile, exploited every opportunity to break onto the national scene. Offering answers to the many problems which beset the country, he became Germany's *'man of steel'*. Such was his success that in July 1932, the Nazis won 230 seats in the *Reichstag*.

Hitler in Power - Dictatorship

On 30th January 1933, President Hindenburg appointed Hitler Chancellor. As Chancellor, Hitler led a 12-man ministerial cabinet which contained only two other Nazis, Göring and Frich. The belief that Hitler could easily be contained proved within a short time to be nothing more than a vain hope. Hitler's first move was to announce news of a forthcoming general election, on 5th March 1933. Before this took place, on 27th February, the *Reichstag* building conveniently went on fire. A Dutch Communist, Marinus van der Lubbe was blamed and, on the following day, Hitler managed to persuade Hindenburg to pass a decree for the Protection of People and State. Civil liberties were suspended and the police were given widespread powers of arrest and detention. The election campaign was dramatised as a struggle to save Europe from the *'Red Threat'*. Despite a daily barrage of Nazi propaganda, terror and violence, the Nazis gained just 44% of the votes - 288 seats. Hitler was, nonetheless, empowered to pass the Enabling Act on 23rd March. This allowed Hitler to govern by decree. The Nazis were well and truly in the saddle. German trade unions were now banned, political parties dissolved and federal states and the civil service controlled. The first real threat to Hitler's totalitarianism came from within the party itself, namely from Ernst Röhm and the SA. Increasingly critical of Hitler, Röhm and the SA began to call for a second revolution and for the merging of the SA and the regular army. Hitler acted swiftly. On 30th June 1934, the *'Night of the Long Knives'*, Röhm and around 400 members of the SA were killed. Decimated and leaderless, the SA was now replaced in importance by the SS and the *Gestapo*, the secret state police under Göring and Himmler. Hitler's dictatorship was further aided by the death of President Hindenburg in August 1934. Hitler as *'Der Führer'* inherited the presidential powers, including supreme commander of the armed forces.

Life in Nazi Germany

In power, Hitler aimed towards economic self-sufficiency, autarky. A vast modernisation programme took place which included a scheme of public works. New motorways, the *Autobahnen*, were built, railways were improved and cheap houses were constructed for workers. As industry flourished, consumer goods became more plentiful. Employment, which had stood at 6 million in 1933 was negligible by 1939. The expansion of the armed forces, the state bureaucracy and the Nazi Party all helped to create this 'miracle'. Agriculture was not quite so successful, however, and there was an over-importation of foreign goods. The diversion of money from agriculture to armaments led to the famous *'guns or butter'* controversy. Meanwhile, propaganda played a tremendous role in projecting Nazi ideology and ensuring loyalty to Hitler and the party. Every aspect of the media was controlled, mass rallies were held and short memorable statements such as *''Deutschland, Deutschland, über alles'.* (Germany, Germany above everything) were frequently heard. Nationalism was brought onto what could only be considered a spiritual level. And through the manipulation of school curricula, indoctrination became an everyday occurrence. Youth movements taught loyalty and devotion to *'Der Führer'*. Those who spoke out were brutally dealt with. Undoubtedly, those who suffered most were the Jews whom Hitler believed to be the *"eternal fissure fungus of humanity"*. A Jew was automatically deemed to be *"a parasite, a sponger"*, responsible for Germany's ills. Anti-semitic legislation included the Nuremberg Laws of 1935. Not only were Jews deprived of German citizenship and civil rights, they were also forced to wear the identifying Star of David. Increasingly, they were denied all but the most menial of jobs. Then on 9th-10th November 1938, *'Crystal Night'*, Jewish premises were wrecked, synagogues burnt and 91 Jews killed. Worse persecution was yet to follow.

Foreign Policy

Hitler's foreign policy was ambitious and dynamic. His aims of destroying the Treaty of Versailles, uniting all Germans into a single country and of providing Germany with *Lebensraum*, or living space, in Eastern Europe could not but bode ill for the future. They involved taking risks and showing force. Hitler's first move on the international front was to walk out of the League of Nation's Disarmament Conference in October 1933 when other powers refused to disarm. Hitler subsequently withdrew from the League of Nations. In January 1934 a ten year Non-Aggression Pact was signed with Poland. The following year, January 1935, another diplomatic triumph was scored when the inhabitants of the Saar voted by 90% to return to Germany. In that same year Hitler spoke openly about a new German airforce, the *Luftwaffe*. He also announced plans to conscript an army of over half a million. The common political Stresa Front of Britain, France and Italy against German aggression came to nothing when Britain signed the Anglo-German Naval Pact of June 1935 by which terms Germany promised not to exceed 35% of Britain's naval strength. Hitler's biggest gamble to date was taken in March 1936 when he marched his troops into the Rhineland. Although he had instructed his forces to withdraw at the least sign of resistance, no effort was made to stop them. Improved relations between the two Fascist leaders, Hitler and Mussolini, could be seen in October 1936 when they signed the Rome-Berlin Axis. The following month, the Anti-Comintern Pact was signed.

During the Spanish Civil War, 1936-1939, Hitler and Mussolini engaged in joint military action. Then in 1939, the *'Pact of Steel'*, a formal military alliance, was signed between the two.

The Road to War

The union of Austria and Germany, the *Anschluss*, was forbidden by the Treaty of Versailles. Yet Hitler, who was himself Austrian, saw the union as the fulfilment of a lifetime ambition. In 1934 he had considered taking over Austria but when the other powers, including Italy, made known their opposition, Hitler held back. In 1938, feeling more confident of his ability to pull off the union, Hitler used 'bully boy' tactics on the Austrian Chancellor, Schuschnigg, who was eventually forced to resign. He was replaced by a leading Nazi, Seyss-Inquart. Then on 12th March 1938, the German army marched into Austria. When, a month later, a plebiscite was held, over 99% of Austrians approved the Greater Germany. Hitler proclaimed that this was *"the proudest moment of my life"*. The Sudetenland in Czechoslovakia, which contained 3 million German speakers, was Hitler's next focus of attention. Prompted by Hitler, Konrad Henlein, a leading Sudeten Nazi, began to stir up trouble. The Czechs were accused of discrimination against the local German inhabitants. Hitler demanded justice for the *"tortured creatures"* against intolerable Czech rule. Riots, demonstrations and calls for self-government brought the threat of war all too close. In September 1938 a conference of the great powers was held in Munich. Czechoslovakia, which was not invited to attend, was forced to concede the Sudetenland to Germany. That Hitler's pledge of no further aggression was but an empty promise was made all too clear in March 1939 when a German army of occupation took control of the remainder of Czechoslovakia. Hitler's next move was to sign the Nazi-Soviet Pact of August 1939. Germany and Russia agreed not to fight with each other for a 10-year period. Secret clauses allowed for the partition of Poland. With his rear secure, Hitler invaded Poland on 1st September 1939. On 3rd September, Britain and France declared war on Germany. International diplomacy had failed. The Second World War had begun.

World War II

The German war, 1939-45, was very much Hitler's war, controlling, as he did, the war department and the armed forces, consisting of the army, navy and airforce (*Luftwaffe*). The forces at his disposal were formidable, although perhaps not as powerful as Hitler made others believe. In any case, Poland was overrun in four weeks. From October 1939 to April 1940 there was very little real or substantial fighting, so that people began to speak in terms of a *'phoney war'*. But in April 1940, the Germans occupied Denmark and Norway. The invasion of Belgium and Holland on 10th May 1940 opened the period of *'Blitzkrieg'*, or lightning warfare. Penetration by German tanks and the use of air power ensured the fall of the Netherlands within four days, Belgium within three weeks and France within seven weeks. Hitler's defeat of France provided the revenge he sought for the humiliation of 1918-1919. The Battle of Britain, which began in July 1940, proved to be Germany's first big military setback. Unable to win that war, the Germans moved eastwards. Yugoslavia and Greece were invaded in April 1941. Operation Barbarossa, the German invasion of Russia, began on 22nd June 1941. Hitler never had any intention of being bound by the Nazi-Soviet Pact. Believing the Red Army to be *"no more than a joke"* his troops relentlessly advanced through Russia. The three main areas of attack were Leningrad, Moscow and Kiev. By December 1941, Hitler was within an ace of achieving his objective. Kiev had been taken and German forces were 20 miles from Moscow. The Russians counter-attacked, however, and increasingly the Germans were put on the defensive. The defeat of Rommel and his desert forces at El Alamein in North Africa in October 1942, defeat in the battle of Stalingrad, January 1943, the fall of Mussolini in July 1943 and the successful D-day landings on 6th June 1944, were bad blows for Hitler. The last major offensive in the Ardennes, December 1944 to January 1945, ended all possibility of success.

Conclusion - Horror - Defeat - Death

Life in occupied Europe was difficult, to say the least, but it was in the treatment of the Jews that Nazism was revealed in all its horror. The extermination of all the Jews in Europe was Hitler's *'final solution'*. Mass extermination camps, poison gas chambers, the use of human guinea pigs for experimentation, was the fate of 6 million Jews who lost their lives. Annihilation of gypsies and *'inferior'* Asiatics was also part of Hitler's solution. Ultimately, however, defeat awaited Hitler. In March 1945, the Allied armies crossed the Rhine while the Russians began their invasion of Germany from the East. The Battle of Berlin began on 19th April of that year. It was marked by bitter street fighting and strong German resistance. Hitler, who had spent the last month of the war in an underground bunker beneath the Reich Chancellery in Berlin, had no alternative but death. On 29th April 1945, he married his mistress, Eva Braun. The following day they were both dead, having committed suicide. On instructions dictated by Hitler beforehand, their bodies were burned. Hitler's nominated successor, Admiral Doenitz, who was not a high-ranking Nazi, agreed to the *"unconditional surrender of all German forces"* on 7th May. The following day, VE Day (Victory in Europe Day), all military activity in Europe ceased. Thus it was that Hitler and all he represented, his memory of horror, was destroyed. In a biography of Hitler, Alan Bullock maintained of his career that it *"did not exalt but debased the human condition, and his twelve-year dictatorship was barren of all ideas save one - the further extention of his own power and that of the nation with which he had identified with"*. It is perhaps the great tragedy of the Third Reich that the millions secretly critical of Hitler did not join with the handful in open opposition. Rather, they *"looked on, while a pack of fools, against whom destiny had long since decided, let the whole wonderful Reich be transformed into one single garbage heap"* (German writer).

31. Account for Hitler's Rise to Power in Germany

Introduction - Establishment of the Nazi Party

During the years 1933 to 1939 Hitler and the Nazis turned Germany into a one-party totalitarian state where the state wielded as much power over the individual as any other state in recorded history. But what enabled Hitler to rise to power in Germany and to subject the German people so thoroughly to the state machine? The answer can only be found in a look at post-war Germany, in the establishment of the Nazi party, the economic crisis resulting from the depression of the late 1920s and early 1930s, the failure of Weimar politics and of course, in Hitler's own skill and ability. Defeat for Germany in the First World War created a disturbed restlessness throughout the country which the new Republican regime based in Weimar found difficult to contend with. For all too many people, Weimar was *"the greatest villainy of the century"* and those responsible for it, and for accepting the Treaty of Versailles, were *"degenerate traitors"*. In addition, Weimar was handicapped by its own constitution which allowed for the development of a multiplicity of parties. Elections resulted in weak coalition governments where sectional interests were all too often more important than the national cause. Adolf Hitler (1889-1945) was among those ardent nationalists who scorned the *'November criminals'*. He dreamed of overthrowing the Republic and restoring Germany as the greatest power of continental Europe. With this goal in mind, Hitler in the post-war period was against joining an established party, preferring instead to find a struggling political group easy to take over and to mould into his own party. His opportunity to do just that came in September 1919 when Hitler was instructed by the Political Department to investigate the activities of the German Workers Party, one of the many political malcontent movements of the time. Hitler soon joined this small and obscure party. Renamed the National Socialist German Workers Party (Nazis), Hitler assumed the leadership position and slowly and painfully, he pushed the movement forward. His ability to exploit opportunities, his gift of oratory which allowed him to draw the crowds and to hold audiences spellbound, as well as his power to attract influential and powerful personalities to the party are of undoubted importance in the rise of the party to power some years later.

1923-1929

By 1923 the Weimar Republic was on the point of collapse. Hitler hoped to turn the political and economic crisis of that year to his advantage by staging a coup d'état or *'March on Berlin'* in imitation of Mussolini's *'March on Rome'*. Hitler's putsch started in a Munich beerhall in November 1923. Declaring that *"The national revolution has begun"*, Hitler, with the backing of General Ludendorff and other Bavarian nationalists, marched through Munich. The police and the army had been alerted and when they opened fire, the Nazis fled in disorder. In the trial which followed, Hitler received much publicity and ensured that his name was not forgotten. Released from prison after nine months, Hitler was convinced that *"Instead of working to achieve power by armed conspiracy, we shall have to hold our noses and enter the Reichstag against the Catholic and Marxist deputies. If outvoting them takes longer than outshooting them, at least the results will be guaranteed by their own constitution"*. Thus it was that Hitler sought to rebuild his near disintegrated and divided party. In particular, he concentrated on giving the party organisational structure and unquestioned leadership. The SA, semi-military defence squads under the leadership of Captain Ernst Röhm, rapidly developed. These groups were uniformed (Brownshirts) and were composed of ex-servicemen and *Freikorps*. More frightening was the elitist SS, Hitler's personal paramilitary bodyguard. Yet the years 1924 to 1929, the *'Golden Age of the Weimar Republic',* were lean years for the Nazis. Consequently, while membership of the Nazi party grew from 27,000 members in 1925 to 178,000 members in 1928, the movement remained a fringe group in German politics. In the 1928 elections, for example, the Nazis won only 12 seats. The years thereafter, however, were crucial in the decline of Weimar Germany and the rise of Hitler.

The Economic Crisis

It was the depression, which began in the USA in 1929, that tipped the scales against the Republic and for the first time since 1923 shifted the weight of advantage to Hitler's side. Because the prosperity of Weimar Germany was based primarily on borrowing rather than productivity, no country in the world was more susceptible to the depression which threatened the breakdown of the entire economic system. Economic symptoms were manifold and included contracting trade and production, the cessation of foreign loans and investments, the recall of money already lent, falls in prices and wages, the closing of factories and businesses, unemployment and bankruptcy as well as the forced sale of property and farms. Unemployment figures which stood at 1,320,000 in 1929 increased to 3,000,000 in 1930 and peaked at 6,000,000 in 1932. Alongside this was the incalculable human anxiety and embitterment which now burned in the minds of millions of ordinary German men and women who saw the apparently solid framework of their existence cracking and crumbling. In such circumstances, men were no longer amenable to the arguments of reason which seemed to get them nowhere. Rather, they began to entertain extravagant hopes and hatred which was exploited by the demagogy of Hitler, who realised all too well that drastic situations require drastic measures. With his cure-all policies, Hitler and the Nazis used the economic crisis to good effect. At the same time as the Nazi Party became the mass party of protest, it offered jobs to the unemployed, more land to the peasants and large government contracts to big businesses. Hitler insisted that *"If the economic experts say this or that is impossible, to hell with economics. What counts is will"*.

Political Weakness and Instability [I]

The fact that the depression years were those in which Hitler and the Nazis became a major factor in national politics is not accidental because the economic crisis produced a political crisis. The Weimar Republic, born out of defeat, was severely tested and in the final analysis, overwhelmed. What was especially obvious about Weimar Germany in the depression years was the refusal of political parties to sink their differences, unite in the face of emergency and jointly assume responsibility for the unpopular measures which had to be taken. A turning point in the history of the

Republic was the fall of Hermann Müller's coalition government in March 1930 as thereafter no party combination came into existence that could control a majority in the *Reichstag*. Heinrich Brüning, who succeeded Müller as Chancellor, persuaded President Hindenburg to invoke Article 48 of the Constitution which allowed rule by decree. But Brüning's position became increasingly precarious as the economic situation worsened and extremist parties, such as the Nazis, increased their support. In the September 1930 elections, Nazi numbers in the *Reichstag* went from 12 to 107. This ensured that the Nazis became the second largest party in the state and that Hitler, on the threshold of power, had become a politician of European importance. More than ever before, the party was turned into a highly organised machine. Between 1931 and 1933 membership of the party more than doubled, reaching a figure of 900,000 in January 1933. The SA also became increasingly efficient (as did the SS) and its illegal campaign of running street battles, and violence, complemented Hitler's legal campaign, *"Possession of the streets is the key to power in the state"*.

Political Weakness and Instability [II]

Brüning's efforts to balance the budget and cut expenditure proved very unpopular and increased hardship and discontent. It was clear that, under Brüning who was known as the *'Hunger Chancellor'* parliamentary democracy had failed. The Nazis continued to exploit Germany's, and indeed Brüning's, problems. Brüning was attacked as the embodiment of all the evils of the 'system' by which Germany had been governed since 1918. In April 1932, Hitler tested his popularity by contesting the presidential election against Hindenburg, who, aged 84 and very senile, was seeking re-election. Although Hitler lost, his personal vote of nearly 13 million was a considerable achievement. Brüning lasted only another month, decreeing belatedly the dissolution of the Nazi armed bands and continuing to grapple ineffectually with the economic crisis. Brüning was succeeded by Franz von Papen in June 1932. This right-wing Chancellor who ruled over a *'cabinet of barons'* lifted the ban on the SA and SS and tolerated the revival of Nazi party activities. The run-up to the July 1932 elections witnessed some of the worst political riots in the history of the Weimar Republic. The Nazis won 230 seats and became the largest party in the *Reichstag*. Von Papen, relying on Nazi support, made approaches to Hitler about Nazi participation in government, even offering Hitler the Vice-Chancellorship but Hitler refused to accept anything less than the position of Chancellor. This precipitated the resignation of von Papen and the November 1932 election in which the Nazis lost 34 seats. In spite of the drop in Nazi support and the appointment of General Kurt von Schleicher as Chancellor in December 1932, Hitler was to show that he was far from being a spent force and that his finest hour was not too far away.

The Rise of Communism

The Communists or Undemocratic Left, like the Nazis, won huge support during the depression years. In May 1928 they had a total of 54 seats in the *Reichstag*. This figure jumped to 77 seats in September 1930, to 89 seats in July 1932 and to 100 in November 1932. Such rapid increase in support gave rise to the spectre of Communism and the fear of a Communist revolution. Germany was, after all, the country designated by Karl Marx, where the Communist revolution would begin.

Added to that was the fact that there had already been a number of Communist risings in Germany. That Communism had succeeded in Russia at a time of crisis was a powerful reminder of just what could happen. Many people, consequently, began to turn to the Nazis as the only alternative to Communism. Banking, big businesses and large landowners all looked to the Nazi Party as a bulwark against the rising tide of Communism. They poured money into the party organisation as they realised that the party's socialism was not to be taken seriously, whereas its nationalism was impeccable. The Communists were further hindered by the manner in which they deliberately limited their appeal to one class, by their rigid doctrinaire beliefs and their international character. Nor did the Left in Germany do itself any favours by the refusal of the Communists and the Social Democrats, until 1932 the largest single party in the *Reichstag*, to present a common front against the Nazi challenge. This may be explained, in part, by the Communist view that Nazism would serve as the prelude to the proletarian revolution. Communists who adhered to this belief, almost 'willed' the Nazis to power. This, in time, would prove to be a fatal error.

Propaganda - Popular Policies

The importance of propaganda in increasing the Nazi vote and helping Hitler to power cannot be overlooked. The Nazis, under Goebbels, were masters of propaganda, using every modern means of communication to bring across their message. The walls of towns were plastered with Nazi posters, the Press was used to great effect, sensational charges and counter-charges generated interest and enthusiasm for the movement while mass meetings and demonstrations were frequent. Nuremberg, a city with strongly 'Germanic' buildings and fortifications, was the scene of mob oratory. Audiences were worked up to hysterical enthusiasm of the most unrestrained kind. Seeing thousands of Hitler's followers in their brownshirts and jackboots and the columns of Hitler Youth marching through the town, Germans were given the impression, as early as 1929, that the Nazis were numerically much stronger than they really were. Films of Hitler were made and shown everywhere and in the Presidential campaign of 1932, Goebbels' ingenious mind devised a novel electioneering device which involved sending Hitler from meeting to meeting by aeroplane in a *'Hitler over Germany'* campaign. The effect was startling. Hitler's insight into mass psychology was also used to great effect in his public oratory. As well as offering protection to the privileged, Hitler promised support for the middle classes, the 'little man', the worker and the peasant. He cleverly pilloried certain factors as being responsible for Germany's troubles. The Allies and their demands, the hated Treaty of Versailles, the Jews, the Communists and a succession of incompetent ministries were all used as scapegoats.

Miscalculation of his Enemies - Hitler in Power

Meanwhile, von Schleicher as Chancellor ruled without a parliamentary majority but also without much support from President Hindenburg, who refused to allow him to rule by decree. Schleicher's attempts to split the NSDAP (the Nazi Party) by offering posts to leading Nazis, proved unsuccessful and in January 1933 he resigned. By then, Hitler and von Papen had reached agreement. Von Papen would persuade Hindenburg to appoint Hitler as Chancellor of a minority government in which von

Papen and the right-wing nationalists were represented. It was intended by von Papen that Hitler would become a puppet, that he could be held in check and tamed. Thus, while Hitler's name was to go top of the bill, the real decisions would be taken by those who outnumbered him in the cabinet. Accordingly, on 30th January 1933, Hitler was appointed Chancellor. The reality of the following months showed just how bad the judgement of Hitler's political opponents and rivals was, for instead of being controlled, Hitler took the driving seat. Having increased Nazi representation in parliament and excluded the Communists, Hitler passed the Enabling Act of 23rd March 1933 by which he established himself as dictator of Germany. Thereafter, the Weimar Republic ceased to exist. In July 1933 the Nazis were declared to be the only legal political party within the *Reich*. The following year, upon the death of Hindenburg, Hitler merged the offices of Chancellor and President and became known simply as *'Der Führer'* (the leader). Terror, repression and propaganda penetrated all areas of life so that increasingly Germany became a totalitarian state. The Nazi *'bloodless'* or legal revolution had ensured that the despised prophet, *'the fool'*, entered into his inheritance. Hitler could well maintain that *"we are the result of the distress for which the others were responsible"*.

32. Hitler's Domestic Policy, 1933-1939

"We who are becoming a people, we are the raw stone
You, our leader, should be the stonemason .....
... For your stern hand wants to give us shape"
— Heinrich Anacker

Hitler Takes Power

On 30th January 1933, President Hindenburg appointed Hitler Chancellor of Germany. As Chancellor, Hitler led a 12-man ministerial cabinet which included two other Nazis, Wilhelm Frich as Minister of the Interior and Hermann Göring, Minister without Portfolio. It was believed at the time that Hitler could be controlled, Vice Chancellor von Papen boasting that *"we have hired him"* and *"within two months we will have pushed Hitler so far into the corner that he'll squeak"*. But Hitler had no intention of being manoeuvred by his cabinet colleagues. He was resolved to escape the conservative restraining influence of parliament and to subordinate the whole machinery of the state to his own will and direction. One of Hitler's first moves was to call for a general election to be held on 5th March 1933. Before this took place, on the night of 27th February, the *Reichstag* building went up in fire. While the Nazis may well have been themselves implicated in the fire, the Communists were blamed. A Dutch Communist, Marinus van der Lubbe, faced trial and execution for the crime. Hitler now spoke of the need to save Europe from the *'Red Threat'*. By the morning of 28th February, 4,000 Communist officials and party members had been arrested. Later on the 28th, Hitler persuaded the President to pass the Decree for the Protection of People and State. This gave the government the power to suspend the basic rights of citizens, to act outside the law and to arrest and execute those suspected of plotting against the state. Meanwhile, the election campaign of March 1933 was fought against a background of violence and intimidation. In spite of this, the Nazis fell short of an absolute majority, winning only 288 seats out of 647 in the *Reichstag*. A majority was obtained, however, by denying their seats to 181 Communist deputies and by combining with the Nationalist Party.

The Consolidation of Power

The *Reichstag* passed the Enabling Act by a two-third majority on 23rd March 1933. In this way, *"created by democracy and appointed by parliament"*, Hitler became a dictator. He was empowered to begin the Nazi revolution, the process of *Gleichschaltung,* or *'putting into the same gear',* all aspects of German life. Between March and April 1933, Hitler destroyed the quasi-independence of the German states by giving their parliaments a Nazi majority and by appointing a Reich Governor in each state. Then on 30th January 1934, Hitler abolished altogether the principle of federal government. Hitler also set about purging the civil service. Realising just how easily an independent civil service could sabotage the intentions of a government, a law for the Restoration of the Professional Civil Service was passed on the 7th April

1933. This, along with other such laws, established Nazi control of appointments, promotions and dismissals within the civil service. The Communist Party had been proscribed in February 1933. Between May and July, other political parties were dissolved, forcibly or voluntarily. A law of 14th July 1933 declared that the Nazi Party was the only legal party in Germany. The formation of new parties was forbidden. In February 1934 the *Reichstag* was dissolved. By then, all political alternatives to Hitler's dictatorship had been removed. Totalitarian rule as it applied to industry ensured that all trade unions were abolished in May 1933. They were replaced by the Nazi dominated German Labour Front (DAF). Under Robert Ley, the DAF served as a control mechanism for workers and employers alike. Wages and working conditions were fixed while strikes were forbidden. The Front provided its members with cheap holidays and instituted social welfare schemes.

The Night of the Long Knives, June 1934

Hitler had come to power with the help of the SA *(Sturm Abteilung)*, the brown-shirted Storm Troopers, commanded by Ernst Röhm. By 1933, the SA numbered 2-3 million. This mass movement had strong radical and anti-capitalist leanings, and was becoming an embarrassing legacy of the years of struggle, grumbling, as it did, that the Nazis had gone respectable. Röhm wanted the Nazi Revolution to continue and became increasingly critical of Hitler for his refusal to do so, *"Hitler is a swine"*. Röhm also called for the merging of the SA and professional Reichswehr (army) into a new People's Army. Hitler knew that the Reichswehr would never allow itself to be submerged in the *'brown flood'* and showed himself determined to preserve the unique position of the army in the state. Hitler's decision was undoubtedly influenced by the need he would have of army generals for their technical skill in the future re-armament of Germany. Their support would likewise be necessary when the aged President died, if Hitler was to be allowed to succeed him. Thus Röhm's pretensions to become the nucleus of a new army were rejected with contempt. Friction between the two sides led to a showdown. On 30th July 1934, the Night of the Long Knives, Hitler, with the backing of the army, struck. SA commanders were arrested all over Germany and, although the number killed has never been agreed, it may be as many as 400. In addition to the deaths of Röhm, Heines and others, people with no connection with the SA lost their lives. These may have been suspected dissidents or victims of private quarrels. The SA, crushed and without leadership, was replaced in importance by the SS and the Gestapo. When, on 2nd August 1934, President Hindenburg died, Hitler used the occasion to merge the offices of Chancellor and President. He became head of state, known simply as *'Der Führer'*. Simultaneously, Hitler became supreme Commander of the Armed Forces, army members swearing *'unconditional obedience'* to him.

The German Economy

The economic objectives of Nazi Germany were concerned with growth and self sufficiency, *autarky*. The task of modernising and reorganising the economy was to be by means of two Four Year Plans. The first plan, under the direction of Georg Hans

Reinhardt ran from 1933-1936, the second plan, 1936-1939 was largely executed by Hermann Göring. Also of immense importance in the early years of economic development was Hjalmar Schacht, Finance Minister and President of the *Reichsbank*. The German economy was helped by the fact that by 1933 the worse effects of the depression were over and by the system of state directed capitalism. A vast public works programme took place. Four lane highways, the *Autobahnen*, were built, creating employment for over 200,000 men. Railways and other means of transport were likewise improved but the most spectacular achievement occurred in the motor industry. Over 1 million people were employed and the *Volkswagen,* or *'people's car'*, was produced at a price that everyone was to be able to afford. New cheap housing for the German working class was constructed and slums were cleared. The civil service, the Nazi Party organisations and the Army were all expanded. Armament production, especially important in the second Four Year Plan, created high employment. Waste products were recycled and substitute goods, such as synthetic wool and rubber, were produced. In the agricultural sphere, Hitler's economic programme was less successful and there was a constant shortage of home produced products. The famous battle over *'guns or butter'* showed Hitler's determination to press ahead with reform and the building of Germany's armaments industry. Unemployment, which stood at 6m in 1933, was eliminated by 1939. Such material progress helped to build up German national morale and confidence.

Education - Youth Movement

Nazism had a profound impact on German education. Intellectual activity was sneered at by 'good' Nazis and creative or independent thought was not allowed. All teachers were required to belong to the Nazi Teacher League and their teaching had to reflect Nazi educational policies. Indoctrination was thus a constant feature of schooling. Children were taught that Germany was the greatest country in the world *"Germany, Germany above everything"*, and that Hitler was the greatest person ever born. They learned about the superiority of German people and the inferiority of other races. They were taught that they had a right and duty to conquer and destroy 'inferior' peoples. History, geography, language, literature, music and art were twisted to enforce Nazi ideology. In 1937, for example, Hitler declared *"works of art that cannot be understood will no longer openly reach the nation. The end has come of artistic lunacy and the artistic pollution of our people"*. In music, excerpts from Wagner's classics were constantly repeated and incorporated into Nazi ceremonies while Mendelssohn, being Jewish, was forbidden. The youth of Germany was particularly important to Hitler. Young people had to be taught robot-like obedience to the regime. The various branches of the Nazi Youth would be the means by which this would be done. From the age of 6 - 10 a German boy was given a performance book in which was noted his progress in athletics, outdoor activity and Nazi ideology. At 10, he progressed to the *Jung Volk* and swore his willingness to give up his life for Hitler. At 14, the boy entered the Hitler Youth which by 1939 had a membership of 6 million. Girls were forced to join a parallel organisation, the League of German Maidens. Their importance lay in the fact that they must become fit mothers.

Anti-Semitism

"We want no more stupid, absurd statements to the effect that the Jew is a human being". One of the most consistent features of Hitler's political thinking was his anti-semitism. Jews were the enemies of the German people, they *"spread as a pestilence spreads"* and in so doing, the Jew *"pollutes the blood"* of the Aryan. The Jew became the universal scapegoat in Nazi Germany, anti-semitism being part and parcel of state policy. In 1933, for example, Jews were expelled from the civil service and German universities. In October of that year they were forbidden from practising law. Simultaneously, a campaign of violence against the Jewish *"parasite"* was waged. Window smashing, looting and assaults were commonplace. In time, Jews were excluded from the legal, medical and teaching professions. In 1935, the Nuremberg Laws came into force. Jews lost their German citizenship. Marriage or sexual relations between Jews and Aryan Germans were forbidden and Jews were forced to wear the Star of David as an identifying sign. The anti-semitic campaign eased somewhat in 1936 as the Nazis tried to present a more tolerable face to the world during the Olympic Games of that year. When a Polish Jew, Herschal Gryuszpan, murdered Ernst von Rath, a German diplomat in Paris, on 7th November 1938, a further wave of persecution broke out. During the *'Night of the Broken Glass'*, 9th-10th November, 7,000 Jewish shops were wrecked, synagogues were burned, thousands of Jews were arrested and 91 were killed. Such persecution resulted in over 300,000 Jews emigrating from Germany by September 1939. The war years, 1939-1945, witnessed Hitler's *'final solution'* - the annihilation of 6m Jews.

The Churches in Nazi Germany

Although brought up a Catholic and greatly impressed by the power and organisation of the Catholic Church, Hitler soon abandoned formal religion, believing that Nazism should be the only creed of the German people. The launching of a full or frontal attack on the Church was dangerous in that it could create martyrs. Hitler opted instead for a campaign of deliberate deception by which the Churches were promised security and were then steadily deprived of their power and influence. The Church, for its part, was grateful to Hitler for saving Germany from Communism. In 1933, Hitler concluded a concordat with Pius XI by which he promised to give Catholics the freedom to practise their religion, to recognise the right of the Church to manage its own affairs, to continue state subsidies to the Church and to allow Catholics control of their own schools. In return, the Catholic Church undertook to stay out of politics. Yet in the following years, priests were arrested, monasteries closed, Catholic charities suspended, publications banned and its organisations harassed or suppressed. Realising that his concordat was a mistake, in 1937 Pius XI issued an encyclical, *'With Burning Anxiety'*. This was concerned with the evils of Nazism which were condemned as incompatible with Church teaching. In his dealings with the Protestant Churches, Hitler sought to unite the 281 different Protestant Churches into one national Church, *Reichskirche*. This would have a Nazi-appointed bishop at its head and be responsible for regulating Christian practice. Many Protestants opposed this subordination of the Church to the State. Led by Martin Niemöller, they organised themselves into a confessional Church. Like many others, Niemöller was arrested for his anti-Nazism.

He was kept in solitary confinement for 7 years. Largely due to figures like Niemöller and Cardinal Galen, the Churches in Germany, although severely handicapped, were not destroyed.

Totalitarianism

Between 1933 and 1939 Hitler and the Nazis turned Germany into a totalitarian state in which the individual became a mere cog in the state machine. Every aspect of German life - politics, education, law, work, church, army - was expected to succumb utterly to Nazi ideology. Propaganda played an important part in the totalitarian regime as it was the means by which the minds and bodies of German citizens were enslaved. The Nazis, under Goebbels, were masters of propaganda. They specialised in rallies, marches, slogans, posters, and flags. From 1933 on, each September, a party rally, lasting several days was held at Nuremberg, a city with strongly 'Germanic' buildings and fortifications. Hundreds of thousands of people listened to mass choirs, brass bands and speeches. Hitler, understanding the importance of mass psychology, used the medium of speech to bewitch an audience. He left behind him an extraordinary impression of force and people could not but be impressed by the immediacy of his passion, the intensity of his hatred. He was, after all, their Saviour. Press, radio, cinema and theatre were all controlled and used to great effect, while nationalism was raised to an almost spiritual level. No falsehood was too blatant to gain acceptance. Those who would not allow themselves to succumb to Nazism through propaganda found another 'inducement', namely the *Gestapo*, or state police. Established in 1933, the Gestapo ensured, through repression and brutality, that no one would dare oppose the regime. The *Gestapo*, led initially by Göring, came under the total control of Heinrich Himmler in 1936. Its powers were unchallenged and, like the SS, it considered itself to be above the law. Enemies of the state - Communists, Socialists, members of the clergy, gypsies, Jews and political dissidents - were sent to concentration camps where ill treatment was the norm rather than the exception. Dachau, Sachsenhausen, Buchenwald and Lichtenburg were some such camps. State control in Nazi Germany was absolute.

33. Hitler's Foreign Policy, 1933-1939

Aims - Guiding Principles

The basic principles of Hitler's foreign policy were formulated in *'Mein Kampf'*. They show that his would be an aggressive or dynamic foreign policy centering around three main aims. In the first place, Hitler wished to destroy the Treaty of Versailles, to make Germany free from its restrictive clauses, *"No human being has declared or recorded what he wanted more often than I. Again and again I wrote these words - the Abolition of the Treaty of Versailles"*. A second aim of Hitler's was to unite all Germans in a single country. Of his *Grossdeutschland* theory, Hitler wrote *"To demand that the 1914 frontiers of Germany should be restored is a political absurdity .... The confines of the Reich as they existed in 1914 were thoroughly illogical"*. Hitler sought rather to extend the frontier of Germany to include the Germans of Austria and the Sudeten Germans of Czechoslovakia. The one exception to the Greater Germany was the German population of South Tyrol, which was to be sacrificed to the needs of a future alliance with Fascist Italy. Finally, Hitler demanded *"land and territory for the nourishment of our people and for settling our surplus population"*. This would involve expanding eastward *(Lebensraum)* to the rich plains of Poland, the Ukraine and Russia. The empire of the *Herrenvolk* would be based upon the slave labour of the inferior Slav races. In the pursuit of these aims, which could not but bode ill for the future of Europe, Hitler showed himself to be an opportunist, turning events whenever possible to his own advantage. He avoided the complete isolation of Germany at any one moment and was prepared *"to make a pact with the devil"* if it suited his purposes. But Hitler was not going to be deterred by agreements with others. Over and over again, he used a policy of dissimulation, repudiating agreements entered into or pretending to know nothing about a pending German act of aggression. Hitler could also appear mild and conciliatory, even reasonable, in order to allay the fears of other powers.

Withdrawal from League of Nations - Non-Aggression Pact

Hitler believed that *"German misery must be broken by German steel"*. The first and indispensable step towards his dynamic foreign policy was to re-arm. Re-armament would have to take place, however, in such a way that it would not lose him the support of the German people. At the same time, the other powers should be made to feel that Germany was acting within the bounds of acceptable behaviour. Hitler's first gamble on the international front, therefore, took place within the context of the Disarmament Conference in Geneva, 1932-1933. Hitler presented Germany as the one nation which had so far disarmed and accused others of treating her like a second class citizen by refusing to do likewise. The denial of equal rights left him with no option but to withdraw from the Disarmament Conference and the League of Nations. Both moves were taken *'in sorrow rather than anger'* on 14th October 1933. As Hitler had sensed, none of the other governments were willing to seek reprisals against Germany. The 12th November plebiscite in Germany on the issue of withdrawal from the League secured a 95% approval for Hitler's action and was pronounced as a *'day of salvation'*. Hitler had now manoeuvred himself into a strong position within which he could begin re-armament. In the meantime, Hitler signed a ten-year Non-Aggression Pact with Poland on the 26th January 1934. This, though never popular in Germany, was an astute move by Hitler. Not only did it substantiate his claim to peaceful intention but it brought about a relaxation of tensions on Germany's eastern frontier with Poland over the city of Danzig and the Polish Corridor, while simultaneously, it destroyed the Franco-Polish alliance of 1921. Of the Pact, Hitler maintained that *"All our agreements have a purely temporary significance"*.

The Saar - Germany Rearms - Naval Pact, 1935

1935 started well for Hitler. The Saar, a coal mining area placed under the control of the League of Nations for 15 years, held a plebiscite in January 1935. This resulted in a 90% vote for the return of the area to the *Reich*. Feeling ever more confident, Hitler notified foreign governments on 9th March that a German airforce, the *Luftwaffe*, was already in existence. Then, on 16th March, the German government proclaimed its intention of introducing conscription and building up a peacetime army of 36 divisions to an approximate numerical strength of 550,000 men. Hitler pre-empted any criticism by insisting that Germany was following the example of her neighbours. This did not prevent the governments of Britain, France and Italy sending representatives to Stresa on 11th April to consider the German announcement. The three powers issued a declaration of solidarity as they jointly condemned the German announcement, reaffirmed their loyalty to the Locarno Treaty and intimated that they would stand firm against further treaty violations. A week later, the League of Nations censured Germany. Yet shortly afterwards, in June 1935, Britain and Germany signed a Naval Agreement which bound the Germans not to build beyond 35% of Britain's naval strength while at the same time recognising her right to begin naval re-armament and to build up to 100% of the submarine strength of the British. This treaty was an affront to Britain's Stresa Front partners and showed clearly that the Treaty of Versailles was no longer sacrosanct. The solidarity of the Stresa Front was further destroyed by the Italian invasion of Abyssinia, October 1935. Hitler, as always, would be the one to profit from such actions.

The Rhineland - Co-operation with Other Powers

In March 1936, Hitler judged the moment opportune for another coup in foreign policy. France and Britain were preoccupied with Mussolini's Abyssinian adventure when Hitler, on 7th of the month, took his biggest gamble to date by marching 35,000 troops into the demilitarised Rhineland. He justified sending troops into the Rhineland, forbidden under the Treaty of Versailles, on the grounds that the Franco-Soviet Pact of May 1935 had brought *"legal insecurity into the Locarno Pact"*. Although Hitler had instructed his troops to withdraw at the least opposition, knowing full well that the military resources at Germany's disposal were inadequate for even moderate resistance, the forces were unchallenged. Once again, Hitler had shown that aggression paid *"The world belongs to the man with guts! God helps him"*. Thereafter, Hitler's foreign policy continued to disturb European affairs. The Spanish Civil War, which began on 17th July 1936, saw Hitler sending men and military supplies, experts and technicians of all kinds as well as the Condor Air Legion to Spain. His excuse for involvement on the side of Franco and the Nationalists was that the war in Spain was part of an international fight against Bolshevism. The reality was that Hitler was not interested in a victory for Franco. He sought rather to prolong the war and to use it as a laboratory for testing German weapons and military techniques. Mussolini's involvement in Spain, on the same side, ensured that the two Fascist leaders were brought closer together. In October 1936, they signed the Rome-Berlin Axis, a friendly agreement within the context of which there would be growing co-operation between the two nations on a number of issues. The Anti-Comintern Pact, November 1936, of Germany and Japan, and later Italy, worked towards the defeat of Communism. Clearly, the dissatisfied powers of the world were drawing together.

Austria

The union of Austria and Germany, known as the *Anschluss*, although forbidden by the terms of the Versailles treaty, had always been one of Hitler's ambitions, himself an Austrian by birth. Hitler thought about uniting the two in 1934 when an abortive Nazi putsch in Vienna led to the death of the Austrian Chancellor, Dollfuss, but decided against such action when the other powers made their opposition clear. Tension between Austria and Germany was relieved in July 1936 when the Austro-German Agreement was signed. Intended to put relations on a more even footing, the Agreement reaffirmed Hitler's recognition of Austria's full sovereignty, but the clause relating to foreign policy, which acknowledged Austria to be a *'German State'* was used by Germany as a lever with which to exert increasing pressure on the Austrian government and whittle away at Austria's independence. In February 1938, at a meeting between Hitler and the Austrian Chancellor, Dr. Schuschnigg, Hitler demanded the legalisation of the Nazi Party in Austria, an amnesty for imprisoned Nazis and the appointment of leading Nazis to key government positions. Schuschnigg had little option but to agree to the demands. Fearing that the Austrian government would cease to be master of its own house, Schuschnigg decided that a plebiscite on the question of unity would be held on 15th March. Hitler, furious and unsure of the outcome of any vote, insisted that the plebiscite be delayed and that Seyss-Inquart, the leader of the Austrian Nazis, replace Schuschnigg as Chancellor. Rather than drive Austria into a civil war, Schuschnigg agreed to resign. Seyss-Inquart thereupon 'discovered' a Communist plot and invited Hitler into Austria to restore order. German troops marched into Austria on 12th March. When a plebiscite was held in April 1938, 99% of those who voted approved the *Anschluss*. It was, according to Hitler, *"the proudest hour of my life"*.

Sudetenland - Munich Conference

There was no appreciable pause between the liquidation of the Austrian problem and the beginning of the campaign against Czechoslovakia. The means by which Hitler would undermine Czechoslovakia was by exploiting the grievances of over three million German inhabitants, living in the western fringe area known as the Sudetenland. He was helped in his goal by the existence of a ready-made Nazi movement in Czechoslovakia, under the leadership of Konrad Henlein who proved to be nothing short of a *"Trojan horse within the walls"*. Henlein was briefed by Hitler. He realised that *"we must always demand so much that we can never be satisfied"*. Thus while the Czechs, urged by the West, sought to make the utmost concessions to the Sudeten Germans, the situation there remained one of permanent unrest. Hitler spoke of the Sudeten Germans as *"tortured creatures"* and of the Czechs as *"oppressors of Germans"*. At a speech in Nuremberg in September 1938, Hitler launched a brutal attack on the Republic and its President, Benes, concluding that *"The Germans in Czechoslovakia are neither defenceless nor are they abandoned"*. Hitler's speech was followed by a rising in the Sudetenland. Although the rising was put down, the situation remained tense. Hitler threatened war if his demand for total annexation of the Sudetenland was not met. German divisions already massed on the Czech border while the Czechs had ordered full mobilisation. Three visits by Chamberlain to Hitler had failed to resolve the crisis. Then on *'Black Wednesday'*, 28th September, when all hope of avoiding war seemed gone, Mussolini, acting as mediator, proposed a conference of Hitler, Chamberlain, Daladier and himself. Czechoslovakia was not invited to attend. The Munich Conference, 29th September 1938, allowed Germany to take over the Sudetenland. Hitler promised that *"It is the last territorial claim which I have to make in Europe"*.

Czechoslovakia - Pact of Steel/Non-Aggression Pact, 1939

The Munich Agreement soon proved to be little more than a sell-out to Hitler. The Czech government had lost its system of fortification to Germany as well as much of its industrial area and vital communications. The Slovaks thereafter demanded their autonomy, seeking Hitler's help for their demands. This proved to be a vital mistake as it strengthened Hitler's hand as he sought to make life difficult for the new Czech President, Emil Hacha. Hacha was told that the disorder in his country was a threat to Germany. He was forced, through threats and bullying, to invite Hitler into his country to restore order. If Hacha did not sign the agreement *'Prague would be bombed to rubble'*. On 15th March 1939, Hitler's army marched into Czechoslovakia and completed *'the rape of Czechoslovakia'*. Ten days later, Hitler seized the predominantly German city of Memel from Lithuania. Appeasement was now well and truly dead, war only a matter of time. Further preparation for war on Hitler's part included the Pact of Steel with Mussolini in May 1939 and the Nazi-Soviet Ten Year Non-Aggression Pact with Stalin in August 1939. The Pact of Steel was a formal military alliance whereby Germany and Italy pledged *'to act side by side'* in the task of *'safeguarding the foundations of civilisation'*. The Pact with Russia was an extraordinary agreement in view of how both powers regarded each other but it was a cynical alliance of convenience which allowed Germany to avoid fighting a two-front war and Russia to buy time with which she would build up her defences and prepare for war. Secret clauses gave the Russians the chance to take over the Baltic states and to divide Poland with Germany.

Invasion of Poland - Conclusion

"The victor will not be asked afterwards whether he told the truth or not. In starting and waging a war, it is not right that matters, but victory". With the conclusion of the Nazi-Soviet Pact, Hitler's preparations for the next phase of his Eastern drive were complete. Demands to Poland, exposed on three sides to Germany since the destruction of Czechoslovakia, included the return of the port of Danzig to Germany and the construction of an extra-territorial highway across the Polish

Corridor. Failure to comply would lead to invasion. Such an invasion began on 1st September 1939. The next question was, how would Britain and France react? For too long they had shown an almost pathetic readiness to believe in Hitler's professions of peaceful intent, their anxiety to prevent war had put them on the defensive, allowing them to engage in an extraordinary amount of wishful thinking as, again and again, Hitler had defused potentially dangerous situations by saying all the things that peaceful people wanted to hear. The invasion of Poland, however, showed that this would no longer be the case. It was the 'straw that broke the camel's back' for, on 3rd September, the two powers declared war on Germany. The Second World War had begun. War was the culmination of six years of Hitler's foreign policy where increasingly he had let his ideas expand as he reached out further and further, taking bigger risks and shortening intervals between coups. This, coupled with Hitler's belief in his own infallibility *"who says I am not under the special protection of God?"* would mark the deterioration of his judgement and ultimately prove to be his undoing because World War II, the most destructive in history, avenged itself completely upon its author, leading to his death and the destruction of the Third Reich.

Hitler's Germany: Past Exam Questions

1995

D1. Adolf Hitler

Account for Hitler's rise to power in Germany.

1994

C5. National Socialism

Treat of the origins and growth of National Socialism in Germany up to Hitler's accession as Chancellor, 1933.

1992

D2. Hitler

Describe how Hitler and the Nazi party turned Germany into a totalitarian state.

1991

D1. Hitler's Foreign Policy

Discuss the reaction of European States to Hitler's foreign policy up to the outbreak of World War II.

1987

D3. Hitler's Foreign Policy

(i)   Treat of Hitler's foreign policy during the period 1933-1939.

(ii) Estimate the extent to which this policy caused World War II.

FASCISM

34. Discuss the Principal Characteristics of European Fascism in the Inter-War Period

Introduction

Fascism was essentially a post World War I phenomenon which in the inter-war period enjoyed a considerable vogue. Although Fascism flourished in markedly different backgrounds, the conditions which perhaps best lent themselves to the development of the philosophy include the inability of post-war governments to deal with the problems of unemployment, inflation and poverty which beset many countries. This was aggravated by a disillusionment with, and reaction to, liberal trends, as well as a fear of Communism. In its most restricted sense, the word *'Fascism'* applies to the political regime in Italy from the period 1922-1943. The term comes from a Latin word *'fasces'* meaning *'bundles'* which harks back to the days of Ancient Rome when law enforcement officers there carried a bundle of rods bound tightly together, with an axe in the middle. Undoubtedly the symbol was representative of authority and strength. To limit Fascism to the Italian context, however, would be to do it an injustice. It would discount Fascism as a major force in post-war Europe and neglect its universal character. As Mussolini insisted *"Fascism as an idea, a doctrine, a realisation is universal, never before have the people thirsted for authority, direction, order, as they do now. If each age has its doctrine, the innumerable symptoms indicate that the doctrine of our age is the Fascist one"*. Nonetheless, it is no easy matter to pinpoint Fascism precisely. Every country where there was a Fascist party had peculiarities duly reflected in its local political organisations. Furthermore, Fascism in its various forms was confined in the main to the role of a political movement; only in Italy and Germany did it go on to the actual seizure of power, consequently showing itself in its most dramatic and complete form. Yet the differences between the various Fascist movements and the much confused talk about its philosophy should not overlook the fact that the Fascist movements also had a good deal in common and that certain concepts or ideas might be pinpointed as, in some way, characteristic.

Totalitarianism

Totalitarianism is the very essence of Fascism, and Fascism is without question the purest example of a totalitarian ideology. Setting out, as it did, to create a new civilisation, a new type of human being and a totally new way of life, Fascism could not conceive of any sphere of human activity remaining immune from state intervention. Mussolini's interpretation of Fascist totalitarianism was of *"a state which controls all forces acting in nature. We control political forces, we control moral forces, we control economic forces... everything in the state, nothing against the state, nothing outside the state"*. For Mussolini, the Fascist state was not only a living being, an organism, but a spiritual and moral entity. This total conception of national, political, economic, social and spiritual life was such that Fascism might be likened to a laboratory from which a new culture, a new way of thinking and a new kind of person would emerge. Because they allowed too much freedom, liberalism and democracy were not to be tolerated in the Fascist state. Only one political party would exist in the totalitarian state and for this, everyone would vote. The true Fascist would be courageous, serious, tenacious, hard-working but above all, he would be loyal and obedient to his regime, to the absolute rule of a single man. Both Fascist Italy and Nazi Germany aspired to the attainment of such a state. In reality, however, Hitler's Germany was undoubtedly much more totalitarian than Mussolini's Italy which, by retaining the monarchy and the papacy, impeded the *'total revolution'*.

Nationalism

The cementing force of Fascism was nationalism. As the Socialist Marcel Deat observed, *"the driving force of revolution has ceased to be class interest, and has become instead the general interest; we have moved from the notion of class to that of nation"*. A national rather than an international experience, man 'existed' in the Fascist state insofar as he was sustained and determined by the community. Instead of *'society for the individual'* there was *'individuals for society'*. The Hitler Youth slogan, for example, maintained of the individual *"You are nothing. Your state is everything"*. The state thus became its own judge. But the nationalism of Fascists did more than stress the authority of the state and insist that people exist for its benefit, it tended towards an ultra or chauvinistic nationalism. The Fascists had an exalted view of their own importance. They believed in their spiritual superiority and the corresponding inferiority of the rest of the world. Germans were taught slogans such as *"Germany, Germany above everything"* while Mussolini asserted that *"A people which soars has rights towards the nations which are falling into decay. And these rights are chiselled in letters of fire into the leaves of our book of fate"*. Inevitably this exaggerated view of the importance of one's own national identity led to a highly dangerous militarism or aggressiveness. The Italians wished to expand into Southern Europe, the Balkans and North Africa. The Germans wished not only to unite all Germans into a *Gross Deutschland* but to acquire *Lebensraum* (living space) in Eastern Europe. The general belief was that *"The soldiers of the Fascist must have will to achieve their end at all costs"*.

Superman - Super Race

Fascism incorporated the idea of a *'Superman'*, a leader who was assigned a unique authority, who based his rule on power and might and who, if not himself a God, was at least God given. Such a man was a supreme egotist who despised egalitarianism and democracy. He was wise, heroic, a great genius, perhaps even omniscient, infallible. Mussolini *(Il Duce)* was described in *Il Popola d'Italia* as a demigod who knew everything, a statesman whom Italian people should revere and honour. He was depicted in a diversity of activities - fencing, riding, driving, playing the violin, working in the fields, holding children. His picture was widely displayed and a key catch phrase of the regime was *"Mussolini is always right"*. *Der Führer*, too, was shown to be a man of special purity, of wonderful courage and readiness for sacrifice. He was a kind man with a brilliant mind whose pleasures were few and simple. The cult of leadership went hand in hand with the master race theory. Italians were heirs to the greatness of Ancient Rome. An Italian could *"glory in the fact that I am Latin"* and *"recognise a barbarian in every man of non-Latin blood"*. The German Aryan race was pure bred, typically tall and blond. They were an elite group, a *"super-race" (Herrenvolk)*. Such racial theories believed in the necessity to remove impurities. Hitler's society was one in which *"The weak must be chiselled away... A young German must be swift as a greyhound, as tough as leather and as hard as Krupp's steel"*. A policy of 'mercy killings' (euthanasia) was undertaken against the physically and mentally handicapped. *"Polluters of racial purity"* such as Jews met a still worse fate.

The Anti-Character of Fascism

In many respects, Fascism might be regarded as an anti-movement, defining itself by the things against which its stands. The basic anti-dimensions of Fascism include its anti-democratic stance. This could be seen in its authoritarian leadership, the banning of political parties, the summoning of parliament less and less, as well as the use of threats to achieve results. Central to the growth and success of Fascism was its anti-Communism. Fascism was at pains to emphasise the opposite of everything Communism purported to be. It opposed its internationalism, its materialism, its fixation with class, concentrating instead on loyalty to one's own country as the supreme good, a sense of idealism, heroism, self-sacrifice and the blurring of class divisions. Although there was some ambiguity in the position of Fascist parties towards religion and the churches, there was, undoubtedly an anti-clericalism underlining many Fascist organisations who were opposed to the international character of the Church, the power it had over large sections of the population and the interference of Vatican politics in national political life. It was only in Germany, however, that a really explicit anti-Christian component was present. Anti-semitism was not originally characteristic of all Fascist movements but is central to many of them. Again this found its clearest expression in Nazi Germany where just to be a Jew became a crime. The Nuremburg Laws of 1935 deprived Jews of many basic rights while Hitler's *'final solution'* concerned itself with the mass extermination of 6 million Jews. Mussolini did not have the same antipathy for the Jews but under Hitler's influence and prompting, a Racialist Manifesto was proclaimed in 1938. Many restrictions were placed on Jews.

Economy

A further characteristic of Fascism was its distinct political economy. Above all, the Fascists sought to modernise and develop the economy. They would do so by means of a policy of autarky, or self-sufficiency. Fascists tended towards a savage repression of Socialist parties and Labour movements. Trade unions were banned, strikes and lock-outs forbidden. The corporate state was the means by which Mussolini sought to establish Fascist control over the economy. Each profession and industry had its own corporation which consisted of employers, employees and three Fascist members. The Nazi equivalent was the German Labour Front *(DAF)*. Both organisations set prices, wages and general conditions of work. Workers benefited from schemes of insurance covering unemployment, sickness and accident. Such systems aimed to preserve a basic capitalist system while ending the class struggle. A common cliché of Fascism was that whereas all other political parties concentrated on the issue of the ownership of capital, Fascism concerned itself with whether capital was put to a socially productive use, regarding its ownership as a less important matter. In the inter-war period, the Fascists gave a high priority to the reduction of unemployment. This was helped, in part, by means of public investment. Investment in hydro-electric schemes, railway improvement, construction of express highways and land reclamation all absorbed enormous sums of money. Employment was also found in the Fascist party organisations, the civil service and the army. Preparation for war was an important priority of Fascist economic policy. In both Italy and Germany, economic growth was partly a by-product of an economic policy designed to promote territorial expansion. The approach to national self-sufficiency in food supply, though not especially successful, fitted in with the desire to be independent of strategic imports in a future war.

Propaganda/Repression/Youth

The Fascist government made use of every modern technical achievement of propaganda. Radio, cinema, newsreel and newspapers were all used to great effect. The importance of speech-making was likewise recognised. The voice of the charismatic Fascist leader would be familiar to its people. Passion, repetition and superb showmanship were used to produce an almost hypnotic power over an audience. Hitler was particularly gifted and was frequently able to arouse the masses to a fever pitch. The principle of *'group dynamics'* was exploited at every opportunity for the fascists understood only too well the herd instinct *"Mass assemblies are necessary because they have a strengthening and encouraging effect on most people"*. The insecure, lonely and lost individual *"becomes a member of a community"* through the organisation of mass parades and rallies. Modern amplification and new, more powerful lighting were commonly used. The process of subtle indoctrination permeated every aspect of the Fascist regime so that the super-leader became like a sculptor, moulding his material into shape. Those who remained aloof, critical or overtly reactionary were dealt with through a process of repression. Italy established a secret police force in the form of the *OVRA*, Germany established the *Gestapo*. Such forces were themselves above the law. Special courts had the power to sentence people to death for treason while concentration camps and penal settlements were other means of enforcing discipline and uniformity of thought and action. Fascists also recognised the importance of youth in furthering the ideology of Fascism and creating loyal servants of the state. Mussolini's *Balilla* had a membership of 3 million, Hitler's Youth Movement had 6 million members by 1939. The importance of physical strength was emphasised.

Conclusion

The success of Fascism in the inter-war period was such that in the 1930s hardly a European nation was without a native Fascist party and events towards the end of that decade seemed to indicate that a Fascist Europe was a very real possibility. Fascist movements outside of Germany and Italy included the *Action Française* and *Croix de*

Feu in France, the British Union of Fascists under the leadership of Sir Oswald Mosley, the Rexists in Belgium and the Falangists in Spain. Greece, Romania, Bulgaria and Ireland all had their own movements. Other than the few Fascist groups which were directly German creations, most notably those in Austria, Switzerland and Czechoslovakia, these movements were not mere imitations or by-products. Rather, they were native and indigenous, with roots in the soil of their own country. Because local Fascist groups adopted their political colour to suit their environment, the elements of Fascism thus far mentioned could be seen in varying combinations, being more obvious in some movements than in others. One further characteristic of Fascists that tended to be widespread, was their love of uniform leading to the use of shirts of different colours as well as their use of symbols and a straight arm salute. But Fascism sought not to be too precise and did not have a sound or obvious footing in any particular class. It wished to offer something to everyone. Consequently its principles were often unclear, even to its own members. *"A chaos of contradictions"*, Fascism frequently integrated elements from the political creeds that it so violently attacked. It might also be argued that there was frequently a discrepancy between ideology and practice. Mussolini maintained *"I have a horror of dogma and Fascist dogma is an impossibility"*.

35. Treat of Relations between Fascist Italy and Nazi Germany during the Period 1933-1945

Introduction - Early Antagonism

"I should be pleased I suppose, that Hitler has carried out a revolution on our lines. But they are Germans. So they will end by ruining our idea". Thus spoke Mussolini of Hitler's attempt to launch the German answer to Fascism by means of the National Socialist Workers Party. The success of Mussolini's *'March on Rome'* in October 1922 offered an example and a happy augury for the success of a similar attempt in Germany. Yet Hitler's ride to power proved thornier than Mussolini's and it was not to be for another decade that he was allowed to take power. Like Mussolini's Government of 1922, Hitler's Chancellorship of January 1933 ensured that he became head of a coalition government where the Nazis were in a minority. Rather than allowing themselves to be controlled, both leaders had soon dispensed with their coalition partners and set themselves up as dictators. The many parallels that existed between the careers of the two men were no guarantee of unanimity of thought or movement, however. Thus, while Hitler was initially admiring and even a little in awe of Mussolini, wishing to forge closer ties between the two countries, Mussolini sought to dismiss Hitler as *"a mad little clown"*. Of his master race, Mussolini raged that the Germans were illiterate when the Romans had a Caesar. Mussolini resented Nazi imitations of Fascism, conspicuously obvious in the uniform, drill, titles of leadership, aspirations to totalitarianism, use of violence and propaganda that the Nazis had adopted. He maintained at this point of early antagonism that *"Fascism is not an article for export"*. Mussolini's feelings were undoubtedly prompted by fear. He was especially anxious to quell the tide of German foreign expansion for this could lead to demands concerning the return of the South Tyrol to Germany in a union of all German speaking people. Accordingly, Mussolini was opposed to the idea of union between Austria and Germany, preferring a weak Austria on Italy's borders than a mighty Germany.

Austria - Stresa Front, 1934-'35

On 17th February, 1934, the governments of France, Great Britain and Italy published a joint declaration to the effect that they took *"a common view of the necessity of maintaining Austrian independence and integrity in accordance with the relevant treaties"*. Then, in Venice on 14th of June 1934, at the first of many celebrated meetings between Hitler and Mussolini, the latter was once more pressing on the subject of Austria. Although Hitler disclaimed any intention of attacking Austria, Mussolini's suspicions remained. Meanwhile, the illegal Nazi party in Austria continued to operate. Trouble came to a head on 25th July when the Austrian Nazis murdered the Austrian Chancellor, Englebert Dollfuss, a personal friend of Mussolini. It was believed that Hitler would march into the country and take over. Before he could act, Mussolini, furious at what he regarded as Hitler's bad faith, ordered four Italian divisions to the Austrian frontier, the Brenner Pass, and sent a telegram to the Austrian Government promising Italian support in the defence of their country's independence. Hitler, realising that the Nazis had overreached themselves, repudiated all connections with the conspiracy. The initial announcement of the official German news agency, which had been enthusiastic, was now hurriedly suppressed while the German Minister in Austria was recalled in disgrace. But Mussolini remained outspoken in his dislike and contempt for the *"barbarians"* north of the Alps, and at a meeting at Stresa on 11th April 1935, Mussolini co-operated with France and Britain in the condemnation of Germany's unilateral decision to re-arm. The united front committed itself to *"close and cordial collaboration"* in maintaining Europe's status quo. What was becoming increasingly clear to Hitler, therefore, was that he was not yet in a position where he could afford to use high-handed methods, and that opposition to his schemes would have to be divided before it could be overcome.

Abyssinia - Rhineland - Spain

Mussolini had long been contemplating an invasion of Abyssinia. Not only was it prompted by a desire to acquire valuable resources but it may also have been stimulated by a sense of rivalry with Hitler. Confident that Britain and France would keep an eye on Germany, the invasion began in October 1935. As the Italians approached the capital, Addis Ababa, Hitler decided in March 1936 to use the crisis to occupy the Rhineland. His gamble paid off, for apart from condemning Hitler's defiance, no action was taken. In May 1936 Addis Ababa was captured and King Victor Emmanuel III of Italy was proclaimed emperor of Abyssinia. Aggression had paid off but it was not without repercussions. Italy's action brought an end to the Stresa Front and the driving of Italy into a position of isolation. Hitler proved to be the ultimate beneficiary. The first sign of a rapprochement between the two powers came when Mussolini gave his approval to the Austrian-German Agreement of 11th July 1936. Designed on the surface to place Austro-German common relations on a level satisfactory to both sides, the Agreement marked a big step forward in the policy of capturing Austria by peaceful means. The outbreak of civil war in Spain on 17th July created a situation from which Hitler was able to draw still more advantages. In the course of the war, Germany sent men and military supplies, as well as the famous Condor Legion. German aid to Franco and the Nationalists was never on a major scale. It never, for example, equalled the forces sent by Mussolini, which in 1937 reached 70,000 men. Hitler's aim, unlike Mussolini's, was not to secure Franco's victory, but to prolong the war while at the same time providing a valuable training for his troops. The policy of the League of Nations with regard to the war was one of non-intervention. Thus, at the very moment when Mussolini might have been trying to establish better relations with the Western powers, intervention in the Spanish Civil War kept the quarrel alive.

Growing Co-operation

There could be no doubting that in terms of their foreign policies, Italy and Germany, by 1936, were beginning to follow parallel courses. Hitler, who had spoken of his desire to ally with Italy in *'Mein Kampf'*, felt that the time had come to exploit more fully the situation in which Mussolini had placed himself. In September 1936, he sent his Minister of Justice, Hans Frank, on an exploratory visit to Rome. Frank, who happened to speak Italian fluently, stressed Hitler's anxiety that the Italians should know that Hitler *"regards the Mediterranean as a purely Italian sea"*. Frank also referred to the necessity of increasing collaboration between Germany and Italy. A month later, Ciano, Mussolini's Foreign Minister, set out for Germany. The resulting agreement between the two sides was the Rome-Berlin Axis, October 1936. Announcing the agreement on 1st November, Mussolini used the famous simile of an axis, *"This vertical line between Rome and Berlin is not a partition but rather an axis around which can revolve all those European states with a will to collaboration and peace"*. The Axis was followed in November 1936 by the Anti-Comintern Pact of Germany and Japan. Italy joined in 1937. Although its stated aim was defeat of the Communist *'world conspiracy'*, there can be no doubting that it was targeted against Russia. Of the Pact, Ribbentrop, the German Foreign Minister, declared *"Japan will never permit any dissemination of Bolshevism in the Far East - Germany is creating a bulwark against the pestilence in Central Europe"*. Finally, Italy, as the *Duce* informs the world, would hoist the anti-Bolshevik banner in the South. These friendly alliances of 1936 and 1937 would become the foundation of a future military alliance between the two Fascist dictators. As far as the League of Nations was concerned, both Hitler and Mussolini expressed their contempt for the organisation by simply withdrawing from it and ignoring its decisions. Germany left the League in 1933, Italy in 1937.

Anschluss - Sudetenland, 1938

By 1938, Hitler felt that the time had come to bring relations with Austria to a head. The ability of the Austrian Chancellor, Dr. Schuschnigg, to be master of his own house was reduced. When Schuschnigg, in a last attempt to save Austria, announced plans for a plebiscite in March 1938, Hitler, fearing the vote would not go his way, moved troops to the border. Before this action was taken, however, Hitler, in a letter to Mussolini, gave his reasons for a proposed German takeover of Austria as well as assurances that the border between Germany and Italy would not change. *"It is my unalterable will and my bequest to the German people that it shall regard the frontier of the Alps, raised by nature between us both, as forever inviolable"*. Hitler hoped by such promises to quell any anxiety the Italians might have about South Tyrol. Mussolini informed the *Führer "that Italy watches the events with absolute calm"*. Schuschnigg was now forced to resign. He was replaced by Seyss-Inquart, a leading Nazi, who in March 1938 invited German troops into the country to maintain order. When in April the Nazis organised their own plebiscite, 99% of Austrians opted for union with Germany. This was the fulfilment of a dream for Hitler. His gratitude to Mussolini for remaining silent was expressed in a telegram, *"Mussolini, I shall never forget you for this"*. Soon after, Hitler turned his attention to Czechoslovakia and in particular to the Sudetenland, an area of Czechoslovakia containing three million Germans. He accused the Czech government of mistreating the Sudeten Germans and demanded the total annexation of the Sudetenland. The crisis threatened to escalate into war. Mussolini stepped in. Attempting to defuse the situation, a conference of Britain, France, Germany and Italy was called in Munich, in September 1938. Mussolini could bask in the glory of having saved Europe when the conference decided that Hitler would be allowed to take the Sudetenland. Hitler promised no further aggression.

Aggression - Pact of Steel - War

Hitler's aggression continued. In March 1939 Germany took over the remainder of Czechoslovakia. Although the action was resented in Italy, Mussolini protested that *"We cannot change our policy now. After all, we are not political whores"*. At the same time, Hitler's success filled Mussolini with envy. He decided to seek compensation. In April 1939, Italian troops overran Albania. Hitler was delighted, for the Italian action underlined the common interest of the two dictatorships. He began to press for the signature of a military alliance. The result was the Pact of Steel, May 1939, which declared that *"the German and Italian nations are determined to act side by side and with united forces for the securing of living space and the maintenance of peace"*. But when in September 1939, as a result of the German invasion of Poland, World War II began, Mussolini, believing that Italy was not ready for war, was forced to renounce the Pact of Steel arrangement and declare Italy's non-belligerence. Hitler, annoyed, maintained that *"the Italians are behaving just as they did in 1914"*. Over the following months, relations between the two leaders were strained. Fearful of a German invasion, Italy built costly fortifications on her northern frontier. Mussolini fluctuated between hopes for a German defeat and thoughts of intervention on Germany's side. The thought of being left out of a division of the spoils was unbearable to him. At the famous Brenner Pass meeting, March 1940, Hitler overwhelmed Mussolini. He described at length the course of the war and spoke with great confidence of a German victory. The conflict in Mussolini's mind between fear and the desire to play a historic role was at last resolved. In June 1940, Italy entered the war.

World War II

Italy's first military involvement in World War II was an attack on southern France. At a time when France was already preparing for an armistice with Germany, the Italians failed to distinguish themselves, making little real headway. Not surprisingly, Hitler declined Mussolini's suggestion for joint German-Italian negotiations with France. He had no intention whatsoever of sharing his triumph. Hitler subsequently impressed on the Italians the need to delay any designs that she might have on Yugoslavia and Greece. Rather, all the Italian resources should be devoted to an attack in Egypt and North Africa which began in September 1940. By then, it was already clear that Germany was losing the Battle of Britain. Mussolini, at this point, rejected offers from Hitler of 250 heavy tanks for the Desert Campaign. He hoped instead to wage an independent parallel war. Acting against Hitler's wishes, Mussolini launched the invasion of Greece on 28th October 1940. *"Hitler always faces me with a fait accompli. This time I am going to pay him back in his own coin. He will find out from the newspapers that I have occupied Greece"*. The Greek attack was a massive blunder. It meant that the Italians had to open up a second front, it led to major losses in Greece, Albania and Egypt and forced the Italians to accept German aid. From then on, Italy's status was increasingly reduced and she became a German satellite. Economic assistance, for example, was given only on the condition that German experts should go to Italy and advise on its use. But, German intervention on Italy's behalf did not save her empire. In April 1941, Italy lost Abyssinia and Italian East Africa. On 12th May 1943 at Tunis, the Italian North African army surrendered.

The invasion of Sicily and mainland Italy then began. For Hitler, North Africa had been *"a sideshow by comparison with the real war in the East"*. But Operation Barbarossa, launched belatedly in June 1941 as a result of the necessity of going to Italy's assistance, was by 1943 proving to be the beginning of the end for Hitler.

The Last Years - Analysis

During the Allied Sicily campaign, July 1943, the Fascist Grand Council and King Victor Emmanuel III took the decision to dismiss and subsequently arrest Mussolini. The news of his fall, though foreseen by Hitler, was, nonetheless, a great shock. Realising that his own prestige was directly involved, Hitler sought to rescue Mussolini and restore the Fascist regime. The rescue of Mussolini by a German Commando Unit came about on 12th September. Three days later, Mussolini, old and shrunken, became head of the Salo Government in Northern Italy. This government had neither real independence nor authority. Mussolini was, at best, a puppet of the Germans, agreeing, under pressure to play the part for which he was cast. While Hitler may have retrieved a disastrous situation in 1943, the ugly and awkward facts of war and ultimate defeat for Germany could not be held at bay forever. Perhaps the essential condition of Hitler's ability to continue the war for as long as he did was that he refused to see or admit what was happening outside the magic circle of his headquarters. But by April 1945, the situation was hopeless. On 28th April, Mussolini, along with his mistress, was murdered by Italian partisans. The news must have confirmed Hitler in his decision to end his own life, which he duly did on 30th April. Thus ended the career of the two dictators. Any evaluation of their relationship shows that Hitler's early fascination with Mussolini turned, later on, to hatred. Mussolini, for his part, always felt a sense of inferiority and anxious deference in Hitler's presence. Because Hitler handled him with such remarkable skill Mussolini became a prisoner of his own actions - the more he tried to imitate Hitler, the more dependent he became on him. It was a dependence of which Mussolini was profoundly resentful and which was, in time, to be his undoing.

Fascism: Past Exam Questions

1995

D2. Fascism in Europe, 1919-1939

Discuss the principal characteristics of European fascism in the inter-war period.

1993

D1. Dictatorships

"Conditions in Europe during the period 1919-1939 favoured the rise of dictatorships." Discuss.

1990

D3. Fascism

Account for the growth of fascism in Europe, 1919-1939.

RUSSIA UNDER STALIN

36. Stalin, 1879-1953

"He will strangle us. He is an unprincipled intriguer who subordinates everything to his appetite for power. At any moment he will change his theories in order to get rid of someone."
— Bukharin

Background - Rise to Power

Born Josef Djugoshvili in Georgia on 21st December 1879, Stalin *('man of steel')* became Josef's adopted name in 1913. Stalin's father was a cobbler and a drunk so that his origins were indeed humble. In 1894, Stalin was sent to a seminary to study for the priesthood. Stalin, however, was an atheist and only stayed at the seminary to avail of the education it offered him. Thereafter, he turned to revolutionary Marxism. In 1901, Stalin joined the Social Democrats. He organised a spate of armed robberies and the following years are a tale of arrests, escapes and terms of exile in Siberia. 1912 was a turning point for Stalin. In that year, he was appointed editor of the Bolshevik newspaper, *Pravda,* and he was elected to the inner group of Bolsheviks, the *Politburo.* Stalin was in Siberia when the February revolution broke out but in its aftermath he made his way to Petrograd. His chief role in the October revolution was as a propagandist. When the Bolsheviks assumed power in 1917, Stalin was appointed Commissar for Nationalities. He was also made a member of the Urgburo Organizational Bureau. In 1922, Stalin was appointed party General Secretary, a position he used to build up a network of loyal supporters. In the years immediately preceding Lenin's death in January 1924, Stalin became *'Lenin's voice'.* The leadership struggle now came into the open. Trotsky was perhaps the main contender. Stalin used Zinoviev and Kamenev to help him destroy Trotsky's influence. He was helped by Trotsky's illness and his theory of *'world permanent revolution'* which won less support than Stalin's *'socialism in one country'.* Zinoviev and Kamenev were disposed of on ideological grounds and by 1927 all three opponents were expelled from the party. Bukharin, the right-wing leader, was removed from the politburo in 1929. Russia, with Stalin as its master, stood on the eve of a new revolution.

Economic Policies

Stalin wanted to develop Russia into a modern industrial society. He believed that industrialisation was the key to survival in a capitalist world and that if the USSR did not catch up and indeed overtake the West, that the Soviet Union would be crushed. The New Economic Policy was therefore replaced by Five Year Plans. The first of these started in 1928 while the third was cut short in 1941 by the German invasion of Russia. Targets for production were set. In this way the whole of Russia was hurled into a gigantic struggle to transform. Emphasis was on heavy industry, iron, steel, transport and machinery. The second and third plans also sought to increase armaments production. Consumer goods were seriously neglected. But the plans resulted in an astonishing transformation. Between the First and Second World War, industrial output had increased by 400%. In 1939 the USSR was second only to the US as an industrial power. This had been achieved through the ruthless accumulation of capital, the limitation of personal consumption and the manipulation of labour. Simultaneously, Stalin sought to organise an agrarian revolution. This would be done through collectivisation. 25 million smallholdings were to be taken from peasants and turned into collective units. These larger farms would be more efficient and productive and could make better use of labour and machinery. Collectivisation proved very unpopular, especially among the *Kulaks*, or larger farmers. Stalin insisted that *"we must annihilate them as a social class"*. Terror and repression became widespread in the countryside. Kulaks responded by the burning of crops and the killing of cattle. Stalin pressed ahead, ignoring the human tragedy. While he could claim 100% collectivisation by 1940, food production was only then creeping up to the 1928 level, in spite of the fact that the Russian population had grown from 150 million to 170 million.

The Purges and Show Trials

The fierceness and cruelty which Stalin used to get his economic plans underway dismayed many Russians but it is the terrible bloodletting of the 1930s, resulting in hundreds of thousands of deaths, for which Stalin's reign of terror, unparalleled in modern Russian history, is best remembered. Stalin suffered from extreme jealousy, suspiciousness, insecurity and even paranoia. This worsened after the suicide of his wife, Nadezhda, in 1932 . Repression was the means by which his terrorist state would be maintained. In 1933 the first round of purges took place. 'Undesirable elements' were to be eliminated, a situation that ensured that the party was reduced by a third. A lull in 1934 came to an end on 1st December of that year when Serge Kirov, a senior member of the Politburo, was assassinated. Supposedly a close friend of Stalin, the murder was used to justify a further, more brutal campaign of terror. This time, senior members of the party were arrested. Mass executions also took place. The Show Trials of 1936-1938 saw all the great names of the 1920s - members of Lenin's Politburo, chiefs of the Red Army and Soviet navy - step into the dock. Confessions were incredible. People 'confessed' to plotting to kill Stalin or to overthrow the state and were consequently found guilty. Zinoviev, Kamenev, Rykov and Bukharin were just some of those executed. Yagoda, the head of the NKVD*, masterminded the trials but he was himself executed in 1937. His successor, Yezhov, was committed to a lunatic asylum in 1938 and was later executed. In this way, Stalin *'the man eater'* established himself as dictator of totalitarian Russia. From then on, only reliable henchmen would be appointed to key positions.

Foreign Policy

Stalin's belief in *'socialism in one country'* ensured that he was not prepared to make any sacrifice of Soviet state interest for the sake of promoting revolution abroad. In any event, Stalin was suspicious of the West. He believed that the USSR had no natural allies and that she was better to adopt a defensive rather than offensive approach

---

* Until 1934 the NKVD was known as the OGPU. It was the successor to Lenin's *Cheka* (secret police)

to international relations. Until 1934, the Treaty of Rapallo was the anchor of Russian foreign policy. The treaty allowed for the re-establishment of diplomatic relations between Germany and Russia, the *'two black sheep of Europe'*. At the same time, it provided for mutual trading and military benefits. In 1928, the USSR signed the Kellog-Briand pact 'outlawing' war as a means of solving disputes. Russia's peace loving image was reinforced by the fact that in the 1930s non-aggression pacts were signed with many powers. Increasingly, Russia was becoming an accepted member of international society. It was, however, the rise of Hitler that marked a turning point in Stalin's foreign policy. In 1934, Russia became a member of the League of Nations. She preached the necessity for a strong League, the principles of collective security and the indivisibility of peace. During the Spanish Civil War, 1936-1939, Stalin sent sufficient aid to the Republican side in Spain to prolong rather than to win the war. But Russian foreign relations undoubtedly suffered from the impact of the purges and Stalin's weak international standing in the late 1930s could be seen from the fact that he was not invited to attend the Munich Conference, September 1938. Thereafter, Stalin was convinced that the only way to save his country was to enter an agreement with Hitler. In the Nazi-Soviet pact, August 1939, each power agreed not to attack the other for ten years. Secret clauses allowed for the partition of Poland.

World War II

The Nazi-Soviet pact was entered into cynically but it allowed Stalin time and space. War began on 3rd September 1939. In return for peace and territories allocated to him, Stalin supplied Germany with war materials. Stalin knew that war with Hitler was inevitable. He hoped the conflict could be delayed until late 1942. When Operation Barbarossa, the invasion of Russia, began therefore on 22nd June 1941, Stalin was taken unawares. The speed and success of the first German moves ensured that after only a fortnight, Russia had lost 1 million men, nearly the whole of its airforce and thousands of tanks. Yet, though badly shaken, Stalin recovered and began to give inspirational leadership and tireless energy to the task of the war, *"The whole Soviet people must fight for every inch of Soviet soil, fight to the last drop of our blood for our towns and villages"*. The German army of 3 million men adopted a three-pronged attack:

1. Leningrad in the north
2. Moscow in the centre
3. Ukraine and then the Caucasus oilfields in the south.

By September 1941 the northern prong had reached Leningrad and there began a 900-day siege. The centre force took Smolensk while the southern group took Kiev. By December, Hitler was within sight of his objective. But the Germans failed to take Moscow. Thereafter, while Hitler had some further successes, the Battle of Stalingrad, August 1942 to January 1943, was the turning point, the beginning of the end for the Nazis. The Russians, under Marshal Zhukov counter-attacked, forcing a German surrender. The Russians were increasingly on the offensive. Once victory was certain, Stalin's main concern was to make sure that, after the war, Russia could keep lands gained in 1939 - Latvia, Estonia, Lithuania and eastern Poland. He was also determined that the other states of Eastern Europe should fall under Soviet influence.

Post War Foreign Policy

Even before war had ended, the Yalta Conference, February 1945, had made plans for post-war development. Stalin agreed to Soviet participation in the United Nations and to a promise of free elections for Poland and other 'liberated' countries. Agreement was also reached on the division of Germany - and Berlin - into four spheres of influence: British, French, American and Russian. The Potsdam Conference, July 1945, reiterated many of these agreements and proved to be a personal triumph for Stalin in terms of the benefits and advantages that he secured. Thereafter, relations between Russia and America began to break down particularly when Stalin began to tighten his control over Eastern European countries. The free elections never materialised. In their place Soviet-supervised elections were held. Stalin proceeded to direct East European countries on how to develop. Farms were collectivised, industries nationalised and Communist parties purged. By the end of 1949, Romania, Bulgaria, Czechoslovakia, Hungary and Albania all had Communist-advised regimes. Yugoslavia resisted Stalinist dictatorship. Western opposition led to the *'Iron Curtain'* and the *'Cold War'*. The Cold War centred on Berlin in 1948. Stalin, fearing the formation of a powerful West Germany, attempted to starve the Western Powers out of Berlin. The blockade failed as the Allies air-lifted supplies into the city, and it was called off on 29th May 1949. Tensions between East and West had, nonetheless, deepened. The Korean War, 1950-1953, further threatened relations. Korea was a divided country: the North was Communist, the South was anti-Communist. In June 1950 the North Koreans made an all-out attack on the South. It was thought that the attack was ordered by Russia. Open war between the US and the USSR was a real possibility. This was prevented when Communist China rather than Stalinist Russia became directly involved in the conflict.

Post War Economy

The Soviet Union had emerged victorious in 1945. Stalin's position was strengthened as was the position of Communism in general. Yet the human and economic cost of the *'Great Patriotic War'* was devastating. At least 20 million Soviet citizens had died, millions more were wounded and maimed. The number of homeless stood at 25 million. Towns were shattered ruins while the countryside was reduced to grinding poverty and misery. Stalin made the huge task of rebuilding a major priority. In 1946 he announced plans for a fourth Five Year Plan, a fifth followed in 1951. The emphasis was once more on heavy industry and soviets were encouraged to work night and day. New towns were created, power stations and railways built and canals constructed. Stalin was obsessed with quantity and by 1950 production figures were 70% higher than those in 1940. Simultaneously, a build up of military equipment took place. As well as producing conventional weapons, tanks and MIG fighters, nuclear industry was encouraged. The first Russian atomic bomb was developed in 1949. The advances in agriculture were less spectacular, however. Collectivisation was again forced on the Russian people but this time it was enlarged to join several villages together. By 1953, there were less than 100,000 collectives in the USSR. In spite of this, production still did not increase. By 1950 Russia had only one fifth of the number of tractors in the US. The average harvest for the early 1950s was several million tons less than it had been in 1913.

Conclusion

In the last years of his life, Stalin continued to control every aspect of Russian life. The secret police, led by Beria, remained in existence and there was a return to pre-war tyranny. The Jews, in particular, suffered under Stalin and their persecution was every bit as severe as it had been under the Tsars. Jewish newspapers were banned and Jews themselves removed from top positions. This coincided with what could be deemed *'a purge of intellectuals'*. Zhdanov, secretary of the Leningrad party, launched a campaign to make artists, writers, musicians, scientists and historians follow party lines. They were expected to produce works of *'socialist realism'*. Those who did not conform faced punishment and exile. To that extent, it might be argued that Stalin was robbing the country of its brains but even more so, its heart and soul. Meanwhile, the cult of Stalin was being fostered. His portraits were hung everywhere, the flood of praise flowed unceasingly and towns were renamed - Stalingrad, Stalinabad, Stalinsk, Stalino and Stalinogorsk. His official biography stated that *"Stalin is a brilliant leader and teacher, the greatest strategist of the socialist revolution..."* But the elderly Stalin became ever more suspicious and rarely left the Kremlin. Plans were afoot for another bloody purge late in 1952. Doctors and Jews were a special target. Stalin, however, died on 5th March 1953, aged 73 years. While reaction to his death was mixed, Alexander Solzhenitsyn insisting that he could have *"howled for joy"*, the event was momentous, in one way or another, for all Soviet citizens. Stalin's economic achievements were indeed great. Nobody can dispute that under his control, Russia moved from the wooden plough to the atomic era, yet his terror and brutality cannot be masked. He left behind *"a country paralysed by fear, dullness and suspicion"*.

37. Stalin's Domestic Policy

Rise to Power - Aims

The death of Lenin in January 1924 led to an intra-party struggle. Potential leaders included Trotsky, Stalin, Zinoviev and Kamenev. Stalin's strategy was to undermine the position of potential rivals, to exploit (and distort!) past associations with Lenin and to play his rivals off against one another. Trotsky was the first of his opponents to be disposed of. His theory of *'permanent revolution'* was less tangible and less appealing to ordinary Russians than Stalin's *'socialism in one country'*. Stalin suggested that is was possible to construct socialism in Russia and leave the international revolution to take care of itself. His theory gave the Russian revolutionaries, who were unsure of what direction to go, a new *raison d'être*. By the time that Trotsky was expelled and Zinoviev and Kamenev realised just how dangerous Stalin really was, their reputations had already suffered. Zinoviev's downfall came because of his part in the Leningrad-Moscow rivalry (i.e. which city, Leningrad or Moscow, should emerge as the centre of power) and his belief that agriculture should be put ahead of industrialisation in the modernisation of Russia. Kamenev's belief that no one leader should try to replace Lenin as sole ruler of Russia proved to be his undoing. By December 1927 all three candidates had been expelled from the party. Other potential leaders, including Bukharin, were got rid of over the following years. Thus it was that *"the party's most eminent mediocrity"* emerged as sole leader of Russia. As well as his aim of socialism in one country through which Russia would become self-sufficient, Stalin sought to de-westernise the USSR and to make himself supreme dictator.

Industrialisation [I]

"We are fifty or a hundred years behind the advanced countries. We must make good this distance in ten years. Either we do it or be crushed". Stalin's objective was not just to catch up on the West, however, but to overtake it. Industrialisation would be the key to the gigantic leap forward, it would be the means by which Russia would be transformed. Five-Year Plans were launched to replace Lenin's NEP. The plans were not so much a programme as a law. Targets of production were laid down by *Gosplan,* an organisation which planned and controlled Russian industry and agriculture (under the Five-Year Plans). Failure to achieve required standards met with stiff penalties. The first plan which ran between 1928 and 1933 was directed at heavy industry, iron, coal, steel, transport and machinery. During this five-year period alone, 1,500 new industrial plants were built. The second plan lasted from 1933 to 1938. As well as heavy industry, there was a build up of armaments. Munition factories were established in the Urals. The third plan which began in 1938 was interrupted by Germany's invasion of Russia in 1941. Already by this stage, the plans had resulted in what amounted to an economic revolution. A vast iron works was built in Magnitogorsk in the Urals, a large hydro-electric plant was constructed on the river Dnieper, tractors and automobiles were produced. Railways, roads, air routes and canals were all developed. Simultaneously, towns were enlarged and new towns sprung up.

Industrialisation [II]

Just before the Second World War broke out, Russia had increased her industrial output by 400% since the beginning of World War I. Electricity output showed a tenfold increase between 1928 and 1940. This phenomenal progress, at a time when production was falling in many other countries, ensured that by 1939 the USSR was second only to the US as an industrial power. Such was the success of the *'leap forward'* that the unemployment of the NEP period gave way to labour shortages. This was overcome by the release of surplus labour from the land, an increase in the hours of work and by the use of forced labour. So-called *'criminals'* provided a cost-free labour force. Meanwhile, the necessary capital for industry was achieved through the ruthless accumulation of profit and a limit on personal consumption. Those whose performance was judged as poor, who were late, absent or incompetent were regarded as saboteurs. Punishment included imprisonment and death. On the other hand, the best workers were publicly honoured and formed part of a propaganda campaign. In 1935, Alexis Stakhanov supposedly succeeded in producing 102 tons of coal in a six-hour shift (14 times the average). For this all-time record, he was awarded the *'Order of Lenin'* and *'Hero of Socialist Labour'*. As well as public recognition, rewards included extra pay and free holidays. But for the ordinary Russian, living conditions remained deplorable. Standards of comfort and amenities were non-existent.

Collectivisation [I]

At the same time as the industrial revolution was taking place, there was to be an agrarian revolution. Stalin believed that this could best be achieved through collectivisation. This involved the abolition of small private holdings, of which there were 25 million and uniting them into larger collective units - the *kolkhozes*. This would allow for the modernisation and organisation of Russian agriculture and make optimum use of labour and of machinery. Quotas for production were fixed and as with industry, failure to meet targets met with punishment. State-owned farms, *Sovkhozes*, were established as early as 1919 and they were to lead the way. Few peasants, however, wished to give up their farms. The greatest resistance came from the *Kulaks*, the better-off farmers who stood to lose most by collectivisation. Opposition was such that millions of Russian peasants burned crops and killed their livestock - *"kill, it's not ours! kill, the state butchers will do it if we don't"*. Grain was hidden after the harvest. The result was that between 1928 and 1933, the number of horses declined from 33m to 15m, cattle numbers decreased from 75m to 34m, pigs from 26m to 9m and sheep and goats were reduced from 146m to 42m. The grain harvest declined from 73.3m tonnes to 68.4m for the same period.

Collectivisation [II]

Stalin made clear that opposition was not to be tolerated. He declared that the *Kulaks* should be *"annihiliated as a class"*. The OGPU were ruthless in their suppression and once more, the Russian countryside became a battlefield. Stocks of grain were confiscated, recalcitrant peasants were deported into Siberia or labour camps. Millions were killed. Famine returned to Russia and from 1932 to 1933 its spread reached frightening levels. In some areas, the peasants were reduced to cannibalism. But Stalin continued to pursue his policy of collectivisation relentlessly and up to 10m people are said to have *'met unnatural death'*. While in 1928 only 2% of farms were collectivised, by 1932 the figure had reached 62% and by 1940 the government announced 100% collectivisation. There now existed about 300,000 collectives, each with an average of 80 families. Stalin did make one concession to the peasants. He allowed each peasant employed on a collective to own a small private allotment of 2.5 acres and a cow. This was jealously guarded by the peasant and yields from private plots were much higher than from the collectives. Although overall production did increase gradually, in 1939 food production was only just creeping up to the 1928 level, in spite of the fact that the population had grown from 150m to 170m.

Purges

In the 1930s a new black phase of Russian history began as Stalin sought to 'cleanse' the Communist party. *"How long are you going to kill people?"* Stalin was asked to which he replied *"As long as it is necessary"*. Many reasons have been put forward as to the causes of this massive bloodletting. These include Stalin's personal depression. 1932 saw the suicide of Stalin's wife and the attempted suicide of his son. Thereafter, he became increasingly isolated. Stalin was also very suspicious and insecure. His dullness contrasted markedly with the flair, imagination and popularity of other party members. At the same time, Stalin was very paranoid believing that his enemies were everywhere. Undoubtedly, there was widespread dissatisfaction and oppositionist sentiment, particularly among *'old Bolsheviks'* or founder members but this was insufficient to justify the reign of terror which Stalin initiated. Elimination of enemies started in earnest in April 1933 when a resolution was passed to get rid of 'undesirable' elements within the party. The criteria laid down for these 'undesirables' was broad enough to embrace practically anybody. The results of this first round of purges, which sought to eliminate ordinary party members, was that by the end of the year one-third of the party had been expelled or had left of its own accord. 1934 saw a lull in the purges but the assassination of Serge Kirov, a popular member of the Politburo and a likely contender for leadership, on 1st December of that year gave Stalin a new licence to kill. Those in high positions fell victim to arrests, deportations and executions. One noticeable feature of this second phase of purges was that many people were prepared to denounce each other.

The Show Trials, 1936/1938

Starting in August 1936 a series of public show trials took place. These were the brainchild of Yagoda, the head of NKVD. The chief prosecutor was Andrei Vyskinsky, well known for his demand *'Shoot the mad dogs'*. Those put on trial were accused of plotting against the State, being agents of the *Gestapo*, planning the murder of Stalin, even of poisoning water supplies. They were then found guilty on their own confessions. Undoubtedly they were forced confessions - victims were terrorised, beaten, blackmailed, brainwashed. Major public and army figures were executed. Zinoviev, Kamenev and 14 others were found guilty of being *'agents of the German-Polish Fascists'* in August 1936 and thereafter they were executed. Anyone suspected of being a Trotskyite was also tried, as was the whole of Lenin's Politburo with the exception of Stalin and Trotsky. Many chiefs of the Red Army and admirals of the

Soviet navy also came under attack. Yagoda lost his position as head of the NKVD in September 1936 and was subsequently executed. His successor, Yezhov, met a similar fate. In 1938 he was condemned to a lunatic asylum and in 1939 he was executed because *"he killed many innocent people"*. Such was the totality of Stalin's purging that it is estimated that as many as 10% of Russia's population *"passed through the penitential system"*. By 1939, when a halt was called to the terror, the Politburo was made up entirely of Stalin's henchmen, among which were Molotov, Khrushchev, Zdhanov and Beria, the new chief of police. A final postscript to the purges came on 20th August 1940 when Trotsky was assassinated by Stalin's agents in Mexico.

Totalitarianism

By the 1930s the growing totalitarian nature of Stalinist Russia could not go unnoticed. The means by which the economic revolution was achieved and the elimination of all potential enemies through the policy of purging were just some of the ways in which Russia was forced into a totalitarian state. Others include the suppression of religious beliefs, the confiscation of Church property, the ill-treatment of priests and the steady flow of anti-religious propaganda to the press. Simultaneously, the cult of Stalin was fostered. Towns changed their name in recognition of their new 'God' - Stalingrad, Stalinabad, Stalinogorsk, Stalinsk. Statues were erected to testify loyalty to Stalin. Meanwhile, the family was exploited as a unit of social service. The USSR continually proclaimed the virtues of a stable family and married life. There was also the state sponsored creation of Youth Clubs. The Young Pioneers, the *Komsomol* and the *Osoaviakhim* were some such organisations. The freedom of individuals was severely restricted, ensuring that there was no scope for even limited discussion of the nature or aims of society. In such a context, Soviet patriotism became paramount. Strict censorship guaranteed that culture was 'hijacked'. Education, literature, art, music were made to glorify the State. History was revised. In 1936 a new constitution gave everyone over 18 years the right to vote by secret ballot but the only party allowed to stand for election was the Communist party (so that the result was hardly a surprise). Such was the means by which Stalin achieved his totalitarian dictatorship.

38.   Stalin's Foreign Policy

"We do not want a single foot of foreign territory but we will not surrender a single inch of our territory either".
— Stalin

Aims - Attitude

The Russian revolution of 1917 brought into existence a new political and economic system. This, along with the Soviet aim of promoting revolution abroad, ensured that the USSR was regarded with great hostility by the West. Likewise, Russia was suspicious of Western powers. All capitalists were regarded as a threat to Communism. A further problem which underlay relations with other powers was the essentially negative memories of Western interference in the Russian civil war. This was complicated by the fact that Stalin had rarely been outside Russia and was largely ignorant of 'foreigners'. Stalin also knew that as the only Communist state in the world, the Soviet Union, had no natural allies. But Stalin's belief in *'socialism in one country'* was such that the defence of the USSR was more important than spreading revolution. Stalin was not prepared to make any sacrifice of Soviet state interest. Thus it was that Stalin, whose aim was primarily defensive, sought to keep the capitalist powers at bay as he won breathing space which would allow him to build up his country. A belief in the necessity of peace created a fear of war which was *"of an incredible intensity"*. Stalin could be as cold-blooded in foreign matters as he was with dealing with events at home. He knew, however, that it was to his advantage to play the diplomatic game. Stalin was helped in this by the fact that in 1924 the Soviet Union had been recognised *de jure* (rightfully) by a whole host of important powers including Great Britain, France, Italy, Norway, Sweden, Denmark, Austria, Hungary and Greece. The US continued to withhold recognition.

Rapallo Agreement - International Co-Operation

As early as 1922, the two outcasts of Europe, Germany and Russia, drew together in a treaty that greatly alarmed the rest of Europe. This was the Rapallo agreement whereby Germany became the first country to give Russia full recognition. Both countries agreed to renounce financial claims on each other and to exchange trade and military advice. The Rapallo agreement was renewed in 1926 and despite its smooth surface being ruffled from time to time, it remained the anchor of Soviet foreign policy until 1934. Stalin agreed to provide the bases for German military experiments and to allow for the establishment in Russia of German factories for the production of poison gas, aeroplanes and artillery shells. In return, Russia was familiarised with the most progressive Western techniques in a vital area of defence. To Germany, Rapallo constituted a weapon in the struggle against Versailles whereas for Russia it meant that a united capitalist front against her was impossible. Meanwhile, Russia's attempt to create a *'barrier of peace'* was taken a step further when in 1928, her Foreign Minister, Maxim Litvinov, called for total international disarmament. In that same year, Russia signed the US inspired Kellog-Briand pact 'outlawing' war as a means of solving disputes. When in 1933 America granted official recognition to the USSR, it seemed that the Soviet Union was increasingly becoming an accepted member of international society.

Relations with Communist Movements

An important feature of Russian foreign policy under Stalin was relations with Communist groups outside of Russia. Stalin saw himself as supreme master directing the activities of other left-wing movements and consequently insisted on total control over, and total obedience from, all foreign Communist parties. He insisted, through a Comintern directive in 1928, for example, that the German Communist Party (KPD) remain distinct from the more moderate Social Democratic Federation (SDP). This weakened the Left in its dealings with Hitler. Stalin, for his part, hoped that a weak Nazi government would give way to a Communist revolution and dictatorship. Only when Hitler came to power in 1933 and the Communist party was banned and persecuted did Stalin realise his mistake. This prompted a new policy which was first publicly declared in 1935 at the Congress of the Third Communist International. Stalin now made known his approval of Communist co-operation with Liberals and Socialists. This was known as the Popular Front. The idea was that the spread of Nazism and Fascism threatened all liberal and left-wing forces everywhere. Therefore, despite their individual differences, they should unite to defeat these forces which would destroy them all. France and Spain were two countries where Popular Front governments were formed in the 1930s. All too often these movements were suspected of being Russian-led, for the reality of the situation was that the interests of foreign Communist parties were continually subordinated to the interests of Stalin.

Stalin's Response to the Rise of Hitler

The rise of Hitler to power in 1933 brought further changes to Stalin's foreign policy. In particular it meant an end to German-Russian co-operation. Attempts to breathe life into the Rapallo agreement were futile and by 1934 Rapallo was nothing more than 'a corpse'. Already by then, Litvinov had negotiated non-aggression pacts with Poland, Finland, Lithuania, Estonia and Romania. September 1934 saw Russia looking for further collective security, this time through her entry to the League of Nations which she had earlier condemned as a *"capitalist club"*. Russia was also elected permanent member of the Council and seemed to have well and truly moved over to the 'side of the angels'. Above all, Russia feared being caught on her own in a war against Nazi Germany. Every diplomatic device had to be exploited to prevent this. Litvinov sought to put teeth into the League as he preached the necessity for strength and firmness against Fascism as well as the indivisibility of peace. Simultaneously, he drew the League's attention to the aggression of Fascism. In 1935 the Soviets gave added emphasis to their policy of collective security by concluding mutual assistance pacts with France and then Czechoslovakia. A clause in the Franco-Soviet treaty allowed for assistance to Czechoslovakia only if both countries united in action. But the weakness in Russia's position was obvious from the fact that she was not invited to join the Stresa Front in 1935 and by the failure of the Western powers to resist Hitler's occupation of the Rhineland in 1936.

The Spanish Civil War, 1936-1939

When the Spanish Ccivil War broke out in 1936 and Germany and Italy sent troops to help Franco and the Nationalists, Stalin decided to aid the Republicans. There was, however, strict limitations placed on the nature and quantity of Soviet aid offered. This was because of Stalin's overriding desire for peace and his fear of open conflict with Fascist Germany and Italy. Stalin also realised that the triumph of Communism in the midst of a hostile capitalist Western Europe was not a practical solution and could have the effect of uniting Britain, France, Germany and Italy against the great *'Red Peril'*. Stalin also felt that Spain was too removed from the USSR for him to be able to control its Communist development. Communism without Stalin was not a realistic proposition for him. His policy, therefore, was to send sufficient aid not to win the war, but to keep it going as long as possible in the hope of distracting the Fascist powers. Tanks, fighter planes and military advisors were sent in limited numbers. The number of Soviet personnel sent to Spain, for example, never exceeded 2,000. In this way Stalin ensured that Soviet Russia would not be militarily exhausted before the onslaught of the feared German invasion. One 'success' for Stalin in terms of his involvement in Spain was that he managed to get the Republican government there to send its gold reserves to Russia for 'safekeeping'. The gold was conveniently retained after the war.

Towards War

Russian foreign relations undoubtedly suffered from the impact of the purges as questions were asked about the type of state that could allow such treachery and cruelty. The result was to leave the Soviet Union isolated. While isolated the Russians saw the progress of the British policy of appeasement and the success of Hitler at the Munich Conference, September 1938, to which Stalin had not been invited. The German seizure of Czechoslovakia in March 1939 represented to Stalin the start of *Lebensraum,* but without French help, Stalin maintained that he was unable to help Czechoslovakia in her hour of need. The failure of collective security led Stalin to state *"Let every country defend itself against the aggressor as it will and can, our interest is not at stake, we shall bargain with the aggressor and with their victims"*. Soon afterwards, *Pravda,* the official newspaper, declared that Russia saw *"no difference between German and English robbers"*. Such was the context in which Stalin turned away from the West and sought an accommodation with Hitler. This came in the form of the Nazi-Soviet Non-Aggression Pact of August 1939. The pact was the combined work of Molotov* and Ribbentrop, the German Foreign Minister. It was meant to last for 10 years during which time both countries agreed not to attack each other. Secret additional clauses allowed for the partition of Poland and adjoining Baltic states. Although the pact was entered into cynically, Stalin had bought valuable time to complete his preparation to defend his country while Hitler ensured that Poland would not be helped by Russia when the Germans invaded.

* Molotov replaced Litvinov as Foreign Minister in May 1939

Involvement with China and Japan

Stalin also had to keep a constant watch on Russia's frontiers in Asia and the Far East. Japan was Russia's old enemy and had been the last foreign power to leave Russian territory during the civil war. Though Stalin's Far Eastern policy in the period before the Second World War sought to make the most of the differences between imperialist Japan and weak China, its operation was largely one of support for China. Yet Stalin was not above playing a double game when it suited him. Consequently he bought off the Japanese at various stages. They gained from oil protection rights in Northern Sakhalin and in 1935, Russia's interest in the Chinese Eastern Railway was sold to the Japanese puppet state of Manchukuo at a fraction of its real value. Nonetheless, the Japanese joined with Germany (and later Italy) in November 1936 in the Anti-Comintern Pact which was directed specifically against the Soviet Union. In 1937, Stalin welcomed Japan's war with China, hoping that Japan would be weakened by it. When in 1938 the Japanese invaded the People's Republic of Mongolia - a Russian sphere of influence - war broke out between Russia and Japan, lasting until the summer of 1939. Stalin took the war seriously and sent a large army, under Marshal Zhukov, to Mongolia. Modern tanks and aeroplanes helped to ensure that a crushing defeat was inflicted on Japan. Thereafter, Japan refused to be drawn into Germany's war with Russia when it came in 1941.

The Outbreak of War

World War II broke out in September 1939 following Hitler's invasion of Poland. Stalin could breathe easily, for a time at least, knowing that the Soviet Union was safe from German aggression. Russian armies moved forward as Stalin sought to gain for Russia everything that was permitted (and more!) under the Nazi-Soviet pact. Part of Poland was taken while strategic areas of Finland were also seized by force. The Baltic States were likewise annexed. The occupation of these lands gave Stalin the feeling that Russia was now secure against German attack and, throughout 1940, relations were friendly. Russia supplied Hitler with enormous quantities of oil, grain and war materials as well as allowing Hitler's warships to use Russian naval bases. This was of huge benefit to the Germans during their successful campaigns up to 1941. In 1941, however, relations worsened. Talks between Molotov and Ribbentrop in Berlin over what Germany should or should not be allowed to occupy, insofar as Russia was directly effected, broke down. Then in June 1941 Hitler gave orders for Operation Barbarossa, the German invasion of Russia. Stalin was stunned and horrified. In spite of the bad relations between the two countries in that year and 76 separate warnings of a German attack, Stalin had not expected invasion, at least not until Britain had been defeated. So nothing had been done to prepare the Russian army and people. This in turn allowed for the speed and success of Hitler's first moves. But Stalin, and indeed the whole of Russia, fought back and eventually *"tore the guts out of the German army"* (Winston Churchill).

Russia Under Stalin: Past Exam Questions

1992

D1. Stalin

"From the death of Lenin, 1924, up to Hitler's invasion of Russia, 1941, Stalin consolidated his personal power and transformed the USSR." Discuss.

1990

E4. Essay

(v)   An assessment of the part played by Stalin in the history of the USSR.

1988

D1. Stalin

Assess the part played by Joseph Stalin in Russian affairs,

1985

D1. Stalin

Discuss (i) or (ii):

(i)   Stalin's rule in the USSR. during the period 1927-1941.

(ii)   Stalin as war-leader and statesman during the period 1941-1953.

CIVIL WAR IN SPAIN

39. The Spanish Civil War

Introduction - Outbreak of War

A Republic was declared in Spain, for the second time, in 1931 when Alfonso XIII went into exile. But the divisions and unresolved problems, so much a part of 20th century Spain, remained. In particular, there was the Left-Right conflict. Power had traditionally rested with the Right, the army, the Catholic Church and the wealthier landlords and industrialists. These were supported by the Fascists *(Falange)* and the Royalists and collectively they made up the National Front. They sought to save 'traditional Spain' from disorder and left-wing domination. The Left consisted of the Republicans, Socialists, Communists and the navy, and received the backing of the mass of workers and peasants as well as the Basques and Catalans, separatists who sought more independence for their regions. The February 1936 election swept this Popular Front coalition to power. Headed by Manuel Azaña and referred to as the government of the *'Godless Republic'*, the Popular Front immediately set about re-introducing the reforms of 1931-1933, which included the introduction of a democratic constitution, the granting of some measure of local autonomy to Catalonia, a reduction in the power of the Catholic Church and an attempt to break up large estates and redistribute land. The Popular Front also released thousands of political prisoners. Soon, however, disturbances of all sorts began to occur. The general indecision of the country was such that violence was followed by counter-violence and in such a climate, the Nationalists decided that a military coup was the only way of saving Spain. General José Sanjurjo, Emilio Mola and Francisco Franco, all of whom had been 'transferred' outside Spain, drew up plans to seize power. As they did so, they received an added impetus when on 13th July, José Calvo Sotelo, a leader of the *Falange* and CEDA (Catholic party) was assassinated. Within days, Spain had been plunged into civil war.

Phase One: July-December 1936

The civil war erupted in Melilla, Morocco, where some army officers seized important buildings. Franco flew to Morocco from the Canaries and took command of the Nationalist forces there. Meanwhile, revolt and war had spread to the mainland of Spain. The Nationalists had the advantages of surprise, of superior armed might and experience and of greater organisation. They were also helped by the refusal of the Republican government to arm the workers. Yet the Nationalists faced some serious setbacks in the early days of war. These included the death of General Sanjurjo who was killed in an aircrash, and the problem of finding transport for the African forces, so difficult because the navy had remained loyal to the Republicans. This last problem was overcome by the use of 20 German transport planes. On 6th August Franco arrived in Seville with 10,000 African troops. He soon began to make headway against the Republican forces. Seville, Granada, Cordoba were taken, as were Badajoz and

Talavera after fierce sieges and bitter fighting. Simultaneously, General Mola was working from the north. He managed to capture Pamplona, Salamanca, Valladolid and Burgos, which now became the headquarters of Nationalist forces. The aim was to link up the northern and southern sections at Madrid. Progress was hampered by the well defended mountainous regions through which Mola's troops had to pass and the Republican offensive at Toledo. This, more than anything else, delayed the capture of Madrid and gave the capital time to strengthen its defences.

Siege of Alcazar at Toledo - End of Phase One

Toledo was a medieval city on the banks of the river Tagus which, from the first week of civil war, experienced fierce fighting between the Nationalists and Republicans. In the battle for control of the city, the Republicans appeared to be getting the upper hand. The Nationalists, pressurised, retreated to Alcazar, the great stone fortress of Toledo. The besieged garrison, led by General Moscardo, had a good supply of water, arms and ammunition, and hoped to hold out in spite of the fact that their food supplies were inadequate and they were cut off from the outside world. Largo Cabellero, the new Republican Prime Minister, came from Madrid to supervise the siege. But the Republicans found the walls of Alcazar difficult to penetrate. They thus began, on 21st September, to dig a tunnel under the fortress with the intention of placing mines there and blowing up Alcazar. Although some mines did go off, Moscardo refused to surrender. Franco, at this point, was obliged to change direction and go to the relief of Alcazar. On 27th September, one of his armies, under General Varela, arrived with artillery. The Nationalists were thereby enabled to win the ten week siege. Attention was again focused on Madrid. The capital was besieged and bombed but the Republicans had had time to prepare for a siege and held on. The inability of Nationalist forces to advance beyond the suburbs meant that the triumphant *'March on Madrid'* had not been accomplished and the war dragged on. In the first six months of fighting alone, 100,000 people were killed, many of them innocent victims. In addition to Madrid, the Republicans continued to control Valencia, Barcelona and the Basque region.

Phase Two: 1937

The Nationalists re-opened their offensive in the new year by attacks on Malaga and Valencia. The Republicans hit back. In the Jarama valley both sides suffered terrible casualties before the Nationalists conceded defeat. Then in March 1937, at Guadalajara, near Madrid, the Nationalists suffered another setback. The campaign against the Basques proved more successful. Bilbao, the Basque capital, had iron ore deposits, metalworks and shipyards, all of which were very important to the war effort. Slowly but surely, the Nationalists made their way. On 26th April the town of Guernica, the spiritual capital of the Basque region, was bombed by the German Condor Legion which, in its *Blitzkrieg* tactics, dropped 100,000 pounds of bombs. Over a thousand people were killed and many more were injured. The destruction of Guernica, immortalised by Pablo Picasso in his famous painting *'Guernica'* caused a wave of horror around the world and undoubtedly damaged the Nationalist cause. Nonetheless, the ruthlessness and horror continued. Growing disunity among the disparate Republican forces ensured that in May 1937, they fought amongst themselves in Barcelona in what has been described as a miniature civil war within the Civil War. The Communists succeeded in establishing control over the city. Upon this followed a major crisis in the government, leading to the formation of a new government, under Juan Negrín. The death of General Mola in June 1937 did not halt the campaign against the Basques. On 19th June Bilbao was taken, on 25th August Santander fell and on 21st October, Gijon, the last town to hold out in the north, fell. The Basque dream of independence was well and truly over.

Phase Three: Battle of Teruel, December 1937-February 1938

A key battle and one of the hardest fought of the civil war was at Teruel. Teruel was a Nationalist stronghold but in an attempt to relieve pressure on the northern front and on Madrid, the Republicans mounted an offensive. On 15th December 1937, the campaign began. The Nationalists, led by Colonel d'Harcourt, were taken by surprise. They had 18,000 troops by comparison to the Republicans 100,000 troops. Led by El Campesino, the early successes were for the Republicans. This, however, was their last gain. A counter-attack began on 15th January 1938. A fierce battle raged during the worst winter Spain had had for many years. Sub-zero temperatures ensured that many people died from frost-bite. Franco sent help in the form of 80,000 troops. The Nationalists were further aided by German and Italian planes and artillery which proved superior to the Russian tanks used by the Republicans. The tide of war consequently turned in favour of the Nationalists, so that on 22nd February 1938 the Nationalists captured Teruel. By then the town had been reduced to ruins by shells and bombs, 14,000 people were dead and 20,000 wounded. Teruel must be seen as the beginning of the end for the Republicans, as from now on they were in retreat.

Phase Three Continues

Following the Nationalist success at Teruel, Franco decided on a sudden drive towards Valencia. The Republicans made a last offensive by attempting to cut off Franco's troops at the river Ebro. From July to November 1938 the battle of Ebro was fought. It, too, was fiercely contested. The Republican army was, by then, exhausted. Shortage of men, artillery and aeroplanes and a people who were half-starved meant that the battle cry of *"Resist, Resist, Resist"* became increasingly meaningless. When at last the Nationalists were able to re-cross the Ebro, helped, as they were, by Franco's superior air power, even the severe winter could not hold back their final sweep to victory. The war, which had been one of lightning offensives and wearisome delays, conformed to type to the very end. An offensive in Catalonia, begun in December 1938, soon developed into an attack on Barcelona, from where the Republican government was now operating. Menaced from both north-west and south-west, Barcelona fell at the end of January 1939, after a campaign of just over one month. The government fled north to Figueras. In February, when 62 members of the parliament met, Negrín hurled defiance at the enemy. Yet, where earlier when he spoke in terms of peace proposals he had formulated 13 points as his irreducible minimum, those 13 points were now reduced to 3. Franco continued to insist that nothing short of unconditional surrender would be accepted. As the Republicans lost the rest of Catalonia, hundreds of thousands of refugees poured into France. Meanwhile, the government moved to a village near the French frontier before finally Negrín and his cabinet returned to Madrid.

Phase Four: Siege of Madrid

The battle of Madrid had actually started in November 1936 and had involved heavy hand-to-hand fighting and high casualties. Yet the city had refused to fall and stalemate had ensued. The main reasons why the Nationalists had failed to capture Madrid included the delays caused by Toledo and Teruel, the tough resistance put up by the Republicans and Franco's refusal to allow the city to be bombed to pieces. Franco's strategy for the last two years of war was to surround Madrid and starve its inhabitants into surrender. Four columns of troops surrounded the city. Perhaps more important was the *'fifth column'*, consisting of secret supporters inside the city. As the tide of war turned against the Republicans and the situation in Madrid gravely worsened, this *'fifth column'* grew. By 1939 and with no fuel inside the city, only two ounces of food daily and hundreds dying of starvation, attack proved unnecessary. On 5th March 1939, Negrín and his government were ousted by a military junta of Socialists and Anarchists. Led by Colonel Casado, the Junta formed a Council of National Defence which sought to obtain better terms of surrender than Negrín. This coupled to more division and in-fighting among the Republican supporters and a revolt against the Council resulted in over a thousand deaths. The Republicans had come to the end of the road. The Council addressed itself to surrender but failed to achieve improved terms from the Nationalist leaders, other than to allow their own junta officials to leave Spain. On 28th March 1939, 200,000 Nationalists entered Madrid in triumph. On 1st April, the war officially ended.

Conclusion

The Spanish Civil War lasted two years and 254 days and was estimated to have cost 1,000,000 lives, *"un millon de muertos"*. In addition, over 300,000 Republicans went into exile and a remaining 250,000 were imprisoned. The Civil War was not just national but international in character, attracting to each side the sympathies and active support of men in other countries. On a simplistic level, it was believed that the war in Spain was between Civilian Government and Totalitarian Dictatorship, between Communism and Fascism, Left and Right. While the reality was slightly more complicated, the extent of foreign intervention was decisive. On the Nationalist side, Hitler sent 16,000 troops and the Condor Legion of aircraft tanks and artillery. Mussolini sent as many as 70,000 troops and the Portuguese President, Salazar, sent 20,000 men. On the other side of the fence, Stalin sent 2,000 men, tanks and raw materials. Volunteers, forming part of the International Brigades and numbering around 40,000, also sided with the Republicans. France, though sympathising with the Republicans, opted, alongside Britain, for a policy of non-intervention. Superior foreign aid, the presentation of a united front and strong leadership guaranteed a Nationalist victory. Franco, who opted for a policy of neutrality in the Second World War, now became *El Caudillo* (the leader). He established an authoritarian, pro-Spanish and Catholic state. In time, Spain gradually began to assume an aura of respectability. This allowed for international acceptance. Following the death of Franco in 1975, a peaceful transition to monarchy took place.

Civil War in Spain: Past Exam Questions

1994, 1989

E4. Essay

The Spanish Civil War, 1936-1939.

1992

D3. Franco and Spain

Account for the victory of Franco in the Spanish Civil War and assess the significance of that victory for Spain.

1990

E4. Essay

(iv) International involvement in the Spanish Civil War.

1985

D2. The Spanish Civil War

Treat of the origins of the Spanish Civil War and discuss international reaction to events in Spain, 1936-1939.

Franco with Mussolini at Bordighera

Josef Stalin

Adolf Hitler

Hitler and Mussolini, 1938

WORLD WAR II

40. Assess the Part Played by Great Britain in World War II

"Victory - victory at all costs, victory in spite of all terror; victory, however long and hard the road may be".
— Churchill, 1940

Introduction - September 1939-May 1940

At the end of several years of tension, war came in September 1939 when Hitler's forces, on the first of the month, attacked Poland. By that stage there was a feeling that something evil had been let loose in Europe and a belief that peaceful solution had been carried to the limit of honourable negotiation. This, combined with a promise of military assistance to Poland, ensured that on 3rd September, Britain and France declared war on Germany. But the Allies proved unable to help the Poles. The British Royal Air Force (RAF), for example, did not have the necessary fuel capacity to fly over such distances. Consequently, Hitler with his *Blitzkrieg* (lightning war) tactics was enabled to carry out the swift conquest and partition of Poland. Defence measures taken in Britain included black-outs, rationing, evacuation from London as well as the extension of military conscription. Abroad, the British Expeditionary Force (BEF) took up positions at the north end of the Maginot Line. *'Operation Yellow'*, however, the code name for an attack on the West through the low countries was postponed a number of times and people began to speak in terms of a 'twilight' or 'phoney' war. This was because, apart from occasional skirmishes on the Maginot Line and considerable activity at sea, things were uncannily quiet and there was no bombing. Hitler even held out an olive branch to the West in October and November 1939 but this was mainly for the purpose of propaganda inside Germany and was promptly rebuffed. Meanwhile, the German *Sitzkrieg* (sitting war) created a false sense of security, prompting Chamberlain to speak in terms of Hitler having *"missed the bus"*. This all changed on 9th April 1940 when the Germans launched an offensive against Denmark. The country almost immediately fell. Only days later Norway was in the grip of the Nazis. British and French help to Norway came too late and in May 1940, they were forced to withdraw.

May-June 1940 - From Chamberlain to Churchill

The unsuccessful attempt to save Norway from falling into Hitler's hands led to general disenchantment with Neville Chamberlain's conduct of war. He was accused of showing little enterprise and of lacking the personality to inspire a nation at war. On 10th May, Chamberlain resigned. Winston Churchill, who had earlier served as First Lord of the Admiralty, now aged 65, became Prime Minister of a national or coalition government. While he warned that *"I have nothing to offer but blood, toil, tears and sweat"*, Churchill showed an indomitable spirit and great confidence. He announced his policy *"to wage war, by sea, land, and air, with all our might and with all the strength that God can give us"*. Hitler's Germany was the enemy and nothing should distract people from the task of effecting defeat. That nothing should be allowed to stand in the way of the nation's total prosecution of war became more immediate on the very day of Churchill's appointment, as German troops swept into the Netherlands and Belgium. On 14th May, the Netherlands surrendered, Belgium capitulated on 28th May. Such was the effectiveness of the *'scythe sweep'* that the Maginot Line was rendered useless as Hitler, by-passing it, made his way through France. The failure of Allied counter-attacks meant that there was no alternative but to evacuate by sea as many British and French troops as possible that were cut off in the north-west. Between 27th May and 4th June hundreds of little boats took part in the evacuation of 340,000 men, 224,000 of whom belonged to the BEF. The evacuation took place in the midst of shell fire and aerial attack and led to talk of the Dunkirk *'miracle'*, whose spirit was one of bold improvisation, endurance and of attempting the impossible. Thereafter, the surrender of France towards the end of June 1940 left Great Britain alone and seemingly defenceless in the face of the European conqueror.

The Battle of Britain

'Operation Sea Lion' was the name given to the German invasion of Britain. In order to successfully invade Britain, control of the air was required. The task of achieving this was entrusted to Göring's *Luftwaffe*. On 10th July the first heavy bombing in Southern England took place. For a month bombing was concentrated on shipping and ports, for another month on airfields and London. Although the British had roughly the same number of fighter planes as the *Luftwaffe*, they had far fewer bombers than the Germans. Nonetheless, production of British Spitfires and Hurricanes increased dramatically. The British were further aided by radar which warned of approaching attacks and guided the RAF towards the *Luftwaffe*. In addition, the fact that the British fought mainly on home ground meant that they did not have the same fuel problems as the Germans and could remain in the air for longer periods. The skill and sacrifice of many of her bravest pilots also deserves mention and in time, these pilots retaliated by heavy bombing raids on Germany. Not surprisingly, losses on both sides were high. During the *'Blitz'* about 60,000 people were killed. Between August and September, the *Luftwaffe* lost 1,244 planes and crews. These were losses it could not afford. Hitler, realising that air superiority over England was proving more difficult than originally thought, decided on 17th September to postpone *'Operation Sea Lion'* indefinitely. While bombing continued thereafter, Churchill speaking of the Battle of Britain, could well maintain that *"Never in the field of human conflict was so much owed by so many to so few"*. Churchill himself had played an important role in the battle. Seemingly everywhere, he was at fighter headquarters, visiting victims of the *Blitz*, broadcasting frank reports to the nation. The victory of the British in this, *"their finest hour"*, meant that though the road to survival was still long and painful, they had set out resolutely.

War in North Africa - Balkans

Mussolini brought Italy into the war in June 1940, when France was clearly in collapse. He saw the war as an opportunity to expand his empire. Consequently, in September 1940, a strong Italian force numbering around 300,000, and under the command of Marshal Graziani, invaded Egypt. This move threatened the British hold on the Suez Canal and led to a British counter-attack in December. Under General Wavell and numbering only around 60,000, the British pushed the Italians back 500 miles westwards to Benghazi. With very small losses to his troops, Wavell managed to take 130,000 Italian prisoners. He subsequently withdrew to Egypt, leaving a small Australian garrison to hold Tobruk. These startling land victories helped to raise British morale but Wavell was unable to follow up the successes. There were many reasons for this. In the first place, Churchill halted the British defeat of Italian forces when he ordered Wavell to dispatch his forces to Greece which had been invaded by Axis powers. Churchill also demanded that an attack of Italian East Africa take place. The third obstacle to Wavell's continuing success was the arrival of a strong German army in North Africa under the command of General Rommel, the *'Desert Fox'*. Meanwhile in Europe the Italians suffered still more reverses in the Balkans when they attacked Greece and Yugoslavia. German intervention quickly brought the expulsion of British troops from Greece and even Crete. Before long, Germany occupied the whole of the Balkan peninsula. In the North African desert, however, the British made fresh gains against the Italians. In January 1941, two British columns advanced against Eritrea, Italian Somaliland and Abyssinia. Throughout all of this, the sea battle raged intermittently. In November 1940 a British air attack from the carrier *Illustrious* on the naval base at Taranto knocked out three Italian battleships. Then in March 1941 British naval units inflicted heavy losses on the Italian fleet off Cape Matapan in Southern Greece.

The Grand Alliance - Continued Fighting in North Africa

The huge financial burden that these battles placed upon the British taxed her heavily. Some relief came in the ingenious *'Lend Lease'* Act of March 1941 which authorised President Roosevelt to put American resources at the disposal of any state whose defence was regarded as necessary for the security of the US. Britain's position was further helped when Hitler invaded the Soviet Union in June 1941, bringing that country into the war on the side of the Allied powers. Of his alliance with the USSR, Churchill declared that he would not *"unsay"* any word he had previously spoken about Communism but insisted that *"the Russian danger is .... our danger"*. In December of the same year, the Japanese bombing of the US base at Pearl Harbour brought America into the war. The *'Grand Alliance'* was now in place and the balance of advantages tipped sharply in Britain's favour. An Anglo-American agreement on basic strategy gave priority to the defeat of Germany over Japan. But the tale of reverses was not yet done. In North Africa Erwin Rommel captured Tobruk in June 1942 and then advanced to El Alamein, as he made ready to capture Egypt. El Alamein proved to be the decisive battle of the desert war. Fought in October 1942, General Montgomery, Commander of the British Eighth Army, after some fierce fighting, managed to break through Rommel's lines. Rommel's *Afrika Korps* and the Italian armies were completely routed with the loss of 60,000 men, 1,000 guns and 500 tanks.

On the importance of this victory, Churchill maintained that *"Up to Alamein we survived. After Alamein we conquered"*. In fast follow-up to this victory, Anglo-American forces landed in Morocco and Algeria, forcing the Vichy authorities there to abandon their carefully cherished attitude of neutrality. Then in December the battle of Tunisia was fought. A triumph of combined Anglo-American-French forces under Montgomery and General Alexander took place. More than 250,000 Germans and Italians were taken prisoner. *'Operation Torch'* came to an end on 12th May 1943.

Bombing of Germany - Operation Husky

After the Tunisian victory, the *"soft underbelly of the Axis"* had been exposed. The war in the East, meanwhile, had reached a turning point in the Winter of 1942 with the Battle of Stalingrad, which was of undoubted importance in the eventual defeat of Germany. There now remained two ways of striking at the Axis, short of opening up a second front in France. One was to strike at German communications and industrial centres by air attack. The other was to strike from the south of Italy. In terms of the former, the RAF made its first thousand-bomber attack on Cologne on 30th May 1943. This was followed during the summer by others on Essen and the Ruhr, a centre of steel production. The autumn of 1943 saw the bombing campaign against Germany stepped up. The docks of Hamburg, and Berlin itself, suffered. American bombers went at high altitude by day, the British by night. Many cities were left in ruins. The attack on Italy, *'Operation Husky'*, began on 9th July 1943. The American Seventh and British Eighth Armies landed on the coast of Sicily. Within weeks, the Germans were driven out. As the Allies moved northwards, many Italian garrisons showed themselves all too ready to quit. Mussolini was himself deposed on 25th July 1943 and although he was restored for a while as leader of a puppet German government, the end was in sight. Marshal Badoglio, Mussolini's successor, was forced to make peace with the Allies and on 16th September, he turned his forces against the Germans. Slowly but surely the Allies advanced. Naples was liberated on 1st October 1943, Rome in June 1944 and in April 1945, the Allies broke through into the Plain of Lombardy. The defensive Gothic Line was now broken.

Operation Overlord

Following a conference in Teheran, November 1943, between Roosevelt, Churchill and Stalin, it was agreed to open up a second front and invade France. The D-Day landings were preceded by the smashing from the air, or by local sabotage, of German coastal defences, radar installations and interior communications. At the same time, the United Kingdom was turned into a vast airfield, port and base in which men and equipment were accumulated for the great invasion. Some 1 million American troops had been trained and transported to Britain in readiness. Then on 6th June 1944 the largest seaborne invasion in history took place when a mighty armada of 4,000 ships converged upon the beaches of Normandy. General Dwight Eisenhower was placed in command of *'Operation Overlord'*. On the first day, he landed 130,000 men, by the sixth day, 326,000 men had successfully landed on a bridgehead some 50 miles wide. By 2nd July, 1 million men were in France. Although there were 61,000 casualties, only 9,000 had been killed. At the end of July the Allies had 2 million men in France. As well as the British and Americans, these included Canadians and Frenchmen.

Against them the Germans had mustered a quarter of their entire army. Led by Field Marshal Karl von Rundstedt, they put up fierce resistance. Nonetheless, they were driven back to the old Siegfried Line in the Rhineland. Paris was liberated in the latter days of August. In the following months, the Allies freed the rest of France and much of Belgium and the Netherlands, and this in spite of such setbacks as that at Arnhem in the Netherlands.

End of War - Conclusion

The Germans made a last desperate attempt to halt the Allies. In mid-December, General von Rundstedt began a surprise counter-offensive in the Ardennes. At first he was successful and the Allies were driven back so that a huge 'bulge' appeared in their lines. The Allies got reinforcements and by late January, the Germans had retreated. This became known as *'The Battle of the Bulge'*. In February at the Yalta Conference, Churchill, Roosevelt and Stalin met to decide on the future of Europe. It was at this conference that a promise was made whereby in return for Russia's entry into the Japanese war, the USSR was to gain extensive territorial gains in the Far East. Meanwhile in March 1945, the Allied armies, having captured Cologne, crossed the Rhine. In April the Allied forces closed on Berlin and finally on 8th May, the Germans formally surrendered. The war in Europe was over but the war in the Pacific had yet to be fully resolved. British Hong Kong, Singapore, Malaya and Burma were overrun by the Japanese. Led by Admiral Lord Mountbatten, British forces, combined with Indian, Chinese and African troops, cleared Burma and then moved on to take Malaya while the Australians recovered Borneo. The campaign against Japan itself culminated in the dropping of two atomic bombs on 6th and 9th of August. Days later, Japan asked for peace. Thus ended the Second World War, the most destructive war in human history. In so far as Britain was concerned, war had cost 303,000 lives in the armed forces, 30,000 members of the Merchant Navy and 60,000 civilians. The severest material loss was financial. Great areas of the country were laid waste and in addition to the general dislocation of ordinary life, people experienced high taxes, rationing and desperation. In the midst of the Potsdam Conference, July 1945, Churchill was replaced as Prime Minister by Clement Atlee. Upon him and his Labour government rested the task of steering the country through the difficult early years of the post-war period.

41. Treat of the Part Played by the USSR in World War II

"There is nothing more maddening than being interrupted just as you are completing the roof of your hut: if only we had five more years! But if war comes then we shall fight it with a fierceness and anger the like of which the world has never seen".

— *'In the Ukrainian Steppes',* a Russian play

Introduction, 1939-1941

The Nazi-Soviet Non-Aggression Pact of 23rd August 1939 promised ten years non-aggression between the Soviet Union and Germany. In addition, secret clauses allowed for the division of Poland. Although entered into cynically by both partners, it did allow Stalin breathing space during which time Russia could strengthen her forces. Meanwhile, Hitler with his rear secure, invaded Poland on 1st September 1939. This led to the outbreak of the Second World War. While Soviet Russia was not officially involved in the war, she did, nonetheless, invade Eastern Poland on 17th September 1939. That blow in the back sealed Poland's fate, for there were scarcely any troops there to oppose this second invasion. Poland was partitioned between Germany and Russia and by 5th October, the country no longer existed. The Soviet Union now sought strategic control of the Baltic states. By 10th October 1939, Estonia, Latvia and Lithuania were induced to allow Russian forces to take over. On 12th October, Stalin demanded that Finland sign a mutual assistance pact and that it hand over some territory to the USSR. The Finns refused these demands and on 30th November, the Soviets attacked at various points along the frontier. This *'winter war'* was one in which the Finns, under the leadership of Marshal Von Mannerheim, fought bravely. Yet even the inferior Russian weapons, snowy mountainous conditions and heavy loss of life, could not prevent the overwhelming numbers of Russian troops from finally breaking through. In March 1940 the Finns surrendered and the Peace of Moscow was signed, by which strategic areas of Finland were ceded to the USSR. As the war in Europe continued to be fought, Stalin provided the Germans with vital materials, such as petrol, iron-ore, timber and wheat. He also turned a blind eye to the Luftwaffe's activity over Russian soil and consistently refused to believe intelligence reports of an impending German invasion of Russia.

Operation Barbarossa

Hitler had always contemplated the overthrow of the Soviet Union. The Nazi-Soviet Pact was simply a matter of expedience. Consequently, in December 1940, Hitler issued directive No. 21, *'Case Barbarossa'*, which declared that *'The German armed forces must be prepared to crush Soviet Russia in a quick campaign before the end of the war against England'*. Hitler's reasons for invasion included his deep anti-Communist convictions, his need for greater supplies and resources than Russia would give him voluntarily and his desire to acquire more living space for German people *(Lebensraum)*. Mussolini's abortive aggression in the Balkans, which resulted in Hitler's decision of 1st April to send forces against Greece and Yugoslavia, entailed the postponement of Operation Barbarossa from May to late June 1941. The attack on

Russia, when it began on 22nd June, took the world by surprise as it was not preceded by a declaration of war. About 3,200,000 German soldiers were involved. These were divided into 3 major groups. The Northern force was led by Field Marshal Von Leeb. His plan was to advance through the Baltic region and capture Leningrad. The Central group, under Field Marshal von Bock, struck towards Smolensk and Moscow while the Southern group, commanded by Field Marshal Von Rundstedt, planned to drive into the Ukraine and press on to the Caucasian oil fields. Such was Stalin's shock at the invasion that leadership gave way to despair as he realised that the warnings he had angrily spurned were true. Only on 3rd July had he sufficiently recovered to address the nation on radio and to resume effective control.

The Siege of Leningrad

The *Luftwaffe* bombers with their *Blitzkrieg* tactics had, within 48 hours of their Russian invasion, inflicted devastating losses on the Red Air Force even before the planes could get off the ground. Simultaneously, defence units at the border disintegrated and the mechanised armies of the *Wehrmacht* swept into Russia. Battles moved swiftly and confusingly and heavy tolls were exacted. The initial success of the Germans was such that in October 1941 Hitler announced that *"the enemy is already broken and will never rise again"*. The Germans on the Northern front, for example, succeeded in breaking through the Baltic provinces and by September had reached the outskirts of Leningrad. Hitler hoped to besiege the city, strangling it with hunger and destroying it with artillery bombardment. Three million people were trapped inside the city. There were about 200,000 soldiers who were, in turn, aided by the People's Militia. But although the people of Leningrad did what they could to defend the city, they were severely handicapped by limited supplies of weapons, ammunition and food. The only supply route for the inhabitants was across Lake Ladoga, the *'Lifeline Road'*. The barges which crossed the lake in summer and the lorries which drove over the ice in winter were bombed by the Germans. The city itself was bombarded for an average of 9 hours a day. January to February 1942 was the worst period of the war for Leningrad, as during these two months 200,000 people died of cold and hunger. Water and sewage pipes froze and there was no electricity. In May 1942 fresh troops crossed Lake Ladoga to strengthen the exhausted garrison. Although the Germans continued their artillery attacks through 1943, on 27th January 1944, after 900 days of bombardment, the enemy retreated. Up to 1 million people had died during the siege.

Central Forces/Moscow

Meanwhile, within 5 days of the onslaught of battle, Army Group Centre had covered 320 km and captured 300,000 Russians between the frontier and Minsk. Only weeks later, another 200,000 prisoners were taken near Smolensk which was seen as *'the key to Moscow'*. So fierce was the fighting there that the Germans called it *'the bloody furnace'*. The actual attack on Moscow was delayed by several weeks as Hitler directed some of Army Group Centre's force to assist the assault on Kiev. In October, however, the Germans reached Khimki, halfway between the airport and the Kremlin. On the 19th of the month, Moscow was declared to be under siege, and the civilian population was organised to build anti-tank defences around the city. As temperatures continued to drop, reaching 20°C below freezing in November 1940, the Germans found themselves ill-equipped for the Russian winter. Their clothes were unsuitable and their artillery unable to function properly. A large scale Russian counter offensive, prepared and directed by General G. K. Zhukov, began early in December with the 31st Army attacking to the south of Moscow and the 29th Army to the north. The Red Army maintained its attack into the New Year, suffering over 400,000 casualties. Finally, on 15th January 1942, Hitler permitted the German Army Group Centre to withdraw 100 miles and more from Moscow.

Battle for Stalingrad

Hitler's goal to capture Moscow and Leningrad and destroy the Soviet armies in 1941 proved unattainable. Consequently, he decided that the South was to be the main theatre of operation in the summer campaign of 1942. The Caucasus produced three-quarters of Russia's oil, a great deal of iron-ore and some coal. Hitler could gain much needed supplies for the Germans while, at the same time, he could bring Russia to its knees. He was, in particular, obsessed with the capture of Stalingrad, symbolic as it was of Stalin and the Soviet regime. Before *'Operation Blue'* got underway, a disastrous Russian offensive in the Ukraine had been launched by Timoshenko in May 1942. Approximately 350,000 Russians and 12,000 tanks were captured. On 28th June the attack on the Caucasus began. Voronezh fell on 6th July, Rostov was taken on the 23rd July. Hitler then split his forces, ordering the Sixth Army under General von Paulus to capture Stalingrad. While the army that faced Stalingrad was a good deal weaker than it needed to be, it still consisted of 400,000 men. The city was defended by 100,000 men under Zhukov, now a Marshal. Over the weeks ahead, the Germans advanced, wave after wave, against Stalingrad, the Russian Verdun. The fighting was horrific and, as buildings were reduced to rubble, troops were reduced to eating rats. The Russians fought doggedly. Although they were driven back into the centre of the city, civilians crawled out of their cellars and fought alongside the troops. Zhukov reformed his army and on 19th November a Soviet counter-attack began, taking the Germans by surprise. The slaughter continued through until the beginning of February 1943, when von Paulus surrendered with the 22,000 men still with him.

Russian Determination and Triumph

The Battle for Stalingrad was a turning point in the war and marked the beginning of the end for Nazi Germany. In addition to *'General Winter'* which ensured that *Blitzkrieg* tactics came unstuck, there were many other reasons why the Russians managed to hold on to their major cities. One such was the *'scorched earth'* policy which the Russians adopted. This involved burning haystacks and grain and driving their animals with them as they disappeared into the woods or swamps to form guerilla bands. Nothing of value was left for the enemy. Another important element contributing to Hitler's defeat was the dismantling of some 1,500 factories from western Russia and their movement to the Urals, Siberia and Central Asia. There they were rebuilt and produced vital materials necessary for the war effort. The loyalty and determination of the Russians played a part in the eventual triumph. Sometimes this was forced, but more often it was as a direct result of German brutality which fired the patriotism of the Russian people. Stalin's leadership was, after the initial shock of invasion, inspirational and his speeches rousing. Even as the Germans advanced on

Moscow, he refused to leave the Kremlin. The German underestimation of the strength of the Red Army disadvantaged the aggressors. They were also taken by surprise to find brilliant military Russian leaders, most notably Zhukov and Timoshenko, opposing them. Above all, however, Hitler had expected to deal with the Soviet Union in isolation. Yet, after *'Operation Barbarossa'* commenced, an Anglo-Russian alliance was formed. Then in December 1941, the US entered the war and Hitler had to contend with the formidable opposition of the *'Big Three'*.

Turn of the Tide

Although the tide had turned after Stalingrad, the war was by no means over. Russia's success thereafter was helped by the flow of western aid. Huge numbers of planes, tanks, jeeps and chemicals tipped the balance in her favour. By April 1943, the Germans had been driven back some 600 miles. Rostov and Vorenezh were among the towns recaptured. Hitler now insisted upon another German offensive, believing a spectacular victory necessary for army morale. *'Operation Citadel'* chose Kursk as the scene of the engagement. This time the Russians, forewarned by the British, were ready. An elaborate anti-tank defence all around Kursk had been prepared when the assault began on 5th July 1943. The biggest and fiercest tank battle of the war took place but the Germans failed to break through the Russian line and had to call off the attack. More Russian successes followed. On 23rd August, the Germans were forced to evacuate Kharkov. By September, the Russians had advanced as far as the River Dnieper in the Ukraine. In October, Smolensk and Kiev were recaptured. The relentless pursuit continued through the winter months. In January 1944, the 900 day siege of Leningrad came to an end. During the spring the last remaining pockets of enemy resistance were mopped up. Odessa was recaptured in April and the Crimea in May. In June 1944, the long awaited *'second front'* that Stalin had impatiently been demanding was opened as an Anglo-American task force landed in Normandy. Soviet troops simultaneously crossed the Polish frontier at several points.

War Comes to an End - Conclusion

Henceforth, the Russians used the Red Army to gain political as well as military advantage. The Russians proceeded to enter Romania and capture Bucharest. Freed from the Nazis, Romania made peace with Moscow and declared war against Germany. Bulgaria, Yugoslavia and Hungary told similar stories. With the exception of Greece, which the British occupied, Soviet troops had liberated the entire Balkan peninsula and assured their own predominance in the post-war period. In January 1945, Warsaw was liberated. Soviet troops drove the Germans out of Vienna in the spring of 1945 and then pushed into Czechoslovakia. The Russians also advanced into Germany, pressing relentlessly towards Berlin. A last desperate effort by the Germans along the line of the Oder proved futile. In April, Soviet and American forces met at Targau on the river Elbe. The Russians were given the honour of taking Berlin in May 1945. On 8th May, the Germans formally surrendered. As war in Europe came to an end, the conferences of Yalta and Potsdam 1945 sought to determine the continent's future. In addition to the agreement on the division of Germany, it was decided that Stalin, in return for joining the war against Japan, would be given considerable territorial gain. With Japan's surrender only days after the USSR's involvement there, this was to prove a costly error on the part of Britain and the US. In the meantime, Russia, the emerging Superpower, had to count the very considerable cost of war. With as many as 20 million Soviet citizens reported to have died in action or as a consequence of the occupation, and huge devastation to towns, villages, factories, schools, railroads, electrical power and the countryside itself, the Eastern Front might well refuse to be *'the forgotten chapter of World War II'*.

World War II: Past Exam Questions

1995

D3. The U.S.S.R. and World War II

Describe the part played by the U.S.S.R. (Union of Soviet Socialist Republics) in World War II, 1939-1945.

E4. Essay

(iii) Naval warfare in World Wars I and II.

1994

D3. World War II

Account for the initial success and the ultimate defeat of Germany in World War II.

1993

D2. Winston Churchill

Assess the part played by Winston Churchill, British Prime Minister, 1940-1945, in bringing about the Allied victory in World War II.

1990

D4. Warfare, 1939-1945

Describe the main developments in warfare during World War II.

1989

D4. Great Britain, 1939-1945

Assess the part played by Great Britain in World War II.

1988

D5. Warfare

"Science and technology altered the nature of warfare in the twentieth century". Discuss.

1987

D4. The U.S.S.R. and World War II

Treat of the part played by the U.S.S.R. (Union of Soviet Socialist Republics) in World War II.

POST-WAR FRANCE

42. Charles de Gaulle, 1890-1970

Background - Army Career

Charles de Gaulle was born, the son of a lecturer, in Lille on 22nd November 1890. On leaving school, De Gaulle entered the military academy of St. Cyr where he proved to be a brilliant student. During the First World War, De Gaulle fought under Marshal Pétain. In 1916 he was wounded at the Battle of Verdun and subsequently taken prisoner. Released in 1918, De Gaulle resumed his military career. In the early 1920s, De Gaulle taught military history at St. Cyr. 1925 saw his promotion, by Pétain, to the staff of the Supreme War Council. He also became a member of the National Defence Council. Throughout the 1930s, De Gaulle expressed his strong reservations about France's defence policies. In a series of books including 'Vers l'Armée de Métier' (Towards a Professional Army), De Gaulle spoke of the foolishness of relying on the fortifications of the Maginot Line as the means of defending France from future invasion. De Gaulle warned that tank and air power rendered the Maginot Line obsolete. This, along with De Gaulle's insistence on the need to develop a modern, mechanised French army with specialised armoured divisions, was largely ignored by his superiors. With the advent of World War II, France's ill-preparedness was quickly realised. De Gaulle was then a Colonel, but in May 1940 he was promoted to the rank of General. The following month he was appointed Under-Secretary for War in the French government. In this latter capacity he flew to London twice and so impressed was he by Churchill's determination to defeat Hitler that, with the impending French defeat at the hands of the Germans, he announced the formation of the Free French Movement.

French Resistance

France fell to the Germans in June 1940. When on the 22nd of the month the armistice was signed, defeated France was divided in two. The north and west were occupied by German forces while the south and east became a puppet state ruled from Vichy by Marshal Pétain. De Gaulle refused to accept that France had been defeated maintaining that *"we have lost a battle but we have not lost the war"*. From England, where he was condemned by Pétain and sentenced to death by a French court martial, De Gaulle continued to fight against Germany, carrying on what amounted to a guerilla war. Acts of sabotage and the disruption of communication guaranteed that, in time, resistance was to grow from tiny seeds into a powerful movement. In the meantime, however, De Gaulle faced many problems. Not only were French exiles in London unable to make an impact in occupied France or in pro-German Vichy France, but De Gaulle was also disliked and distrusted by the Allies who saw him as a *"prickly general"* who might attempt to establish a military dictatorship in the future. 1941 improved De Gaulle's position. Vichy rule was becoming increasingly distasteful and the French Communist party, militantly anti-Nazi since the start of Operation Barbarossa, supported De Gaulle's resistance. The Allied landings in French North Africa in 1942, De Gaulle's establishment of a power base there, the liberation of Corsica by his forces and the formation of the machinery of local government in preparation for a takeover of administration of liberated France ensured the continued growth and success of De Gaulle's movement. And although De Gaulle was kept in the dark about D-Day landings in Normandy on 6th June 1944, his return to France thereafter furthered his position. De Gaulle was determined that France would not be led by either the Allies or the Communists. The Germans surrendered Paris on 26th August 1944. The following day, De Gaulle led a victory parade down the Champs Elysées, the acknowledged liberator of the overjoyed Parisians.

De Gaulle as Head of State, 1944-1946

On 10th September 1944, De Gaulle announced the setting up of a Provisional Government of which he was the head. This government received formal recognition from the Allies in October but, as far as international co-operation was concerned, the Allies remained wary of De Gaulle. Consequently he was not permitted to attend either the Yalta or Potsdam Conferences in 1945. He did, nonetheless, gain an occupation zone of influence in defeated Germany and was represented at the signing of Germany's unconditional surrender on 7th May 1945. At home, De Gaulle had to deal with a number of problems, the most immediate of which was what to do with the Vichy officials and collaborators. Special courts were set up and 767 people were shot after official trials. Among those was Vichy Prime Minister, Pierre Laval, who became a scapegoat for all the evils of the Vichy years. Vichy Head of State, Pétain, was sentenced to death but this was later commuted to life imprisonment because of his age and his record of service in World War I. At local level, a savage campaign or witch hunt against collaborators also took place. The number who lost their lives in this way is unknown but Alfred Cobban, the British historian, estimates as many as 30,000. As far as the economy was concerned, the Resistance Charter demanded *"A more just social order....the subordination of private interests to the general interest"*. In a referendum of October 1945, the people voted by a majority of 96% against the revival of the Third Republic. The new government, of which De Gaulle was Prime Minister, had to draw up a constitution. Yet De Gaulle, who was lacking in political experience, failed to come to terms with the party system. In particular, he refused to allow Socialist or Communist deputies hold key positions even though between them they had gained 48% of the vote. Constant difficulties existed but the breaking point, in so far as De Gaulle was concerned, came over the issue of presidency. De Gaulle failed to win approval for a strong presidency and resigned suddenly on 20th January 1946.

Retirement and Return to Power, 1946-1958

Later in 1946, the French electorate approved a new constitution. The Fourth Republic proceeded thereafter to repeat many of the mistakes of the Third Republic, lurching from one governmental crisis to another. Lack of strong decisive government and *'Immobilisme'* perhaps best characterise the years 1946-1958. In April 1947, De Gaulle founded his own party, the *Rassemblement du Peuple Francais (RPF)*. This was a conservative group to the right of French politics which aimed to destroy the parliamentary system and to change the constitution. Its slogan was *"Power to De Gaulle"*. While the RPF did have some success at the polls, becoming the largest group in parliament by 1952, it failed to form a single party government or to bring De Gaulle back to power. In time its followers began to play the parliamentary system. As a result, De Gaulle announced his second retirement from public life in 1953, declaring that he would only return in the event of a national crisis. Such a catastrophe originated in Algeria, a French colony since 1830. Algeria was a prized colonial possession. Not only had oil and natural gas been discovered, but 1 million French settlers lived there. A further half million French Algerians were living and working in France. In 1954 the Algerian National Liberation Front under the leadership of Ben Bella demanded independence. When the French refused to comply, a long and costly war followed. By 1958 the war was costing the French £2,000,000 a day. But when it was rumoured that the government of Prime Minister Pflimlin was considering a settlement with the Algerians, the regular army rose in rebellion and demanded the return of De Gaulle, the one man they considered to be strong enough to keep Algeria French. In May 1958 Pflimlin resigned and De Gaulle was invited to become Prime Minister. He agreed on condition that he could rule by decree for six months and that he could draw up a new constitution.

Fifth Republic - Solution in Algeria

When De Gaulle became Prime Minister on 1st June 1958, the Fourth Reublic was essentially dead, all that remained was to bury it. This was done in September 1958 when a national referendum was held and 80% of Frenchmen voted acceptance of a new constitution. The constitution of the Fifth Republic differed radically from those of the Third and Fourth Republics. In particular, it greatly strenghtened the powers of the President and reduced those of the Assembly. No longer a mere figurehead, the President could appoint the Prime Minister, control defence and foreign policy, dissolve parliament, rule by decree in times of crisis and appeal directly to the people by referendum to support his decisions. In December 1958 De Gaulle was elected to the office of President. He retained the position, being re-elected in 1965 by popular vote, until his resignation in 1969. Meanwhile De Gaulle's handling of the Algerian crisis was going to be of upmost importance to his future. Although the army and the Algerian settlers had been the ultimate cause of his resumption of power, De Gaulle never committed himself to keeping Algeria French. Realising that a military victory was impossible, De Gaulle in 1959 offered Algeria independence within five years. The Secret Army Organisation (O.A.S.) and those in the French army who had earlier supported De Gaulle now turned against him. In 1961 the O.A.S. attempted a military coup of Algeria but De Gaulle appeared on television and succeeded in getting widespread support for his handling of the situation. Several attempts were made on his life but in March 1962, when De Gaulle put the Algerian question to a national referendum, 92% of the French people voted in favour of granting Algeria independence. De Gaulle's success in disentangling France from the Algerian debacle is undoubtedly one of his greatest achievements.

Foreign Policy

De Gaulle's dream of grandeur or greatness for his country was such that he aimed to give France a key role in international affairs. He also sought, whenever possible, to establish the independence of France. In particular, De Gaulle wished to make France independent of the American and Soviet blocs. He envisaged France as a *'third force'* between the Superpowers. Not surprisingly, De Gaulle resented American domination of NATO. He disliked Britain as a country with too close ties with the USA. His resentment of these two powers was likely to be linked with their treatment of him as leader of the Free French during the war. In any event, starting in 1959, De Gaulle gradually withdrew France from NATO. All formal ties had been broken in 1966 and NATO had to move its headquarters from Paris to Brussels. In 1963 and 1967 De Gaulle used his power of veto to block Britain's entry to the EEC. Relations were, however, improved between France and Germany. Both De Gaulle and Adenauer worked towards co-operation and reconciliation. This led in 1963 to the Franco-German Treaty of Friendship. As President, De Gaulle undertook several foreign trips including a visit to Latin America in 1964, to Moscow in 1966 and to Canada in 1967. His goal was to enhance France's image as a world power. To this end, De Gaulle worked towards the development of independent nuclear weapons. France exploded her first atomic bomb in 1960. Thereafter, she refused to sign a nuclear test ban and by 1968 she possessed hydrogen bombs and a nuclear strike force. Although of little practical value, this force cost 1,000 million dollars a year.

Economy

The post-war economic boom, initiated by the governments of the Fourth Republic, reached its peak under De Gaulle so that it was now possible for France to become a modern industrialised society. Having taken office, De Gaulle persuaded the French people to subscribe to a *'patriotic loan'*. This enabled him to introduce cuts in public spending, to bring about currency reform and to stabilise the economy. By 1963 France had accumulated considerable gold reserves and had solved her balance of payments deficit. New industries such as plastics, chemicals and electronics were established, while shipbuilding, motor and aircraft industries were all expanded. Agriculture was modernised. In 1961, for example, a law was passed to enable young modern farmers to buy land. Pensions were awarded to older farmers to encourage them to retire. Meanwhile the state set up an agency to buy land and resell it to younger people. French agriculture also benefited from membership of the EEC and from the Common Agricultural Policy which gave guaranteed prices and subsidies to farmers. Big farmers fared much better than smaller ones. A rapid increase in population was accompanied by a shift of population to urban areas. Simultaneously, there was an increase in social services. Hospitals, schools and houses were all developed. Town planning was improved. Yet problems remained, and economic progress all too often varied from area to area. In the west of France, for example, the average income was half what it was in the east.

1968 Revolution - Resignation - An Evaluation

From the mid-1960s there was growing discontent with De Gaulle's style of leadership. A new generation of French people questioned the relevance of his economic and political policies. This was especially obvious in the student revolts of 1968. The French university was old fashioned in its structures, philosophy and curricula. Students were critical of accommodation, relevance of academic courses and the impossibly high standards demanded. Under the leadership of Daniel Cohn-Bendit, students began to strike in February 1968. By May, huge demonstrations led to serious clashes with the police. Tear gas was used against the students who put up barricades and threw bricks, stones and Molotov cocktails. The students were joined by about 10 million workers, discontented with poor wages, censorship and discrimination. Having assured himself of the army's support, De Gaulle appeared on national television and called for the defence of the Republic against militant communism and anarchy. His formula worked. De Gaulle was helped by the fact that the students and workers had little in common. Workers were bought off with a pay rise and order was restored. But De Gaulle's prestige was damaged. He tried to recover lost ground by introducing change in the Senate and by creating regional councils. A positive vote, for these measures, was to be regarded as a vote of confidence in his presidency. When he lost by 12 million votes to 11 million, De Gaulle resigned in April 1969. He retired to Colombey-les-Deux-Eglises where he wrote his memoirs. De Gaulle died in November 1970. *"Respected rather than loved"*, De Gaulle was unbending in his drive to force his will on the French nation. His was an authoritarian or military-like discipline. Excessively nationalistic, he had an unshakeable confidence in his own judgement, so much so that towards the end of his presidency his advice to the French was *"Find another De Gaulle"*. Yet there can be no doubting De Gaulle's untiring devotion to France's interests. The enduring nature of the Fifth Republic is a monument to its creator, General Charles De Gaulle, the *"male Joan of Arc"*.

43. The Fourth Republic, 1946-1958

Origins of the Fourth Republic

France's defeat at the hands of the Germans in 1940 and the signing of an armistice in June of that year ensured the collapse of the Third Republic. The humiliation of total collapse was followed by the moral ambiguity of divided allegiance. On the one hand, there was Vichy France and its supporters, while on the other, there were the followers of the Resistance movement. Four years of divided loyalties could well have been followed by civil war when France was liberated in 1944. That such was not the case was largely due to General de Gaulle, who for 14 months headed a provisional government. As he sought to restore law and order, De Gaulle faced enormous problems. In particular, he had to deal with collaborators, as well as setting about restoring the economy and gaining international recognition. In October 1945 a referendum was held. The overwhelming desire for a new beginning was shown from the fact that 96% of the French voters rejected the idea of continuing, or reviving, the Third Republic. De Gaulle now headed a parliamentary government but it was a task he was not suited to by either training or beliefs. He failed to come to terms with the Left or to include Communists in key ministerial positions. Breaking point came over the issue of a new constitution. De Gaulle stood for a presidential, as opposed to a parliamentary, executive. His vision of a strong President who could decide policy was along American lines. But De Gaulle's views were not shared by others and in January 1946 De Gaulle suddenly resigned. He was convinced that the constituent assembly would fail to draft an acceptable constitution and that he would be recalled. This was not the case, however, for while the new constitution did have a difficult birth, its first draft failing to find acceptance by the French people, a final version was accepted in October 1946. Thus began the Fourth Republic.

The Constitution

The constitution of the Fourth Republic was accepted by 9 million votes to 8 million. That the Republic had not got off to a flying start but was rather dogged by apathy was seen from the fact that over 8 million voters (1/3 of the electorate) abstained from casting a preference. Thereafter the Fourth Republic was to follow so closely in the steps of the Third that the observer might well feel that it had merely changed to remain the same. Parliament was to consist of two houses, the National Assembly and the Council of the Republic. This second chamber was more a symbol that an effective political force and was perhaps best described as a *'chamber of reflection'*. The President, who was to have only limited power, was elected for 7 years. The Socialist, Vincent Auriol, became the first President. Because of his personal prestige and political skill, Auriol was able to play an important role behind the scenes, although his functions remained largely those of prompter and scene shifter. His successor, Coty, was even closer to the presidential tradition of the Third Republic. The Prime Minister, for his part, had to command the confidence of the Assembly. Felix Gavin first held the position. Yet attempts were made to remove some of the weaknesses of the old regime. The right of *'interpellation'* by which a deputy would call for the resignation of a government minister was dropped. Parliament itself could be dissolved only by a vote of no confidence. And in order to avoid instability, the constitution favoured the creation of large parties. But while all of this was effectively contrived on paper, the reality was that it was to prove easier to change a nation's laws than its habits. Governments fell without having received the fatal vote of no confidence, the group system gradually re-emerged and all too often while governments changed, their personnel remained the same.

Political Parties - Immobilisme

Between September 1944 and June 1956 there were six general elections in France. During the same period, 27 separate governments were formed. Most of these were coalitions. In the early days of the Fourth Republic, the National Assembly was dominated by three groups. These were the Communists (P.C.F.), the Socialists (S.F.I.O.) and the *Mouvement Républicaine Populaire* (M.R.P.). This latter party was a new Christian Democrat group led by Georges Bidault. Participation in government by the P.C.F. soon led to various disputes. Fear of dictatorship coupled with opposition from the Americans, who were unwilling to give Marshal Aid to France if Communists continued to hold high places, led to their dismissal from cabinet in 1947. For over 30 years, the Communists did not hold any government positions. Other groups in French political life included the Radicals, who made up the centre, and the right-wing *Rassemblement du Peuple Français* (Rally of the French People). Established by De Gaulle in April 1947, the RPF was opposed to Communism and to the constitution. Although the group performed quite well at the polls, it was never large enough to form a single party government or to bring De Gaulle back. In 1953, De Gaulle withdrew from the party. Meanwhile, the overriding characteristic of successive governments was their failure to govern properly - *Immobilisme*. Time and time again, governments were incapable of decisive action or imaginative reform in case of offending one or other coalition partner. An attempt was made by the government of Pierre Mendès France to provide strong dynamic government and to break out of *immobilisme* but the effort proved impossible and Mendès France lasted only 7 months in office. Bargaining and compromising on policies ensured that support for big parties sagged. A host of smaller ones appeared, some only lasting one election. Into this rather confusing political arena appeared Pierre Poujade in the mid 1950s. His was a party of the extreme Right that denounced taxation, the bureaucracy, the unions, big business and Jews.

The Economy

The French government faced serious post-war economic problems. Growing inflation, for example, threatened to get out of hand, leading as it did to the government printing more and more bank notes. The result was that between 1945 and 1947 the *franc* lost one third of its value. Yet the re-shaping of the French economy met with remarkable success, much of this because it was the one area of French life that was largely free from the vagaries of party politics. Recovery was especially helped by the infusion of Marshal Aid from America. In one form or another, the flow of credit from the US continued up to 1955. The appointment of Jean Monnet as head of Planning Commission was a major success. Monnet was an outstanding economist who in 1946-47 launched the plan for economic expansion. Railways, mines and electricity were all nationalised, while investment in modern machinery and technology was stressed. Targets for growth were set. With the slogan *"Modernisation or downfall"* his ideas quietly but efficiently penetrated French industry and business. France's steel and electrical industries grew, while French cars, railways and aviation proved tremendously successful. A second plan was adopted in 1954. Economic co-operation with the other European states came in the Schuman Plan, 1950, and the establishment of the EEC in 1957, of which France was a founder member. Agriculture did not share in the boom. It was not until the Fifth Republic that the benefits of the common market made themselves felt. In spite of an annual growth rate of 4% in the 1950s, problems remained. These included a balance of payments deficit, the devaluation of the *franc* in 1958 and the slow development of social reform.

Foreign Policy - Colonial Problems (Indo China)

The Fourth Republic had some achievements in European international relations. In particular, France played a significant role in building powerful institutions for European security and trade. In April 1949 France signed a treaty with other Western European countries to form the North Atlantic Treaty Organisation (NATO). In that same year, France agreed to the creation of West Germany. In 1950, French Prime Minister René Pléven had plans for a European defence community to consist of an army made up of contingents from each member state. While this ultimately failed, France played a part in the re-integration of Germany into the Western Military Alliance. France was also responsible for the European Coal and Steel Community (ECSC) which originated in the Schuman Plan, and in 1957 France was a founder member of the EEC which was to work towards *"an enduring and closer union between peoples"*. But it was overseas commitments that most preoccupied French foreign policy. Indo-China, which comprised Vietnam, Cambodia and Laos, was one such concern. It had been part of France's overseas empire since 1884 and had been run primarily for the good of the French settlers. All too often the native population endured harsh and depressed conditions. In 1946 the Communist leader, Ho Chi Minh, and his military commander, General Giap, started a campaign for Vietnamese independence, using the Communist guerilla organisation, the Vietminh.

Indo-China

The French refused to recognise Vietnamese independence and an eight-year war followed, 1946-1954. By 1951, 250,000 French troops, led by General Navarre, were in Vietnam but the guerilla tactics used by the Vietminh proved impossible to overcome. The struggle was all too often played out in the swamps and jungles of the area and the cost in money and men was appalling. The decisive battle was the siege at Dien Bien Phu which lasted from March to May 1954. Giap won the day because he managed to get supplies through 800 kilometres of jungle, swamps and blown bridges. He used 20,000 native labourers to make a tough, bicycle-pushing human supply column. For the really heavy material 600 Russian-built $2^{1/2}$ tonne trucks were used. Aerial attack was avoided when Vietnamese peasants tied the tops of the trees together to provide a leafy corridor hidden from the pilots above. In such circumstances, the French could do little and on 7 May 1954 they gave up. By then, approximately 95,000 French men were dead, still more were wounded. Late in 1954, the Geneva Settlement was reached. Laos and Cambodia became independent. Vietnam was partitioned into Communist North Vietnam and independent non-Communist South Vietnam. When in

1956 a Communist group tried to seize power in the South, civil war broke out which dragged on until 1975. American intervention was humiliating and unsuccessful.

Algeria

The loss of Indo-China had important repercussions in North Africa. Tunisia and Morocco, which were protectorates rather than colonies, demanded independence in 1956 and the French felt compelled to grant it. In that same year the ill-fated Suez war ensured that the French and British lost control of the strategic waterway, the Suez Canal, to the Egyptians. The Algerian demand for independence proved much more difficult and was to mark the final blow to the Fourth Republic. Algeria had been a French colony since 1830. Some 1 million or 10% of Algeria's population were French settlers, known as *Colons*. These had prospered while the Arabs remained poor. France's resolve not to depart from Algeria was strengthened by the discovery of oil and natural gas in the Sahara and by the fact that the French army saw Algeria as their last imperial stronghold. Tension snapped late in 1954 when an independent Moslem group, the National Liberation Front (FLN), led by Ben Bella, began guerilla warfare against French rule. Consisting of 150,000 soldiers, the FLN were expert in ambush warfare, had the sympathy of the local people, the help of neighbouring countries and were difficult to find in the mountainous interior. But the 350,000 French troops in Algeria were determined to preserve French rule. The Secret Army Organisation (OAS) was a guerilla force comprising French settlers. War consisted of terror and counter-terror. Bombs were planted at bus stops, dance halls, shopping centres, and stabbings of men, women and children were all too common. By 1958 the war was costing the French £2,000,000 a day, stability at home was threatened while French international influence was suffering.

Algeria - Collapse of the Fourth Republic

Algeria was a political hot potato. It was also the issue which divided French public opinion. Realising that *"we are sitting on a volcano"*, Prime Minister Pierre Pflimlin decided in May 1958 to arrive at a settlement with the FLN. In Algeria, the French army, led by General Salan, revolted. The rebels then captured the island of Corsica and there was every danger that they would invade France itself. They called on De Gaulle to assume control. It was believed that De Gaulle was the only man capable of providing strong presidential government. The army was confident that De Gaulle would keep Algeria French. Even opponents of De Gaulle saw him as a solution - albeit a temporary one! - to a crisis which threatened law and order and was on the verge of escalating into civil war. De Gaulle held himself in readiness. On the 29th May, President Coty accepted Premier Pflimlin's resignation. De Gaulle was thereupon asked to set up a government of national safety. He agreed on certain conditions, namely that he be allowed to draw up a new constitution to be submitted to the French public for approval. De Gaulle's terms were accepted. In this way, the Fourth Republic empowered De Gaulle to end that Republic. The demise of the Republic in June 1958 was followed by its burial in September 1958 when the constitution of the Fifth Republic was accepted by some 80% of the population. De Gaulle now set about creating a strong presidency, extricating France from the Algerian debacle and promoting economic well being.

44. The Fifth Republic, 1958-1969

Origins of the Fifth Republic

The Fourth Republic lasted from 1946 until 1958. During that time it had a chequered career. In particular it had a great deal of political instability, carrying over, as it did, virtually the same political system as the Third Republic. This led to short-lived governments and to *immobilisme*. The situation was further complicated by impossible overseas commitments but it was the Algerian crisis which dealt the final blow to the Fourth Republic. The Algerian National Liberation Front (FLN) had demanded independence in 1954. France's refusal to grant this led to a four-year unwinnable guerilla war. By 1958 the war was extremely unpopular. In May of that year, Prime Minister Pierre Pflimlin was considering a settlement with the FLN. The French army in Algeria, refusing to tolerate withdrawal, mutinied. Led by General Salan, a self-elected revolutionary committee seized control. The rebels then succeeded on 24th May in getting control of the French island of Corsica. There was a threat that a military coup of Paris was next unless General Charles De Gaulle was appointed Prime Minister. While De Gaulle pronounced his readiness to return to power, he refused to take part in a military coup. The situation became increasingly tense, leading to the resignation of Pflimlin and De Gaulle's appointment as Premier. On 1st June 1958, De Gaulle was given the power to govern by decree for six months, during which time he put into law a host of badly needed reforms which it had hitherto proved impossible to get through the Assembly. De Gaulle also made preparations for a new constitution which was submitted to a referendum in September 1958. Its acceptance by a majority of almost 80% of the voters ensured that the Fourth Republic was dead and buried, and the Fifth born.

The Constitution

De Gaulle had consistently argued that France could only recover political stability and national strength by means of a government based on a presidential, rather than a parliamentary, executive. Thus it was that the constitution of the Fifth Republic differed radically from its predecessors in that the balance of power was transferred from the assembly to the President. The President was no longer a mere figurehead. Rather, he became the real ruler of France. Elected for a 7-year term of office by an electoral college of delegates from local councils, the powers of the President included his right to appoint or dismiss the Prime Minister, to control defence and foreign policy, the ability to dissolve parliament, to rule by decree in times of emergency and to appeal directly to the people by referendum in order to gain a mandate for his policies. De Gaulle was himself elected President in December 1958. In 1962 he used a referendum to amend the constitution and provide for direct election of the President by the people. De Gaulle was re-elected President in 1965, this time by popular referendum. During his presidential reign, De Gaulle appointed two Prime Ministers, both of whom were dedicated followers. Michel Debré served from 1959 to 1962, Georges Pompidou from 1962 to 1969. Parliament, meanwhile, continued to have two houses, the National Assembly and the Senate, while France was itself divided into 465 constituencies. Perhaps De Gaulle's greatest asset throughout his presidency was that parliament generally supported his rule. In this, De Gaulle was helped enormously by the electoral success of his own party, the *Union Pour la Nouvelle République (UNR)*. De Gaulle's presidency also witnessed a revolution in political personnel.

Algeria

The war in Algeria, which De Gaulle inherited from the Fourth Republic, was the supreme test of his skill as a politician, leader and statesman. Having refused to be drawn on the Algerian question in the early months of the Fifth Republic, De Gaulle was, nonetheless, realistic enough to realise that a military victory was impossible. Consequently, in September 1959, De Gaulle offered Algeria self-determination within five years. This proved too much for the French army and the *Colons* in Algeria. In January 1960 these 'die-hards' carried out an armed demonstration which was poorly organised and easily dealt with. A much more serious revolt took place in April 1961. Led by Generals Salan, Jouhaud and Challe, power was seized in Algeria while military action against metropolitan France was threatened. For a while all was uncertainty. Would 1958 repeat itself? Would De Gaulle go as Pflimlin had? With superb showmanship and firmness, De Gaulle appeared on national television and appealed directly to the nation for support. Such was De Gaulle's authority in France and the hostility to the army rebels that the navy, air force, rank-and-file soldiers and the French public gave him overwhelming backing. The Algerian coup failed and most of its leaders were arrested. The Secret Army Organisation (OAS) went underground and although terrorist acts continued, including several failed assassination attempts on De Gaulle, they became less frequent. In March 1962 a negotiated settlement was hammered out. Algeria was to be granted independence on condition that French oil interests were protected. This received the backing of 92% of French voters. That De Gaulle solved the Algerian debacle without promoting civil war, is one of his greatest achievements.

Foreign Policy [I]

Now that France had lost her colonies, De Gaulle sought a new role for his nation in world affairs. Believing *"France cannot be France without greatness"*, his goal was to make France leader of an independent Europe. De Gaulle wished especially to assert French independence of the two Superpowers, the US and the USSR. The EEC was the means of enhancing France's prestige. Under French influence, it could present a *'Third Force',* or bloc, in world affairs and rival those of the Americans and Russians. Especially obvious in terms of De Gaulle's foreign policy was his resentment of the US and Britain. Originating in their treatment of him as leader of the Free French movement, De Gaulle's anti-American feelings were deep-rooted and full of spite and suspicion. He argued that huge American commercial companies had too much influence in France and that through friendships with Britain and West Germany, the Americans were trying to gain influence in Europe and ultimately threatening France's bid for leadership of the EEC. Of Britain, De Gaulle believed she was basically untrustworthy and that she was too keen on safeguarding her own interests and those of the empire. She was also regarded as too close to the US. As a result, France twice vetoed Britain's entry into the EEC. Years of enmity between Germany and France were, however, ended. A series of state visits led to Adenauer and De Gaulle signing the Franco-German Treaty of Friendship in January 1963. This had promises of cultural, military and political co-operation. The treaty was followed in 1964 by French recognition of China's Communist government.

Foreign Policy [II]

In order to strengthen France's image abroad, De Gaulle undertook several foreign tours. In 1964, for example, he travelled to ten South American countries. A visit to Moscow was undertaken in 1966 and the following year, De Gaulle travelled to Canada. The visit was a controversial one in that De Gaulle, by exclaiming *"Vive le Quebec Libre"* (Long Live Free Quebec) to French separatists in the province, offended the Canadian government. Another important aspect of De Gaulle's dream of grandeur or greatness for France was the development of an independent nuclear striking force, *'force de frappe'*. In February 1960, France exploded its first atomic bomb in the Sahara. In 1963 France refused to sign the US-sponsored nuclear Test Ban Treaty because it would prevent France from developing an independent nuclear capability. Having refused to allow French troops to take part in NATO exercises as early as 1959, France's complete withdrawal from NATO took place in 1966. NATO was then forced to move its headquarters from Paris to Brussels. By 1968 France had sponsored the hydrogen bomb. Such a defence programme cost some 1,000 million dollars a year but regardless of cost, De Gaulle refused to be deflected from his purpose. Yet the reality of the situation was that although France's position reached great heights of prestige in the 1960s, it never quite matched De Gaulle's dream. Complete independence proved impossible.

The Economy

De Gaulle believed that financial stability was the key to France's continued economic growth. Upon taking office, he got the French people to subscribe to a *'patriotic loan'*. The enthusiastic response was such that within seven weeks the French had donated 140 tons of gold. Simultaneously, cuts in public spending were introduced and there was a revaluation of the *franc*. Consequently by 1963 France had accumulated considerable gold reserves and had solved her balance of payments problem. The Monnet plans initiated during the period of the Fourth Republic were continued with the adoption of a third plan in 1958 and a fourth one in 1962. These, along with the ending of colonial wars and political squabbles, ensured that France now became a modern industrialised society. Heavy industry led the way. This was spearheaded by the aircraft, car manufacturing and shipbuilding sectors. Technological innovation was widespread and new industries such as electronics, chemicals and plastics thrived. The economic benefits of membership of the EEC helped to ensure that exports doubled between 1959 and 1962. Social objectives such as housing, hospitals and schools appeared more prominently on the list of priorities and there was considerable improvement in town planning. But while living standards undoubtedly improved, they varied in different areas, and wages of state employees generally lagged behind those of the private sector.

Agriculture

Edgar Pisani was appointed to do for agriculture what Monnet had done for industry. His law of 1961 was a bold step intended to haul French farming into the modern world. The government set up pension funds to encourage old farmers to retire early; it lent money to marketing co-operatives and established SAFERS, or regional agencies, to buy land as it came on the market, improve it and resell it at moderate prices to younger farmers willing to use modern methods. Reform did take place. Among the most notable was the clearing and drainage of land at Guiche in the Adour valley which extended acreage from 865 to 1,850 and doubled production. Co-operatives such as that at Beauce near Paris encouraged efficiency and led to an increase of output by 400% in 20 years. Another example of reform was the vast Midi scheme on the coastal strip west of the Rhone delta. A far-reaching programme of irrigation made a whole area fertile, effectively making *'a desert bloom'*. In spite of such reform, however, the problem of *'two agricultures'* remained. The rich wheat and cattle farms of the Paris Basin and north-east plains all too often contrasted markedly with the small farms of the rest of the country. And the benefits of the Common Agricultural Policy which gave subsidies and guaranteed prices, effectively ensured that the big farmers got richer, and small farmers poorer, thus widening the gap. Meanwhile there was a significant shift of population from rural to urban France.

Unrest - Resignation - Fifth Republic Survives

Early in 1968 France seemed untroubled, peaceful and prosperous. Below the surface, however, there were serious rumblings. Discontent first made itself felt in the universities. Under the leadership of Daniel Cohn-Bendit, students voiced their criticism of academic courses, university authorities, impossibly high standards, overcrowding and the high failure rate of the system. They were also opposed to the spiritual sterility of their society and to De Gaulle, whom they regarded as an anachronism. Student sit-in strikes and demonstrations began at Navarre and soon spread to the Sorbonne. Before long, virtually all students in Paris were engaged in a massive revolt. On 13th May, approximately 10 million factory workers entered the struggle with wage demands. Clashes with the police intensified. A massive strike threatened to cripple the country. De Gaulle then made his famous broadcast on national television, calling for support against anarchy. This, along with disunity among the strikers, a pay rise to the workers and the associations of the strikers with Communist militants, ensured that the strike soon ran out of steam. Elections at the end of June gave an extra 90 seats to the Gaullists. But the revolt had left a trail of difficulties and unanswered questions. Perhaps sensing that his days were numbered, De Gaulle resigned in April 1969, following defeat for his referendum on regional development. He was succeeded by Georges Pompidou, a strong Gaullist supporter. Meanwhile, the Fifth Republic survived and has continued to do so to this very day. It stands as a monument to its creator, representing the history of modern contemporary France.

Post-War France: Past Exam Questions

1994, 1992

E4. Essay

Charles De Gaulle.

1989

D3. Charles De Gaulle

Treat of the part played by Charles De Gaulle in the history of France.

1988

E4. Essay

(iv) The career of Charles De Gaulle.

1986

D4. The Fall of France

Account for the fall of France in 1940 and describe the consequences of the fall for France.

POST-WAR GERMANY

45. *"Both as a national leader and as an international statesman, Konrad Adenauer had outstanding achievements to his credit."* Discuss.

Introduction - From Basic Law to National Leader

Konrad Adenauer (1876-1967) came from a German middle-class Catholic background. He served as Mayor of Cologne from 1917 until the advent of the Nazis to power in 1933. Restored for a time to that position after the war, in October 1945 Adenauer was removed by the British, who believed him to be too independent-minded. By that time Adenauer had already taken part in the foundation of the Christian Democratic Union (CDU), the most important post-war party to emerge. Adenauer now directed his energies into building up the CDU which, under his leadership, became the strongest political party in Germany. He presided over the Parliamentary Council which met in September 1948 in Bonn. The Council was responsible for naming the new West German state the *'Federal Republic of Germany'* and for the drawing up of a new constitution, known as the Basic Law. The Basic Law sought to steer a careful path between establishing a government that was too weak to rule effectively and an all-powerful government. It did so by creating a Federal Republic of eleven *Länder,* or regional governments, with two houses of parliament, the *Bundesrat* and the *Bundestag*, the latter being made up of popularly elected deputies. This constitution, which contained various safeguards, was passed by 53 votes to 12 and come into force on 23rd May 1949. The first elections for the *Bundestag* were held on 14th August of the same year. The CDU-CSU (Christian Social Union) combination won a slight majority over the Social Democrats (SPD) - 139 seats as opposed to 131. A month later Adenauer was elected President by a majority of one vote. Thus, with no real experience of national politics, Adenauer assumed centre stage and although he may have had all the signs of a temporary leader, he was, in fact, over the next 14 years to accomplish some considerable achievements, both in national politics and as an international statesman.

Economic Growth

A major priority of the Adenauer government was to make Germany prosperous again by rebuilding the economy from the ruins of war. From 1949-1963 the Minister for Economic Affairs was Dr. Ludwig Erhard. Best known as *'the wizard'*, Erhard sought to encourage investment, to aid private enterprise and to stimulate exports. Marshall Aid amounting to $1.3 billion, for example, was carefully invested while simultaneously, West Germany handed back state control of industry to free enterprise as it allowed for the development of a market economy. Such an approach appealed to business people and German firms like Krupps, Siemens, Volkswagen, Daimler-Benz and Bayer became worldwide symbols of a new German boom. By 1961 Volkswagen was exporting over 1 million cars each year. Germany also became the world's third largest producer of steel. High annual growth rates were helped by the introduction of a new *Deutschmark* in 1948, the general shortage of consumer goods in the early years of the Federal State and by the *co-determination* laws of 1951 and 1952. These gave workers a say in running industries and enabled trade unions and employers to work in greater harmony than in any other Western European nation. A restrained wage policy was practised by trade unions and strikes were generally avoided. Further benefits to the economy came from the co-operation of banks with industry and from the good organisation and policy of hard work that was prevalent. The result, an *"economic miracle"*, must be hailed as an outstanding achievement for Adenauer. A new confidence arose and in the period from 1950 to 1963 exports rose from 8.4 billion *marks* to 52.3 billion. For the same period, industrial production rose by 300%. A huge reduction in unemployment, a steady increase in standards of living and one of the best social services in Europe can be added to the list of achievements.

Politics

The failure of the democratic system under Weimar and the dictatorial Nazi regime of the period 1933-1945 meant that Germany was a country with little faith in its political self. That Adenauer succeeded in selling democracy to the West Germans in such a climate was a considerable achievement. His persuasive manner and gift for political tactics, together with a directness and simplicity of expression guaranteed that whereas the words *'republic'* and *'democracy'* meant surrender, humiliation and misery in the 1920s, now in the 1950s they coincided with bringing order out of chaos. Adenauer, governed firmly (his period in government was often called *'Chancellor Democracy'*) and he showed a readiness to assume responsibility for decisions. The result was rising prestige, reflected by a growing stability at the polls. The CDU-CSU gained 244 seats in the Bundestag in the 1953 elections and 270 seats in 1957. Meanwhile, other political parties, most notably the SPD, had to take cognisance of Adenauer's political and economic success by re-evaluating their own programme. The 1959 SPD party conference at Bad Godesberg marked an abandonment of Marxist policies as the SDP worked increasingly towards a reformist course within a liberal political state. Adenauer also had some success in dealing with the emergence of Neo-Nazi groups in the 1950s, as he sought to absorb many of them into the CDU. Perhaps reflective of Adenauer's achievement as a politician and the general stability and prosperity of post-war Germany was the attraction to the country of many millions of refugees, particularly from East Germany, and their assimilation into the country. By 1959, however, the tide of Adenauer's achievements as a national leader were beginning to turn.

Foreign Policy - Co-operation with the West

Adenauer quickly made it clear that his predominant concern was with foreign policy and that it took precedence over other matters. Accordingly, he acted as Foreign Minister between 1951 and 1955 and it was as an international statesman that he best distinguished himself. Even after 1955, when Heinrick von Brentano assumed the position of Foreign Minister, major decisions were reserved for Adenauer. The Chancellor's strong anti-Communist stance and his desire to restore West Germany as a sovereign, independent state meant that he adopted a pro-Western European outlook. And because of the history of antagonism and hatred between Germany and France, Adenauer realised that the key to European co-operation was France, for if that country could accept Germany's friendship, other European nations would follow suit. This approach led to a quick improvement in Federal Germany's international status. As early as November 1949 the Western occupying powers of Britain, France and America decided that Germany's powers of self-government should increase. She was, for example, given the right to sign trade agreements with other countries. Days later, West Germany was allowed to join the International Ruhr Authority, whose purpose it was to oversee industrial production in the Ruhr. The Petersberg Agreement of 22nd November 1949 brought about a reduction in the amount of reparations taken from Germany, thereby giving her greater economic freedom. Following this, limitations on steel output and shipbuilding were lifted. Protection was also given to West Germany against attack as the Western powers increased their forces there. The increasing independence of the Federal Republic was again recognised in January 1950 when Adenauer was permitted to open consulates in London, Paris and Washington.

Social, Cultural and Economic Co-operation

Under Adenauer, West Germany was allowed to join the Council of Europe. This was an organisation which held its first meeting in Strasbourg in August 1949 and whose aims included the fostering of social and cultural co-operation between member states as well as the protection of human rights. Economic co-operation, in the form of the Schuman Plan of 1950 led to the Treaty of Paris, 1951, by which France, Germany, Belgium, the Netherlands, Luxembourg and Italy formed the European Coal and Steel Community (ECSC). The ECSC established a common policy on coal and steel and led to huge increases in production. Advocates of European integration, Adenauer included, wished to go still further. In the negotiations which followed, Adenauer, acting as an international statesman, made major concessions to France. On 25th March 1957 the six members of the ECSC signed the Treaty of Rome. This treaty created the European Economic Community (EEC) which came into effect on 1st January 1958. The EEC aimed to remove tariff barriers between member states and to work towards the free movement of goods, capital and labour. A common agricultural policy was to be established and the European Social Fund would work towards reducing unemployment and improving standards of living throughout the community. Adenauer's contribution earned him the praise of Belgian Prime Minister, Paul Henri Spaak, who maintained that *"without him the dream of a united Europe would not have become a reality"*. In this area of economic co-operation Adenauer's achievements are indeed 'outstanding'.

Defence - Rearmament

The issue of German re-armament, first raised in the 1950s, was hotly debated. The outbreak of the Korean War (1950-1953), the expansion of the *'People's Police'* in East Germany, and the Cold War combined to convince Adenauer and his government that it must organise its own military force. The *Bundestag* voted in favour of doing just that in 1952. But the French and British were worried about the emergence of a new German national army and both Churchill and Pléven (of France) proposed the establishment of a European army called the European Defence Community (EDC), in which German units would be integrated under European command. Although the idea of the EDC was ultimately rejected, Adenauer continued to work towards convincing the West of his trustworthiness. That he succeeded in doing so was a major accomplishment. Meanwhile an alternative solution to the problem of German re-armament became necessary. By the Paris agreements of October 1954 which came into force on 5th May 1955, West Germany became a sovereign state with power to establish full diplomatic relations with other countries. She also became a full member of the North Atlantic Treaty Organisation (NATO). Re-armament of a volunteer federal army, air force and navy would take place within the NATO framework and would be under the supervision of the Western European Union. Through treading warily, Adenauer had achieved a great deal. Another triumph of some significance was the winning back of the Saar to West Germany. Since the war this area had been under French control but when a referendum was held on the future status of the Saar in January 1957, an overwhelming majority of voters opted to be reunited with Germany.

Relations with East Germany, Russia, America and Others

Adenauer, like so many Germans, deplored the division of his country and had as an avowed aim the unification of the two Germanies. Refusing to adopt a neutral stance, however, Adenauer as a realist knew that he would have to accept division for an indefinite period of time. The policy that he chose to adopt with regard to East Germany was the Hallstein Doctrine, devised by a foreign office official. The doctrine sought to prevent international recognition of East Germany by refusing to maintain diplomatic relations with countries that recognised the GDR. It was a policy that made discussion on Berlin impossible and actually widened the gulf between East and West. It could not, therefore, be considered one of Adenauer's 'achievements'. The construction of the Berlin Wall in 1961 to stop the flood of refugees from the East became a sinister symbol thereafter of the divide between the Federal Republic and the GDR. With the USSR, relations were more complicated. In 1955 formal diplomatic relations were established between the two countries in return for which Adenauer secured the release of thousands of German prisoners who had been in Russia since the war. In 1958 when Khrushchev demanded the withdrawal of all Allied troops from Berlin within six months, under threat of his transferring the control of the routes of access to the East German authorities, tensions deepened. Adenauer refused the demand and relations deteriorated still further with the erection of the Berlin Wall. Adenauer was more successful in his dealings with the US who believed that in Adenauer's Germany it had a firm European ally on whose partnership it could count. Relations could not, nonetheless, be deemed outstandingly successful. A greater achievement was the attempt by Adenauer to make partial material atonement for the death of 6 million Jews during the war years, and his efforts to establish the Federal Republic as a non-colonial power which supplied capital goods and technicians as well as export credits in the emergent states of Asia and Africa.

The Last Years - An Assessment

It has been argued that the triumphs of the late 1950s marked the climax of Adenauer's political career. Certainly rumblings of discontent with Adenauer's chancellorship were heard thereafter and his achievements, though by no means at an end, were less. Increasing antagonism between Adenauer and Erhard coincided with calls for the retirement of Adenauer who, then in his 80s, was accused of hanging on to power too long and preventing younger, more talented men coming to the top. Perhaps not surprisingly, the elections of 1961 saw the CDU-CSU lose a number of seats in the *Bundestag*. In order to form the next government, Adenauer had to bring the Free Democrats back into coalition with his own party but they insisted that, in return for their support, Adenauer relinquish his position before the end of the parliamentary term. A final and significant achievement of Adenauer before he retired was the cementing of relations between Germany and France and the breaking down of remaining antipathies. This was done through the Franco-German Treaty of Friendship of January 1963 which promised collaboration in economic, political, military and cultural matters. The treaty was seen as a great contribution to peace in Europe. But Adenauer's end was in sight. Amidst the *Der Spiegel* controversy which led to the dismissal of Defence Minister, Franz Josef Strauss, for charges of treason against the paper's editorial staff which could not be substantiated, Adenauer himself resigned in October 1963. During his 14 years as Chancellor of the Federal Republic, Adenauer had presided successfully over a transitional period in Germany's history. His achievements were many and sometimes 'outstanding' and they gave to West Germany security, prosperity and dignity. He was also responsible for enabling Germany not just to be absorbed into the contemporary world but to play an active and independent role. For this the country owed him a great debt. Yet problems remained to be worked out by his successors. To them was left the task of building, consolidating, maybe even at times negating, the work of their predecessor.

Post-War Germany: Past Exam Questions

1994

D4. Konrad Adenauer

"Both as a national leader and as an international statesman Konrad Adenauer had outstanding achievements to his credit". Discuss.

1988

D3. West Germany, 1949-1966

Treat of economic and political reconstruction in the Federal Republic of Germany under Konrad Adenauer and Ludwig Erhard, 1949-1966.

POST-WAR BRITAIN

46. British Foreign Policy, 1945-1966

Introduction - Post War Position/Potsdam Conference

Although Britain had emerged victorious from World War II, she was no longer the predominant power in the world. Her involvement in war since 1939 had left her broke, weak and exhausted. Meanwhile, the power and status of the US and USSR had grown immeasurably. Their swollen military forces and the vast resources at their disposal ensured that they were now brought to the leadership of nations, that they had emerged as the Superpowers. Such was the change in the world at large that Britain had to reassess and redefine her role in international affairs. Britain's relations with the two new giant powers, with Europe and especially her western neighbour, and with her colonies and the countries of the Commonwealth, all had to be determined. As she did this, the role of Foreign Minister became increasingly exacting and necessitated an unending series of journeys to an unending series of conferences. In Atlee's post-war Labour government, 1945-1951, Ernest Bevin held the position of Foreign Minister. When the Labour government came to power, the Potsdam Conference, July 1945 was already in progress. Defined as the 'Versailles' of the Second World War, it was attended by the *'Big Three'* - Britain, the US and the USSR. The conference was mainly concerned with the future of Germany, with the question of Poland and with arranging a Conference of Ministers to draft peace treaties with the other defeated powers, Hungary, Bulgaria, Romania, Finland and Italy. From the outset differences between the powers emerged. Bevin, whose proletarian origin and long struggle on behalf of the workers might have endeared him to the Soviet Union, soon came to abhor Stalin and his tactics in spreading Communism in Eastern Europe. Consequently, he adopted a policy of close co-operation with the US.

Closer Ties to the US and to the West

In her role as 'protector' of the Free World, British troops had helped to restore the monarchy in Greece in 1944. Troops were thereafter used to hold off Communist guerillas but in 1947 Britain informed Washington that she could no longer afford the economic burden of supporting Greece. Truman promised the necessary military and economic aid, maintaining that *"It must be the policy of the US to support free peoples who are resisting attempted subjugation by armed minorities or by outside pressure"*. The Truman Doctrine was followed in June 1947 by the Marshall Plan, by which America promised considerable financial aid for Europe. Bevin took a vigorous initiative in assembling the Organisation for European Economic Co-operation (OEEC) which played a huge role in accepting and administering Marshall Aid. In other ways, too, Britain drew closer to the US and Western Europe. The Dunkirk Treaty of March 1947 was a *"Treaty of Alliance and Mutual Assistance"* between France and Britain against Germany. A year later, the Brussels Pact was signed by representatives of Britain, France, Belgium, the Netherlands and Luxembourg. This was a promise of joint Western union for mutual co-operation in economic and military matters. It was particularly directed against the Soviet Union who only a month earlier had added Czechoslovakia to her *'Iron Curtain'* countries. The USSR's attempt to make the West's position in Berlin untenable by a blockade of the city, 1948-1949, strengthened Britain's resolve to side with the US in the Cold War between East and West. Britain also played a leading role in the formation of the North Atlantic Treaty Organisation (NATO). Consisting of 12 countries originally, it provided for collective action in case of attack on any one of those countries. Bevin was delighted that the US had been persuaded to drop its traditional opposition to participation in European alliances.

Concerns Regarding Total Commitment

In the Western policy of *'containment'* of Communism, it soon became clear that defensive alliances were not enough and that Britain would have to increase its defence expenditure. This became more immediate in September 1949 when it was announced that an atomic explosion had occurred in the Soviet Union. This and the emergence of Communist China meant that more than ever, there was a hardening of world relationships along the lines of the ideological schism between Communism and Democracy. Thus, when the Communist forces of North Korea invaded the South, Britain's commitment to democracy and to the United Nations meant that, after the US, she had the largest troop contingent in the Korean War. But not all British people were in agreement about the country's strong support for America and particularly of the more aggressive strategies of some of the US generals. At home, talk of spending £1,500m a year on rearmament opened up old wounds within the Labour Party and divided members according to their allegiance to *'guns or butter'*. Then in March 1951, Herbert Morrison took over the Foreign Office from Bevin, who died a month later. Morrison's term was brief and inglorious and there could be no doubting that the Korean War, which dragged on until 1953, had important domestic repercussions for Britain and hastened the fall of Labour. In terms of her commitment to full European integration, Britain moved cautiously. Involvement in the Council of Europe fell short of forging political union. Britain refused to become involved in the European Coal and Steel Community, arguing that it was likely to lead to cartels or to technocracy. She also failed to become involved in the European Defence Council.

Decolonisation

In line with a more general movement towards decolonisation, the Labour government handed over power in Jordan in 1946. This had been a mandated territory given to Britain after the First World War. The issue of Indian independence was one which became steadily more immediate throughout the 20th century. Mahatma Gandhi, leader of the Hindus urged Britain to *"Get off our back; walk by our side"*. The existence of a Moslem group complicated the situation, however, and made it impossible to preserve Indian unity. Consequently, when the country was granted independence on 15th August 1947, India was divided into two - a Hindu dominated India and a Moslem dominated Pakistan to the north. Palestine, another British mandate, presented still more serious problems. This was as a result of conflict between the Arab population and the Jewish one. The attempt to secure a national homeland for the Jews meant that, since the outbreak of war in 1939 and their persecution at the hands of the Nazis, numbers fleeing to Palestine rose steadily. In 1945 they comprised approximately 30% of the population. British proposals for a two nation state were rejected and having referred the issue to the UN, the British withdrew from Palestine in May 1948. A state of open war did not prevent the establishment of the state of Israel by the Jews and its subsequent recognition by the UN. Other countries that received their independence under the Labour government were Burma and Ceylon, both in 1948. In 1949, Ireland left the Commonwealth and declared herself a Republic.

Conservative Power - Suez Crisis

The Conservative governments of Churchill, Eden, Macmillan and Douglas-Home, 1951-'64 maintained the American alliance and the link with NATO. The problems of Russian intransigence, a divided Germany, emerging nationalism in Africa and Asia and the degree of British participation in the various European organisations remained as acute as ever. Nonetheless, tensions did ease somewhat in 1953 with the death of Stalin and the ending of the Korean War. Khrushchev's policy of *"peaceful co-existence"* was also looked upon favourably. A personal triumph in diplomacy for Eden were the Paris Agreements of 1954, which were ratified in April 1955. In place of the French-proposed European Defence Community it was agreed that a Western European Union should be formed. West Germany would be admitted and she would be allowed to re-arm within the context of NATO to which she now became a member. Britain further undertook to maintain four divisions and the Tactical Air Force on the Continent. It was by involvement in the Middle East that Eden's policy was to meet its greatest challenge, and by misjudgement of international reactions, to run into temporary ruin. The building of the Aswan Dam was a project close to the heart of Colonel Nasser, leader of Egypt. The American offer of 56 million dollars towards its cost was withdrawn in protest at Egypt's increasing co-operation with Communist states. Nasser reacted by nationalising the Suez Canal Company on 26th July 1956. Eden, obsessed with the image of Nasser as a second Hitler devised a plan with France and Israel. This led to an Israeli attack on Egypt in October 1956 and the occupation of Egypt by French and British troops as they sought to *'restore order'*. The vehemence and extent of public reaction forced the British and French governments to halt their operation. An international UN task force policed the area but the Suez Canal remained in Egyptian hands.

The Winds of Change

The Suez Canal crisis was an episode which did little for Britain's reputation worldwide. Diplomatic disaster, combined with ill-health, led to Eden's resignation in January 1957. He was succeeded by Harold Macmillan under whom most of the remaining British colonies became sovereign states. In 1957 the Federation of Malaya became an independent country within the Commonwealth. By the Cyprus Act, 1960, the island became an independent Republic with a Greek Cypriot President and a Turkish Cypriot Vice-President. The Maltese government also sought sovereignty which it duly received in 1964. But it was in Africa that 'the winds of change' were blowing most vociferously. The Gold Coast was the first of the African dependencies to achieve independence. It received statehood as Ghana in 1957. In quick succession, other colonies followed suit. Nigeria's independence was declared in 1961, as was that of Tanganyika and Sierre Leone. Uganda's independence in 1962, came next. Then Kenya and Zanzibar in 1963, Nyasaland and Northern Rhodesia in 1964 and Gambia in 1965. Some areas of British Africa presented fundamental obstacles to independence. This was especially true in relation to Kenya and Southern Rhodesia. Both states had large scale European populations. In Kenya the British had the monopoly of the best farming lands. This was resented by native Kenyans and led to outbursts of savage tribalism. The violence of the *Mau Mau*, in particular, led to continued warfare. Finally in December 1963 Kenya was granted independence with Jomo Kenyatta as leader. Rhodesia likewise underwent a military campaign before it was set up as the independent state of Zimbabwe in 1980.

Defence and Nuclear Weaponry

One of the ways in which Britain sought to reinstate herself as a major power was through the development of an independent nuclear programme. The manufacture of the atomic bomb was first authorised by Atlee and Bevin and thereafter the Conservatives remained loyal to the concept of an independent deterrent for Britain. The first atomic test took place at Monte Bello in October 1953. These weapons were shortly superseded by the successful testing of the hydrogen bomb in the US and USSR. Churchill declared in 1955 that *"To make our contribution to the deterrent we must ourselves possess the most up-to-date nuclear weapons and the means of delivering them"*. Accordingly, the British developed ballistic missiles armed with nuclear warheads. Britain then tried to develop its own system but because of the enormous cost, it soon became clear that Britain could hardly expect to keep pace with the nuclear giants. The nuclear debate was one which seriously split the Labour Party and led to emotional opposition within the country. In 1958 the Campaign for Nuclear Disarmament (CND) emerged with the aim of getting rid of all nuclear weapons. It was a campaign, however, which received the support of middle class intellectuals and students rather than the population as a whole. In December 1962, talks between Macmillan and John F. Kennedy led to an agreement whereby America promised to supply *Polaris* missiles for use in British submarines. The British would supply the nuclear warheads. Following this, the Test Ban Treaty of 5th August 1963, signed between the US, USSR and Britain, banned all forms of nuclear testing except underground tests. This marked an important advance in the campaign for nuclear disarmament.

EEC Membership - Conclusion

By 1957 plans for closer political and economic integration were reaching fruition on the Continent. The Treaty of Rome, signed by France, West Germany, Italy, Belgium, the Netherlands and Luxembourg (the *'Six'*) was responsible for establishing both the European Economic Community and the European Atomic Energy Community. Although Britain was invited to become a part of this, she declined. She did so because of her view of a global Commonwealth and because she wished to retain power of independent decision. Instead, Britain began negotiations for a more limited European free trade area, consisting of the *'Outer Seven'*. But however hard Britain might try, the reality was that she could not avoid an intimate involvement in the affairs of Europe. Consequently, in the 1960s applications to join the EEC by Macmillan and Wilson were made. These were vetoed by France, and particularly by De Gaulle. Only in 1973 did Britain actually become a member. Any evaluation of Britain's role in world affairs after 1945 must acknowledge that in terms of Britain's status, there was a displacement of power and she could no longer rate as a front rank power. Her inability to compete in the arms race and the loss of her empire are evidence of this. Yet the reality was that Britain's long-established instincts and attitudes were not easily altered. Nonetheless, time showed that a change in her isolationist ways would be in her interest. Only slowly, and sometimes painfully, did she commit herself more deeply to her European partners and adjust to a somewhat different role in world affairs.

47. Treat of the Domestic Policies pursued by successive British Governments during the period 1945-1966

Introduction

The Second World War ended in May 1945. It was a war which had cost Britain greatly, financially and otherwise. In its aftermath, the country was on the brink of bankruptcy, many industries were struggling for survival and massive damage necessitated a huge rebuilding programme. The desire to break with the past ran deep, for as well as the sacrifices and severities of war time, there was little nostalgia for the insecure and difficult Thirties. Thus people looked ahead to the future and especially to a society which incorporated the desire for fuller social justice, a lessening of class difference, and greater security and peace. This dream of a more just society had found expression in the Beveridge Report of November 1942. Far reaching and ambitious, it planned *"to establish full social security for all from the cradle to the grave"*. The mood, as expressed in 1945, did not desire the continuance of the wartime coalition. Rather it favoured wholeheartedly a Labour Government. Consequently, in the July 1945 election, Labour rocketed to power with a total of 393 seats as opposed to 213 for the Conservatives and 12 for the Liberals. Clement Atlee assumed the position of Prime Minister. Helping him to implement the Socialist objectives of a welfare state, full employment and nationalisation of key industries, was a host of brilliant men, some of whom had held office under Churchill. Among them were Hugh Dalton, Ernest Bevin, Sir Stafford Cripps, Aneurin Bevan and Arthur Greenwood.

The Welfare State

The Welfare State required a large cash flow but the Government had a deficit of £750m in 1946. This was partly offset by borrowings from the US and Canada and subsequently from the substantial payment made to Britain as part of the Marshall Aid programme. These cash injections helped the Government to meet its spending targets. A notable Labour achievement was the National Insurance Act of 1946 which offered protection against unemployment, sickness and old age. While this was not an innovation, it was important in that it was not means-tested. Everyone paid the same contributions and drew the same benefits. The Industrial Injuries Act, 1946, also helped to improve the welfare of British citizens by giving compensation for those injured or killed at work, as well as for those suffering from industrial diseases. In that same year, a revolutionary idea in the form of the National Health Service Act came about. This set out to provide free medical service for all and took over responsibility for the voluntary hospitals, now placed under regional boards. England and Wales were divided into 14 regional Health Board areas, Scotland had 5 regions. Simultaneously, drugs, medicines, spectacles and false teeth were provided, at first free but later for relatively small charges. Further reform came in 1948 when the National Assistance Act drove the last nail in the coffin of the old Poor Law. It set up boards to assume responsibility for those not already covered by the National Insurance Act - the handicapped, homeless, deserted, insane, dependents of prisoners, unmarried mothers.

Education/Housing/Other Reforms

The Butler Education Act of 1944 was partly implemented in 1947. The school leaving age was raised to 15 and a special examination, known as the *'Eleven Plus'*, divided students into categories according to age, ability and aptitude. The existence of Grammar, Technical and Secondary Modern Schools ensured that a full national system of education was constructed. Other proposals in the Act, such as the extension of higher education to many young people, were postponed because of shortages of money and staff. Perhaps more urgent was the question of housing. The Housing Act of 1946 increased subsidies to local authorities who were given permission to restrict private buildings and limit costs. Between 1947 and 1950 an average of 170,000 new houses were completed every year. The pressing need for new houses could not be separated from the need to decide how towns were to develop. An innovation in planning, the New Towns Act of 1946, empowered a central authority to build completely new towns, complete with schools, factories, shopping centres and housing estates. Harlow, Stevenage and Crawley are examples of new towns built to relieve the pressure on the big congestions of population. In addition to these major measures, a host of others were passed. These included the Representation of the People Act, 1948, which abolished the double vote for graduates and owners of business premises; and the Parliament Act of 1949 which curtailed the power of the House of Lords in holding up bills to one year instead of two.

Nationalisation/Unemployment - Fall of Labour

In line with the long-established socialist principle that public services should be placed under public control and not run for private profit, key industries were placed under government control. Herbert Morrison, leader of the House of Commons, was responsible for the programme. In 1946, the Bank of England was nationalised, then in 1947, coal, electricity, civil aviation and the communication industries were taken over. This was followed in 1948 by the nationalisation of public transport in its various forms, and gas. The attempt to bring iron and steel under state control in 1949 met with huge opposition yet while Labour pressed ahead, some 80% of the country's industry was still in private hands. Nationalisation of the remaining 20% secured no effective 'commanding heights'. In terms of the government's policy of securing full employment, Labour was very successful. No post-war slump occurred and unemployment rarely rose above 2%. Nor was there any hard core of long-term unemployment. But for all that, everything was not well. Strains and stresses of the post-war years included an inadequate supply of money, the continuance of rationing, shortages of fuel and of housing, and increased taxation. In 1949 the Pound Sterling was devalued and in the February 1950 election, Labour secured only a small working majority. High defence spending, and increased prices as well as a slackening of legislature momentum ensured that popular support for Labour declined. This was compounded by a cabinet rift and the resignation of key ministers. In this climate, Labour lost office in October 1951. The Conservatives now secured 321 seats to Labour's 295 seats.

Churchill Returns to Power

Churchill returned to power in 1951 with the promise of *"setting the people free"*. He was 76 years of age and it was his first experience of the office of Prime Minister during peace time. The mainstays of his ministry were Sir Anthony Eden, Lord Salisbury and Rab Butler. Although there were fears that the Conservatives would give less attention to the social services than the Labour Party, these fears soon proved unfounded and not only was the legislation setting up the Welfare State preserved but in some details, such as family allowances, it was improved. The reality was that the electorate now demanded all parties to have a social conscience. Only the iron and steel industry and most of the road haulage business returned to private ownership. The costs of the Welfare State and the high defence expenditure, caused especially by the continuance of the Korean War until 1953 and the uneasy relations with the USSR, meant that Rab Butler, as Chancellor of the Exchequer, had to contend with a balance of payments crisis of nearly £700m. He adopted a cautious policy of raising interest rates, restricting credit and cutting down on imports. The result of these measures was that within a few years there was a credit balance of under £300m. The resurfacing of old problems of inflation, industrial disputes and falling exports in the 1954-1955 period led to Butler reverting to the restrictive measures that had seemed to work in 1951. But there was much criticism of these 'stop-go' economic policies. More successful was Harold Macmillan's housing policy. Controls on private building were removed between 1952 and 1954 so that there was a spectacular increase in the number of houses built. In 1953, an annual target of 300,000 was actually exceeded. Other achievements of the period included the dispensing with food rationing and the passing of the Television Act in 1954 which allowed for commercial television, financed by advertising, to be set up.

Eden's Premiership

In 1953 Churchill suffered a serious stroke and increasingly he was forced to rely on his deputy, Anthony Eden. At the age of 80, Churchill retired from active political life in April 1955. When Eden formed a new ministry, many regarded it as a continuation, under new management, of the former firm. A decision to hold a general election in May 1955 had the desired result because the Conservatives gained 344 seats, Labour 277. Continuing disputes within the Labour movement meant that it was unable to present a united front capable of forming a government. Eden's domestic policy was generally to promote *"a property owning democracy"* and *"partnership in industry"*. This involved the sharing of responsibility and profits between employers and employees. It was an appeal aptly geared to the realities of the changing social structure of Britain. Despite the increase in national prosperity, however, Eden's domestic policies were troubled by an increase in inflation, balance of payments problems and a poor showing on the industrial front. In 1955 alone there were rail, docks, and newspaper stoppages. Macmillan, as Chancellor of the Exchequer, cut government expenditure and set out to stabilise prices and wages. He also introduced Premium Bonds, a government fundraising scheme which involved monthly draws for large money prizes. By 1956 a credit balance of £192m existed. A major increase in small savings, mainly through Building Societies, took place. Eden's foreign policy, and particularly the Suez Canal debacle, did little for his reputation. He was accused of being *"a curious mixture of strength and weakness"* and of *"forever changing his mind"*. This, combined with continuing bad health, led to his resignation from office on 9th January 1957.

The Era of Macmillan

The 62-year-old Harold Macmillan now became Prime Minister. He proceeded to lead the country at a time when she was experiencing an unprecedented prosperity and constantly rising living standards. It was an *'affluent society'* and millions of pounds were spent on consumer goods such as cars, televisions, radios, washing machines and refrigerators. Gambling, liquor, tobacco and entertainment were all part of the material success. Symptomatic phrases were Macmillan's *"You've never had it so good"* and the workers' *"I'm all right, Jack"*. Popularly dubbed *'Supermac'*, Macmillan had a strong combination of intellectual ability, imperturbable temperament and reputation for efficiency. In the 1959 general election, the Conservatives emerged with a majority of 100 seats. *"Expansion without inflation"* remained Macmillan's aim and this necessitated an *"investment in men"* rather than things. The Macmillan government also concerned itself with long-term economic planning. But in spite of the variety of fiscal prescriptions and tonics, the affluent society was unable to sustain itself. In the early 1960s the boom began to end. Under Selwyn Lloyd, interest rates were once again increased, purchase tax was added and import duties raised. Attempts to introduce a pay policy to control wages were unsuccessful. A 'purge' of seven cabinet ministers in 1962 failed to improve the situation. In March of that year, the Conservatives had already lost a 'safe' seat at Orpington to the Labour Party. Meanwhile, unemployment continued to rise and in January 1963 it exceeded 800,000. In June 1963, Jack Profumo, Minister for War, was compelled to resign following his affair with Christine Keeler who was simultaneously involved with a Russian diplomat. The Conservative's image was seriously harmed and this combined with Macmillan's own ill-health led to his decision to step down. Alec Dougles-Home succeeded him. Under him the fortunes of the party continued to decline.

Wilson Government - Conclusion

Douglas-Home remained in office for just a short time as in the 1964 general election Labour secured a slight majority and returned to power. The party was then led by Harold Wilson, who is said to have adopted a *'dictatorial'* or *'presidential'* attitude, particularly towards his cabinet. In any case, Labour had returned to power with promises of adopting a professional or planned approach to the economy. Yet the Wilson government had inherited a huge balance of payments deficit. Steps taken to remedy the situation included increased personal taxation, wealth taxes, 15% surcharge on imports, a sharp increase in the lending rate and a prices-and-incomes policy. In line with electoral promises, old age pensions were raised and prescription charges abolished. Other steps that were taken were the Rent Act, the Trade Disputes Act, the Redundancy Payments Act and the Race Relations Act. This latter Act sought to ensure that the large number of immigrants to Britain were not subject to discrimination on grounds of race. But although Labour secured a larger majority in the 1966 general election and remained in power until 1970, they failed to keep their promises of economic growth and improved planning. Inflation remained high and strikes were common. Any analysis of the post-war period thus shows that while the British people had committed themselves to ensuring greater social justice and less extreme inequality, they were subject to frustration, economic problems, bouts of economic upsurges, rapid social changes and varying successes and dilemmas.

Post-War Britain: Past Exam Questions

1995

D5. Great Britain, 1945-1966

Treat of the domestic and foreign policies pursued by successive British governments during the period 1945-1966.

1994

E4. Essay

(iv) The welfare state in Great Britain from 1945 onwards.

1992

D5. Britain, 1945-c.1966

"Britain, in the years after World War II, saw her empire decline but the standard of living of her people improve significantly." Discuss.

48. Nikita Khrushchev, 1894-1971

"We must help people to eat well, dress well and live well. You cannot put theory into your soup or Marxism into your clothes. If, after forty years of Communism, a person cannot have a glass of milk or a pair of shoes, he will not believe that Communism is a good thing, no matter what you tell him".

— Khrushchev

The Rise of Khrushchev

Khrushchev was born on the 17th April 1894 near Kursk in southern Russia. His father was a poor peasant. The young Khrushchev worked as a mechanic in the coal mines of the Ukraine. He joined the Communist Party in 1918 when he was still an *"unpolished, uneducated"* worker. Thereafter, Khrushchev fought with the Red Army against the Whites in the Civil War. He rejoiced in the Communist victory. Trained by the party in economics and Communist theory, Khrushchev's rise to a position of power was rapid. He made an invaluable contribution to the reconstruction work of the Stalinist era and had particular responsibility for the construction of the Moscow underground, an undoubted marvel of Soviet technology. Khrushchev also played a leading part in the purging of anti-Stalinists in the 1930s and served as party secretary to the Ukraine and Moscow. When Stalin died in 1953, he was recognised as one of the leading figures in the government and in the Communist Party. Fearing the rise of another dictator, it was decided that party posts should be split. Thus it was that a five-man collective leadership was formed with the top posts being held by Malenkov as Chairman or Prime Minister and Khrushchev as Secretary. Beria, head of the state police, was eliminated as a potential rival for leadership when he was arrested in June 1953 and executed some months later. Khrushchev now began to build up a strong body of supporters. In particular, he sought to limit Malenkov's position and in February 1955, after attacking Malenkov's policy of consumer goods at the expense of heavy industry and agriculture, Malenkov was forced to resign. The post of Prime Minister was taken by Nikolai Bulganin from 1955 to March 1958 whereupon Khrushchev, the real ruler of Russia, took the two top positions.

Secret Speech - De-Stalinisation

Wishing to give the Russian people a richer and fuller life and to depart from the tyranny of Stalinism, Khrushchev selected a private session of the Twentieth Party Congress on the 25th February 1956, to make his *'secret speech'*. This was a remarkable three hour speech entitled *'On the Cult of Personality and its Consequences'*. It was largely an attack on Stalin's crimes, his *"intolerance, brutality and abuse of power"*. Not surprisingly, it said nothing about Khrushchev or his 'faithful' service to Stalin. Lenin's Will, which had criticised Stalin, was read. Details of the purges were given and *'Beria's gang'* was exposed. Stalin was also implicated in the Kirov murder, 1934. The failure to prepare for Hitler's invasion and the draconian economic policies were further areas of criticism. The speech was the beginning of a process of de-Stalinisation. Statues and portraits of Stalin were removed. The city of Stalingrad was renamed Volgagrad and Stalin's body was taken from the mausoleum in Red Square to some obscure position in the Kremlin wall. The more relaxed and liberal regime made way for the release of thousands of political prisoners. Simultaneously, millions of people in forced labour camps were allowed home. The KGB, which had taken over from Stalin's secret police, was reformed. The reduction of censorship ensured a new freedom for Soviet writers. This was known as *'The Thaw'* after a novel by Ilya Ehrenburg. Alexander Solzhenitsyn's *'One day in the life of Ivan Denisovich'* describes vividly life in one of Stalin's *gulags* or labour camps. But the state refused to publish Boris Pasternak's *'Doctor Zhivago'* because it was concerned with the *'sacred'* Communists of Lenin's era.

Agriculture

Khrushchev launched a massive campaign to build up agriculture and made regular inspections of agricultural areas. He advocated the amalgamation of collectives into huge state farms, *'agro cities'*, initiated a scheme to grow wheat in the previously uncultivated virgin lands of south-west Siberia, proposed a major increase in maize and meat production questioning *"what kind of Communism is it that has no sausage?"*. Khrushchev's reforms seemed initially to be successful and production increased by 50% between 1953 and 1958. Record harvests, for example, in 1956 seemed to augur well for the future as did the figures for meat production in 1958. But these figures were artificially high, resulting from the slaughter of whole herds of dairy and beef cattle. Moreover, Khrushchev's hope of developing some 75m acres of virgin land failed. Problems of soil erosion, dust storms, and severe climate ensured very poor yields. His insistence on maize growing in order to provide fodder for cattle proved equally disastrous. It was grown in largely unsuitable cold areas. All of this combined to ensure chronic agricultural problems, in spite of the fact that state investment in agriculture increased fourfold in ten years. 1962 saw sharp increases in meat and butter prices. In the same year, food riots were put down only when at least 70 unarmed demonstrators were shot in one town. 1963 led to the introduction of bread rationing and the importation of large quantities of grain from abroad. Interference by party officials in farm management and an attempt to do away with the system whereby the peasant owned a private plot further combined to earn Khrushchev the hostility of the peasant.

Industry/Technology

The sixth Five-Year Plan was started in 1956, but its targets were found to be over-optimistic and it was abandoned in 1958. By this stage, Khrushchev had sought to de-centralise planning. In 1957 the sixty Moscow ministries were abolished and replaced by 104 regional councils. This, however, did not lead to greater economic output, as Khrushchev had hoped. Activities were unco-ordinated so that certain goods were over produced while others were virtually unattainable. By 1962 it became necessary to set up a co-ordinating body. The number of economic councils was also reduced.

Meanwhile, in 1958 a Seven-Year Plan was announced. Although heavy industry was given priority, consumer goods were to receive some emphasis. Yet again targets were not met and while the standard of living did increase during the 1953-1964 period, huge problems remained. Khrushchev made too many rash promises to the Russian people which he was unable to fulfill. Technological progress under Khrushchev was, nonetheless, impressive. The railway system underwent a major electrification programme while the national airline *Aeroflot* greatly expanded. New routes were also opened up. Even more significant was the Soviet space programme, undoubtedly helped by the system of free education and the large numbers that attended universities. October 1957 saw the first earth satellite, *Sputnik*, being launched and in 1961 Yuri Gagarin became the first man in space.

Eastern Europe

The states of Eastern Europe in the post-war period had been forced to adhere strictly to the Moscow line. In the period after 1956, however, with the downgrading of Stalinism and Khrushchev's talk of *"different roads to socialism"*, there were calls for increasing independence among some Communist bloc countries. In June 1956 workers' riots in Poland took place. Calls for a higher standard of living and more freedom from Russia were made. Gomulka, who had been imprisoned by Stalin, was made Party Secretary, in defiance of Moscow. Khrushchev flew to Warsaw and demanded Gomulka's replacement. The Poles refused to comply and Khrushchev gave in. The Polish government was allowed to handle internal affairs although it was not possible for Poland to follow an independent foreign policy. Then in October 1956 the people of Budapest revolted. Leading members of the hated Communist Party were forced to flee and Imry Nagy became the new Prime Minister. Nagy promised elections in which the Communist Party would stand against other parties. He also announced that Hungary would break defence arrangements with the USSR. This was too much for Khrushchev who had already come under attack for his softness with Poland. On 4th November 1956, Soviet troops and tanks returned to Budapest. Bitter fighting followed. Over 30,000 Hungarians were killed, 200,000 went into exile. Nagy was himself arrested by the Russians and shot some months later. Such ruthlessness prevented the break-up of the Soviet bloc. But Khrushchev did not always need to take such a hard-line approach in his dealings with satellite states. Bulgaria, for example, was a strong supporter. And although not without their problems, the governments of East Germany and Czechoslovakia were close to Moscow.

Relations with the West

Khrushchev showed a new and more pragmatic view of the modern world than Stalin had. Realising that both the US and the USSR were *'armed to the teeth'* he believed that a certain caution was necessary if the world was to be saved from a nuclear holocaust. This view helped to bring about a 'thaw' in the Cold War between East and West. Yet while Khrushchev could be sincere, even friendly, in his dealings with the West, he could also be inconsistent and contradictory. Many of his decisions proved to be hasty and ill-considered. 1955 showed that the Soviets were willing to withdraw their forces from Austria. In July of that year, Khrushchev attended his first summit meeting of great powers in Geneva. While no agreements were signed in

Geneva, disarmament was discussed. In that same year, Russia formed a Soviet bloc defence organisation known as the Warsaw Pact. This was in response to the West's establishment of NATO some years earlier. Then in 1956 Khrushchev spoke of the possibility of peaceful co-existence. This suggested that there was room in the world for two Superpowers to live side by side. Khrushchev, introducing a new balance in world affairs, visited Britain in 1957. September 1959 witnessed a visit to the US Khrushchev addressed the United Nations Assembly in New York, met President Eisenhower at Camp David and agreed to a summit conference to be held in Paris in 1960. Just weeks before the summit meeting, the good relations formerly established were destroyed when a Soviet anti-aircraft unit brought down an American U2 plane flying over the Soviet Union. This ensured that the Paris Conference was a failure. In September 1960 Khrushchev, in a return visit to the US, proved to be abusive and provocative. The following year (1961) he ordered the building of the Berlin Wall to stop the flood of refugees to the West.

Cuba - China

Friendly relations were established between Cuba and the USSR. Khrushchev welcomed the prospect of a Communist Soviet-supported state off the US Coast. But the Americans, alarmed by what they considered to be a danger to their state, invaded the Bay of Pigs in April 1961. The attack was a disaster for the US and in its aftermath, Khrushchev pledged military support to Fidel Castro of Cuba. Between the spring and summer of 1962, 42 Russian-made missiles capable of reaching any city in the US were being installed in Cuba. The Americans demanded removal and when Khrushchev refused, it seemed as if major conflict was about to unfold. Only at the last moment did the Soviets give way. Thereafter, Khrushchev seems to have returned to his policy of peaceful co-existence. In 1963 a 'hot-line' was established between the White House and the Kremlin. Its purpose was to provide easy access of contact and prevent future crisis. There was also in 1963 a test ban treaty signed between the two powers. It outlawed nuclear tests in the earth's atmosphere. Relations with Communist China were more strained and while Khrushchev was in power a China-Soviet war was threatened. This was especially obvious in the period after 1958. Mao Tse-tung, the Chinese leader, disliked Khrushchev's denunciation of Stalin and his desire for co-existence with the West which was contrary to accepted Communist thinking. Khrushchev for his part, condemned Mao Tse-tung as a *"madman determined on nuclear war"*. The final break between the two powers in 1960 ensured that the Communist Party was split in two. Approximately 20 of the 65 Communist parties in the world supported China.

Fall of Khrushchev - Evaluation

Khrushchev was at the height of his popularity in the late 1950s. Thereafter, opposition grew. He was accused of putting forward one 'hair-brained' scheme after another. Criticism focused especially on his failure to sustain the reform programme at home and to win success abroad. He was also blamed for practising nepotism and for fostering a personality cult. In October 1964, he was recalled from holiday and told that neither government nor the central committee had confidence in him. Having no option but to resign *"in view of his health and age"*, Khrushchev lived quietly in retirement in Moscow until his death on the 11th September 1971. Denied a state funeral and burial within the Kremlin, Khrushchev under the pro-Stalinist joint leadership of Brezhnev and Kosygin became a 'non-person'. Yet in spite of his many failed schemes, Khrushchev was a symbol for a more humane and less repressive Communism. He showed a genuine wish to improve conditions and to that extent he was *"the people's hope, the forerunner of the New Time"*. The eyes of the Soviet people were opened to many of their problems, attention was focussed - albeit unsuccessfully - on agriculture and the need for consumer goods and in spite of his instability and lack of subtlety in foreign affairs, the world had moved from the *"snarling hatred and distrust of the early days of the Cold War"*. A staunch Communist, Khrushchev could be ruthless in the pursuit of his goals but he was never dictatorial or tyrannical.

Post-War Russia: Past Exam Questions

1994

D5. The USSR, 1945-1966

Discuss the part played by the USSR in international affairs during the period 1945-1966.

1991

D2. Khrushchev

Treat of the part played by Nikita Khrushchev in the history of the USSR.

POST-WAR GENERAL TOPICS

49. The United Nations

Origins and Aims

The concept of a United Nations had already taken root after the First World War in the form of the League of Nations. But by 1940, having failed in its primary objective, the League of Nations was disbanded. Although the need for a collective organisation remained, it was not possible, either practically or emotionally, to revive the old League. A new organisation, the United Nations (UN) emerged. This had its origins in the Atlantic Charter, August 1941, when the US President, Franklin D. Roosevelt, met British Prime Minister, Winston Churchill, in secret, on board the warship *Missouri*. Both men agreed on the need for a *"wider and more permanent system of general security"* and had as their ideal *"that all men in all lands may live out their lives in freedom from fear and want"*. In January 1942, the ideas expressed in the Atlantic Charter were accepted by 26 nations, all of whom agreed to unite against the Axis powers of Germany, Italy and Japan. It was then that the name United Nations was first adopted. Thereafter, in the autumn of 1944, a conference of the *'Big Four'* (US, Britain, USSR, Nationalist China) met at Dumbarton Oaks near Washington to draw up plans for a Charter and to decide on the structure of the UN. This scheme was approved at the Yalta Conference, February 1945. A general conference was held in San Francisco from April to June 1945. The final form of the UN Charter was now decided and on 26th June, it was signed by 57 nations. The UN organisation officially came into being on 24th October 1945. It has as its symbol a light blue flag with a polar map and two olive branches, representative of its aim of international peace and co-operation. In addition, the UN aspired to protect fundamental human rights, to work towards social, economic and cultural matters. Its headquarters is in Manhattan, New York on a site donated by John D. Rockefeller, Jnr.

Principal Organs [I]

The General Assembly, or parliament of the UN, occupies a central position in the functioning of the organisation. It is the one body in which all UN members are represented and while a member may send as many as five representatives, each member has only one vote. The Assembly is the main debating chamber and can discuss almost any topic. It also has supervisory, financial and elective functions. Convening annually, the Assembly's rules permit a calling of special sessions at short notice. Decisions on substantive questions are taken by a majority or by a two-thirds vote, depending on the importance of the matters involved. The Security Council is often likened to the cabinet of a national government. It originally consisted of five permanent members (US, Britain, USSR, Nationalist China, France) and six non-permanent members. In 1963, the non-permanent members were increased to ten. These are elected from the General Assembly for a period of two years. Each of the permanent members has the power of veto but because the powers repeatedly used this veto and it became closely bound up with the Cold War, a resolution was passed by the General Assembly in November 1950 that allows it to override a veto if it can obtain a two-thirds majority on emergency resolutions. The Charter assigns the Security Council primary responsibility for maintenance of international peace and security. In the task of preserving peace, the Council may apply diplomatic or economic sanctions and even send peacekeeping forces to international trouble spots. Members of the UN agree to carry out the decisions of the Security Council.

Principal Organs [II]

With responsibility for the day-to-day administration of the UN, the Secretariat is a civil service whose staff is chosen from all nations of the world. It is headed by a Secretary-General, the most important figure in the UN. The first Secretary-General was a Norwegian, Trygvie Lie. The principal judicial organ of the UN is the International Court of Justice based at the Hague in the Netherlands. It consists of 15 judges, of varying nationalities, elected by the Assembly and the Council voting independently. The Court deals mainly with international disputes and with interpretations of international law and treaties. Accordingly, cases must be brought by member states rather than individuals. The administration of territories, not yet independent in 1945, was left to the Trusteeship Council. Acting under the authority of the General Assembly, the Council receives reports from the administering authorities and petitions from the trust territory itself, as well as providing for periodic visits to the trust territories. It helps these territories towards independence. Finally, there is the Economic and Social Council. It originally consisted of 18 members but in 1965, the number was increased to 27. Members are elected by the General Assembly for three years, with the possibility of re-election. This Council was given the task of overseeing *"international economic, social, cultural, educational, health and related matters"* and for co-ordinating the work of the various specialised agencies concerned with such matters.

UN Agencies

There are approximately forty agencies and other bodies associated with the UN. These include the International Labour Organisation (ILO) whose job it is to improve working conditions in industry worldwide. It does so by the drawing up of regulations which member states are expected to adopt and abide by. Safety standards, good labour relations and effective management are all emphasised. The United Nations International Childrens Emergency Fund (UNICEF) is concerned with all aspects of children's welfare - education, health and general care. The United Nations Education Science and Cultural Organisation (UNESCO) helps to improve international co-operation in the fields of education, science and culture. It tries to disseminate information, to remove illiteracy and to do away with propaganda and bias offensive to given national groups. The World Health Organisation (WHO), for its part, promotes positive health measures, provides information on drugs and medicine, co-ordinates medical research, works towards the elimination of disease as well as providing equipment and trained personnel. The Food and Agricultural Organisation (FAO) tries to combat world hunger and to raise living standards. Agricultural education is a high priority. Concerned especially with exchange rates and the stabilisation of international currencies is the International Monetary Fund (IMF). A World Bank was also founded. This helps to fund projects in developing countries. The task of promoting world trade and settling disputes between trading nations is left to the General Agreement on Trade and Tariffs (GATT).

Peacekeeping - Palestine/Indonesia

During the first 20 years of its life - and thereafter - a large number of disputes came before the Security Council and the General Assembly, reflecting the unsettled conditions in the world after World War II. The UN succeeded in helping to settle some of them; others remained unsolved and were a continuing concern. In its handling of Palestine, the UN has been accused of *"showing neither firmness nor consistency in the face of a dynamic new nationalism"*. After World War I, Palestine was severed from Turkey and given to Great Britain to administer as a mandated territory. Large-scale Jewish migration to Palestine, caused by the intense desire among Jews for a national homeland, led to growing hostilities between Jews and Arabs. Unable to keep both sides apart, Britain announced its desire to end its mandate in April 1947. The problem was handed over to the UN which, on 29th November 1947, voted in favour of the division of Palestine into two independent states, Jewish and Arab. The Arabs opposed the plan. Nonetheless, when Britain gave up its mandate on 15th May 1948, the Jews proclaimed the state of Israel. The following year, Israel was admitted to the UN. Meanwhile, the Arabs refused to recognise Israel as a state and would not negotiate with it directly. Disputed territory in the Sinai Peninsula, the Golan Heights and the Lebanon led to open hostilities between Jews and Arabs and continuous violations of cease-fire agreements. Not until 1974 did the General Assembly recognise Palestine's rights to nationhood. Since then, in September 1993, the Israelis and the Palestine Liberation Organisation have agreed to recognise each other's claims. The UN was more successful in its handling of Indonesia. The UN intervened in fighting between Dutch troops and Indonesian nationalists in spite of Dutch claims that the matter was within its *"domestic jurisdiction"*. The result was the recognition by the Netherlands of Indonesia's independence. The formal transfer of sovereignty took place on 27th December 1949.

Korea, 1950-53

Shortly after the end of World War II the northern half of Korea was occupied by the USSR and the southern half by the US. When the two nations proved unable to agree on how to achieve a united democratic Korea, the General Assembly called for the holding of free elections in both parts of Korea. These elections were held only in the southern half and the Republic of Korea was proclaimed. The Soviet Union, having refused to allow free elections, set up a Communist regime, the People's Republic of Korea, in the northern part of the country. During 1948-1949 both US and USSR troops were withdrawn from Korea. Then in June 1950 the armed forces of North Korea invaded South Korea. The UN immediately called for their withdrawal but the request was refused. The Security Council (with Russia absent) called on the members of the UN to *"furnish such assistance to the Republic of Korea as may be necessary to repel the armed attack and to restore international peace and security in the area"*. A large UN force, comprising mainly US troops but also containing troops from around 14 other nations was sent to Korea. This led to a prolonged struggle in which the North Koreans were eventually driven back and their capital Pyongyang, taken. Communist China which assisted the North was labelled an aggressor. Fighting continued until July 1953 when an armistice was signed at Panmunjon. Both sides agreed to a partition based on the thirty-eighth parallel. The Korean War was a crisis point in the Cold War and because of apparent US domination of the UN, one of the most controversial operations of the organisation.

Suez Canal - Congo - Cyprus

When on 26th July 1956, President Nasser of Egypt announced that his government had nationalised the Suez Canal Company, there developed a sharp military conflict over the control and operation of the canal. Britain and France were heavily involved, as was Israel, which ensured that the dispute became merged with the long-standing Israeli-Arab tensions. But Britain and France agreed to withdraw their troops if the UN created a force to take a position between the Israelis and Egyptians. Consequently, a peacekeeping force from 10 nations was sent to guard the borders between Egypt and Israel. The withdrawal of the participating armies was a triumph for the UN. The former Belgian colony of the Congo (Zaire), which became an independent state on 30th June 1960, posed another problem for the UN. Shortly after independence, violence broke out and spread quickly through the country, ensuring that Belgium immediately rushed troops back to protect its interests. On 11th July, the province of Katanga seceded. The Congolese government appealed to the UN for military assistance. The UN responded by sending a force of well over 20,000 troops. Following this the UN, in December 1962, having already adopted a resolution declaring that all secessionist activity should *"cease forthwith"* moved against Katanga in force. On 17th January 1963, President Tshombe of Katanga ceased resistance. In February, the Secretary General of the UN announced that the organisation had *"largely fulfilled"* its mandate in the Congo. On 30th June 1964 the last UN forces were withdrawn. The UN also became involved in Cyprus which became an independent country in 1964. Location and population, however, meant that fighting broke out between Greeks and Turks on the island. The stationing of a peacekeeping force there from March 1964 helped to prevent major conflict on the island during the 1960s and 1970s.

Conclusion

As well as the conflicts already mentioned, the post-war years brought a series of local wars, none of which the UN was able to prevent. Examples of such wars include the hostilities between India and Pakistan over Kashmir, fighting between Communist and Nationalist China about Formosa and guerilla wars in Malaya, Kenya and North Africa. The UN also became involved in conflicts between the rival blocs of the world, the US and USSR, which threatened global peace. The rapid advance in nuclear weaponry and the world's destructive capacity was, likewise, out of harmony with the UN aim *"to have succeeding generations free from the scourge of war"*. To that extent, the UN failed to live up to the high hopes of its founders. Friction also arose from the fact that not all members were prepared to pay, in full, the required contribution to the UN. Another problem with the UN was that all too frequent use was made of the veto, held by permanent members, to prevent decision and action by the Council. This, however, did, in time, allow for the enhanced role of the General Assembly. Apart from its various agencies, positive aspects of the UN include its increasingly universal character. By 1963, it had 113 members. And because the US and USSR were both in the UN from the start, the real balance of power - with few exceptions - was reflected in its structure. In this, and in other ways, the UN learned from the mistakes of its predecessor. Perhaps the greatest tribute to the UN is that a third World War has been avoided. For all its apparent failures, the UN as mediator, negotiator and keeper of peace is constantly called upon. As it *"continues to be a symbol of humanity's eternal yearning for a world at peace"* (Francis T. Holohan), few could doubt that the world would be worse off if the UN did not exist.

50. Treat of the Movement towards European Unity from 1945 to 1966

"We must build a united states of Europe".

— Churchill, 1946

Introduction

Although the idea of a united Europe was not a new one, it was only in the period following the Second World War that practical steps were taken towards the voluntary achievement of that aim. More than ever before, Europeans showed a new readiness to come together. Advocates of a united Europe included Jean Monnet and Robert Schuman of France, Konrad Adenauer of Federal Germany, Alcide De Gasperi of Italy and Paul Henri Spaak of Belgium. These were motivated by idealism and national interest. Above all, they were determined that the destruction and devastation caused by World Wars in 1914 and again in 1939 should not occur again. Since these wars had been largely caused by national rivalries and ambitions, it was believed that European unity, by drawing nations together, was the key to averting future wars. The containment of Germany within a framework of European unity was also seen as the best insurance against future aggression and the revival of her military might. Added to this was the desire to put Europe back on the international map. In the post-war period, the US and USSR dominated the world stage. A united Europe could provide a strong third grouping and thereby act as a balance in world affairs. This was seen as especially necessary in the case of Soviet Russia. Its growing strength was a threat to the weakness and vulnerability of individual European states. Only through co-operation could they present a formidable enough force, capable of offsetting the danger they faced. An even greater argument in favour of unity was the immediate practical benefits to be derived. Through sharing resources, real and dramatic growth could be achieved. Economics provided a 'lower level link' through which other forms of co-operation could come about.

Organisation for European Economic Co-Operation (OEEC)

Even before the war had ended, the governments of the Benelux states, Belgium, the Netherlands and Luxembourg, had provided a salutary example of how economic measures could break down political barriers. The first practical step towards integration, in the post-war period, took place in 1947. It had its origin in the Truman Doctrine and the resulting plan put forward by General George Marshall, in June 1947, for a European Recovery programme based on American aid. Known as the Marshall Plan, the programme demanded a joint American-European action rather than a series of individual agreements between the USA and various European nations. Although the USSR and the Communist states of Eastern Europe were invited to participate, the Russians refused. Western Europe, badly in need of funds, reacted enthusiastically. In accordance with American wishes, a properly structured body, the Organisation for European Economic Co-operation (OEEC) was established in April 1948. Consisting of 17 European nations, all of whom received help, the OEEC was set up to administer the recovery programme. $12,000m were made available and each country was expected to contribute an amount towards economic recovery, equal to what they received from the US. In addition to administering monies, the OEEC did excellent work in trying to meet the desperate need for food, houses and jobs. Europeans had at last found common ground in their shared need. By 1952, the aims of the OEEC were largely accomplished. It did, nonetheless, go on to encourage trade among members by advocating the reduction of tariffs. To this end, the OEEC was helped by the General Agreement on Trade and Tariffs (GATT) and the European Payments Union (EPU). A doubling of trade among OEEC members had taken place by the mid 1950s. Thereafter, the movement widened to include non-European states. It adopted the name Organisation for Economic Co-Operation and Development (OECD).

Military Unity

On a certain level, military togetherness came more quickly to Western Europe than political or economic unity. In March 1947 the Dunkirk Treaty was signed by Britain and France. Aimed at countering the possible revival of German military aggression, it soon became clear that the threat was coming from another level, namely the USSR. In the aftermath of the Prague coup by the Communists, a more general defensive treaty was signed by Britain, France, Belgium, the Netherlands and Luxembourg at Brussels on 17th March 1948. The five nations agreed to build up a common defence system in the face of a possible *"armed attack in Europe"*. The necessary machinery was set up at Fontainebleau, near Paris, with Field Marshal Montgomery as head. They also agreed to *"strengthen economic, social and cultural ties by which they are already united"*. But as Soviet military strength continued to grow at an alarming rate, the five European nations realised that, on their own, they would not be able to stand up to the USSR. Consequently, the Brussels Treaty was used as a springboard, a step forward in a still wider defence arrangement that would include Western powers on both sides of the Atlantic. In Washington, on 4th April 1949, 12 nations joined the North Atlantic Treaty Organisation (NATO). As well as the 'Brussels' signatories, original members of NATO were America, Canada, Iceland, Norway, Denmark, Portugal and Italy. Members called for the peaceful settlement of disputes, economic co-operation and the strengthening of military defence. Forces were to be kept in a state of readiness *"by means of continuous and effective self help and mutual aid, in order to resist armed attack"*. Parties agreed *"that an armed attack against one or more of them shall be considered an attack against them all"*. And while NATO was not strictly European, it was an important inroad on the path to European unity. In particular, it gave Western Europe a new sense of security and helped to end the era of narrow nationalism.

Council of Europe

In the political field, too, organisations sprang up to seek European unity. At the Hague in 1948, a great Congress of *"Europeans"* was held. Churchill, Adenauer, Schuman, De Gasperi, Spaak and many other famous politicians attended. In all, 750 delegates were present. The Congress proposed the setting up of a European parliament open to all democratic states in Europe which protected human rights. A year later, in May 1949, the Council of Europe was formed with its headquarters at Strasbourg in eastern France. The statute was signed by 10 states, Britain, France,

Belgium, the Netherlands, Luxembourg, Denmark, Ireland, Italy, Norway and Sweden. West Germany joined in 1950. Spaak became the Council's first president. The Council consists of two bodies, the Consultative Assembly and the Council of Ministers. The former has its representatives chosen by members of parliaments from various states and meets in public, the latter is the real authority and meets in private. British opposition to the idea of supranationalism and political entanglements meant that the powers of the Council of Europe did not go as far as European federalists or integrationists would have wanted. Its main work is concerned with social and medical services, working conditions, education, travel and human rights. It seeks to develop a common approach among members in dealing with problems. Questions of defence are excluded from the Council's business. Lacking the power to enforce its decisions, the Council has been described as a *"talking-shop"*. To see it as no more than this is to underestimate its true worth, however, for as well as being the first European assembly, the Council has made important findings and recommendations on a wide range of issues. The establishment of the European Court of Human Rights is a further achievement of the Council. Another council, the Nordic Council, was formed in 1952. It sought further co-operation among the Scandinavian states, Norway, Sweden, Denmark, Iceland and Finland.

The European Coal and Steel Community

Economic unity was pushed ahead by the French Internationalists, Jean Monnet and Robert Schuman. In the Schuman Plan, 1950, it was proposed to make industry more efficient in Western Europe by establishing a common policy on coal and steel production. The argument used here was that if Europe's coal and steel industries could be brought under genuine supranational control, war between states would be almost impossible as the aggressor would be directly hindering his own interests. From June 1950 to March 1951 negotiations for such a plan took place. Then, on 18th April 1951, six nations, France, West Germany, Italy, Belgium, the Netherlands and Luxembourg signed the Treaty of Paris which created the European Coal and Steel Community (ECSC). Britain refused to participate, fearing loss of national sovereignty. The ECSC began to function in August 1952 from its headquarters in Luxembourg. It functioned through a High Authority to which was attached a consultative committee representing producers, workers, dealers and consumers. The ECSC also had a Council of Ministers and an Assembly. Its first president was Jean Monnet. The ability of *'the six'* to buy and sell coal, iron, ore, steel and scrap unhindered by duties, quotas or privileges meant that in the first ten years, trade in those commodities increased among members by 170%. For the same period, prices rose by only 3%. Investment, research and long-term planning were all part of the duties of the ECSC. When old and expensively run mines were closed, care was taken to provide jobs for displaced workers. A limited common market, in the form of the ECSC, could act as a bridge to an all-European Economic Community. That goal, present from the start of the ECSC was given an added push when, in the late 1950s, increased demand for oil as an energy source began to make itself felt.

The European Defence Community

The issue of re-arming Germany became more immediate in 1950 as a result of US pressure, caused especially by the outbreak of the Korean War and the need to provide a strong army in Europe to counter-balance the Soviet threat. The French were fearful of rapid West German rearmament, however, and sought to prevent her development of an independent military force. A compromise solution was put forward in October 1950 by French Prime Minister, René Pléven. The Pléven Plan suggested the formation of a European Defence Community (EDC) made up of contingents from each member state, including West Germany. There would be a common budget to finance the EDC and a European Defence Minister to control it. Such an organisation would alleviate the need for a separate West German national army. Negotiations for the Plan dragged on for two years. In May 1952 the EDC Treaty was signed by France, Belgium, the Netherlands, Luxembourg, Italy, West Germany. Britain remained as opposed to supranationalism in defence as she was in economics and politics. Her refusal to participate combined with the French insistence on playing a dominant role and restricting the German contribution caused considerable difficulties. Consequently when the tensions of the early 1950s began to slacken with the death of Stalin and the ending of the Korean War in 1953, the need for the EDC was reduced. When the French National Assembly, then under the leadership of Pierre Mendès France, took a vote on the issue of the EDC, in August 1954, a majority voted against it. This spelled the end of the EDC. New conferences, thereafter, resulted in West Germany becoming a sovereign, independent state and a member of NATO on 5th May 1955. Although West Germany was to rearm, all her forces were under NATO command. In addition, Britain and America promised to keep forces on German soil indefinitely.

The European Economic Community - Euratom

Although the collapse of the scheme for a European Defence Community came as a bitter blow to 'European-minded' statesmen, it did not signal the end of European integration. A committee set up under Belgian Foreign Minister, Paul Henri Spaak, was established to discuss ways of creating closer European unity. Spaak and his team of experts worked hard and, after several meetings, Spaak's proposals formed the basis for formal treaties creating the European Economic Community (EEC) and the European Atomic Energy Commission (Euratom). The two treaties were signed in Rome on 25th March 1957 by the six members of the ECSC. In the treaty relating to the EEC, the signatories agreed

1. to remove all tariffs and restrictions on trade amongst member states,
2. to have an agreed common tariff and trade policy towards other countries,
3. to arrange for the free movement of capital, services and people,
4. to establish a common agricultural and transport policy,
5. to allow for fair and free competition within the EEC.

The EEC sought to strike a balance between the supranational interests of its commission and the national interests of individual states. It had its own constitution and came into operation on 1st January 1958. With its headquarters in Brussels, the EEC proved to be a major step in creating a union of over 160 million people, working in close economic co-operation. Euratom, for its part, aimed to co-ordinate all future development, production and use of nuclear energy. It was to be concerned only with its peaceful uses and control of the fissionable material would be supranational.

EEC/EFTA - An Assessment

When the EEC was first set up, many countries were reluctant to join it. Some states opted to join the European Free Trade Association (EFTA), established in July 1959 in Stockholm and consisting of Britain, Sweden, Norway, Denmark, Portugal, Austria and Switzerland. As distinct from the *'inner six'* of the EEC, these became known as the *'outer seven'*. EFTA was a trading agreement which did not seek political or economic union. Yet, although trade between EFTA countries did increase, membership of the Association was no real substitute for the possibilities of the EEC. In any case, the success of the EEC, though not without its share of difficulties, is such that it has gradually broken down early reluctance. In 1961, Britain first applied for membership of the EEC. Her application was vetoed by the French who argued that Britain was not truly 'European'. Only in January 1973 did Britain, along with Ireland and Denmark, enter the Community. Since then, the EEC has become the European Union (EU). An enlarged organisation, the EU has moved European unity beyond that which was envisaged by the Treaty of Rome. Any assessment of the issue of unity cannot fail to see that while there have been many different strands of opinion as to what direction Europe should go and how she should proceed, great progress had been made by 1966. Changes, scarcely envisaged in 1946, have taken root, albeit at times, slowly and painfully. Co-operation has involved 'burying the hatchet' in terms of past animosities and looking anew at the role of one's own country in a united Europe and indeed, world. But as well as the three main areas of unity written about here, there has also been much co-operation in social, sporting and technological fields. The establishment of European Broadcasting, Eurovision, the European Athletic Championships, the European Organisation for Nuclear Research, European Space Research Organisation and the European Launcher Development Organisation are just some such examples.

51. Treat of Decolonisation from 1945 onwards

Causes of Decolonisation [I]

European imperialism began late in the 15th century and continued through to the First World War, undergoing an astonishing revival between 1870 and 1914. Although little new colonisation took place after 1914, it was not until after the Second World War that the end of Europe's great colonial empires in Asia and Africa came about. The process of decolonisation between 1945 and 1966 witnessed a series of events which can only be described as *'momentous'* for Europe and the world at large. Yet the *'colonial revolution'* did not develop suddenly or without warning. Nor was it simply the by-product of war. Its roots went much deeper, perhaps even to the age of imperialism itself. The drive for independence, however, received added momentum during and after the Second World War. In the first place, the spectacle of Europeans fighting a vast war may have lost them the respect of some of their colonial subjects. Certainly, the myth of European invincibility, the unbeatable white man, was broken. In the period 1940-1943, European powers suffered humiliating defeats at the hands of the Japanese. The French were ousted from Indo-China, the British from Malaya and Burma and the Dutch from Indonesia. Although the Japanese were eventually driven out, the resistance groups had little intention of calmly handing back power to their former white masters. They demanded independence and were prepared to fight for it. Another contributing factor in the cause for decolonisation was that the Second World War had been fought to save democracy and freedom from the evils of Nazism and its horrific racist theories. In the aftermath, it became harder to justify the continuation of empires. Unease must also have been felt about the racist ideas towards some of the colonists themselves.

Causes of Decolonisation [II]

Any assessment of the causes of decolonisation would be incomplete without a look at the *'revolution of expectations'*. By 1945, colonial peoples were more than ever aware of what was going on in the outside world. The days of ignorance, illiteracy and superstition were rapidly passing away and people realised that disease, hunger and poverty were not inevitable. Neither was it essential that they were politically dependent, racially inferior and economically subservient. The growth of a national consciousness was exploited by the emergence of leaders and the formation of colonial nationalist parties. Examples of the *'white'* colonies of the British empire which had already moved towards self-government - Canada, South Africa, Australia, New Zealand, Ireland - were cited. That the newly emerging Superpowers, the US and USSR, were anti-imperialist also played into the hands of the colonised. The US, herself a former colonial subject, felt a natural dislike for the system. She argued that imperialism offered an excuse for Communist agitation in the colonial world and that the best way of preventing Communism was to grant independence. The US led the way by her recognition of the Philippines as an independent republic on 4th July 1946 and her subsequent help of that government. The Soviet Union, for her part, argued that imperialism was nothing more than a platform for capitalism. Little was said of the USSR's imperialist ambitions throughout Eastern Europe. In any case, these factors combined to create a new willingness to rethink and reshape colonial relations. They were helped, too, by the emergence of political parties in Europe promoting the idea of decolonisation.

Britain's Withdrawal from Asia

Although Britain was one of the victorious powers in the Second World War, she emerged from the fighting exhausted and weakened. Her foreign policy in the twenty years following the war was largely one of withdrawal from her empire for the 'winds of change' had indicated that, no matter how painful, there could be no going back to the pre-war colonial status position. The first event in the transformation was the independence of India. Demands for Indian independence had grown steadily throughout the 20th century. By the time the war had ended and Labour had given its promise of early independence, the only important question was how Britain would leave. The difficulty lay in the existence in India of two religious groups, the Hindus comprising 330m people and led by Mahatma Gandhi, and the Moslims, consisting of 70m people and under the leadership of Ali Jinnah. Admiral Lord Louis Mountbatten, acting as Viceroy, sought to prepare the country for independence. Like so many others, he became convinced that partition was the only answer. Consequently when independence was granted on 15th August 1947, India was divided into two. The Hindu state continued to be called India, the Moslem state to the north assumed the name of Pakistan. But independence was accompanied by considerable violence, bloodshed and civil war. Only with time did things begin to settle down. Meanwhile, India and Pakistan, like Ceylon, an island of 8m people which received independence in February 1948, opted to remain within the British Commonwealth. Not so with Burma which became independent in January 1948 and chose to follow a solitary path. Independence for Malaya came a little later, in August 1957, after the British had successfully beaten Chinese-backed Communist guerillas in the country.

Britain - Middle/Near East

The force of Arab nationalism undoubtedly impinged on British Mediterranean interests. In 1946, Britain handed over power in Jordan. Other interests were the islands of Cyprus and Malta, the former attaining independence in August 1960, the latter in 1964. The British League of Nations mandate in Palestine proved more troublesome as a result of continuing conflict between the Arabs and the Jews, who were seeking a national homeland. Each side suspected the British of favouring the other and the British proposal for the establishment of two nations was rejected. So intractable was the problem that the British referred the issue to the UN and on 15th May 1948 they withdrew from Palestine. Thereafter, the Jews proclaimed the state of Israel. Early in 1956, Britain's joint interest with Egypt and the Sudan was ended and the country became independent. What happened subsequently with regard to British involvement in the Suez Canal Company seemed to be a reversal of her withdrawal from *'Imperial Power'* status. Trouble arose when Colonel Nasser, a fervent Arab nationalist, nationalised the Suez Canal Company on 26th July 1956. Britain believed her interests in the Middle East to be threatened and, along with France and Israel, devised a plan leading to war between Egypt and Israel, and occupation by Britain and France in order to 'restore order'. World opinion was swift in condemning British action and, on 6th November 1956, the operation ended. The endeavour had cost Britain £250m and Sir Anthony Eden's resignation as Prime Minister.

Britain - Africa

With African politicians calling for independence for black African states in the wake of the Second World War, it was not the principle of independence which remained to be disputed so much as when and how this was to happen. The Gold Coast led the way. There the national leader, Kwame Nkrumah, received huge support and in 1951 he was enabled to become Prime Minister of the colony. Some years later an independence motion was passed without opposition in the legislature so that in March 1957 the Gold Coast was declared independent. It became known as Ghana. In rapid succession, other colonies followed suit. 1961 saw the declaration of independence by Nigeria, Tanganyika and Sierra Leone; Uganda in 1962; Kenya and Zanzibar in 1963; Nyasaland and Northern Rhodesia in 1964 and Gambia in 1965. In terms of the attainment of the ideal of independence, Kenya and Southern Rhodesia proved most problematic. Both states had large-scale European settler populations. In the case of Kenya, for example, these numbered some 40,000. The largest and most politically aware of the Kenyan tribes, the *Kikuya* competed with Europeans for land in the White Highland. A secret terrorist organisation *(Mau Mau)* was also in operation and from 1952-1956 the British had to wage constant war against them. The demand for independence could not be stilled, however, and in December 1963, Kenya gained independence with Jomo Kenyatta as leader. In Southern Rhodesia, too, the Europeans wanted to remain in control. Because the Europeans refused reforms, it was a military campaign that finally resolved the matter. In 1980 an independent state of Zimbabwe was created.

The Netherlands/France - Indonesia/Indo-China

The Dutch in Indonesia and the French in Indo-China reaped what has been described as *"the sorry harvest of Japanese occupation"*. The Dutch controlled the second largest European empire in Asia. It consisted of the Indonesian islands of Sumatra, Borneo, Java and New Guinea. Following Japan's occupation and subsequent defeat in the war, Indonesian nationalists proclaimed an Indonesian Republic only two days after Japan's surrender. The Dutch wanted to resume control, however, and negotiations took place. When these broke down in 1946, fighting started and continued intermittently until 1949. From the beginning, the Dutch task was hopeless. 80 million people could not be subdued by a small European state. The UN Security Council, to whom the matter was referred, recommended independence. Thus in August 1949, the Dutch agreed to recognise the independence of the Indonesian Republic. Sukarno became its first President, Hatta the Prime Minister. In 1963, the last bit of Dutch territory in the area, West Irian, was handed over to Indonesia. The French fought longer and more stubbornly to preserve their power in Indo-China. In the aftermath of war, negotiations with the French on the issue of independence failed and in 1946 open warfare began. The Viet Minh under the leadership of Ho Chi Minh and General Giap waged a guerilla campaign against the French. War continued until 1954 when, between March and May, the decisive battle was fought at Dien Bien Phu. This led to the dramatic fall of the French garrison and to the Geneva Agreement, 1954, by which Laos and Cambodia became independent, and Vietnam was partitioned along the 17th Parallel into the Communist North and non-Communist South.

France - Algeria/Africa

Shortly after the Geneva conference on Indo-China, the French Prime Minister, Pierre Mendès France, arranged a settlement concerning one of her North African possessions. Accordingly in March 1956, Morocco and Tunisia received their independence. The Suez crisis of that same year ensured that France, along with Britain, lost control of the Suez Canal to the Egyptians. A solution for Algeria proved much more difficult to find and revolution there resulted not just in a long bloodstained war but also in the fall of the Fourth Republic and the return of De Gaulle to power. Algeria contained 1m settlers, *'Colons'*; it also had valuable supplies of oil and gas. In 1954, the National Liberation Front (FLN) led by Ben Bella began a terrorist campaign with the aim of securing independence for Algeria. It fought especially hard against the Secret Army Organisation (OAS). Both sides engaged in torture and murder and the war became steadily more brutal. May 1958 proved to be a crisis point when the French army, led by General Salan, rebelled. De Gaulle was recalled, most people believing that he would keep Algeria French. But in spite of an army revolt in January 1960 and an even more serious one in April 1961, De Gaulle worked towards ending the war and granting independence. A negotiated settlement led to Algeria's independence in March 1962. The remaining French possessions in 'black' Africa centered around French West and Equatorial Africa. These possessions contained only 80,000 Europeans out of a total 20 million inhabitants and France conceded independence more readily and peacefully. By August 1960 power was transferred to all colonies. A host of new states appeared on the map, most of them choosing to remain in close friendship with France.

Belgium/Portugal - Conclusion

The movement towards freedom spread across Africa to the Belgian Congo, an area particularly rich in minerals and rubber. Although the Belgian government was not anxious to hand over power, it hastily reconsidered its position in the climate of the dramatic explosion of tribal nationalism and some serious rioting. Consequently, in January 1960, at a conference in Brussels, it was announced that the Democratic Republic of the Congo would come into being in June 1960. Yet because it did so without adequate preparation, independence in the Congo caused enormous difficulties. An army mutiny and tribal warfare necessitated the dispatch of Belgian troops to the Congo to restore order. They were succeeded by UN troops who remained in the Congo until July 1964. Events in the Congo led to a nationalist rebellion in neighbouring Angola in 1961. The Portugese dictator, Dr. Antonio Salazar, crushed the rebellion with considerable severity. He insisted that the states of Angola and Mozambique were part of Portugal itself and refused to give them up. Only in 1975 did they gain independence. In conclusion, however, it must be acknowledged that within a relatively short period of time, European rule in Asia and Africa almost completely disappeared and a vast shift in world relationships took place. That the process of decolonisation should have contained interludes of considerable violence is hardly surprising. Perhaps more surprising was the extent of the peacefulness of the transition and the manner in which colonisers and colonised, in many of the cases, have remained on good terms. And while political Westernisation was forced to retreat, other aspects of Western civilisation and economy continued to bear influence.

52. The Cold War

"Since 1945, relations between West and East were dominated by a series of real crises and recurrent tensions." Discuss.

Introduction

The Western powers and Russia had appeared to work closely together during the Second World War. Their alliance, however, had been formed because of the presence of a common enemy (Germany) and once that threat disappeared, the 'marriage of convenience' proved unable to survive. The post-war years saw a division of West and East into two separate camps. The East was dominated by Russia who now sought to dominate the Eastern states she had liberated from the Germans as they became her buffer zone or defensive barrier against the West. America, the other Superpower, continued to play a part in European affairs, acting as 'Big Daddy' to the West. Essentially, the struggle between East and West was an ideological conflict between complete opposites which could not be reconciled - Communism and Capitalism. It took the form of unfriendliness, recurrent tensions and real crises and became known as the *'Cold War'*. This phrase was coined by an American statesman, Bernard Baruck. The word 'cold' is used to distinguish this war from a 'hot' or shooting war. Thus, although many bullets and bombs were fired, the two giants avoided becoming directly involved in an all-out war with each other. The roots of the Cold War went very deep and, as the *'Iron Curtain'* descended across Europe, every move on the part of East and West was regarded suspiciously by the other. Likewise, every gain by one was a loss to the other and every problem was tackled with the purpose of advantage in mind. At first, the deterioration of relations was confined to increased tensions and fierce exchanges across conference tables but, in time, these tensions took the form of real crises.

Greece - Turkey - Economic Aid

Greece became the first real arena in which the Superpowers struggled for supremacy. Civil war developed in Greece when Communists there challenged the right-wing, British-backed government. Even though Greece threatened to fall into the Communist grip, Britain, encountering her own post-war problems, informed the US that, through necessity, she would relinquish her role in Greece. She invited the US to take over the responsibility. This crisis, along with the mounting pressure in Turkey from the USSR to hand over disputed territory and to allow the Soviet Union access to naval bases, precipitated an important decision in Washington. The question was whether US resources should be put behind a general effort to check any further extension of Soviet and Communist power. The Truman Doctrine, March 1947, committed the US to do just that. $400m was given to assist Greece and Turkey, economically and militarily. The break between East and West became even more pronounced with the Marshall Plan, June 1947, by which the US advanced $12,000m to assist the economic recovery of Europe. West European countries responded enthusiastically and in April 1948 established the Organisation for European Economic Co-Operation (OEEC) to administer the monies. Stalin sensed an American trap, believing that US money would only enslave the borrowers. Therefore, he declined the money and compelled the Eastern European governments under his control to do the same. When Czechoslovakia hesitated, a savage Soviet-backed coup took place. A further countermove by Stalin was the establishment of *Comiform* in September 1947, through which he established more firmly, control over Eastern satellite states. The setting up of a Council for Mutual Economic Assistance (COMECON) in 1949 to help the economies of Eastern Europe was still more evidence that the tension of the Cold War had definitely come into being.

Crisis in Berlin - The Berlin Blockade

The lines of the Cold War hardened thereafter. Insofar as defeated Germany was concerned, the country, in the aftermath of war, was divided into four spheres of influence, American, British, French and Russian. Berlin was inside the Russian zone but because of its important position, it too was divided into four sectors. Real crisis arose when the Western powers united their zones in June 1948 and then introduced a new *Deutschmark*. The Russians, fearing a strong, self-supporting German economy were annoyed by the decision and refused to take part in the scheme. On the 24th of the month, they imposed a blockade of the city by cutting off all road, rail and canal access to Berlin. The West responded by supplying the 2 million people living in West Berlin by air, *'Operation Vittles'* at a cost of over £200m. As the blockade continued for 11 months there was every possibility that some exchange of fire might provoke full scale war but Stalin was finally made to realise that it was impossible to strangle West Berlin and on 12th May 1949 he called off the blockade. The East-West divide had other repercussions for Germany, however. Perhaps most significantly, it led to the creation of two Germanies, the Federal Republic of West Germany (FRG) and the Democratic Republic of East Germany (GDR). Each Germany was created in the image of one of the opposing sides in the Cold War and emphatically demonstrates the recurrent tensions that were present. The building of the Berlin Wall in August 1961 to stem the flood of refugees from East to West was still more evidence of a Cold War.

NATO - Warsaw Pact

The Berlin Blockade and the intensification of the Cold War convinced the Western powers that the only answer to the might of the Soviet armies was a definite military alliance. A decisive step towards the achievement of that aim was taken in Washington on 4th April 1949 when 12 countries - USA, Canada, Britain, France, Belgium, the Netherlands, Luxembourg, Italy, Portugal, Denmark, Norway, Iceland - established the North Atlantic Treaty Organisation (NATO). A defensive alliance, NATO, nonetheless, pledged itself to using *"armed attack"* if necessary. Article 5 of the Treaty stated that *"an armed attack against one or more shall be considered an attack against them all"*. NATO gave its members a new sense of security and proved successful in preventing the spread of Communism in Western Europe. Greece and Turkey signed the Treaty in 1952, West Germany in 1955. Although the Russians denounced NATO as an imperialist aggressive plot, they were undoubtedly impressed by the show of Western unity. Ensuring that tension remained a persistent current in the Cold War, the Soviet Union formed the Warsaw Pact in May 1955. This Pact placed the Communist nations of Europe - Albania, Bulgaria, Czechoslovakia, East

Germany, Poland, Romania - under Soviet military command. All the states agreed to the placing of Soviet forces within their territories and to the appointment of a Russian general as commander of the forces. Joint action against an aggressor was a condition of membership. In this way, the recurrent tensions of the Cold War guaranteed that the Iron Curtain became a grim reality.

Korea, 1950-1953

The spread of Communism ensured that the Cold War was not just 'fought' in Europe and that relations between East and West became steadily more icy and bitter. Korea, a country divided into North and South in the wake of Japan's surrender, became another point of *'real crisis'*. South Korea, reflecting an American presence there, became the Republic of Korea, while its Northern counterpart, with Russian help, became the Communist Democratic People's Republic. Between 1948-1949 American and Soviet forces left Korea. Then on 25th June 1950 the North Koreans, armed with modern Soviet weapons, attacked the South. America asked the United Nations for help and, in the absence of the USSR, the UN Security Council authorised and instructed its members to use force. With American forces the most numerous, around 15 countries were represented in South Korea. They were commanded by General Douglas MacArthur. Fierce fighting took place but the Communist advance was halted and, as the UN forces crossed the boundary into North Korea, the army there was put on the defensive. Chinese help for the North Koreans led to a general fear of a third World War. When MacArthur sought to extend his authority by extending the war into China, President Truman, anxious that the crisis would not escalate, had him dismissed and replaced by General Ridgway. Peace talks began in July 1951 and dragged on, with spasmodic fighting, until 1953. An armistice at Panmunjon in July 1953 left Korea as it was prior to the hostilities, divided along the 38th parallel into North and South Korea. By then over three million people had been killed and relations with China, the other major Communist world power, were now as cold as they were with Russia.

A Partial Thaw

The year 1953 saw a general thaw in the Cold War. Reasons for this included the change of leadership in both America and Russia. In January 1953, Eisenhower succeeded Truman as President of the US. Then in March 1953, Stalin's death led to a power struggle and the emergence of Nikita Khrushchev as USSR leader. Khrushchev encouraged friendly relations between East and West and spoke in terms of peaceful co-existence. The new more relaxed phase of the Cold War may also have been prompted by the nuclear escalation inherent in the development of hydrogen warheads by both Superpowers. Signs of peaceful co-existence included the Korean armistice, the withdrawal by the USSR of claims to Turkish territory, the acceptance of the Austrian Peace Treaty which resulted in the withdrawal of occupying forces and the declaration of the permanently neutral state of Austria, as well as the withdrawal by both the US and USSR of objections to a number of countries from rival blocs becoming members of the UN. The period also witnessed a number of summit talks to discuss arms control, but before too long, there was a return of Cold War patterns. This was, in part, caused by Western objections to the cruel suppression by the USSR of risings in East Germany in 1953 and Poland and Hungary in 1956. Heavy domestic pressure in the Soviet Union to give up the policy which led to such unrest in the satellite states also prompted a new aggressiveness. The Suez Crisis, 1956, and the Russian completion of the Aswan Dam did little to ease tension. Likewise, American involvement in Communist Vietnam served to prolong East-West divisions.

Cuban Missile Crisis, 1962

Cuba became Communist when Fidel Castro led a guerilla movement to power in January 1959. Quarrels with the US, thereafter, led President Eisenhower to break off relations with Cuba and to cut trade links. Then in April 1961 Cuban refugees staged an American-backed invasion of Cuba, landing at the Bay of Pigs. This failed invasion prompted Castro to turn to the Russians for help. He asked the Soviets for rockets to defend the island against a second attack. The Russians proceeded to build missile launching sites in Cuba which, when operational, would be capable of delivering warheads within striking distance of all major US cities. The Americans, then led by President Kennedy, could not tolerate this threat to their security. On 23rd October, Kennedy, having already demanded that the Russians dismantle the missile sites, authorised a naval blockade of Cuba. Russian ships approaching the island would be stopped and searched. Tension now increased as arguably the worse crisis between the Superpowers began. Again the world hovered on the brink of a world war. Khrushchev, however, in the face of such overwhelming American strength, decided to back down. Soviet ships were ordered to turn around before open confrontation took place and the bases were subsequently dismantled. Khrushchev's wisdom in backing down was praised by Kennedy. A positive outcome of the crisis was the installation of a direct telephone 'hotline' between the White House in Washington and the Kremlin in Moscow. Its purpose was to improve ease of communication.

Conclusion

Although the East-West divide spread to Asia, Africa and South America as the struggle between Communism and Capitalism sought to play itself out, it was in Europe that the Cold War had begun and where it always had its clearest expression. Part and parcel of the conflict was the arms race. This involved not just the development of the hydrogen bomb but the successful testing of Intercontinental Ballistic Missiles (ICBM) and the spending of vast sums of money on military forces and nuclear weaponry. Space exploration was another area of rivalry and tension between the Superpowers. Yet the realisation by both states that they had the power to destroy the world and that they had already brought it to crisis point, called for some caution. Consequently in 1963, a Test Ban Treaty was signed between the US and USSR. This was but one of a number of treaties which in the years after 1963 sought to curtail the actual number of missiles held by both sides and to prevent the spread of atomic weapons. This, coinciding with new and sometimes more cautious leadership, as well as the emergence of an even more complicated pattern of international relations which allowed for the rise of new Centres of Power, augured well for East-West relations and allowed for a détente or relaxing of tension. Since 1963, the mighty power struggle has subsided or 'frayed out'. Real crises of relations have been pushed further and further into the past.

Post-War General Topics: Past Exam Questions

1995

D4. European Unity

Treat of the principal factors since 1945 that have contributed to the movement towards European unity.

1993

D.3. European Unity (also 1988 E4)

Treat of the movement towards European unity from 1945 to 1966.

D.4. Decolonisation (also 1989 E4)

Account for decolonisation - the withdrawal of European powers from their territories overseas - from 1945 onwards.

D.5. The Superpowers

"In 1945 there were two superpowers, the United States of America and the Soviet Union."

Describe how the United States and the Soviet Union became superpowers and how they related to each other in Europe during the period 1945-1966.

1991

D.4. The Cold War

"Since 1945, relations between West and East were dominated by a series of real crises and recurrent tensions". Discuss.

D.5. The E.E.C.

Trace the origins and development of the European Economic Community, 1945-1966.

1990

D.5. The Superpowers

Treat of relations between the two superpowers, the U.S.A and the U.S.S.R., during the period 1945-1966.

1987

D.5. Europe, 1945-1950

Treat of the problems facing Europe in the post-war period, 1945-1950, and assess the attempts made to solve them.

Winston Churchill

Charles de Gaulle

Nikita Khrushchev

Western European leaders with American ally: Eden, Adenauer, Acheson, Schumann.

Churchill, Truman and Stalin at
Potsdam 1945

Harold Macmillan became
Prime Minister of Britain in
1957

Konrad Adenauer, Chancellor
of West Germany, 1949-1963

De Gaulle with the Soviet
Leader, Mr. Khrushchev, who
paid an official visit to France
in 1960

RESEARCH TOPIC

The current Higher Level Leaving Cert. History examination allows the student to prepare an essay beforehand, based on a topic of his/her own choice. The following guidelines will be of assistance to students preparing this Special Topic essay.

Guidelines for *Research Topic* in European History

1. The essay must be kept within the time period specified for the Leaving Cert. Course II i.e. European History 1870-1966.

2. Topics must be kept within the European context of the course.

3. The subject chosen should be worthy of an essay i.e. it should be of some significance to the course.

4. The *'Research Topic'* essay should not be too broad e.g. the topic *'Adolf Hitler'* is too broad. Instead the student should narrow the focus e.g. *'Hitler and the Generals'* or *'Hitler's Jewish Policy'*. Likewise, the essay should not span too many years. *'World War II, 1939-1945'* does not allow for adequate depth, but *'The Mission of Count Claus von Stauffenberg'* is acceptable.

5. The title of the essay must be clear and concise.

6. There should be adequate and suitable sources/resources available which should be reflected in the body of the essay. Students should use an average of 3-6 sources which should be of a *primary* and *secondary* nature.

7. The essay should follow a logical line of argument. The conclusion, which is crucial, should be in line with the content of the special essay topic.

8. Around 30 minutes should be spent writing this essay.

9. The *Short Questions* which accompany the Research Topic are generally quite simple. A few sentences will suffice as an answer to each of these questions. They are intended to indicate a comprehensive study of your chosen topic. The following information will help you to answer the short questions:

Some useful definitions

(a) *Primary source material* is any evidence from the past that relates to the period of time being studied. In relation to the Special Topic for Leaving Cert. History, this would include press cuttings, letters and diaries. On the subject of audio-visual sources, primary material would include *Movietone*, *Pathe News*, radio speeches and interviews with people who witnessed or were aware of the people or events under study.

(b) *Secondary source material* is produced by people who did not witness the events under study. Rather, they rely on primary sources or even on secondary sources to produce their material. Examples of secondary sources include books, magazines, films and TV programmes made or written after the period in question.

(c) *Prejudice* - A preconceived opinion, especially an unfavourable one based on inadequate facts.

(d) *Bias* - An irrational preference or prejudice.

Skills of the historian

(a) *Collecting the sources* - This is the bringing together of as much material as possible on the topic under study. Difficulties associated with this range from the amount of material available to the problem of getting access to it. It is important that sources are then examined and compared so that points of agreement and disagreement can be noted. The collecting of sources is an important skill of the historian.

(b) *Analysing a source* - This is another skill necessary to the historian. It involves breaking down a source into its relevant parts and then examining it in detail.

(c) *Synopsising a source* - This is the ability to condense or give a brief general survey of a source.

(d) *Evaluating a source* - The student needs to assess if a source is relevant. Trivia must be separated from what is important or substantial. It is also necessary to judge whether a source contains prejudice or bias and, if so, to what extent.

(e) *Synthesising of sources* - Often the most difficult skill required of the historian is to combine his/her ideas. The putting together of separate elements must be done in such a way as to produce a connected whole, an effective and worthwhile essay.

The following Research Topics - *"Bleeding the French White" - Gen. Erich von Falkenhayn and the Battle of Verdun (Feb-Dec 1916)* and *The Mission of Count Claus von Stauffenberg* were researched and written by two recent Leaving Cert. students. Their essays are printed here as examples of the type of Research Topic required, and are followed by some suggestions as to how they could be improved. Each Research Topic essay must be **unique** and **a product of the student's own research** at Higher Level - Leaving Cert.

WARNING: It is important that the Research Topic essays provided here are **NOT submitted by other students as their own work. Such action could lead to penalties and loss of marks in the Leaving Cert. History exam.**

Research Topic Essay — I

"BLEEDING THE FRENCH WHITE" — GEN. ERICH VON FALKENHAYN AND THE BATTLE OF VERDUN (FEB-DEC 1916)

Falkenhayn's strategy and decision to invade Verdun

Critics are not agreed as to whether General Erich von Falkenhayn's decision to *'bleed the French white'* at Verdun in 1916 was a brilliant innovation or a strategic blunder. A highly intelligent and rather arrogant man, he had been promoted to the German General Staff because of his brilliance on the battlefield. At the beginning of the war, Falkenhayn did not have any clear policy on where the German attack should be concentrated but his later conclusion was that the outcome of the war would eventually be decided on the Western Front. This view was controversial in that it conflicted with that of his colleague on the general staff, General von Hindenburg, who believed that World War I would eventually be settled in the East. However, it is possible that the officers on the general staff, comfortably settled back at base, were sufficiently removed from the horrors of ongoing trench warfare not to have registered its reality. Falkenhayn's initiative showed in the selection of the salient of Verdun for his attack; he guessed correctly that the French would probably sacrifice a huge part of their army to defend this emotionally significant but strategically unimportant place.

Problems with Falkenhayn's first attack

Verdun is located on what was then the Western Front near the border between modern France and Belgium. The river Meuse flows through it and it was in planning which side of the river to begin his attack from that Falkenhayn's initiative first began to falter. His vacillations eventually meant that he forgot the golden principle of concentration of force, and restricted his attack to the right bank only. Nevertheless, the first day of battle, February 21, 1916, went well for the Germans; Falkenhayn launched a heavy attack, first with long-range shells, then with high-explosive shells and flame throwers. However, they did not succeed in killing all the French gunners, and the German patrols who did gain ground were stranded in no-man's-land because Falkenhayn, unable to make up his mind, had held back the main attack until it was too late.

Early gains on the German side

The battle then went quickly in Falkenhayn's favour; the Germans swiftly captured Fort Douaumont on February 25. It must be noted, however, that this was as much due to French incompetence as to German brilliance - the fort practically fell into the hands of a German sergeant and his ten men. Meanwhile, the Germans were having difficulty transporting the heavy artillery needed for *'bleeding the French white'*. Falkenhayn exacerbated this situation by not giving his troops the reserves they needed.

Falkenhayn extends attack but suffers heavy casualties

Pressure from his superiors finally coerced Falkenhayn into extending his attack from the right bank to both banks of the river Meuse on March 6, as it would not take more troops than it would have a month ago. Thus began the fierce battle for the hill appropriately named *Le Mort Homme*. This attack was finally repulsed by the French on April 10. Within a fortnight of the beginning of the battle for *Le Mort Homme*, there were 81,607 German dead, almost as many as the French. By the end of May, German losses exceeded French ones. Somewhere along the line, the policy of *'bleeding the French white'* had taken a fatal 'boomerang'. Falkenhayn was even beginning to lose interest in the invasion he had planned himself and was only persuaded to continue by Knobelsdorf, the Kaiser's Chief-of-Staff.

Problems with the Austrians

Falkenhayn was at this time distracted by other troubles. Another fault which obscured his military acumen was that of arrogance towards other peoples; unfortunately, he held the Austrians in particular contempt even though they were Germany's only constant ally during the war, Falkenhayn had launched the Verdun offensive without a word to the Austrian Chief-of-Staff, Conrad von Hotzendorf, and his attitude towards the Austrian army was clear enough in his words to the Austrian Archduke Karl *"What is Your Imperial Highness thinking of? Whom do you think you have in front of you? I am an experienced Prussian general!"* He also assured the Archduke that his troops were inadequate, disorganised, and unmilitary. Hotzendorf was sufficiently angered by Falkenhayn's behaviour to launch the Asiago offensive on the Italian border on May 15 without first consulting Falkenhayn. Not only did the offensive fail, but the Russians were also able to get through the denuded Austrian front. Falkenhayn, while doubtless taking great pleasure in Hotzendorf's humiliation, had no choice but to take valuable troops away from Verdun to plug the gap at the Russian front. This was all a costly waste of time which could have been avoided if Falkenhayn had been more sensitive.

Battle stagnates - Falkenhayn does U-turn

The Germans laid siege to Fort Vaux from 1st-7th June, finally capturing it after a week of fighting. Again, this was partly due to French incompetence, as the fort was not properly defended. The Germans advanced steadily after that, as far as Fleury on 23 June. This was the closest Falkenhayn managed to get to Verdun. From July to September, the battle continued without Verdun in sight. Conditions in the trenches were intolerable, and morale was running low. It seemed as if Falkenhayn's policy of *'bleeding the French white'* just wasn't working. Under pressure from his superior, Knobelsdorf, Falkenhayn did a dramatic U-turn on his idea. A new *'big push'* was launched against the French, with the Germans going on an all-out advance. This *'push'* got to within two and a half miles of Verdun before petering out.

Phosgene gas and its failure

The offensive only reached that far (temporarily) because of the introduction of phosgene gas, which the Germans used to poison the French by filling artillery shells with it. The deadly gas effectively silenced the French ranks when it came into contact with them. But Falkenhayn was suspicious of the newfangled substance and he didn't allow his army to use enough of it. Therefore they only knocked out the French guns in the centre, while those on the flanks could still punish the German attackers. In another attack using phosgene gas, the Germans advanced only to find the French artillery very much intact, and intent on destroying them. The phosgene-proof gas mask had been invented.

The Loss of Verdun - Conclusion

After the the failure of that last attack, the Germans had effectively lost the battle of Verdun. After several successful counterattacks in October and November, the French won back Fort Douaumont and Fort Vaux and the German troops lost the little ground for which they had sacrificed so much. Falkenhayn was dismissed by a disillusioned Kaiser. His vision of *'bleeding the French white'* contrasted with the stark reality of the total loss of 800,000 lives. Verdun was a wasteful battle; Falkenhayn's constant indecision and overwhelming arrogance had brought him defeat where an able, intellectual mind should have predicted victory. The man whom Alistair Horne had termed *'the typical Prussian general'* had shown very clearly why the species became a dying breed.

— Susan Lanigan

Sources:
1. *Our Own Worst Enemy* by Professor Norman Dixon. This was my main source on the Battle of Verdun. A psychological analysis of human hostility, it is a fascinating read and while not taking any sides, is whole-hearted in its denunciation of human emotional flaws which lead to war.
2. *The Military History of World War I - Summation: Strategic and Combat Leadership* by George Dupay. This, the last book in a series, was written by a man with military experience and is useful in offering a calm unbiased analysis of Falkenhayn's performance.
3. *Encyclopaedia Americana* Volume 3, entry on Falkenhayn.
4. *August 1914* by Barbara Tuchman. Not relevant to the period in question but useful information on General Joffre, who led the French at Verdun.

Evaluation

This is a suitable, even well-chosen *'Research Topic'* essay and shows evidence of many of the skills of a professional historian. Weaknesses do exist, however.

- Some of the paragraphs are too sketchy. They lack necessary detail.
- Analysis and evaluation are present but not always in the required proportion.
- The term *'war of attrition'* could be used to show the frame of mind that existed.
- Other factors in the German defeat such as the indomitable spirit of the French leader, Marshal Pétain, and the effect of the British diversionary offensive on the Somme might be explored.
- The Battle of Verdun might be placed in the overall context of the war.

Research Topic Essay — II

THE MISSION OF COUNT CLAUS VON STAUFFENBERG

On the 30th April 1945, Adolf Hitler and his long-time mistress, Eva Braun, committed suicide in Hitler's Berlin bunker. It is ironic that it was suicide which ended the reign of this tyrant when so many others had failed to rid Germany of his influence. Throughout his career, even from the early days as a party official, there had been opposition to Hitler and what he represented. This resistance was underground and well-organised and involved some of the most influential names in Germany, for example, Julius Leber; the eminent socialist, Carl Goerdeler, the former mayor of Leipzig and Count Helmuth von Moltke. Numerous plots were suggested for deposing the Nazi regime and seizing power. Eventually, however, most of the conspirators came to agree that it would be necessary to assassinate Adolf Hitler to achieve these aims. Although between 1921 and 1945 there were many significant attempts on Hitler's life (one historian lists as many as 461) the most important one without doubt was the Bomb Plot of July 1944 - the brainchild of Count Claus von Stauffenberg. Although in the final analysis the plot failed in its ultimate aim, its one important effect was to show the world *"that some attempt has been made by Germans to rid themselves of these criminals"* [1].

The group which showed the most determined opposition to Hitler was a small group of high-ranking officers in the General Army Office which made repeated, if unsuccessful, attempts on Hitler's life. Demoralised, the plotters suddenly found a willing hit-man in Count Claus von Stauffenberg, the new Chief-of-Staff. Stauffenberg breathed new life into the resistance with *"his dynamic personality ... the clarity of his mind"* [2]. From the headquarters of the Reserve Army at Bendlerstrasse in Berlin, Stauffenberg and his co-conspirators, General Olbricht, Major von Tresckow and others, began making plans for a complete coup. Plans had to be evolved for wresting control of the entire country and bringing the war to an end. Ironically, a blueprint already existed which could be adapted to this end. It was code-named *'Operation Valkryie'* and it entailed the mobilisation and deployment of the Reserve Army. A *'cover story'* of an attempted putsch by the SS would also be released and all politicians and party officials would be made subordinate to military commanders. Finally, a provisional government would be formed with either Carl Goerdeler or Julius Leber as Chancellor to negotiate a ceasefire with the Allies.

With the successful Allied invasion of Normandy in June 1944, the conspirators wondered whether they should continue with their plans. Another argument put forward was the increased inaccessibility of Hitler. Assassination would have to be attempted at his headquarters in Berchtesgaden or Rastenburg but as of yet none of the conspirators had access to either sanctuary. Despite these obstacles, Stauffenberg and his comrades decided to carry on. As von Tresckow put it *"The assassination must be attempted at all costs"* [3]. On 20th July one of these obstacles was removed when Stauffenberg was appointed to a position as Fromm's deputy and on 1st July he officially assumed the post. He would now have access to the Führer's headquarters personally. However, on 5th July they were yet again thrown into confusion with the arrest of Julius Leber by the *Gestapo*. The authorities had got wind of a conspiracy and were closing in. Plans for the assassination would have to be dramatically accelerated.

Stauffenberg had become the most important figure in the conspiracy, *"On his shoulders alone rested its only chance of success"* [4]. It was up to him not only to plant the bomb but also, as Chief-of-Staff of the Reserve Army, to direct the troops that were to seize Berlin. And he had to carry out both objectives in the one day and at two spots separated by two or three hundred miles. This was only one complication that would arise, another being that the desperate plotters had decided that it would not suffice to kill Adolf Hitler. They must, with the same bomb-blast, eliminate Göring and Himmler, thus ensuring that the forces under the command of these two men could not be used against them. It was this almost unnecessary resolve that led Stauffenberg to miss two golden opportunities on 11th and 15th July. He swore not to fail again and was determined to make the attempt on his next visit to the *'Wolfsschanze'* (Wolf's Lair) i.e. Hitler's headquarters at Rastenburg. He was due to give a report on the Reserve Army on 20th July at 1pm. The key officers in the garrisons in and around Berlin were warned that 20th July would be *'Der Tag'*.

At 7am on Thursday 20th July 1944, Stauffenberg, along with his aide Werner von Häften and another officer, boarded a plane at a military aerodrome south of Berlin. The plane did not arrive at Rastenburg until 10:15. At 11:30, Stauffenberg met with Marshal Wilhelm Keitel, Chief of General Staff for a 45 minute conference. The men were then informed that the meeting with the Führer originally planned for one o'clock had been moved forward by half an hour and Stauffenberg asked to be shown to a washroom to freshen up before his meeting with Hitler. Here he was joined by von Häften, carrying a suitcase containing two bombs. Stauffenberg changed his shirt and, assisted by his aide began to arrange and activate the bombs when they were interrupted by a messenger sent to warn him that the briefing was about to begin. The presence of the messenger undoubtedly prevented him from arming both bombs. However, time was running short - in less than 10 minutes the activated bombs would explode.

Stauffenberg had hoped to be conducted to the Führer's underground bunker, where it was hoped the concrete walls would maximise the blast. But since 16th July conferences had been held in the *'Lagerbaracke'* (conference barracks); a wooden structure of some 16 by 40 ft, in which a blast would be significantly less lethal. When Stauffenberg entered, the meeting had already begun and Lieutenant General Hensigner was giving a report on the situation on the Eastern front. Twenty four other men were gathered around a large, heavy oak table on which were spread a number of maps. Stauffenberg took up a place near Hitler to his right, next to a Colonel Brandt. He placed the briefcase on the ground as near to Hitler as possible and then promptly left the room again on the pretext of a telephone call to Berlin. What happened next can only be guessed at - Colonel Brandt is thought to have moved the briefcase to the far end of the heavy table support, which now stood between the bomb and Hitler. *"This seemingly insignificant gesture saved Hitler's life : it cost Brandt his"* [5]. Within minutes the bomb exploded. Three officers were killed as well as the official stenographer but unknown to Stauffenberg, the intended victim emerged with only burns and punctured eardrums.

Meanwhile Stauffenberg took a plane to Rangsdorf where he landed three hours later at 3:45. As planned, one of his co-conspirators, General Fellgiebel, Head of Communications at Rastenburg, had phoned Berlin and ordered the activation of *'Plan Valkryie'*. He also imposed a blackout on all communications from Rastenburg. When Stauffenberg arrived back at the Bendlerstrasse, he learned to his utter consternation, however, that nothing had been accomplished in the three hours he had been airborne. Word had come from Fellgiebel but they had been unsure whether Hitler was dead or not. It had been 3:30pm before any decisive action had been taken and the orders from *'Operation Valkryie'* had been given by Colonel Merz von Quirnheim. Stauffenberg, having at this stage returned to HQ, was still convinced that Hitler could not possibly have survived the blast. He only began to suspect otherwise when he paid a visit to the office of General Fromm. Fromm maintained that he had just spoken with Keitel who had assured him that the Führer was still alive. Whatever the case was, Stauffenberg recognised the necessity of proceeding with *Operation Valkryie* - he argued that they must go ahead and destroy the tyrant's *'evil rule'*.

The communications blackout was lifted at 4:30 and at 6:30 a news bulletin was released declaring that an attempt on Hitler's life had failed. The war office was now besieged with phone calls and Stauffenberg himself informed all of the them that the bulletin was false. In some places the plan had worked for a few hours at least. In Vienna all SS officers were arrested and the army occupied key positions. In Paris, General von Stülpnagel imposed martial law and imprisoned all SS, SA and Gestapo personnel. In spite of this Stauffenberg now realised the conspiracy was doomed. Around midnight the War Office was overwhelmed and he, Olbricht, Häften and Merz von Quirnheim were placed under arrest by Fromm. General Fromm had been aware of the conspiracy all along but in the months of planning had vacillated abjectly. He sentenced these four main conspirators to immediate execution and his orders were carried out shortly after midnight in the courtyard at Bendlerstrasse. These men could perhaps be called lucky because, in the months that followed, their fellow conspirators were subjected to Hitler's vindictive sadism and were tortured and interrogated, tried by the notorious People's Court and painfully executed. Germany lost almost 4,000 of her best army officers, civil servants and intellectuals during these purges. The Bomb Plot also led Hitler to distrust the Army even more and hastened the day when Germany would be defeated. However of the Bomb Plot it can unfortunately be said *"The revolt, the only serious one ever made against Hitler in the 11¹/₂ years of the Third Reich was snuffed out in 11¹/₂ hours"* [6].

— *Emma Geoghegan*

[1] Count von Uxkull (Stauffenberg's uncle) in *"Secret Germany : Claus von Stauffenberg and the mystical crusade against Hitler"*.

[2] *"The History of the German Resistance, 1933-1945"*.

[3] *"Secret Germany ..."*

[4, 5, 6] *"The Rise and Fall of the Third Reich"*.

Bibliography:

1. *Secret Germany : Claus von Stauffenberg and the mystical crusade against Hitler* by Michael Baigent and Richard Leigh.

2. *The Past is Myself* by Christabel Bielenberg.

3. *The History of the German Resistance, 1933-1945* by Peter Hoffmann.

4. *Hitler : A Study in Tyranny* by Allan Bullock.

5. *Hitler and Germany - Modern Times* by B. J. Elliot.

6. *The Rise and Fall of the Third Reich* by William L. Shirer.

Evaluation

This is a well written and researched essay. Some changes could be made to improve its overall strength and impact, however.

- The essay's introduction could be improved by omitting the earlier lines and including, instead, some discussion on army disaffection and/or some personal background to the key conspirator, von Stauffenberg.

- The short and longer term objectives of the conspirators might be analysed in more detail.

- The July Plot 1944 should be placed in the overall context of German reverses in the war.

- The consequences of the failure of the July Plot need to be examined. It is not enough to look at what happened to the conspirators. An analysis of the implications of failure insofar as they affected the possibility of a compromise settlement, for example, might be made.

- Perhaps above all, the essay needs greater analysis and evaluation. The student needs to draw conclusions.

Notes